ARISTOPHANIC HUMOUR

Also available from Bloomsbury

ARISTOPHANES AND THE DEFINITION OF COMEDY
by M. S. Silk

COMEDY
by N. J. Lowe

GREEK LAUGHTER
by Stephen Halliwell

HUMOUR, OBSCENITY AND ARISTOPHANES
by James Robson

ARISTOPHANIC HUMOUR

THEORY AND PRACTICE

Edited by Peter Swallow and Edith Hall

BLOOMSBURY ACADEMIC
LONDON • NEW YORK • OXFORD • NEW DELHI • SYDNEY

BLOOMSBURY ACADEMIC
Bloomsbury Publishing Plc
50 Bedford Square, London, WC1B 3DP, UK
1385 Broadway, New York, NY 10018, USA
29 Earlsfort Terrace, Dublin 2, Ireland

BLOOMSBURY, BLOOMSBURY ACADEMIC and the Diana logo are trademarks
of Bloomsbury Publishing Plc

First published in Great Britain 2020
This paperback edition published in 2021

Copyright © Peter Swallow, Edith Hall and Contributors 2020

Peter Swallow and Edith Hall have asserted their right under the
Copyright, Designs and Patents Act, 1988, to be identified as Editors of this work.

Cover design: Terry Woodley
Cover image: Heritage Image Partnership Ltd / Alamy Stock Photo

All rights reserved. No part of this publication may be reproduced or transmitted in any
form or by any means, electronic or mechanical, including photocopying,
recording, or any information storage or retrieval system, without prior permission
in writing from the publishers.

Bloomsbury Publishing Plc does not have any control over, or responsibility for, any
third-party websites referred to or in this book. All internet addresses given in this
book were correct at the time of going to press. The author and publisher regret
any inconvenience caused if addresses have changed or sites have ceased to
exist, but can accept no responsibility for any such changes.

A catalogue record for this book is available from the British Library.

A catalog record for this book is available from the Library of Congress.

ISBN: HB: 978-1-3501-0152-4
PB: 978-1-3501-9485-4
ePDF: 978-1-3501-0153-1
eBook: 978-1-3501-0154-8

Typeset by RefineCatch Ltd, Bungay, Suffolk

To find out more about our authors and books visit www.bloomsbury.com
and sign up for our newsletters.

J. T. Sheppard as Peithetairos, the Cambridge *Birds* (1903).

For Ellie and Jess,
Sarah and Georgie

CONTENTS

List of Illustrations	xi
Notes on Contributors	xii
Preface by Edith Hall	xv

1 **Introduction: Dissecting the Frog(s)** *Peter Swallow* — 1

Part One Theory — 11

2 **Beyond a Joke: Making Humour Theory Work with Aristophanes** *N. J. Lowe* — 13

3 **Play as Shared Psychological Register: *Paidiá*, Laughter and Aristophanes** *Edith Hall* — 23

4 **Aristophanic Incongruities** *Craig Jendza* — 39

5 **Laughter, or Aristophanes' Joy in the Face of Death** *Mario Telò* — 53

6 **Laughter and Collective Trauma in Aristophanic Comedy** *Pavlos Sfyroeras* — 69

7 **The Satirist as Troll? Sociopathic Strains in Aristophanes** *Ralph M. Rosen* — 79

8 **The Hilarious Politics of the Supernatural in Aristophanic Comedy** *Edith Hall* — 89

9 **Aristotle on Aristophanic Humour** *Pierre Destrée* — 101

Part Two Practice — 117

10 **Surface and Deep Aristophanic Parody** *Athina Papachrysostomou* — 119

11 **A Grammar of *Para Prosdokian*** *Dimitrios Kanellakis* — 129

12 **Laughing against the Machine** *Maria Gerolemou* — 145

13 **No Laughing Matter? The Comic Potential of Madness in Aristophanes** *Natalia Tsoumpra* — 153

14 **Sexual Violence and Aristophanic Humour** *Peter Swallow* — 167

15 **Aristophanes, Philosopher: The Comedy of Truth in Nietzsche and Freud** *Adam Lecznar* — 183

Contents

16 *Melancholia* and Laughter: Modern Greek Productions of
   Aristophanes in the Twenty-First Century   *Magdalena Zira*   193

17 Saving Classics with the *Clouds*: A Case Study in Adapting
   Aristophanes   *David Bullen*   205

Notes   215
Bibliography   253
Index   279

ILLUSTRATIONS

Frontispiece:	J. T. Sheppard in the 1903 Cambridge University production of *The Birds*, directed by H. J. Edwards and W. Durnford. Available at: www.cambridgegreekplay.com/plays/1903/birds (accessed 7 June 2019).	v
3.1	*Paidiá* playing with a stick in a love-game on a red-figure pyxis of about 415 BCE, ARV² 1238.99. Illustrated by Becky Brewis.	25
3.2	*Paidiá* enjoying athletic sex with the satyr Chorillos on a red-figure dish of about 350 BCE, ARV² 1512.18. Illustrated by Becky Brewis.	26
3.3	*Paidiá* joins battle with the giants alongside a satyr and Dionysus on a red-figure krater of about 400 BCE found in Ruvo. ARV² 1338. Illustrated by Becky Brewis.	28
5.1	Paul Getty Crater, inv. 248778, Museo Archeologico Nazionale di Napoli.	57
5.2	Ghiottoni Crater, inv. A 0.9. 2841. Civico Museo Archeologico, Milano. Copyright Milan Municipal Authority, all legal rights reserved.	57
5.3	Paolo Veronese, *Perseus Freeing Andromeda*, originally in the antichamber at Vaux-le-Vicomte, Musee de Beaux-Arts, Renne.	59
5.4	Yue Minjun, *Expression in Eyes*, No. 168, Xiao Bao Cun, Songzhuang Twonship, Tongzhou District, Beijing.	60
8.1	Fred Düren as Trygaios in *Der Frieden*. Written and directed by Peter Hacks after Aristophanes. AV Documentary by Benno Besson. Edition Mnemosyne 2006 (Digitally Remastered). All rights reserved. 00:14:18.	96
11.1	Graph showing the distribution of *para prosdokian* across *Acharnians*, *Peace*, *Thesmophoriazusae* and *Wealth*.	138
13.1	Heracles in the grip of madness. Red-figure krater from Paestum by Asteas. 350–320BCE. Museo Arqueolólogico Nacional, Madrid.	165
16.1	*The Frogs*, 2012, produced by Fantastico Theatro, directed by Magdalena Zira, set design by Dimitris Alithinos, costume design by Elena Katsouri, presented at the Cyprus International Festival of Ancient Greek Drama. Photographer: Socrates Socratous.	202

CONTRIBUTORS

David Bullen is a writer, director, dramaturg and academic specializing in adapting the plays and myths of the ancient world to the modern stage. A co-founder of By Jove, a London-based socialist feminist theatre company that works with myth, he is currently one of its co-artistic directors. He has written adaptations of plays by Aeschylus, Sophocles, Euripides and Aristophanes, with productions in both the UK and the United States, and has taught at Royal Holloway, University of London, and Rose Bruford College of Theatre and Performance.

Pierre Destrée is Associate Research Professor at the Fonds de la Recherche Scientifique and teaches ancient philosophy at the University of Louvain, Belgium. He is the author of numerous articles on Plato and Aristotle, and has a special interest in the uses of humour in ancient philosophy. He has edited many volumes, most recently (with Franco Trivigno) *Laughter, Humor, and Comedy in Ancient Philosophy* (2019).

Maria Gerolemou is a Leventis Research Associate in Hellenic Studies at the University of Exeter, UK. She is the author of *Bad Women, Mad Women: Gender und Wahnsinn in der Griechischen Tragödie* (2011), and the editor of *Recognizing Miracles in Antiquity and Beyond* (2018) and *Mirrors and Mirroring: From Antiquity to the Early Modern Period* (with Lilia Diamantopoulou, 2020). She is now working on a monograph on automation in classical antiquity.

Edith Hall is Professor of Classics at the University of Durham, UK, and Consultant Director of the Archive of Performances of Greek and Roman Drama in Oxford, UK. Her books on ancient Greek culture and its reception include *The Return of Ulysses* (2008), *Greek Tragedy* (2010), *Adventures with Iphigenia in Tauris* (2013) and *Introducing the Ancient Greeks* (2015).

Craig Jendza is an assistant professor of Classics at the University of Kansas, USA. His research interests include Greek tragedy, comedy, satyr drama, mythology, magic, linguistics, humour and horror. His monograph *Paracomedy: Appropriations of Comedy in Greek Tragedy* examines how Greek tragedians regularly appropriate elements from comedy such as costumes, scenes, language, characters or plots. Some of his recent articles have investigated paracomedy in Euripides' *Orestes* (*American Journal of Philology*), persuasive analogies in Greek magic (*Archiv für Religionsgeschichte*) and Indo-European mythology in Bacchylides (*Journal of Indo-European Studies*).

Dimitrios Kanellakis is a Research Associate at the University of Oxford, UK, where he recently completed his doctorate. His research interests revolve around Greek drama, lyric poetry, theory of literature and classical reception. He is the author of *Aristophanes* *and the Poetics of Surprise* (2020) and editor of *Ancient Greek Comedy: Genre, Texts, Reception* (with Almut Fries, 2020) and of a forthcoming volume on *The Pathology of Love in Greek and Latin Literature*.

Adam Lecznar is Lecturer in Classical Languages and Literature at the University of Leeds. He has research interests across classical reception, intellectual history, and ancient and modern literature. His publications include essays on Nietzsche, Joyce, Aimé Césaire's tragedies and Alejo Carpentier, and he has completed a monograph called *Dionysus after Nietzsche: The Birth of Tragedy in Twentieth-Century Literature and Thought*.

N. J. Lowe is Reader in Classical Literature at Royal Holloway, University of London, UK. His books include *The Classical Plot and the Invention of Western Narrative* (2000) and *Comedy* (2008); a book on the classical roots of science fiction is forthcoming from Liverpool University Press, and he is currently finishing a study of ancient Greece in historical fiction.

Athina Papachrysostomou is Assistant Professor of Ancient Greek Literature in the Department of Philology, University of Patras, Greece, and a Fulbright alumna. Her research interests include Greek comedy, Athenian political history and textual criticism. Apart from several articles and volume contributions, she has published four monographs (two in English: *Six Comic Poets: A Commentary on Selected Fragments of Middle Comedy*, 2008, and *Amphis: Introduction, Translation, Commentary*, 2016; and two in Greek: one on Athenian Democracy in 2014, and one on textual criticism in 2017), and has co-edited one collected volume (*Time and Space in Ancient Myth, Religion and Culture*, 2017).

Ralph M. Rosen is Vartan Gregorian Professor of the Humanities in the Department of Classical Studies at the University of Pennsylvania, USA. He has published broadly in various areas of Greek and Roman literature, with special interests in comic and satirical literary genres, ancient aesthetics, ancient philosophy and medicine, especially Galen. He is co-founder of the Penn-Leiden Colloquia on Ancient Values, and co-editor of six published volumes (Brill) emerging from these occasions. His most recent book is *Making Mockery: The Poetics of Ancient Satire* (2007). He is currently involved in various research projects on Greek comedy, Hippocrates and Galen.

Pavlos Sfyroeras is Professor of Classics at Middlebury College, Vermont, USA. He has published a number of articles on several Greek poets, including Aristophanes, Euripides, Sophocles and Pindar. His forthcoming book *The Feast of Poetry: Sacrifice and Performance in Aristophanic Comedy* (Center for Hellenic Studies) combines his interests in poetic genres, both dramatic and non-dramatic, and ritual performance. His concern with situating poetry in its historical context informs another book-length project that is tentatively entitled *Pindar and Athens: Epichoric Traditions of Mythmaking*.

Peter Swallow is the Tassos and Angele Nomikos Research Associate at King's College London, UK. He teaches Classics at Notting Hill and Ealing High School, and has

Contributors

previously taught at KCL and Goldsmiths, University of London. His doctorate explored the Victorian reception of Old Comedy, and his publications include studies on the translation and performance of Aristophanes.

Mario Telò is Professor of Classics at University of California, Berkeley, USA. He is the author of *Aristophanes and the Cloak of Comedy: Affect, Aesthetics, and the Canon* (2016). In 2018, he co-edited, with Melissa Mueller, *The Materialities of Greek Tragedy* (Bloomsbury). His new book *Archive Feelings: A Theory of Greek Tragedy* is forthcoming in 2020 in the series 'Classical Memories/Modern Identities'.

Natalia Tsoumpra is a lecturer in Classics at Glasgow University, UK. She specializes in Greek comedy and tragedy, and is also broadly interested in ancient medicine, magic, gender and sexuality, and theories of humour. She is the co-editor of *Morbid Laughter* (Illinois Classical Studies 43.2) and the editor of *Costume Change in the Comedies of Aristophanes* (forthcoming in Illinois Classical Studies). She is now working on a monograph on leadership and power dynamics in Aristophanes. She has an ongoing interest in performance and theatre practice, and has worked closely with the Glasgow University Classics Society on producing several classically themed plays.

Magdalena Zira (BA Classics Oxford University, MA Text and Performance Studies King's College London, MFA Drama UC Irvine, PhD Classics King's College London) is a theatre director and scholar of the reception of Greek drama. Her doctoral thesis examines the problem of the Greek chorus in contemporary performance. She has directed over thirty theatre productions in Cyprus and elsewhere. In 2012 she co-founded the independent theatre company Fantastico Theatro, which is committed to approaching classical texts in innovative ways. In the summer of 2017 she directed Euripides' *Iphigenia in Aulis* in the buffer zone of the divided city of Nicosia.

PREFACE
Edith Hall

Aristophanes of Athens is universally acknowledged to be the founding father of comic theatre. Stand-up comedians, humourist essayists, satirists, political speech-writers, authors of librettos of light opera and of situation comedies all study his eleven surviving plays to hone their techniques in provoking laughter. Yet, within the Academy, studies of Aristophanic comedy tend to be anything but funny. His texts have been used to chronicle the realities of everyday life in classical Athens, including the price of sausages; to document the workings of the democratic Assembly, council and lawcourts; and to assess the shifts in attitudes among Athenian citizens towards the protracted war with Sparta, the position of women, the treatment of slaves, and inter-generational conflict. Innumerable studies probe the relationship of Aristophanic comedy to other literary genres, such as lyric and tragedy, to the rituals, cult and festivals of the theatre-god Dionysus, and to contemporary developments in philosophy. But there has been remarkably little work asking the question that must have been at the forefront of Aristophanes' mind – how to maximize the humorous potential of his comic productions. He used every dimension of his theatrical medium to elicit laughter, from complex, punning wordplay, parody and burlesque, to visual, musical and actorly strategies which enhanced the absurd situations his comedies dramatize and the outrageous caricatures of contemporary politicians which are central to the democratic project of Old Comedy.

It was with the overriding aim of analysing the techniques that Aristophanes used to produce humour that, with Peter Swallow, himself an amateur director, actor and singer as well as an expert on the uses to which Aristophanes was put in Britain in the nineteenth century, I convened a conference at King's College London in July 2017. Most of the chapters in this volume began life as papers delivered there. Since Aristophanes is a living presence in contemporary theatre – although his modern reception has been neglected by scholars in comparison with that of Athenian tragedy or Homeric epic – we also encouraged papers that asked whether and how his humour can be translated to the modern stage. There are challenges facing any modern director who wants to make an audience laugh with Aristophanes today. His jokes can depend on knowledge of ancient Greek, or long-dead individuals. Others require an acceptance of the deeply sexist, racist, anti-slave and homophobic views shared by most of his citizen male audience in the late fifth and early fourth centuries BCE. But there can also be significant reward.

Many people have helped bring this book to fruition. Several other scholars and theatre professionals contributed to the conference with papers or interventions, including Helen Eastman, Michael Silk, Francesco Morosi, Isabel Ruffell and Rosie Wyles. Alice Wright and Lily Mac Mahon at Bloomsbury have been enormously supportive, as has Chris Machut in the Classics Department and Alex Creighton from

Preface

the Arts and Humanities Research Institute at KCL. We are also grateful to Marcus Bell, to the catering staff at KCL, and to the cooks and waiters at Pizza Express on the Strand. But we dedicate our book to four young females who have brought endless laughter into our own lives, my daughters and Peter's nieces.

CHAPTER 1
INTRODUCTION: DISSECTING THE FROG(S)
Peter Swallow

The American writer and humourist E. B. White once observed that 'humor can be dissected, as a frog can, but the thing dies in the process and the innards are discouraging to any but the pure scientific mind'.[1] In his book on the metatheatre of Aristophanes, Slater likewise cautions against over-analysing comedy for humour's sake:

> Comedy is notoriously difficult to study and analyze. The creation of taxonomies of jokes or comic techniques risks destroying the very subject it studies, eliminating any sense of what is really funny or creative through the atomization of the dramatic experience into a series of lifeless specimens, pinned onto the collector's display board.[2]

This volume provocatively proposes to disprove such criticisms – or at least to circumvent them. It proposes to take a scalpel to Aristophanes and pin his jokes to the collector's board, not for the purpose of killing the frog but to dissect it and see how it works. Humour, after all, is not only another feature, but the *defining* feature of Old Comedy (else it would self-evidently not *be* comedy); to decide electively not to examine it is short-sighted. The fundamental, guiding question we ask of Aristophanes in this volume is also the fundamental question we should *always* ask of Aristophanes, or of any comedy or satire: *why are you funny*? Because the answer to that fundamental question, as this volume will also demonstrate, can have huge ramifications for how we interpret everything else Aristophanes does.

This may prove a hard task – as we will shortly see, there is as yet no universal humour theory that can perfectly and flawlessly account for what makes something funny and what does not – but that does not make the need to pursue the task any less pressing. And theorists have been thinking about what makes people laugh since Plato (ironic, given the general absence of humour theory from classics), so there is a basis on which we can build. Before turning to an overview of the papers included in this volume, the present introduction will provide a brief overview of the various schools of humour theory which have developed – though I emphasize here that this is only an *introduction* to the theory, designed for readers who may be otherwise unfamiliar with the subject.

And what if, in our over-zealousness to analyse that which we should not, we destroy Aristophanic humour? Well, it is not necessarily the academic's job to preserve the humour of a text if doing so prevents inquiry. A detailed philological reading of *Medea* may likewise run the risk of dimming the affective tragic power of Euripides' drama under the weight of scholarship, but nobody would seriously suggest that philologists

Aristophanic Humour

should therefore stay away from tragedy. And there is every chance that an understanding of how Aristophanes' humour works may make our laughter even louder. My favourite joke in the Aristophanic corpus is from *The Wasps*:

> κελητίσαι 'κέλευον, ὀξυθυμηθεῖσά μοι
> ἤρετ' εἰ τὴν Ἱππίου καθίσταμαι τυραννίδα.
>
> I told her to ride me; she got angry and asked me if I was putting Hippias back in the saddle [lit. establishing Hippias' tyranny].
>
> Wasps 501f.[3]

When I first read this as a schoolboy – in fact it was one of my lines in a performance of the play – I did not find it funny. I didn't know who Hippias was, so while I got the *double entendre*, the pun on a tyrant's name and the surrounding political context of the joke was lost on me. Then the director explained it to me, and I laughed. I still laugh whenever I think of it – or at least smile with appreciation at the (rather crude) wit. Explaining the humour allowed me to see what Aristophanes was doing – to analyse the (rather complex, multi-layered, context-dependent) joke. In fact, even the most basic humour is inherently complicated; as John Morreall has pointed out, to appreciate comedy (and he is specifically talking about Aristophanes here) 'involves higher-order thinking, especially seeing things from multiple perspectives. To get even simple jokes requires that we have two interpretations for a phrase in mind at the same time.'[4] Whenever we hear a joke, we effectively dissect it to see how it works: if we 'get' it, we might laugh; if we don't 'get' it and can't work out how it works, we probably won't. The purpose of this volume is not necessarily to make its readers chuckle, but if we can draw attention to some of Aristophanes' genius and raise a laugh along the way, then all the better.

So there we have it. Scalpels at the ready – let's dissect some *Frogs*.

Theories of humour

Laughter as a physical reaction may have originated in the 'open-mouth display' observed in many mammals.[5] The display of a relaxed mouth, with gums and teeth withdrawn, appears to indicate passivity without intent to attack in many mammals. Smiling, conversely, may be a manifestation of the 'bared teeth display' 'shown by a subordinate to a dominant, a nervous signal of submissiveness common in many species, including many parts of the primate line.'[6] The Play Theory of humour associated with the Dutch cultural historian Johan Huizinga in his influential *Homo Ludens* (1938) draws from such observations of animal behaviour the idea that laughter developed as a social indicator to make clear that playing and joking were not to be taken as hostile acts. Since play activities have been observed in a number of species, they must have some adaptive benefit; evolutionists have suggested play is used to prepare safely for dangerous scenarios and to build sociality. This social function may also be broadly the 'meaning' of the personified figure of 'Play' (*Paidiá*) appearing on some Attic vases contemporary with Aristophanes, and of the constructive recreational activities (*paidiaí*) described in Plato's *Laws* as distinctive to peacetime social life (7.803c).[7] Indeed, one study has found that laughter is 'over 30 times as likely to be performed by subjects in social than in solitary settings' when not stimulated by media.[8] Of course, humour and laughter can be, and often are, targeted and aggressive, but, as Aristophanes shows, there is no easier way to build social cohesion than by sharing a joke about a common enemy. 'The basic ability to perceive humor seems "instinctive"'[9] and 'people of all ages and cultures experience humour in their daily conversation, observation, and imagination',[10] so it seems reasonable to seek an evolutionary explanation.

There is an important distinction to make here between laughter and humour. Laughter is a physiological response which may indicate the experience of humour, but does not necessarily – we also laugh when we are awkward, or very upset, or pretending, or are on laughing gas.[11] In fact, when we laugh, it is quite rarely because we find something funny.[12] Theories of humour typically struggle to account for tickling precisely because the laughter it induces is a response to a physical stimulus, not a response to humour (but tickling *may* be connected to play).[13] Likewise, humour can be experienced without laughter, which is, as we have said, a largely social, group-centred act. This is why the present volume is focusing on humour rather than laughter – it is focused on the stimulus rather than the perceived reception indicated by physical response. Evolutionary explanations of laughter can tell us much about the social function of humour, but may not fully illuminate how humour works in itself.

The Superiority Theory of humour assumes that amusement is derived from the receivers' sense of superiority over the target of the joke. Thomas Hobbes set this out in his political work *Leviathan*, in which he connected humour with a misplaced sense of 'glory':

> *Sudden Glory*, is the passion which maketh those *Grimaces* called LAUGHTER; and is caused either by some sudden act of their own, that pleaseth them; or by the apprehension of some deformed thing in another, by comparison whereof they suddenly applaud themselves. And it is incident most to them, that are conscious of the fewest abilities in themselves; who are forced to keep themselves in their own favour, by observing the imperfections of other men. And therefore much Laughter at the defects of others, is a signe of Pusillanimity. For of great minds, one of the proper workes is, to help and free others from scorn; and compare themselves onely with the most able.[14]

The theory's roots lie with Plato. In the *Philebus*, he argues that humour derives from ridiculing the flaws of the target, and as such is inherently hostile; 'γελῶντας ἄρα ἡμᾶς ἐπὶ τοῖς τῶν φίλων γελοίοις φησὶν ὁ λόγος, κεραννύντας ἡδονὴν αὖ φθόνῳ, λύπῃ τὴν ἡδονὴν συγκεραννύναι' ('when we laugh at our friends' absurdities and mix pleasure with envy, we mix up pleasure with pain', 50a). Aristotle also defined comedy as the 'μίμησις φαυλοτέρων' (the '*mimesis* of baser people', *Poetics* 1449a), although without the caveat that the comic individual is usually just as flawed as their target – for Aristotle, comedy in its narrow sense as theatrical performance is a positive force. (We must remember that we do not have access to his fuller analysis of the *telos* of comedy, which was in the part of his *Poetics* we have lost.)[15] Plato and Hobbes both disdain laughter, but Aristotle asserts that it can be 'ἀνώδυνον καὶ οὐ φθαρτικόν' ('harmless and non-destructive', *Poetics* 1449a).[16] Superiority Theory may explain the aischrology so central to the humour of Old Comedy, offensive language which operates 'as a powerful medium of public ridicule and humiliation'.[17]

In 1709, Lord Shaftesbury published *An Essay on the Freedom of Wit and Humour*, in which he went several steps further than the acknowledgement of the physiological benefits of laughter to be found in ancient medical ideas of Aristotle, Galen and the Hippocratic corpus,[18] by theorizing that humour had a biological function as a physical relief mechanism for bodily fluids and gases.[19] Sigmund Freud later picked up on this concept and reformulated it into a Relief Theory of humour. For Freud, humour creates pleasure by economizing on mental energy, whether that energy is spent on suppressing negative mental thoughts or on maintaining rationality;[20] 'laughter arises when an amount of psychical energy previously used in charging certain psychical pathways has become unusable, so that it can be freely released'.[21] This theory may account well for our fascination with taboo humour on sexual or violent themes, a form of comedy familiar to Aristophanists.

The most popular account for humour today is the Incongruity Theory. There are numerous variants, but in short it argues that amusement is derived from two conflicting ideas, and the act of reconciling these two incongruities:

Why didn't the skeleton go to the ball?
He had no *body* to go with.

Were this joke actually funny, it would work because of the incongruity set up by the two possible meanings of no *body*. When we talk about normal people not going to a social event because they have nobody to go with, we are imagining them as single; the joke invites us to think about a skeleton, so his isolation instead comes down to his lack of corporeality. There is an incongruity established between a normal experience of being date-less – the normal meaning of nobody to go with – and the phrase's different meaning here. Our recognition of this incongruity and its resolution may make us laugh (though probably not in this case).

Aristotle hints at an Incongruity Theory of humour in the *Rhetoric*, arguing that humour can arise when a verbal unit proceeds 'μή... πρὸς τὴν ἔμπροσθεν δόξαν' ('not according to previous expectation', 3.11). But one of its earliest and clearest exponents was Kant, who defined laughter (not humour) as 'an affect arising from a strained expectation being suddenly reduced to nothing.'[22] Of course, not every incongruity is funny – we only have to look as far as the dramatic ironies of Greek tragedy to see this. And the biggest issue with Incongruity Theory comes when mapping it onto extended scenes of comedy, as we find in Aristophanes, where principles familiar to stand-up comedians today – accumulation, repetition, taglines, punchlines, callbacks, running gags, syncopation and crescendo[23] – are paramount in creating the comic effect. Not all humour is verbal, as Charlie Chaplin could attest.

So the Play Theory, the Superiority Theory, the Relief Theory and the Incongruity Theory represent the four major schools of thought on how humour works. This volume aims neither to challenge outright nor adopt wholesale any one of these models. Nor does it attempt to define and advocate its own monolithic new humour theory – although individual papers, especially in the first section, contemplate what minimum core topics and cultural phenomena any proposed 'universal' theory would need to accommodate. Instead, this collection of chapters embraces and discusses the various theories, with all their various benefits and flaws, but to a wider end – acknowledging as it does so that there does not yet exist (and there probably never *will* exist) a single model to explain all forms of humour. It is important to note that these four schools do not necessarily contradict or mutually exclude one another, nor do they by any means attempt to answer the question in the same way. 'With so many theories and approaches, all with their own useful perspective, none monopolizes the truth, and another wrinkle on the elephant always hides awaiting discovery.'[24] Our contributors are unafraid of using concepts ultimately derived from different schools of thought within philosophical and cultural theory if doing so can help us hone our analytical tools in studying Aristophanic plays both as texts and performance. The underlying approach is historicist, indeed culturally materialist insofar as all the essays acknowledge that emotional and psychological responses to theatre are necessarily informed and inflected by the contingent physical, economic and social environments in which performances take place. But this goes hand-in-hand with a conviction that no single paradigm or model can ever be sufficient to the complicated task of analysing performance, especially of 'classic' texts, and that different problems are susceptible to unravelling by different conceptual means. As Hall and Harrop concluded in a volume addressed to the theoretical frameworks used in analysing Greek drama – especially, in that instance, tragedy – in performance, we should never 'be afraid to order our theory eclectically à la carte'.[25]

Aristophanic humour

This volume is specifically about *Aristophanic* humour, and as such, our interest in humour theory extends only as far as it is a useful framework within which to discuss the comedies of Aristophanes. By no means do all contributors frame their discussions around the archetypes we have here discussed. Yet we believe the discussions had here will be of interest to cultural historians and humour theorists more widely, since comedy must form a vital component of any social history, and Aristophanes has lain at the heart of discussions of comedy since the ancient world. Almost every familiar comic technique and tradition, including 'personal satire, philosophical satire, mimicry, parody, puns, *double entendre*, Saturnalian role inversion, Rabelaisian and Bakhtinian carnival, drag acts and cross-dressing, stand-up, bawd and scatology, slapstick, farce and knockabout', has been detected in Aristophanes;[26] his direct or indirect influence has been detected everywhere from the comedies of Jonson and Shakespeare, to the plays and operettas of W. S. Gilbert, to the searing satire *Spitting Image*, a political comedy broadcast on the BBC from 1984 to 1996.[27] Understanding the comic conceptual schemata, the nuts and bolts of Aristophanes' own scripts, can only further illuminate the countless works of comic theory and comic theatre which have analysed and emulated him subsequently.

It is puzzling that, to date, there has been considerable resistance in contemporary classical scholarship to attempting any sort of theory of humour, and it is an irony that while classicists have written endlessly about the structure, themes and context of Greek Old Comedy in an attempt to define what Old Comedy 'means' and in what it essentially consists, they have almost never discussed the fundamental question of how it was (and is, whether 'still' or 'again') funny. Where classicists have discussed Aristophanes' humour, they have inevitably done so through discussion of specific humour techniques: puns, obscenity, metatheatre, and so on. This is a valuable exercise in and of itself, and we focus on some of the more neglected strategies and modes of humour ourselves in the second section of this volume in order to amplify and discover case studies for how Aristophanic laughter did and can still work on the performance ground. But the division of this volume into separate sections on theory and practice is designed to address this cart-before-the-horse tendency. In general, this volume approaches Aristophanic humour in micro- *and* macro-dimensions as the only way holistically to get to grips with the topic.

Since the 1980s, a fashionable approach to Old Comedy has been to explain it as falling, broadly speaking, into the category of Bakhtinian carnivalism; through its topsyturvydom and absurdity, the theory goes, the ancient Athenians could safely celebrate 'a populist, utopian vision of the world which provides through its inversions of hierarchy a critique of dominant culture'.[28] If we wanted to compare this anthropological analysis with humour theory, and at the risk of being provocative by doing so, we might situate it somewhere between the Play Theory and the Relief Theory. It is a tempting thesis because it accounts for comedy's ritualistic origins. As Goldhill points out, Mikhail Bakhtin's original concept of the carnivalesque by no means requires it to be politically and socially innocuous;[29] yet scholars do often cite this theory to explain why Old Comedy cannot be considered a serious, political genre. Halliwell is one such Bakhtinian, arguing that 'the very concept of religious festivity ... is closely entwined in Greek thought with notions of "play", celebration and laughter'.[30] At the same time, however, he resists fully accepting the Play Theory of humour – for, he argues, 'the uncertain, problematic relationships between human laughter and the behaviour of animals and gods ... [demand] a historically nuanced perspective on the status of laughter'.[31]

Michael Silk, for his part, also rejects the utility of humour theory in accounting for Aristophanic comedy. For him, 'through a great variety of theoretical orientations, theorists seem to be assuring us that there is something secondary, special, perhaps inexplicable, about comedy' – his emphasis and ire being on 'secondary'.[32] He criticizes the Incongruity Theory in particular as 'a corollary of a no less fundamental conviction: that comedy presupposes comparison, whereas serious art, such as tragedy, does not'.[33]

But attempting to analyse Aristophanic humour through humour theories in no way diminishes the comic genre or prevents it from having a serious point. If comedy can convey something serious through the use of humour, does that not in fact make it even *more* important to understand how that humour works?

This is not the space to further challenge these views, or the many such views like them written by Aristophanic commentators. Let it simply be said that we hope to lend further complexity and nuance to this debate, and to prove, if not a correction to such positions, then at least a supplement and enrichment.

N. J. Lowe, in contrast, has long championed the application of humour theory to Aristophanes, while acknowledging its limitations. As he argues in his 2008 study on *Comedy*:

> There is still an oddly persistent belief that comedy is intrinsically impervious to analysis, on the grounds either that humour is irreducibly subjective or that comic effect is irreparably destroyed by the act of dissection. Practical experience suggests that the reverse is true: that close analysis of complex humour if anything deepens appreciation of the comic effect, both as an experience of funniness and as a work of artifice.[34]

Sommerstein also seems to embrace humour theory when he outlines three types of laughter (again, not humour) present in Aristophanes. Type one, he argues, 'may be termed *the laughter of derision*';[35] this is essentially a formulation of the Superiority Theory. Type two is '*provoked laughter*, laughter, that is, deliberately induced by a person whose interest is served by it'.[36] In a sense, he is presenting an inversion of the Superiority Theory; by inviting laughter directed at themselves, the speaker of a type-two joke supplicates themselves. Sommerstein's third type is not actually laughter at humour, but the laughter of pleasure.[37] Curiously, Sommerstein defines laughter as '*language* that is unintentionally amusing by its incongruity, either internally or with the speaker or situation' as liminal between types one and two,[38] implying that to speak incongruously is to make *someone*, whether or not the speaker, appear foolish. Thus, he attempts to subsume Incongruity Theory into his larger argument. The director and classicist Alexis Solomos – whose writing on Aristophanes drew explicitly on his experience as practitioner to develop sophisticated theories – embraces incongruity much more simply, putting Aristophanes' funniness down to an inherent, incongruous chaos; 'contrary to what happens in Tragedy, in Comedy not order but disorder is the primary factor'.[39] Aristophanes '[uses] the wrong thing at the right moment'.[40]

Theory and practice

This volume builds on discussions of Aristophanic comedy held at a two-day conference on 'Aristophanic Laughter' at King's College London in July 2017, convened by the volume's editors. It offers insights into potential *theoretical* models for Aristophanic humour alongside discussions of how Aristophanic humour works in *practice*; that is, both by imagining the effect of the plays in their original performance contexts and also the ways in which contemporary performances of Old Comedy have approached the humour present in the text. We feel that this is a vital part of the narrative, since humour always lives or dies in performance – it is never wholly comprehensible on the page alone. As such, the performative turn taken by recent classicists and the new reception-informed focus can only help us to understand Aristophanic humour more deeply.

In our first article, N. J. Lowe addresses in more detail and with greater contextualization many of the issues raised by this introduction. He sets forward a strong defence of using humour theory as a way of analysing and understanding Aristophanes. Turning to Play Theory, Edith Hall asks what play, personified as *Paidiá* on Athenian pottery contemporary with Aristophanes, means in his comedies. Play is at home in the spheres of erotic games and sexuality, and the Dionysiac processional *thiasos*, as well as in both satyric and comic drama. The verb *paizein*, with different shades of meaning, occurs in some revealing passages of Aristophanes. Then Craig Jendza proposes a bold new Incongruity Theory of humour for Aristophanes, which incorporates both verbal and non-verbal forms of comedy to offer a comprehensive model of how Aristophanes *is* and *was* funny.

Our next two chapters throw a new light on the Relief Theory of humour and take a psychological approach to Aristophanic humour. Mario Telò, influenced by Bataille's connection of death with laughter and the Freudian notion of the death drive, explores humour as a masochistic act of self-destruction; Pavlos Sfyroeras is also interested in this connection between laughter and pain, and argues that Aristophanic comedy had an analgesic effect, functioning as a method of processing trauma.

Ralph M. Rosen's chapter offers a constructive comparison between the modern phenomenon of internet trolls and Aristophanes, which may force us to reconsider the licence we allow for *ad hominem* attacks in ancient satire: to what extent is Aristophanic humour conducive to societal cohesion, and to what extent is it merely a destructive source of Hobbesian pusillanimity? Hall's second chapter offers one answer to this challenge, reading Old Comedy as a fantasy for imbuing previously marginalized but newly enfranchised democratic citizens with supernatural power. For Hall, Aristophanes' humour is not destructive but demotic and communal.

Finally, Pierre Destrée rounds off the first half of the volume with a discussion of some ancient humour theory. The second half of Aristotle's *Poetics* is lost; this apparently put comedy at the centre of its analysis in the same way that the extant text discusses tragedy. Destrée's article attempts to reconstruct Aristotle's reception of Aristophanes, to challenge the view that he disdained Old Comedy for its frequent recourse to aischrology.

In the second section of this volume, we begin to look at specific tools for generating humour in Aristophanes. Athina Papachrysostomou's focus is on Aristophanic satire or parody, which she usefully breaks up into surface and deep parody before demonstrating how it functions as a distorting lens through which to view the target. Surface parody offers simple distortion of reality, whereas deep parody recategorizes the target completely. Dimitrios Kanellakis, meanwhile, takes a detailed look at Aristophanes' use of *para prosdokian*, a technique which generates humour through wordplay and the generation of surprise, offering a typography of the technique and contextualization of its dramatic use.

Following this, Maria Gerolemou, Natalia Tsoumpra and myself each take a thematic approach to the topic. Gerolemou explores how Aristophanic comedy approaches mechanization as both a source of humour and a cause of genuine anxiety. Tsoumpra challenges the orthodox view of madness in Greek theatre as inherently tragic, instead offering a persuasive case for its comicality in performance. This provokes the reader to reconsider ideas of paratragedy and paracomedy. My own chapter considers how Aristophanes creates humour in scenes predominated by sexual violence, building on an Incongruity Theory model. I argue that Aristophanes tends to avoid telling simplistic 'rape jokes'; rather, scenes build up multiple layers of incongruity that create humour through complex interactions, often undermining rather than reinforcing the sexual violence.

Our next three chapters focus on Aristophanic humour in reception and performance. Adam Lecznar explores how Aristophanic humour, particularly in comparison with Greek tragedy, has given philosophers – Freud and Nietzsche in particular – a different and more human model for intellectual inquiry. Magdalena Zira looks at how recent modern Greek directors of Old Comedy have emphasized melancholy in their performances, and how this tonal shift away from Bakhtinian carnival in fact reinforces rather than undermines Aristophanic humour.

In our final chapter, David Bullen shares a practitioner's insight into adapting Aristophanes for the modern stage, and as a contemporary political act. His paper offers a personal account of writing an adaptation of *Clouds* for the campaign to save classics at Royal Holloway, and what he learnt about Aristophanic humour in the process. It reiterates this volume's core tenet – the most important thing in any performance of Aristophanes is always, and has always been, to make people laugh. Everything else is secondary.

PART ONE
THEORY

CHAPTER 2
BEYOND A JOKE: MAKING HUMOUR THEORY WORK WITH ARISTOPHANES
N. J. Lowe

Classicists have an uneasy relationship with humour theory. Part of the *raison d'être* of this volume is the fissure that has strangely arisen between classical scholarship on humour and the contemporary field of humour research, which in the last thirty years has reinvented itself as a unified and intellectually rigorous interdisciplinary conversation, but of which classicists have taken a largely sceptical view where they acknowledge it at all. Thus the seminal cultural histories of ancient laughter by Halliwell and Beard are cognisant but deeply wary of the modern field's claims to have identified a universal machinery of humour[1] – no doubt in part because both works are histories less of humour as an affective response than of laughter as a social practice and object of thought in all its cultural contingency, and partly also because both authors happen to be scholars with a long-standing suspicion of tidy, totalizing models and narratives, but mainly because the nearest things to standard models in the field seem inadequate to the task of describing the gelotogenic properties of ancient texts. Even Aristophanists have been only sporadically engaged with this modern phase of humour theory (although this is reciprocated, in that humour theorists for their part have been largely oblivious to developments in Aristophanic scholarship over the same period); while the two conspicuous exceptions, Robson 2006 and Ruffell 2011, have found the models available in mainstream humour theory inadequate to deal with the cognitive plate-spinning of Aristophanic humour in close-reading detail, and have had to look outside the mainstream of humour theory – Robson especially to Gricean pragmatics, Ruffell to Jerry Palmer's pioneering work on popular comedy from the pre-*Humor* era – in their efforts to develop models sufficiently nuanced to be able to analyse the dynamic complexities of humour in the Aristophanic text.

Part of the reason for this breakdown in interdisciplinary communications is that, following a spectacular early surge, the current state of humour theory has grown comparatively becalmed. The year-zero of modern humour studies is 1988, the debut of the International Society for Humor Studies' journal *Humor*.[2] Though the groundwork had been laid twelve years earlier with the establishment of the ISHS conference series (initially triennial, then biennial, and from 1987 annual), it was the journal that formally unified a convergent but still fragmented interdisciplinary conversation into what felt at the time like a glimpse of a utopian future for the humanities and sciences – with linguists and literary scholars publishing in the same journals as neuroscientists and sociologists, united by a common understanding of shared participation in a multi-specialist collaborative project with a large but coherent single object of study. This has not meant that Bergson, Freud, Koestler and their fellow founding fathers have been demoted to chapters in an intellectual prehistory; but the insights and models in those pioneer texts, with which scholarship continues to engage, find themselves now reformulated as part of a newly joined-up project with a large, mature and cohesive theoretical literature, and the longstanding tradition of ignoring predecessors, reinventing the wheel and concocting half-baked totalizing theories of humour from scratch has largely if not entirely fallen away (as has the notion that intellectual progress in the field halted abruptly in 1905[3]).

At the time of its disciplinary integration, the leadership of the humour research community was nucleated in cognitive linguistics. *Humor*'s founding editor was Victor Raskin, whose *Semantic Mechanisms of Humor* (1985) had set out an intellectually robust and explanatorily productive model for the workings of verbal jokes based around the core concept of an opposition between 'scripts' – a term first coined in machine-intelligence circles in the 1970s to denote a set of expectations about how a given scenario will unfold, and whose flexibility, though sometimes criticized for its lack of formal rigour, has been a major factor in its persistence and usefulness in humour models. Raskin's Semantic Script Theory of Humour (SSTH) was widely adopted and extended, most prominently in collaboration with Salvatore Attardo to produce 1991's General Theory of Verbal Humour (GTVH), which sought to scale the model up to more extended kinds of humorous text (Attardo 2001), and latterly in the computationally oriented Ontological Semantic Theory of Humour or OSTH (Raskin 2017). Particularly indicative of the new integrated paradigm for research was Ruch's empirical testing of the model (Ruch, Attardo and Raskin 1993; for a critique of this experiment see Oring 2011: 201f.).

It is important to appreciate that the SSTH and its successors were intended as a conversation-starter rather than -stopper, and that its own authors have repeatedly expressed disappointment at the relatively limited attempts by other researchers to refine the model. Though the GTVH has never quite attained the status of a standard model, with persistent questions over its component claims and explanatory reach,[4] its recentring of humour theory around a version of incongruity-resolution model reflects a wider coalescence of consensus that something-like-opposition of something-like-scripts lies at the centre of a process which is centred on cognitive mechanisms of clash-resolution; and at the very least it has proven a valuable framework and focus for connected debate about the interaction of incongruity mechanisms, inferential logic and social world-knowledge as constituents of the humour process. Its various incarnations have been productive as an analytic tool for describing what individual jokes are doing, and addressing non-trivial challenges such as assessing whether two jokes are the same; and it is a mark of the model's continuing resilience and the thought invested in it that, while many key figures in the field have engaged critically with the GTVH, no serious competitor model has yet emerged to supersede it,[5] and its fundamental assumptions command broad consensus even if its formal specifics do not. As a minimum, most mainstream humour theorists would now agree on the following baseline propositions, none of which was remotely accepted as consensus forty years ago:

1. Humour is a human universal, as are its underpinning psychosocial mechanisms – even while its specific manifestations and uses remain highly susceptible to cultural (and individual) factors.
2. The three canonically recognized types of older theories of humour – superiority, incongruity and release theories – are not competing but complementary, describing different modules of a more extended mechanism with whose sociocultural, cognitive and affective-physiological elements they respectively (though not tidily) align; and the task of humour theory, as opposed to that of the sociology of humour, is to describe the workings of this mechanism.
3. Jokes (finite, isolable comic moments with a single payoff[6]) work by a rapid cognitive spark-jump between scripts that are in some way in tension with one another.

Nevertheless, placing the GTVH and its joke-focused programme of enquiry at the institutional centre of the theoretical conversation around humour has consumed a disproportionate amount of the field's intellectual oxygen, and left some major aspects of the larger humour process comparatively neglected. Consider the joke that Richard Wiseman's 2002 LaughLab survey found to be the joke rated funniest in Scotland:

I want to die peacefully in my sleep like my grandfather, not screaming in terror like his passengers.[7]

This is a joke which depends for its effect on a set of background anxieties in its culture: terror of death, particularly in transport disasters; guilt about valuing our own lives over others'; anxiety over committing our safety entirely to the hands of someone else; and there is perhaps also an element of our own generational survivor guilt over outliving our parents and grandparents. The structure of the joke uses the symmetrical binary form of the utterance to set up a pointed slippage between two conflicting scripts. The initial script here is a banal platitude engaging our fear of death on the level of sanitizing, softening sentiments about its peacefulness, but the word 'passengers' delivers a cognitive shock which forces us into what Attardo calls an 'inferential explosion',[8] reparsing the entire utterance as about much more violent kinds of death and the taboo thoughts they prompt us to think, as we run through an extremely rapid chain of inferences and script-retrievals. (*Wait, what? Who has passengers who would scream in terror, apparently in connection with that person's death? Oh! He's an airline pilot, or possibly a coach driver, or a train driver, or he's giving a group of people a lift home, or maybe there are still further scenarios I can imagine . . . But why then was he asleep? Ah! He must have been dozing on the job! So: The comedian's grandfather died suddenly, with terrible consequences for others, under circumstances which paint him in a dubious light at best; and the comedian is asserting that their own peaceful death is worth a horrible death for many others, and is inappropriately sanguine and non-judgemental about professing this.* **Ha ha,** *that's quite funny; and I have been given permission to indulge taboo thoughts under the licence of humour, all the while assuring myself that I do not share that attitude.* **Hooray!** *Now I feel* *better about death, disaster, selfish thoughts, familial irresponsibility, etc.*) The result is that we feel clever (for having got the joke), entertained (because we have found it amusing), morally reassured (because we do not think like that), and emotionally relieved (because we have nevertheless been briefly permitted to indulge unthinkable bad thoughts).

Much of this may seem self-evident, but I want to point out three elements in this parsing that are surprisingly underemphasized in current models of joke analysis and in humour theory as a whole, yet are crucial to understanding the operations of performed humour in general and of Aristophanic comedy in particular.

First, much of both the inferential sequence and the affective payload is not merely semantic but *mentalizing*. In order to solve the semantic puzzle and get the joke, we are made not only to run through a range of script-matches to the keyword 'passengers' and to construct a narrative scenario around the best match or matches, but to model contrasting mental states (the grandfather's peaceful obliviousness versus the passengers' terror) within it; then, in returning to the moment of the joke performance, to model additionally the state of mind professed by the comedian in their expression of a preference. In doing so, the audience recognizes a gap between the comedian's attitude and their own, and that in permitting themselves to identify with the comedian's perspective (through a combination of performative contract, the poetics of identification constructed over the course of the routine, and the very activity of parsing the scenario by putting themselves inside the heads of the characters to traverse the mental pathways involved), they have been tricked into briefly imagining the satisfaction that might be felt in giving free rein to attitudes they would normally hold to be repugnant. Where humour research has engaged at all with theory of mind, it has been primarily in connection with developmental and psychiatric shortfalls from neurotypical adult humour processing, but there are good grounds to argue that the construction of mental models of other minds is fundamental not just to comic theatre but to basic aspects of humour in general.

Second, the joke does not stop when we get it, but continues to unfold and expand as we play it back and further unpack the implications of the attitudinal contrasts between audience and comedian, grandfather and passengers, traversing the imaginative routes between these four mental vertices in different combinations. The invitation to mentalize does not expire; once engaged, our faculty of gapping conjures multiple disaster scenarios and imagines not only the contrasted states of mind of the pilot and passengers in each, but (our mentalized interpretation of) the comedian persona also imagining and responding to each scenario with variations on the same outrageously inappropriate empathy failure.

Third, the construction and comparison of different mental states is what enables the joke to succeed as a reliever of tensions and anxieties, and to illustrate the uniqueness of humour's distinctive power as a literary mode and cultural practice. To put it at its simplest, humour makes us feel good about the things we feel bad about, taking anxieties and aggressive urges and delivering a powerfully positive affective payload from the temporary permission it grants to engage with the contradictions and slippages we construct around them. And while the ways in which different cultures are attuned to use humour, let alone what they make humour *about*, vary widely, the underlying cognitive-affective process and mechanisms do show every sign of being universal.[9]

Now, there is longstanding recognition within humour theory that while the cognitive element of joke form is now fairly well understood, other aspects of the larger phenomenology of humour remain work-in-progress. In particular, it has become something of a leitmotif in humour studies that jokes appear to be a special and somewhat limited case within the broader field of humour, and that their modelling is neither easily scaled up to more extended forms of humorous text or performance, nor readily exportable to more surreal, bizarre, or nonsense-based kinds of humour. Such model-building and close-reading work as has been done on extended humorous texts (most notably by Chłopicki, Attardo and Ermida) has focused on the comic short story rather than on performed or visual media such as theatre, stand-up, radio and television comedy, comics, or film; it has also been primarily linguistic in focus, with a relatively simplistic model of joke sequencing in terms of successive textual comic beats. Among the particular challenges for joke-based models are the operations of found, unintentional, or authorless humour; the workings of extended comic sequences, routines, performances and narratives, and the question of their reducibility to sequences of atomized jokes; the dynamics of comic arousal in such sequences, including the sensitization of audiences to comic triggers and the escalation of comic beats towards a climax; the iterability of jokes and their ability to be funny, even increase in hilarity, on multiple hearings; the coalescence of multiple comic effects in a single moment; the continuing comic unfurling that takes place in the aftershock of a comic detonation, as its clashing scripts continue to interact; metacomic effects involving jokes about jokes, such as laughing at the failed funniness of a weak or problematic joke; and, I would argue above all, the neglected central role of theory of mind in the parsing and processing of the comic transaction. All but (arguably) the first of these are fundamental to the working of comic performance, yet remain strikingly underaddressed in the present state of humour theory.

In what follows, I want to suggest ways in which these challenges can be addressed through a close reading of how jokes are dynamically constituted within the Aristophanic text, taking a single Aristophanic line (*Acharnians* 104) which seems on the face of it to break humour theory in its current state of sociolinguistic, incongruity-cognitive, joke-oriented understanding – but which in fact offers a glimpse of ways in which that model can be made to work with extended performed texts composed of complex extended sequences involving the mimesis and reconstitution of multiple fictional minds and their associated mental states and attitudes. In the process, I want to build on the pioneering work of Robson and Ruffell to argue four more general claims: that performed comedy (modern as well as ancient) develops comic structures that are fundamentally distinct from those in written texts, and which have not yet been systematically addressed in mainstream humour studies; that these structures are not reducible to the text-based analysis of 'jab lines' and 'punch lines',[10] but involve the coordination of multiple overlapping and interdependent cognitive moves, including the detonation of multiple jokes in a single syllable; that they involve a mode of comic engagement which is apertural rather than closural; and that they make a case for revisiting the arousal models of humour prevalent fifty years ago but marginalized in the discipline's modern phase, for reasons rooted in the history of the field as it followed the trajectory of the mind sciences generally from a psychophysiological phase rooted in behaviourism to a semiotic phase rooted in cognitivism.[11]

One of the questions to which this volume may incidentally frame a collective answer is where the funniest moments are to be found in Aristophanes. My suspicion is that they will turn out to be disproportionately concentrated in the prologues, which are under particular pressure to warm up the audience while simultaneously building characters and world, and constructing relationships of identification and collusion between performers and audience. Thus the prologue of *Acharnians* has a number of simultaneous jobs to do: to tune the audience up with a stand-up-style initial solo routine which will elevate their baseline arousal levels and their sensitization to comic triggers; to map the initially plastic play-world onto the stage space ahead of the *parodos*, where the setting stabilizes; to construct and induct the audience into the play's problem-world and characters; and to establish basic identification relationships configured around the traditional comic hero, his goals and his antagonists. In this instance, Dicaeopolis is keen to see the Athenian assembly discuss peace negotiations with Sparta, and in an opening monologue to the audience (1–42) declares his intention to heckle from the floor of the Pnyx if the speakers deviate from the topic of peace talks (37–9); the assembly then convenes and suppresses the first speaker Amphitheus, who claims to be a minor deity deputed to negotiate peace terms (40–60), in favour of two diplomatic delegations bringing questionable evidence of support from Persia (61–122) and Thrace (134–73). Meanwhile, Dicaeopolis' interventions from the floor escalate from disregarded asides to increasingly active interventions on the platform itself, and a parallel-running side-mission where Amphitheus is dispatched to Sparta to negotiate a private peace treaty for Dicaeopolis and his household (128–33), running the gauntlet of the war-supporting Acharnians on the return (175–203). Over the course of this complex sequence, Dicaeopolis is established as a vicarious agent of the audience's comic desires who will speak truth to power, challenge the subversion of democratic will, and achieve the fantastic rewards of peace – while the conduct of the assembly is then filtered and interpreted through his increasingly confrontational commentary, whose principles were established in his opening monologue which primes, frames and anchors the meeting itself.

Such is the overall dramatic and thematic roadmap; let us now look at one particular moment in this sequence. Here are the exchanges leading into and out from line 104:

Π.	ἄγε δὴ σύ, βασιλεὺς ἄττα σ' ἀπέπεμψεν φράσον
	λέξοντ' Ἀθηναίοισιν, ὦ Ψευδαρτάβα.
Ψ.	ἰαρταμαν ἐξαρξαν ἀπισσονα σατρα.
Π.	ξυνήκαθ' ὃ λέγει;
Δ.	μὰ τὸν Ἀπόλλω 'γὼ μὲν οὔ.
Π.	πέμψειν βασιλέα φησὶν ὑμῖν χρυσίον.
	λέγε δὴ σὺ μεῖζον καὶ σαφῶς τὸ χρυσίον.

Ψ.	οὐ λῆψι χρυσό, χαυνόπρωκτ' Ἰαοναῦ.
Δ.	οἴμοι κακοδαίμων, ὡς σαφῶς.
Π.	τί δαὶ λέγει;
Δ.	ὅ τι; χαυνοπρώκτους τοὺς Ἰάονας λέγει,
	εἰ προσδοκῶσι χρυσίον ἐκ τῶν βαρβάρων.
Π.	οὔκ, ἀλλ' ἀχάνας ὅδε γε χρυσίου λέγει.

Envoy	Come, then, Pseudartabas; speak the message your Emperor sent you to deliver to the Athenians.
Pseudartabas	Narble zarble floopsy weh-weh blerp.
Envoy	Everyone understand that?
Dicaeopolis	*I* bloody well didn't.
Envoy	He says the Emperor is going to send you gold. Tell them more about the gold, clearly this time.
Pseudartabas	**Not getses goldy, big fat arsehole Gweeky.**
Dicaeopolis	Bloody hell, that was clear all right.
Envoy	What did he say, then?
Dicaeopolis	What did he say? That the Greeks are big fat arseholes if they think they're getting any gold from the barbarians.
Envoy	No no, he said 'gold in big fat parcels weekly'.

Acharnians 98–108

A narrowly textual and joke-based model of script collision would have little trouble mapping the comic beats in the text, but a much harder time accounting for the actual comic effect. For one thing, to call line 104 a 'joke' obscures the fact that this is a line with at least four successive comic beats in it, which between them deliver five or more distinct payoffs. The first and largest is the *ou*, which punchlines two strands in a single monosyllable: (a) Pseudartabas turns out to understand and speak Greek after all, and (b) he turns out to be far from a compliant stooge of the envoy but an inconveniently autonomous political and comic agent in his own right. Immediately we revise our models of the mental states of both Pseudartabas himself and the envoy who is trying to use him. This is immediately followed by some amusingly broken Attic supplying the verb and object while demonstrating Pseudartabas' comically garbled Greek. His previous utterance was nonsense Persian, all comedy-barbarian *a*-sounds, which made no attempt even to communicate with his audience; now (c) he shows an ability to communicate when he needs to, but also (d) he betrays an inability to master the Greek inflectional system. Pseudartabas is dimly aware of some morphological features of the Greek verb system, incongruously including the comparatively advanced detail of the future stem of *lambanō*, but not the basic person and number endings of the active; he knows that *chrusos* is a second-declension noun, but not what the accusative ending looks like. But then the next comic beat, which turns out to have been set up by the two preceding words, is that the one Greek word he gets completely correct is the vocative of *chaunoprōktos* – that spectacularly untranslatable piece of verbal aggression based on a winning combination of sexual crudity and male assertion of phallic dominance over pathic passivity – which is then doubled on the final comic beat by being coupled with an ethnic slur in the form of the disparaging and resented Persian word for 'Greek', pronounced here with a comedy Persian accent and with a garbled vocative ending to land (e) a one-two punch of sexual and racial insults which also recapitulate all of (a)–(d) in their incongruous combination of correct and barbarous Greek and their refusal to stick to the envoys' bogus script.[12]

Nor are these cognitive overlaps the most challenging aspect of this sequence for narrowly semantic models of humour. While the line is a showcase for Aristophanes' verbal comic art in its mimetic mix of Greek and barbarism and its swerve into fluent obscenity, the laugh is not in the verbal triggers but in the rapid inferential dance of *minds*. In the space of a single line, we have learned or confirmed a remarkable amount about what is going on behind Pseudartabas' apparently hilarious eye-mask; in particular, that he understands Greek but has the maximum expressible contempt for its speakers, including those on whose behalf he is being paraded. (He will, however, crumble into silent yes/no head-movements at 113–15 when confronted by the universal language of physical violence.) We are used to reminding ourselves that Aristophanic characters are not rounded psychological entities with inner lives and behavioural consistencies of the kind that would be expected from tragedy or Menandrean comedy, but this is not at odds with the invitation to try and imagine what a representative of the Persian empire might think of being paraded at the Athenian assembly by minders to whose charade he feels no particular debt of compliance. Indeed, the more preposterous the character, the more entertaining he is to imagine; and Pseudartabas' characterization is itself framed as the third term in a contest of authority and interest between Dicaeopolis as the audience's vicarious agent of demotic self-assertion and the envoy as the embodiment of elite entitlement and duplicity, into which Pseudartabas is now inserted as a contemptuously autonomous representative of a far superior geopolitical power who will nevertheless in turn acknowledge subjection to Dicaeopolis' forceful expression of demotic authority and control.

Meanwhile, the multiple comic payoffs in line 104 have themselves been set up by processes that have been running all the way through the scene and back to the opening lines of the play. This moment is a pivotal one in the arc of Dicaeopolis' gradual rise to domination of the assembly, which has been building from heckles from the floor which are ignored (67–79), to heckles from the floor which are responded to (83), to interaction with the envoys from the floor (101–9) – which the present sequence will escalate further to see him joining them physically on the platform (110) and coercing the truth out of a now tellingly wordless foreign dignitary by threat of force (111–14a), which in turn will launch a new gag sequence alleging that some or all of the Persian delegation may actually be cosplaying impostors drawn from the local emasculate community (115–22). We never get far enough into this to learn whether this is actually the case, or just a gleeful assertion of unchecked comic control on Dicaeopolis' part, because the herald intervenes desperately to restore some semblance of order and bring this sequence to a close (123) so that Dicaeopolis can set his private plan in motion while the platform is cleared for the next major gag sequence, the parade of Odrysian mercenaries (134–73).

In this single line, then, a whole web of comic strands that have been threaded into the scene as it unfolds are woven together to deliver not a single payoff but a firecracker string of them. There is Dicaeopolis' heckling for peace and personal comic assertiveness and aggression as a focus for the audience's identification and rage; the extended satirical conception of the assembly transparently trying and failing to disguise its own corruption; the conflicting motivations of the four characters, and the expansion of the conflict between the envoy and Dicaeopolis into a tussle over who finally to own and interpret the voice of Pseudartabas. All this is taking place within, and progressively disrupting, the highly formal script of the assembly and its order of business, and it is driven by a series of dark insinuations and anxieties about the very capacity of democracy to deliver on the promise of its name – anxieties which the audience is given permission to endorse, and at the same time aggressively to subvert through the invited identification with the figure of Dicaeopolis and the 'awesomely great idea' (128) he will conceive in the immediate aftermath to secure the rewards that the machinery of democracy has visibly failed to deliver to the demos.

As for the lines surrounding 104's crescendo, these are less dense with comic beats: the surprise gibberish at 100 after the extensive visual and verbal build-up; Dicaeopolis' interjection, more assertive than funny, at 101, and his reaction line at 105; followed by a second comic echo of the main joke at 106f. with his restatement of Pseudartabas' utterance at double length in Attic and quotation of its climactic obscenity (in the process turning the singulars of the Persian's address to the envoy into an inclusive plural targeting all Greeks); and a comic annex to the main joke in 108 as the envoy feebly offers a transparently desperate alternative paraphrase in which the least mistakable word is presented as a mishearing of a Persian unit of volume – which final insult to demotic intelligence will prompt Dicaeopolis to escalate his involvement and bypass the envoy's unreliable mediation by cross-examining Pseudartabas himself under threat of a beating. We might conclude from this that 104 with its multiple comic payoffs has at least a quantitative claim to be judged the funniest line in the sequence, and a peak in the arousal curve whose lingering hilarity elevates the smaller jokes which come after it and allow ripples of its initial comic detonation to be rewardingly replayed from other angles.

None of this is impervious to analysis along lines that have become well established in humour studies, but in shifting the focus from semantic to cognitive structures and preferring to speak of comic beats rather than punchlines, I have tried to foreground the centrality of mentalizing processes to the operation of comedy in performance. While it would be an overstatement to claim that all humour involves some element of consciousness modelling, if only of the fictional mind of the implied speaker, it is doubtful that a text-level model of humour can be functionally complete without a central role for theory of mind. It is especially striking how much complex, multi-level comic work flows through a single line of Aristophanes' text – and in particular, how the comic effect of that single line builds on the audience's application of mindreading skills to a carefully shaped model of three characters' conflicting mental states and motives, as well as on specific violations of expectation and intention set up by earlier priming, framing and anchoring effects, many of them camouflaged as gags in their own right and organized in sub-sequences designed with their own internal comic arcs to keep the audience's arousal levels and susceptibility to hilarity topped up. And once this comic mind-mapping is set working, it continues autonomously past the stop points in the text – a fact that may explain not only the capacity of Aristophanic moments to evoke the laughter response across two and a half millennia of time and difference, but to continue to seem funny, perhaps funnier, on the ninety-eighth or hundredth reading. The achievements of humour theory in the *Humor* era have been transformative, and it is (or should be) no longer acceptable to dismiss them unread. But attention to those lines in Aristophanes which still raise a smile across the vastness of historical and cultural distance that stands between antiquity and our own comic canon and competences is a valuable testing ground for humour theory's claims of universality,[13] and may even show us ways in which humour theory itself can be made to work better.

CHAPTER 3
PLAY AS SHARED PSYCHOLOGICAL REGISTER: *PAIDIÁ*, LAUGHTER AND ARISTOPHANES
Edith Hall

Introduction

This volume investigates how Aristophanic comedy aimed to make its audiences laugh. But comedy was not the only dramatic genre designed to produce this effect. Tragic plays may have been meant to arouse pity and terror in their audiences, but the project of the final play in the tragic tetralogy – the four-part format, three tragedies plus one satyr drama, in which tragedy was produced at the City Dionysia during Aristophanes' entire theatrical career – overlapped with that of comedy.[1] Satyr drama, as the peripatetic critic Demetrius defined it, was *tragōidia paizousa*, 'tragedy at play' (*de Eloc.* 169).

The material of satyr drama may have been mythical and set in the distant past, and the jokes may not have targeted living individuals and institutions. But the response the playwright of satyr drama and his performers wanted to elicit during the final play of the tragic tetralogy was undoubtedly not tears but laughter. And two of the central motifs used to produce laughter – the satyrs' uncontrollable urges to drink wine and have sex, the playful spheres of existence coming under the tutelage of Dionysus and Aphrodite respectively – are the same as those of comedy. The closeness of the relationship of these gods in Old Comedy is surely one of the reasons that they became increasingly associated in ancient Greek culture, their spheres moving inexorably towards one another in Hellenistic art.[2]

The classical Athenians developed a visual system for personifying dramatic genres. By the mid-420s BCE, when Aristophanes' career first took off, both were conceptualized on Athenian theatre-related pottery as maenads in the Dionysiac *thiasos*. Cratinus even wrote a comedy in which *Kōmōidia* herself appeared, as his wife, probably in a maenadic costume.[3] Since *Tragōidia* at this time encompassed satyr drama, there was no separate maenad signifying satyr play, as I have argued in detail elsewhere.[4] *Tragōidia* first appears sedately offering a gift to a child satyr named Kōmos on a red-figure vase dated to about 440 BCE and now in the Vivenel Museum in Compiègne, France.[5] A little later, on the neck of a volute-krater from Gela of about 430 BCE,[6] two satyrs, both named Simos, approach maenads named *Kōmōidia* and *Tragōidia* (with thyrsus) respectively. This scene of pursuit, with its whirling clothes, speed and excitement, is related psychologically to the experience of the dancing chorus central and ancestral to all genres of drama. A famous vase in Oxford (Ashmolean 534) depicts a satyr named Kissos priapically creeping up to a sleeping maenad named *Tragōidia*, thus configuring the relationship of satyrdom to tragedy as one of covert sexual assault.[7]

Aristophanic Humour

These relationships (mother to child, dancer to fellow dancer, serious female subverted by cheeky appetitive male) at some level express the symbiotic relationship of tragic and satyric drama within the tetralogic structure. But satyr play never acquired a distinct maenad to represent it; indeed, it never acquired a feminine noun on the lines of *Tragōidia* and *Komōidia*, but was known, when a generic term was needed, as *saturikon* (or *silēnikon*) *drama* or just 'the satyrs', *saturoi* (e.g. Ar. *Thesm.* 157).[8]

There is, however, an additional female figure who appears in this kind of theatrical pottery. She is named *Paidiá* ('Play') and in Dionysiac scenes looks like a maenad. In the first part of this chapter I use both visual and textual evidence to argue that *Paidiá* is unlike either *Tragōidia* or *Komōidia* because she does not signify a formal genre of theatre in which competitions were held at the Dionysia, and her sphere encompasses rather more than those inhabited by her generic name-label sisters. She denotes, at this time, a collective psychological register in which seriousness is relinquished; the opposite of *paizein* is normally *spoudazein*, to be serious or earnest (Xen. *Mem.* 4.1.1, *Cyr.* 8.3.47; Plato, *Euthyd.* 283b). *Paidiá* signifies a state of mind with heightened responses to hilarity, to anything that might be funny or amusing. It comes as no surprise, then, that the verb *paizein* occurs in some revealing passages of Aristophanes.

Paidiá may have been a minor enough figure in the entourages of Dionysus and indeed, as we shall see in the next section, Aphrodite. But she acquired significance in the twentieth century because classical ideas informed modern anthropological and philosophical discussions of play. In particular, the Greek concept of play was celebrated in Huizinga's *Homo Ludens*. Such has been the influence of this book on subsequent thought that its take on Greek play has remained central to more recent discussions of play in human experience and society. In the second half of the chapter I therefore briefly review modern models of play, and argue that although they have misunderstood ancient Greek play, their misapprehensions can illuminate the distinctive quality of the ancient concept in relation to the comic theatre of Aristophanes.

Paidiá in the world of Aristophanes

The female personification Play, Playing, Game or Game-Playing (for she needs to be translated in all these ways depending on the context) is not often portrayed in ancient art. The exceptions are a cluster of fourteen vases painted between 430 and 390 BCE on which she is name-labelled. In eight of these, she appears in the circle of Aphrodite, where she is not depicted specifically as a maenad, but as an attractive young female alongside other personifications related to the discourses of love and marriage, such as *Peithō*, *Eutychia*, *Eudaimonia*, *Harmonia*, *Hygieia*, *Erōs*, *Pothos* and *Himeros*. Sometimes *Paidiá* appears in such groups when they attend Aphrodite and a lover, for example Adonis. In her excellent article in the *Lexicon Iconographicum Mythologiae Classicae*, Anneliese Kossatz-Deissmann argues that on one group of vases, *Paidiá* plays games which may be interpreted as 'Liebesorakel',[9] like the 'He loves me/He loves me not' game with flower petals still played by English children today; she balances a stick on her

Play as Shared Psychological Register

outstretched hand. The games often belong to the world of the children whom the women owners of this type of pottery wanted to conceive or were already mothers to; *Paidiá* may push a child named Desire (*Himeros*) in a swing, or look quite childlike herself – often younger than the other female personifications portrayed in her company. On the other hand, even games must have rules, especially the potentially dangerous game of flirtation.

On several vases *Paidiá* holds fruit, jewellery or a hair ornament, but is supervised by her companion *Eunomia*, or 'Good regulation'.[10] *Paidiá* here signifies the 'game' of ostentatious flirtation, which must be subject to certain rules if decency is to be maintained. When *Paidiá* is rather firmly embraced by *Eunomia* on a lekythos in the British Museum, Borg argues that it represents not just a tender gesture but the restriction and control of the 'potentially frolicsome game of love by good order'.[11] Moreover, Borg thinks that their relationship signifies the tension felt under Athenian patriarchy between the need for mutual desire in marriage and the cultivation of enjoyment of sex by citizen

Figure 3.1 *Paidiá* playing with a stick in a love-game on a red-figure pyxis of about 415 BCE, ARV² 1238.99. Illustrated by Becky Brewis.

Aristophanic Humour

wives on the one hand, and on the other the condemnation of sexual drive in citizen women that might lead them to stray to extramarital lovers and affairs.

What happens if it is not maintained is strikingly illustrated on a vase that shows a scene belonging to the sphere of Dionysus, rather than Aphrodite. On a dish of about 390 BCE, a satyr whose name, Chorillos, links him to the Dionysiac dancing chorus, enjoys athletic sex with a naked and entirely willing nymph whose name is *Paidiá*.[12] Borg interprets that the nymph's name makes the term *paidiá* virtually equivalent to 'the act of love' and stresses the choral context and the mutuality of the pleasure.[13] Satyrs on vases sexually assault unwilling nymphs name-labelled *Tragōidia*, but *Paidiá* is never shown as a reluctant sexual partner. That *paidiá* in a sexual context could denote activities virtually equivalent to our word 'foreplay' seems apparent from Xenophon's *Symposium* 9.2, where a dancing master from Syracuse provides a soft-porn entertainment for the diners. The Syracusan announces it thus:

Figure 3.2 *Paidiá* enjoying athletic sex with the satyr Chorillos on a red-figure dish of about 350 BCE, ARV² 1512.18. Illustrated by Becky Brewis.

'ὦ ἄνδρες, Ἀριάδνη εἴσεισιν εἰς τὸν ἑαυτῆς τε καὶ Διονύσου θάλαμον· μετὰ δὲ τοῦθ᾽ ἥξει Διόνυσος ὑποπεπωκὼς παρὰ θεοῖς καὶ εἴσεισι πρὸς αὐτήν, ἔπειτα παιξοῦνται πρὸς ἀλλήλους.'

'Gentlemen, Ariadne will now enter the bedroom she shares with Dionysus; after that, Dionysus, a little flushed with wine drunk at a banquet of the gods, will come to join her; and then they will play with each other.'[14]

The form 'παιξοῦνται' is the Syracusan Doric contracted plural indicative future of *paizein* in the middle voice.

One slave then enters, dressed as Ariadne in a bridal gown, followed by Dionysus, to the accompaniment of sensuous Bacchic music on an aulos. At first, they embrace decorously, but soon their kisses and caresses become the real thing ('ἀληθινῶς', 9.5), and their exchanges of affirmations of love seem authentic. They do not appear to be performing theatrical or dance moves they had learned, but to be abandoning themselves to the satisfaction of longstanding desires ('ἐῴκεσαν γὰρ οὐ δεδιδαγμένοις τὰ σχήματα ἀλλ᾽ ἐφειμένοις πράττειν ἃ πάλαι ἐπεθύμουν', 9.6). This foreplay culminates in them making a move towards the bridal couch; so inflamed by the display are the married diners that they leave immediately to find their wives (9.7). The association of the verb 'play' with the erotic games of Dionysus and Ariadne here might lend support to the guess that the mysterious female figure perched on the right of the coach on the Pronomos Vase (which celebrates the success of a chorus in a tragic tetralogy culminating in a satyr drama) is intended to be understood as *Paidiá*.[15]

In one significant Aristophanic passage, towards the end of *Wealth*, flirtation or even physical foreplay seems to be exactly what is meant by *paizein*, although with a rather cruel comic twist. Now that the problem of poverty has been ended, an old woman who used to give a young man expensive gifts in exchange for sexual attention complains that he does not visit her any more. The youth proposed to play a game (*paizein*) with her (1055–9):

Youth	Do you want to play a game (*paisai*) with me for a while?
Old woman	Ooh! You are awful!
Youth	Here, take some nuts.
Old woman	Is this some kind of game (*paidian*)?
Youth	Yes. 'How Many Teeth Do You Have?'
Chremylus	OK, I know the answer! She has three, or possibly four!
Youth	You owe me! You've lost. She has only a single molar.

The game which the old woman anticipates turns out not to be played with her at all, but between two men, laying bets on the number of her teeth.

On the Dionysiac vases, *Paidiá* is usually depicted as a maenad, sometimes with a thyrsus; in her role as member of the *thiasos*, she may hold a wine jug or sportively dance, which is one way that *paizein* sometimes needs to be translated. In Aristophanes'

Aristophanic Humour

Lysistrata the verb means dancing of a specifically maenadic type; the Spartan chorus which concludes the play looks forward to seeing the Spartan girls dancing by the Eurotas again, shaking their hair 'like Bacchants' who wave their thyrsuses and 'play' (the Laconian dialect form of the genitive plural feminine present participle, 'παιδδωᾶν', 312f.). The verb *paizein* plus accusative can also simply mean 'play' a musical instrument; in *Frogs*, Pan plays on his pipe of reeds ('Πὰν ὁκαλαμόφθογγα παίζων', 230). In the Homeric *Hymn to Apollo* 206, however, *paizonta* seems to mean that the god is both dancing and playing his cithara simultaneously. And in art, *Paidiá* may play a musical instrument, like the unidentified percussion instrument she wields on a badly damaged vase from the Athenian agora (*ARV*² 1685, *c.* 420 BCE), on which another maenad seems to have the name *Thymedia* ('Delight') inscribed.[16] As we have seen, *Paidiá* may be depicted enjoying (unlike the oblivious, sleeping *Tragōidia* assaulted by a satyr) fully consensual erotic relations with a satyr. On a fragment of a krater found at Ruvo (*ARV*² 1338), *Paidiá* joins with gusto a battle between Dionysos (who can scarcely be seen) and

Figure 3.3 *Paidiá* joins battle with the giants alongside a satyr and Dionysus on a red-figure krater of about 400 BCE found in Ruvo. ARV² 1338. Illustrated by Becky Brewis.

his satyrs and the giants; holding a thyrsus in one hand and a stone to throw at a giant in the other, she comes to the support of a helmeted satyr. The scene may even be related to a particular satyr drama in which the satyrs fought giants.

Occasionally, *Paidiá* is explicitly connected with theatrical productions, notably on a fragmentary pelike in Barcelona, celebrating a choragic victory (Mus. Arch. 33). Here her relationship with the Dionysiac *thiasos* signifies the agonistic structures and performance conventions within which drama was enjoyed. Apollo and Dionysus, with his *thiasos*, are depicted at a victory tripod. On the left flies a Nike-like figure securely named *Kōmōidia*; there is another winged figure, who might be *Tragōidia*, second from the right, between a satyr holding a jug and a figure definitely name-labelled *Paidiá*. Play may here be closely allied with that satyr, and personify the psychological tenor of satyr play, but in conjunction with the other figures including *Kōmōidia* it is best not to confine her to a function as signifier of just one genre of drama.

Partly for a reason I explore in the last section, *Paidiá* has received meagre scholarly attention.[17] Her connection with Old Comedy is secured by the information that the poet Crates, sometimes said originally to have been an actor for Cratinus (*PCG* Crates I T4), produced a comedy best translated *Games* (*Paidiaí*). One of the two fragments, interestingly, seems to draw a distinction between tragic seriousness and comic playfulness; a character says that a story someone else has referred to is *not* a game, but 'a different sort of story, a serious one (*semnos . . . logos*), for all the tragic poets' (Photius α 1010 = *PCG* Crates I F 28). The other remaining fragment refers to a female who plays a 'kissing game' with male choruses, picking the most handsome ones to kiss (Pollux 9.114 = *PCG* Crates I F 27). Since this fragment survives because it is described in a list of Athenian games in Pollux's *Onomasticon* (9.110–17), it is possible that Pollux's other games were mentioned in that play, or were even personified severally by the chorusmen.

What, then, did *Paidiá* mean for Aristophanes, besides an actual game with a recognized objective, such as the game in *Wealth* discussed above? Despite his fondness for dressing up actors as feminine personifications, such as Peace, Harvest and Festival in *Peace*, Reconciliation in *Lysistrata*, the Muse of Euripides in *Frogs*, Poverty in *Wealth* and Poetry in lost comedies I have discussed elsewhere,[18] his surviving works sadly do not feature a personified Play or a Game. But the verb *paizein* is not infrequent. For Aristophanes, playing usually seems to have a significance connected with the collective ritual function of the comic chorus.

Towards the end of the parabasis of *Peace* – in my view the most metatheatrical of all Aristophanes' comedies – *paizein* comes to denote the entire function of Aristophanes' own comedy within the Dionysia of 421 BCE. The chorus of farmers praises the beauty of Aristophanes' songs, criticizes those of other poets, especially the tragedian Melanthius, and asks the 'Muse Goddess' to spit on bad dramatists but 'play' the festival along with Aristophanes/his chorus (815f):

ὦν καταχρεμψαμένη μέγα καὶ πλατὺ
Μοῦσα θεὰ μετ' ἐμοῦ ξύμπαιζε τὴν ἑορτήν.

Spit on them heartily, far and wide,
Goddess, Muse, and *xumpaize* the festival with me.

Aristophanes is inviting the Muse to collaborate with him at the festival, with its drama competitions, and the verb that naturally occurs to him to signify this is *xumpaizein*. This particular comedy and the whole festival are merged. A similar passage appears at the end of *Thesmophoriazusae* (1226–31), after the chorus say their ungracious goodbye to the Scythian archer:

τρέχε νυν κατὰ τοὺς κόρακας ἐπουρίσας, τρέχε.
ἀλλὰ πέπαισται μετρίως ἡμῖν·
ὥσθ' ὥρα δή 'στι βαδίζειν
οἴκαδ' ἑκάστῃ. τὼ Θεσμοφόρω δ'
ἡμῖν ἀγαθὴν
τούτων χάριν ἀνταποδοίτην.

Go your way and may you waft to perdition!
But for us the festival/comedy has been celebrated/performed enough.
It's time for each of us to be walking home.
May the two goddesses reward our efforts.

The meaning of *pepaistai* here is ambiguous. It depends who is involved in the dative pronoun 'us'. The chorus are saying that they, the women celebrating the Thesmophoria, have finished the performance of the rituals. But their words also embrace, metatheatrically, the entire audience who have watched the comedy being performed and who are also co-celebrants of Dionysus at *his* festival.

It is in *Frogs* that we are offered, however, the most precise dissection of the different facets of Aristophanic *paidiá*, and one particular passage seems to me to be of greater significance for his own analysis of the essence of Old Comedy than has hitherto been understood. For the chorus of Dionysiac/Eleusinian initiates, *paizein* is a key verb that describes their own activities. They decry a long list of political types whom they declare to be ineligible to join these Mysteries because they fan discord, pursue private advantage, take bribes, help public enemies, and commit other civic misdemeanours. But two types of wrongdoing the initiates specify can help us understand Aristophanes' concept of play. The chorus excludes men who 'delight in coarse ribaldry at inappropriate times' ('βωμολόχοις ἔπεσιν χαίρει μὴ 'ν καιρῷ τοῦτο ποιοῦσιν', 358) and 'any politician who reduces the pay of the poets because he has suffered a comic attack in the ancestral rites of Dionysus' ('ἢ τοὺς μισθοὺς τῶν ποιητῶν ῥήτωρ ὢν εἶτ' ἀποτρώγει,/κωμῳδηθεὶς ἐν ταῖς πατρίοις τελεταῖς ταῖς τοῦ Διονύσου', 367f.). There is humour that is overly coarse and there is laughter that occurs at inappropriate times. There are also politicians who object precisely to being made fun of at the Dionysia, which *is* the appropriate time for comic laughter.

And in this appropriate mocking laughter, everyone else is invited to join:

ὑμεῖς δ' ἀνεγείρετε μολπὴν
καὶ παννυχίδας τὰς ἡμετέρας αἳ τῇδε πρέπουσιν ἑορτῇ.
    χώρει νυν πᾶς ἀνδρείως
    ἐς τοὺς εὐανθεῖς κόλπους
    λειμώνων ἐγκρούων
    κἀπισκώπτων
    καὶ παίζων καὶ χλευάζων,
    ἠρίστηται δ' ἐξαρκούντως.

But as for you, stir up the song and the night-long dances, appropriate to this festival.
    Everyone now intrepidly marches
    to the flowery vales and meadows
    stamping in time,
    mocking,
    playing and scoffing;
    We've breakfasted enough.

370–7

Here the participle of the verb *paizein* is sandwiched between two others that mean the type of raillery or jesting, designed to produce laughter, at others' expense – in other words, it is part of the poetic formula that describes the political function of Aristophanic comedy in the democratic city. The chorus now turns to the praise of Demeter:

Δήμητερ ἁγνῶν ὀργίων
ἄνασσα συμπαραστάτει,
καὶ σῷζε τὸν σαυτῆς χορόν,
καί μ' ἀσφαλῶς πανήμερον
παῖσαί τε καὶ χορεῦσαι·
καὶ πολλὰ μὲν γέλοιά μ' εἰπεῖν, πολλὰ δὲ σπουδαῖα, καὶ
τῆς σῆς ἑορτῆς ἀξίως
παίσαντα καὶ σκώψαντα νικήσαντα
ταινιοῦσθαι.

Demeter, queen of our sacred rites,
be present now
and preserve your chorus.
And allow me to play and dance in safety all day long,
and say many funny things
and many serious ones
and, as befits your festival,
may I play and mock and be crowned victor.

384–93

The chorus members want to 'play' in their Eleusinian aspect, too, perhaps giving us a glimpse into the conduct of the processions that wended their way annually at harvest-time from Athens to the Eleusis telesterion. 'Playing' is paired with 'dancing' is this ritual context, but so is 'mocking'; in the same passage, the chorus express their expectation that they will say 'serious' things as well as 'funny' ones. Here the *spoud-* stem, 'serious', often found in antithesis to 'play', is in antithesis, rather to '*geloia*', 'funny'. Perhaps the suggestion is, again, that Aristophanic 'play' can have serious real-world implications, even if the medium requires an attitude welcoming to laughter.

In their next few lines, the chorus invoke Iacchus once more, pairing *paizein* with *choreuein* (409). They conclude by using the idea of *paidiá* in what we might call the 'satyric' sense, meaning physical play with a potential and non-coerced sexual partner. They have seen a beautiful young woman, with a breast partly bared, who is 'partner in our playing', *sumpaistria* (414). Dionysus now speaks up, declaring that, in that case, he is eager to join the procession and 'μετ' αὐτῆς/παίζων χορεύειν', 'playfully dance with her' (418f.).

In the initiates' chorus in *Frogs*, therefore, the term 'play' is associated with (a) processional dance/movement, (b) the type of mockery of individuals central to Old Comedy (which has an earnest purpose even if its joking form, the laughter it seeks to elicit and the festival context do not feel *spoudaion*, 'serious') and (c) erotic, physical reciprocal flirtation. The different significances of the verb *paizein* help Aristophanes define his total project of a physical theatre performed under the sign 'Laughter', which celebrates bodily desires but has, it is lightly suggested, a political purpose too.

But when Aristophanes wants to make a claim that comedy is in its own way as useful as tragedy, and has its own didactic function, he avoids the term *paidiá* and its cognates. His preferred terms are to do with advice and teaching ('ξυμπαραινεῖν καὶ διδάσκειν', famously, in *Frogs* 686f.) and the newly coined generic term for didactic comedy, 'τρυγῳδία', 'wine-lees-song'. Trugedy, as Diakaiopolis insists in *Acharnians*, is socially useful because it knows what is right as well as tragedy does, and Aristophanes makes a claim to be the city's counsellor (*xumboulos*, 499–500).[19] The name of Trygaeus, the protagonist of *Peace*, is undoubtedly related to the poetic genre in which its owner is a hero; namely, trugedy, 'wine-song'. *Trugōidoi* in Wasps denotes comic poets (650, 1537).[20] Aristophanes' rival Eupolis also presented himself as a useful poet whose genre was 'τρυγῳδία' (*Demes* fr. 99); in his *Maricas* he addressed the audience in the voice of a schoolteacher, who claimed he could make his audience both serious and wise (frr. 192.13–15 and 205).[21]

Old Comic *paidiá* does not share the pretensions of 'trugedy', nor claim to be a teacher. The collective games, mockery, inebriation, processional dancing and flirtation involved in Aristophanic *paidiá* may sometimes have a serious underlying thrust, especially when mocking jests are directed against politicians. This *paidiá* is adopted collectively by people who have mutually agreed on an exclusively merry comic register of interaction. But it is a fundamentally light-hearted register, manifested in frequent laughter. It took a specific form in comedy, but was also operative in preparations for marriage and sexual encounters, all Dionysiac festivals (including the exceptionally drunken procession in which Hephaestus was conducted to the temple of Dionysus in the Marshes during the Choes, the second day of the Anthesteria[22]) and, of course, satyr play.

Serious, sober and desexualized play from Plato to game theory

Both the noun *paidiá* and the verb *paizein* are closely related to the Greek world for a child, a *pais*. All three originated in the dim and distant Indo-European semantic past with a word meaning something like 'little'.[23] The same Greek stem produced two other nouns that sounded similar, only distinguished by the slightest of vowel difference and accentuation. Thus the word for childhood, and occasionally the more derogatory *childishness*, is *paidía*, with the stress on the penultimate syllable rather than the last one. Even more confusingly, the term for education, of both children and adults, is *paideía*, as for example at *Clouds* 962, where the Right Argument praises 'the old education' (τὴν ἀρχαίαν παιδείαν). In this noun the penultimate vowel, which is stressed, becomes the longer sound *ei*. The aural differences between the three nouns (*paidiá* (play), *paidía* (childhood, childishness) and *paideía* (education)) will have been much clearer in spoken Athenian Greek than they may seem today.

One meaning of *paizein* was simply to make a joke through wordplay, and is used as such by the scholiasts on Aristophanic comedy (e.g. Σ *Birds* 42; 'οἱ κωμῳδοὶ παίζειν εἰώθασι τὰ τοιαῦτα'). Plato could not resist the temptation to make the venerable Athenian, who in *Laws* is constructing a legislature for the ideal city, self-consciously pun on the similarity between the words for education and play, *paideía* and *paidiá*:

ὅπου δὴ νόμοι καλῶς εἰσι κείμενοι ἢ καὶ εἰς τὸν ἔπειτα χρόνον ἔσονται τὴν περὶ τὰς μούσας παιδείαν τε καὶ παιδιάν, οἰόμεθα ἐξέσεσθαι τοῖς ποιητικοῖς, ὅτι περ ἂν αὐτὸν τὸν ποιητὴν ἐν τῇ ποιήσει τέρπῃ ῥυθμοῦ ἢ μέλους ἢ ῥήματος ἐχόμενον, τοῦτο διδάσκοντα καὶ τοὺς τῶν εὐνόμων παῖδας καὶ νέους ἐν τοῖς χοροῖς, ὅτι ἂν τύχῃ ἀπεργάζεσθαι πρὸς ἀρετὴν ἢ μοχθηρίαν;

Regarding laws that are now, or will in the future be rightly drawn up to regulate education in music and παιδιά, are we to imagine that poets will be permitted such licence that they may teach whatever type of rhythm or tune gives them personally the most pleasure to the children of respectable citizens and the young men in the choruses, regardless of the effect in terms of on virtue or depravity?

Laws 2.656c

The Athenian's interlocutor, Cleinias, agrees that such a proposition would be quite unreasonable. Even to make sense in English, Plato's παιδιά here needs to be translated not by 'play' but by some such bland word as 'recreation'. We may be sure that Plato's play does not include harsh mockery of public men or tipsy amorousness. It does not even need to include the psychological register of which the most frequent manifestation is collective laughter. The gulf between Aristophanic and respectable Platonic 'παιδιά' is huge, but it also helps define the Aristophanic version by way of contrast.

The contrast is made even clearer when the Athenian returns to the theme of παιδιά later, where it achieves a metaphysical as well as a sociopolitical and ethical dimension. Heraclitus had previously speculated that time or eternity 'is a child playing, playing draughts; the power of the child is sovereign' ('παῖς ἐστι παίζων, πεττεύων· παιδὸς ἡ βασιληίη', fr. 52 Diels-Kranz). Plato adapted this idea, to make human beings the playthings of the divine; only god is worthy of supreme seriousness ('σπουδή'):

> ... θεοῦ τι παίγνιον εἶναι μεμηχανημένον, καὶ ὄντως τοῦτο αὐτοῦ τὸ βέλτιστον γεγονέναι· τούτῳ δὴ δεῖν τῷ τρόπῳ συνεπόμενον καὶ παίζοντα ὅτι καλλίστας παιδιὰς πάντ᾽ ἄνδρα καὶ γυναῖκα οὕτω διαβιῶναι, τοὐναντίον ἢ νῦν διανοηθέντας.

> ... but humans are god's toy, and that is the best part of them. So every man and woman should live their lives accordingly, and play the finest games, holding a different view from the one they hold now.

> Laws 7.803c

The reason they need to change their minds, which means preferring peace to war, is that 'in war there is neither play (παιδιά) nor culture (παιδεία) worthy of the name, which are the things we deem most serious':

> παίζοντά ἐστιν διαβιωτέον τινὰς δὴ παιδιάς, θύοντα καὶ ᾄδοντα καὶ ὀρχούμενον, ὥστε τοὺς μὲν θεοὺς ἵλεως αὐτῷ παρασκευάζειν δυνατὸν εἶναι, τοὺς δ᾽ ἐχθροὺς ἀμύνεσθαι καὶ νικᾶν μαχόμενον.

> Life should be lived as play, playing certain games, performing sacrifices, singing and dancing. A man will then be able to propitiate the gods, and defend himself against his enemies, and win the contest.

> 7.803e

But the Athenian now emphasizes that only the supremely decorous kinds of song and dance in austere musical modes, which he has earlier defined, are included in this programme of play. And all theatre arts, drunkenness, sexual banter, ribaldry and verbal assaults on civic leaders are of course out of the Platonic question.

The reason for exploring the radical differences between the Aristophanic and Platonic notion of play is the centrality of Plato's earnest and sober 'παιδιά' to modern discussion of play and game theory. This has in turn made it difficult for philosophers and scholars to penetrate behind the Platonic screen to understand the significance of *Παιδιά* in Athenian fifth- and early fourth-century pottery and the full significance of the verb *paizein* in Aristophanes, especially the genre-defining ludic processional hymn to Iacchus and Demeter in *Frogs*.

Play as Shared Psychological Register

Play was first put at the centre of the modern philosophical radar by Romanticism. In his *Letters on the Aesthetic Education of Man* (1795), Friedrich Schiller made large claims for it, virtually equating it with freedom and with art. He argued that physical play is only made possible when the serious physical work has been done necessary to the support of human life. Work is a response to need, and is unfree, while play is a response to superabundance and occurs in the domain of freedom. Play can take aesthetic forms, at which point it becomes art. In a secular version of Plato's play in *Laws*, Schiller argues that 'Man plays only when he is in the full sense of the word a man, and he is only wholly man when he is playing'.[24] This is an elevated version of play, in which the core Aristophanic elements of inebriation, sexuality and political mockery are nowhere in evidence.

The next momentous claim for play was made by the Dutchman Johan Huizinga, who was born in Groningen in 1872. He studied linguistics at Groningen and Leipzig, writing his doctoral dissertation on the figure of the jester in classical Indian drama, which showed his early interest in joking and play as a fundamental element of culture. He held chairs at Groningen and Leiden, but always tried to reach as wide a public as possible with his work. He was an early and consistent opponent of fascism in Germany, Italy and Spain, and wrote a polemical critique of their ideas in *In the Shadow of Tomorrow* (1935). Two years later he delivered a lecture at the Warburg Institute in London on the concept of play in history and linguistics, published in an expanded version in 1938 as his seminal *Homo Ludens*. But he was about to enter the final and anything-but-playful last period of his life. He was vice-president of the International Committee of Intellectual Cooperation with the League of Nations, which existed to defend western intellectual traditions against totalitarianism. When the Germans occupying the Netherlands closed the University of Leiden and Huizinga delivered a speech criticizing them, he was arrested and sent into internal exile in the village of De Steeg in Gelderland, near Arnhem. He died there in the winter of 1945, never to see the town's liberation.

Homo Ludens is a monumental work of anthropological, social and cultural history, beginning from Aristotle's famous (if not quite true) statement that the human being is the only animal that laughs.[25] Huizinga does not use the title *Homo Ridens*; he is much more interested in play than in laughter. This may explain his neglect of Aristophanes. Yet *Homo Ludens* has much to offer the analyst of Aristophanic comedy, especially in its emphasis on two aspects of play. First, Huizinga stressed the competitive and agonistic element in play, an idea which helps us understand both the rivalry between Aristophanes and the other comic poets with whom he was contending, and the scenes structured around a formal competition, whether a joust between rival orators in *Knights* or the Just and the Unjust Argument in *Clouds*, the replay of the competition between Homer and Hesiod in *Peace*, or the famous altercation between Aeschylus and Euripides in *Frogs*.[26] Huizinga found this idea in the nineteenth-century scholar Jacob Burckhardt, who argued that the ancient Greeks' competitive spirit, *der agonale Trieb*, was uniquely pervasive in their society. Huizinga disagreed, and while acknowledging the centrality of competition to Greek play, presented the agonistic drive as a universal human principle.[27] Second, Huizinga stresses that certain kinds of play are intimately related to wisdom, epistemology and knowledge, as in the popular riddle-solving motif in ancient Greek stories such as the tradition of the competition between Chalcas and Mopsos; this story, which combines the elements of agon and knowledge, also bears a decidedly non-playful force in that Calchas, after losing the competition, either dies of grief or kills himself.[28]

But Huizinga's play is fundamentally different from Aristophanes' because he, like Schiller, was so taken with Plato's rather sombre treatment of play in *Laws*, especially the manner in which the Athenian conflates the identity of ritual and play, and his inclusion of the sacred within the category of play.[29] In the chapter 'Play and Poetry', Huizinga argues that all poetry is born in sacred play and is a play-function operating within a playground of the mind.[30] His emphasis on the erotic aspects of play certainly illuminates one aspect of Aristophanic *paidiá*; lyric love poetry he sees 'as a product of the age-old game of attraction and repulsion played by young men and girls in a spirit of badinage'.[31] He regards all Greek drama as growing out of ritual play; he asks why the Greeks did not use the word 'play' of drama, and decides that Greek society was 'so imbued with the play-spirit' that the spirit never struck the Greeks as something separate and special.[32] This, of course, is not quite correct, as we have seen; 'Play' could be conceptualized, turned into an abstract principle and personified, and to the late fifth-century Athenians signified a psychological register shared by comedy, satyr play and flirtation/sexual foreplay in which laughter is always an appropriate response. The mockery of prominent citizens it encouraged in comedy may have a serious function as a vehicle of democratic accountability, but Old Comic play is infinitely more amusing and light-hearted than the play of Plato, Schiller and Huizinga.

Huizinga's most important critic, the French philosopher and anthropologist Roger Caillois, elevated παιδιά to a different type of importance in his *Les jeux et les hommes* (1958, translated as *Man, Play and Games*). He argues that games take four forms: a formalized rivalry where merit decides the winner ('agon'); games of chance, such as dice (*alea*); imitation (mimesis); and *ilinx* (ecstasy). The first two are 'higher' forms of play that arise in more developed civilizations. But all four can tend towards one of two poles of experience; one is what Caillois calls *ludus*, choosing the Latin word that can be translated 'game', 'play', 'sport', 'pastime', 'entertainment', 'fun' or 'school'. He reserves the Greek term *paidiá* for uncontrolled fantasy, chaos or tumult, originating in early childhood improvisation and energetic gaiety.[33] It is interesting that he intuitively associates the Roman term with orderly play and the Greek term with disorderly rioting imaginations. But Caillois' *paidiá* would have been unrecognizable to Aristophanes, whose chorus of initiates repeatedly stress that they are playing while processing in a strict rhythmical metre during the formal performance of a dramatic genre delimited by myriad rules and conventions, even if those conventions include the celebration of physical desires for wine and sexual encounters.

The importance of play has been constantly re-emphasized, and the concept earnestly defined and debated, across several academic disciplines. American cognitive philosopher George Herbert Mead, in his *Mind, Self, and Society from the Standpoint of a Social Behaviorist* (1934), argued that play and games are what make sophisticated communication and thought possible, since players must be able to adopt in their imaginations multiple viewpoints simultaneously, and predict the responses of adversaries holding those viewpoints. The influential British paediatric psychoanalyst Donald Winnicott saw playing, especially with transitional objects such as teddy bears, as crucial to the development of the individual human psyche and its separation from the parental other.[34] Hans-Georg Gadamer's hermeneutic philosophy saw all understanding – especially clear in the case of our responses to art – as a form of play that takes the form of a dialogue between interpreting agent and what is being interpreted.[35] Moral and political philosophers gravely debate whether the goods intrinsic to play are the achievement of difficult goals and pleasure that derives from play, or the activity of playing itself.[36]

Meanwhile, game theory, a branch of mathematics, has evolved rapidly since the Hungarian John von Neumann proved his theory of equilibria in two-person zero-sum games in the 1920s.[37] Game theorists analyse decision making by two or more people in relation to many different aspects of human life, from economics to biology; a few ancient historians have applied game theory, along with rational choice theory, to the Athenian democracy, with fruitful results.[38] But Aristophanic comedy, I suspect, has nothing to learn from game theory and not all that much from play theory. With the exception of some of Huizinga's discussion of poetry, theories and models of play have ever since Plato, via Schiller, departed ever further from the *Paidiá* familiar to Aristophanes' audiences from their pottery connected with love, wine and theatre and mobilized in his plays to define his comic project. Play in Aristophanes' Athens meant a psychological stance in which two or more humans agreed to play certain types of game in which sex and alcohol figured large and funniness and laughter were obligatory. It took a special, democratic, generic form including political mockery in his theatre. But in all other respects, Aristophanic play had most in common with satyr play and erotic games.

CHAPTER 4
ARISTOPHANIC INCONGRUITIES
Craig Jendza

Many modern theories of humour rely primarily or exclusively on verbal jokes, and when humour theory has been applied to Aristophanes, it has generally been done on a linguistic level.[1] While it is clear that Aristophanic comedy incorporates linguistic humour that violates the 'cooperative principle' (CP) that the philosopher H. P. Grice suggests underpins human conversation,[2] not enough attention has been paid to the role that non-linguistic incongruity plays in Aristophanes and in humour theory more generally. In this chapter, I will propose and apply to Aristophanes a new theory of humour based on a 'broadened cooperative principle' (BCP) that incorporates not just language but the entire set of standards that allow us to navigate our culture successfully: gender, clothing, sexuality, obscenity, violence, and even concepts like literary genre.[3]

Many humour theories developed or evolved out of insights from Grice's influential work on the logic of everyday conversation. Grice argued that people engaging in conversation follow a cooperative principle (CP): 'Make your conversational contribution such as is required, at the stage at which it occurs, by the accepted purpose or direction of the talk exchange in which you are engaged.'[4] This cooperative principle led to a series of so-called Gricean maxims:[5]

1. Those of Quantity:
    (a) Make your contribution as informative as required
    (b) Do not make your contribution more informative than is required
2. Those of Quality:
    (a) Do not say what you believe to be false
    (b) Do not say that for which you lack adequate evidence
3. Those of Relation:
    Be relevant
4. Those of Manner:
    (a) Avoid obscurity of expression
    (b) Avoid ambiguity
    (c) Be brief
    (d) Be orderly

These maxims underpin successful human conversation, and they can be violated in ways that are either acceptable or unacceptable. If you said, 'What's the weather outside today?' and I said, 'I'd wear a jacket if I were you', I would have flouted maxim 3 ('be relevant'). However, this would be acceptable since one could still infer it was cold outside. But if you said, 'What's the weather outside today?' and I said 'Apples', this would be unacceptable and would inhibit effective societal functioning.

Scholars of humour soon realized that that the violation of these Gricean maxims was an important mechanism in generating humour.[6] Of the three original theories of humour (release, superiority and incongruity), only incongruity theory says anything about the *mechanisms* that create humour.[7] Release theory concerns the psychological effects of humour, suggesting that laughter is the release of excess pent-up nervous energy; superiority theory concerns the social function of humour, suggesting that laughter expresses feelings of superiority towards the target of a joke; and incongruity theory concerns the cognitive faculties behind humour, suggesting that laughter is the result of the perception of something incongruous which violates our mental expectations. The violation of Gricean maxims became a prime method of producing incongruities, since an incongruity would naturally emerge between what an interlocutor expected to hear according to CP and what actually was said. This insight prompted a wide range of new humour theories: the script-based semantic theory of humour,[8] the general theory of verbal humour,[9] and the cognitive-evolutionary theory of humour.[10] Yet since these theories largely developed out of a theory about language, they tend to be less successful at analysing the types of humour that are non-linguistic in nature. This is especially problematic in the case of Aristophanes and ancient humour more broadly, since much of the humour is derived from aspects of the performance, visual or otherwise, not the mere recitation of verbal jokes. Thus I propose that we use a broadened cooperative principle (BCP) that includes both linguistic and non-linguistic forms of cooperation. It is certainly the case that linguistic norms are important, but so are other non-linguistic social codes such as gender, clothing, sexuality, obscenity, violence and literary genre. Much as with CP, sometimes we agree to abide by BCP and sometimes we violate it, in both acceptable and unacceptable ways.

BCP helps regulate how a society functions, and its specific manifestation varies from culture to culture. What about the culture of ancient Greece? What norms were strongly prevalent that might be violated for the sake of humour? I submit that the most relevant aspect of Greek thought that would affect their society's sense of humour is their ubiquitous focus on order and balance. A highly desired character trait in Greece was *sōphrosunē*, the virtue of self-restraint and the maintenance of order in one's intellectual and moral character.[11] This facet of Greek thought can be illustrated with a few examples from various parts of their culture. Plato, and at least some of the Presocratics, conceived of the world as a *kosmos*, a perfectly arranged and orderly system.[12] Greek art and architectural projects were constructed with an eye to order and proportion.[13] The Greek language codifies balance through the μέν ... δέ grammatical construction and various other devices such as parallelism, antithesis and parisosis. The rhetoricians said that successful speeches depend on *kairos*, fitting the content of a speech appropriately to the occasion.[14] Given the weight assigned to order and balance within Greek psychology, its violation might be the sort of thing that the Greeks would find particularly funny.

I contend that humour is generated through the violation of BCP, and that this is primarily accomplished through the perception and resolution of incongruities, which regularly violate BCP and the culturally determined expectations based on it. In this chapter, I explicate some of the different types of incongruity in Aristophanes and suggest that they can explain a large part of Aristophanic humour. Next, I examine scenes that synthesize multiple types of incongruity, arguing that a blend of incongruities maximizes humour by appealing to diverse audiences. Finally, I briefly explore some differences between how incongruities are employed in comedy, satyr drama and tragedy.

Since BCP is an expansion of the linguistically oriented CP, I begin with those violations of BCP that operate through linguistic incongruity. Consider the following joke from *Thesmophoriazusae*:

Kinsman νὴ τὸν Δί' ἥδομαί γε τουτὶ προσμαθών.
οἷόν γέ πού 'στιν αἱ σοφαὶ ξυνουσίαι.
Euripides πόλλ' ἂν μάθοις τοιαῦτα παρ' ἐμοῦ.
Kinsman   πῶς ἂν οὖν
πρὸς τοῖς ἀγαθοῖς τούτοισιν ἐξεύροιμ' ὅπως
ἔτι προσμάθοιμι χωλὸς εἶναι τὼ σκέλει;

Kinsman I'm happy indeed to learn this additional lesson.
What a thing it is to have these clever conversations!
Euripides You could learn a lot more like this from me.
Kinsman In that case, I'd love to discover how to learn
An additional good lesson: how to go lame in both legs!

Thesmophoriazusae 20–4[15]

From the perspective of incongruity theory, this joke has two incompatible matrices, which scholars variously term as 'schemas',[16] 'scripts'[17] or 'frames'.[18] The joke works by establishing a 'learning a lesson' frame that is suddenly resolved to a second frame about 'going lame'. That is to say, it violates CP through maxim 3, 'be relevant'. This joke is not just funny because there was a violation – it's funny because there was a particular *type* of violation. Unlike the previous case where a 'weather' frame was unacceptably resolved to an 'apples' frame, this incongruity turns on the fact that it is actually *congruous* in a different sense – it matches in some way. While it is incongruous to switch frames suddenly, it is perfectly congruous that *Euripides* would be the one teaching lessons about going lame, since he so prominently incorporated lame characters into his tragedies (Bellerophon in *Bellerophon*, for example).[19]

While I do not wish to dispute that the insertion of something completely arbitrary can be funny, it is far more often the case that we can detect something congruous within the incongruity that anchors the joke. A relatively recent parody of the Taylor Swift music video 'I Knew You Were Trouble' – a so-called 'goat remix' – replaces the moment when Swift sings a long high note in the song's chorus with a clip of a screaming goat.[20] What makes this video funny is the incongruity of a goat violating our frame of 'watching a Taylor Swift video'. But it is also funny because the goat, in some sense, is perfectly congruous with the original song – the goat's vocalization sounds somewhat like Taylor Swift's, and it even hits an approximately correct musical note. Detecting something congruous within an incongruity is important for humour. For example, if the clip of the screaming goat in the Taylor Swift video were swapped with a clip of a man biting into an apple, it would not be as funny – funny-strange, perhaps, but not funny-ha-ha.[21]

Most setup and punchline jokes involve incongruity, but they tend to stop at the moment when the incongruity is resolved. Consider the following classic joke:

Two fish were in their tank. One turns to the other and says, 'You man the guns, I'll drive.'

At first we follow Frame 1, where 'tank' means a 'fishbowl', but then we realize that we were supposed to be following a latent Frame 2, where 'tank' means a 'military vehicle'. But Aristophanic incongruities often establish an initial framework that is developed further for increased humour. Here's an example from *Acharnians*, which relies on the dual meanings inherent in the word σπόνδαι:

Dicaeopolis	ἀλλὰ τὰς σπονδὰς φέρεις;
Amphitheus	ἔγωγέ φημι, τρία γε ταυτὶ γεύματα.
	αὗται μέν εἰσι πεντέτεις. γεῦσαι λαβών.
Dicaeopolis	Do you have the treaties?
Amphitheus	I do indeed; three samples to sip.
	This one is a five-year treaty. Take a sip.

Acharnians 186–8

Frame 1 involves σπόνδαι as 'peace treaties' and Frame 2 involves σπόνδαι as 'libations'. Unlike the fish-in-the-tank joke, Aristophanes pushes past the moment of initial recognition. Once we realize that that both meanings of σπόνδαι are operative, the properties of one frame can be applied to the other:

Dicaeopolis	αἰβοῖ.
Amphitheus	τί ἐστιν;
Dicaeopolis	οὐκ ἀρέσκουσίν μ', ὅτι
	ὄζουσι πίττης καὶ παρασκευῆς νεῶν.
Amphitheus	σὺ δ' ἀλλὰ τασδὶ τὰς δεκέτεις γεῦσαι λαβών.
Dicaeopolis	ὄζουσι χαὗται – πρέσβεων εἰς τὰς πόλεις,
	ὀξύτατον, ὥσπερ διατριβῆς τῶν ξυμμάχων.

Dicaeopolis	Eww!
Amphitheus	What is it?
Dicaeopolis	I don't like it, since it reeks of pitch and shipbuilding.
Amphitheus	Well, why don't you have a taste of this ten-year treaty?
Dicaeopolis	This reeks too – of embassies to the cities, A very sharp smell, like allies being beaten down.

Acharnians 189–93

This goes beyond the simple frame opposition from the fish-in-the-tank joke. Here, the frames become fused together; the peace treaties can be drunk as if they were libations and the libations can acquire the taste and smell of peace treaties. There is a visual component to the humour as well, since Amphitheus probably brought out a series of libation vessels representing the peace treaties that Dicaeopolis smelled and drank from.[22] The complex set of incongruities in this extended joke originated in the violation of maxim 4b, 'avoid ambiguity'.

Another example occurs in the contest between Aeschylus and Euripides in *Frogs* when Aeschylus suggests that their poetry should be evaluated based on the 'weight' ('βάρος', 1367) of their lines. Dionysus agrees and decides to weigh their poetry literally, like a cheesemonger (1369). In Frame 1 the 'weight' of the lines signifies its poetic value, and in Frame 2 the 'weight' of lines signifies physical mass. This conflict comes to a head when Dionysus assesses one of Aeschylus' lines as weightier than Euripides':

Euripides	'εἴθ' ὤφελ' Ἀργοῦς μὴ διαπτάσθαι σκάφος.'
Aeschylus	'Σπερχειὲ ποταμὲ βούνομοί τ' ἐπιστροφαί.'
Dionysus	κόκκυ.
Aesch./Eur.	μεθεῖται.
Dionysus	καὶ πολύ γε κατωτέρω χωρεῖ τὸ τοῦδε.
Euripides	καὶ τί ποτ' ἐστὶ ταἴτιον;
Dionysus	ὅ τι; εἰσέθηκε ποταμόν, ἐριοπωλικῶς ὑγρὸν ποιήσας τοὔπος ὥσπερ τἄρια, σὺ δ' εἰσέθηκας τοὔπος ἐπτερωμένον.

Euripides	'Would that the ship *Argo* had not winged her way.'
Aeschylus	'O River Spercheius and the haunts grazed by cattle.'
Dionysus	Cuckoo!
Aesch./Eur.	There they go!
Dionysus	This one here's going much lower.
Euripides	Whatever is the reason for this?
Dionysus	The reason? He added a river, dampening his line like a wool seller does to wool, but you added a line with wings.

Frogs 1382–8

As before, the properties from one frame are transferred to the other. Frame 1 is affected by Frame 2, since the spoken lines can be weighed on a scale; Frame 2 is affected by Frame 1, since the quantity of physical mass expressed in the line indicates its literary worth. The lightness of the wings makes Euripides' line inconsequential, and the waterlogged river makes Aeschylus' line serious.

While CP is limited to linguistic incongruities such as these, BCP can accommodate non-linguistic incongruities as well. In order to violate BCP, one simply needs to exploit a frame with standards that are *robust*, *firmly defined* and *easily transgressable*. Not all cultures will have the same frames, nor have them to the same degree. But due to the commonalities between cultures, certain violations are universal or almost universal, and therefore certain types of humour are likely to be as well. For example, Grice's CP affects almost every culture because members of almost every culture desire to cooperate verbally. However, the Malagasy people of Madagascar apparently do not follow the maxim of quantity, since their drive to tell the truth is overridden by the desire to maintain prestige over others by concealing information from them.[23] If so, we would not expect the Malagasy to derive humour from violations of quantity, since those violations would not be abnormal or incongruous among the Malagasy. Analysed in this way, humour can provide a window into culture and vice versa.

Many, if not all, cultures have a robust set of expectations about the differences between humans and animals and could derive humour from human/animal incongruities (this, for example, is operative in the Taylor Swift goat remix video). One obvious human/animal incongruity in Greek comedy appears in the animal choruses of birds, frogs, ants, bees and so on that occurred at least nineteen times throughout the history of Greek comedy, ranging from our earliest comedian Magnes to the numerous fragmentary poets of Middle Comedy.[24] In *Wasps*, Aristophanes characterizes the chorus of old jurors as wasps, blending together aspects of human and animal:

Bdelycleon ἀλλ', ὦ πόνηρε, τὸ γένος ἤν τις ὀργίσῃ
τὸ τῶν γερόντων, ἔσθ' ὅμοιον σφηκιᾷ.
ἔχουσι γὰρ καὶ κέντρον ἐκ τῆς ὀσφύος
ὀξύτατον, ᾧ κεντοῦσι, καὶ κεκραγότες
πηδῶσι καὶ βάλλουσιν ὥσπερ φέψαλοι.

Loathecleon You dope, if someone stirs up that tribe
Of oldsters, it's like stirring up a wasps' nest.
They even have stingers attached to their rumps,
Really sharp, with which they sting people, and they
Leap around and attack, sizzling like sparks.

Wasps 1382–8

While at first an audience member might believe this to merely be a metaphor, the frames soon fuse together and Aristophanes reveals that the old men also have *properties* of wasps, down to their physical features (sharp stingers) and their actions (stinging, leaping, attacking). We find it funny when people act like animals, but we also find it funny when animals act like people. For example, the biggest running jokes in *Birds* derive from the fact that birds are engaging in acts that are typically associated with people: making oaths, fighting for a cause, and establishing a functioning city.

Another robust category is that of gender, and a number of Aristophanes' plays focus on the differences between women and men.[25] *Lysistrata* and *Ecclesiazusae* in particular involve women exercising political power, and it tells us something important about Athenian culture that the idea of women managing a city was just as incongruous for them as it was for birds to do so. *Thesmophoriazusae* features a number of jokes about women going off to the festival to get drunk on wine, and when the Kinsman takes Mica's baby hostage, it turns out that the baby is actually a winesack (689–764). It is certainly incongruous for a baby to be a winesack, but there must be some sense of congruousness in the joke, otherwise it would not have been funny to the Athenians. Consider the following pair of modern jokes:

(1) A: What's the difference between a lawyer and a leech?

B: One's a blood-sucking parasite, and the other's a leech.

(2) A: What's the difference between a firefighter and a leech?

B: One's a blood-sucking parasite, and the other's a leech.

The incongruity in (1) works because we have a cultural perception that lawyers can be blood-sucking parasites, but it fails in (2) because we do not have the same perception about firefighters. From jokes such as these, we can access prominent cultural views about something, but not the truth of the thing itself. In reality, not all lawyers are blood-sucking parasites, but *enough* people from the culture think *enough* lawyers are blood-sucking parasites to make the joke work. The same principle applies to the depiction of women drinking wine in Aristophanic comedy; it may or may not be true, but it reveals a prominent Athenian conception, probably a male conception, about how women behaved at festivals.

Another relatively fixed system with easily recognizable and easily violable standards is genre.[26] People associate certain features with certain genres, and genres supply certain expectations in form and content. Consider the following two examples of comic 'collision', in which there is a sudden contrast between high-prestige and low-prestige language.[27] The first parodies epic language by staging a low-class cook speaking in Homericisms:

ὡς εἰσῆλθε γάρ,
εὐθύς μ' ἐπηρώτησε προσβλέψας μέγα.
'πόσους κέκληκας μέροπας ἐπὶ δεῖπνον';

    For when he entered,
He immediately asked me with a bold look,
'How many men articulate with voice did you invite to dinner?'

Strato, Phoenicides *fr.* 1.4–6[28]

Here, the collision relies on the stereotypically Homeric word 'μέροπες' ('men articulate with voice').²⁹ The second, in a parody of Euripides' *Bellerophon*, involves a collision between paratragic language and obscenity:

Second Slave	τί πέτει; τί μάτην οὐχ ὑγιαίνεις;
Trygaeus	εὐφημεῖν χρὴ καὶ μὴ φλαῦρον
	μηδὲν γρύζειν ἀλλ' ὀλολύζειν·
	τοῖς τ' ἀνθρώποις φράζω σιγᾶν,
	τούς τε κοπρῶνας καὶ τὰς λαύρας
	καιναῖς πλίνθοισιν ἀποικοδομεῖν
	καὶ τοὺς πρωκτοὺς ἐπικλῄειν.
Second Slave	Why are you flying? Why are you acting crazy for nothing?
Trygaeus	You ought to speak well and not utter
	A foolish sound, but raise a cheer;
	And tell all men to be silent,
	And as for the toilets and sewers,
	Wall them off with new bricks,
	And lock up their arseholes!

Peace 95–101

Although these examples of paraepic and paratragedy produce humour via the same mechanism, there is a huge difference in their distribution in Old Comedy; paraepic is relatively rare and paratragedy is quite common.³⁰ What accounts for this discrepancy, I contend, is that tragedy affords far more opportunities for easily observable incongruities than epic. Paratragedy can target all the same types of things as paraepic (such as language, metre, plots, characters) but can *additionally* target all the theatrical elements of a tragic performance: costumes, the chorus, the music, and special effects such as the *ekkuklēma* and *mēchanē*.

The last robust cultural category I will discuss is clothing and costume. Most cultures have strong clothing norms that are associated with different genders, ages, occupations, religions and so on. This plays out on the tragic stage, where costumes can signal information about a character's status, ethnicity or emotional state.³¹ Underlying these costume choices is a form of BCP, in which one should wear clothing that is appropriate to one's context – one's costume should reflect one's identity.³² But this expectation can easily be subverted. Here's one example from *Frogs* involving Dionysus' choice to wear a lionskin:

Heracles	τίς τὴν θύραν ἐπάταξεν; ὡς κενταυρικῶς
	ἐνήλαθ', ὅστις—εἰπέ μοι, τουτὶ τί ἦν;
	…
	οὔτοι μὰ τὴν Δήμητρα δύναμαι μὴ γελᾶν·
	καίτοι δάκνω γ' ἐμαυτόν· ἀλλ' ὅμως γελῶ.

Dionysus	ὦ δαιμόνιε, πρόσελθε· δέομαι γάρ τί σου.
Heracles	ἀλλ' οὐχ οἷός τ' εἴμ' ἀποσοβῆσαι τὸν γέλων,
	ὁρῶν λεοντῆν ἐπὶ κροκωτῷ κειμένην.
	τίς ὁ νοῦς; τί κόθορνος καὶ ῥόπαλον ξυνηλθέτην;

Heracles	Who banged on the door? He hammered on it like a
	Centaur, whoever – hey, what's this all about?
	...
	By Demeter, I just can't help laughing!
	I'm biting my lip, but I'm still laughing.
Dionysus	Sir, come here; I need something from you.
Heracles	I just can't shake this laughter,
	When I'm looking at that lionskin atop a yellow gown.
	What's the idea? Why has a war club been paired up with women's
	boots?

Frogs 38-9, 42-7

This passage is interesting for a number of reasons. First, since the lionskin is uniquely associated with Heracles, the costume incongruity is extraordinarily clear – it can only refer to Heracles and no one else. Second, Heracles explicitly signals that Dionysus' costume choice is incongruous when he mentions 'that lionskin atop a yellow gown'. Third, the incongruity produces laughter, and lots of it. There are additional things that enhance the humour: the fact that Heracles is seeing someone dressed up like himself, the fact that there's a juxtaposition between the gendered costumes of the feminine gown and the masculine lionskin, and the fact that the god of theatre can't seem to get a theatrical costume right. As a broader point, this passage indicates that Aristophanes had brought it to consciousness that incongruity produced humour since he staged a character laughing at the sudden perception of another character's incongruity.

A similar example occurs in *Thesmophoriazusae* when the masculine Kinsman catches sight of Agathon's feminine dress:

Kinsman	καί σ', ὦ νεανίσχ', ἥτις εἶ, κατ' Αἰσχύλον
	ἐκ τῆς Λυκουργείας ἐρέσθαι βούλομαι.
	ποδαπὸς ὁ γύννις; τίς πάτρα; τίς ἡ στολή;
	τίς ἡ τάραξις τοῦ βίου; τί βάρβιτος
	λαλεῖ κροκωτῷ; τί δὲ λύρα κεκρυφάλῳ;
	τί λήκυθος καὶ στρόφιον; ὡς οὐ ξύμφορον.
	τίς δαὶ κατρόπτου καὶ ξίφους κοινωνία;

Kinsman	And you, young man, I want to ask you, like in Aeschylus'
	Lycurgeia, what kind of female you are.
	Where did this sissy come from? What country? What manner of
	dress?

> What disarrangement of living is this? Why is the *barbitos*
> In conversation with a yellow dress? Why is the lyre with a hairnet?
> Why is the oil flask with a bra? How discordant!
> What's the commonality between the mirror and the sword?
>
> Thesmophoriazusae 134–40

Much like Heracles, the Kinsman finds Agathon's costume incongruous with his identity, calling it a 'disarrangement of living' ('ἡ τάραξις τοῦ βίου') and saying that the combination of an oil-flask and a bra is 'discordant' ('οὐ ξύμφορον'). He contrasts a series of predominantly masculine objects with feminine ones: a *barbitos* with a yellow dress, a lyre with a hairnet, an oil-flask and a bra, and a sword and a mirror. Therefore, Agathon's incongruities work on two levels, violating clothing as well as gender norms.

While my categorization has split these incongruities into distinct types, it is clear that Aristophanes can use multiple kinds of incongruity simultaneously. The Agathon scene from *Thesmophoriazusae*, in fact, has a particularly strong concentration of incongruities. In addition to costume and gender, there are incongruities of genre dealing with stagecraft and music; Agathon is rolled out on the *ekkuklēma* in a parody of tragic theatrical practice, and his aria caricatures the musical stylings of the recent phenomenon of New Music.[33] Agathon is aware of the fact that he is behaving incongruously according to his culture's standards about clothing, and he rejects the assumption that one's clothing must coordinate with one's identity:

> **Agathon** ἐγὼ δὲ τὴν ἐσθῆθ' ἅμα γνώμῃ φορῶ.
> χρὴ γὰρ ποιητὴν ἄνδρα πρὸς τὰ δράματα
> ἃ δεῖ ποιεῖν, πρὸς ταῦτα τοὺς τρόπους ἔχειν.
> αὐτίκα γυναικεῖ' ἢν ποιῇ τις δράματα,
> μετουσίαν δεῖ τῶν τρόπων τὸ σῶμ' ἔχειν.
>
> I match my clothing to my thinking.
> For a male poet ought to coordinate his behaviour
> With the dramas he composes.
> For instance, if someone's composing female dramas
> His body must share in female behaviour.
>
> Thesmophoriazusae 148–52

The Kinsman obscenely pushes the joke further:

> **Kinsman** οὐκοῦν κελητίζεις, ὅταν Φαίδραν ποιῇς;
> …
> ὅταν σατύρους τοίνυν ποιῇς, καλεῖν ἐμέ,
> ἵνα συμποιῶ σοὔπισθεν ἐστυκὼς ἐγώ.

> **Kinsman** So whenever you're composing a *Phaedra*, you climb on top?
> ...
> Call me whenever you're composing satyr dramas,
> I'll collaborate with you from behind with my erection.
>
> *Thesmophoriazusae 153, 157–8*

Here we have additional incongruities based on language, sexuality, obscenity and violence. What is unusual about the Agathon scene is that it synthesizes a broad number of incongruity strategies, ranging from the paratragic use of the *ekkuklēma* to Agathon's gender-swapping costume choice to the Kinsman's transgressive threat of violent rape. The humour generated out of incongruity in this scene is incredibly wide-ranging, and it is worth considering what Aristophanes' objective was in using multiple incongruities in this manner.

I suggest that this scattershot approach to humour was chosen because it was more likely to appeal to diverse audiences in terms of social criteria such as gender, ethnicity and class.[34] Comedians have a choice: they can either pitch their humour at a universal audience or a smaller in-group. Obviously, this choice operates on a spectrum, but judging from the types of incongruity that Aristophanes tends to use, Aristophanic humour is fairly expansive, opting for incongruities that are broadly appealing to people with a diverse range of interests and backgrounds. Aristophanes clearly makes obscure jokes; however, he does not employ them exclusively, but rather nestles them within broader forms of humour. For every joke that relies on audience recognition of something esoteric such as a particular line of Euripidean or Pindaric poetry, there are jokes that rely on the more quotidian norms of clothing or sexuality.

How is Aristophanes funny from a modern perspective? This depends on the extent that the modern culture finds the same violations funny that the Athenians did – that is, the extent to which a modern culture's standards match those of ancient Athens. Consider gender; the Greeks recognized two genders (male and female), and even when they occasionally ventured outside of these two genders in their mythological and philosophical thought, it was still filtered through the lens of male and female.[35] These stories either depicted someone changing between the two genders (e.g. Caeneus, Tiresias, Leucippus) or blending the two genders (e.g. Hermaphroditus, those belonging to the third 'androgynous' gender proposed in Aristophanes' speech from Plato's *Symposium*, 189c–193e). Over the last half-century or so, our dependence on this gender binary has begun to crumble, and we now speak of people who are genderqueer and transgender. This cultural shift is beginning to normalize those who do not adhere to a gender binary, and those with this broader view of gender would not find the transgression of gender norms funny, because for them, if a male-bodied person wears feminine clothing, this would not constitute a violation of normal codes, but would be perfectly acceptable behaviour. This implies that not everyone within a culture will find the same things funny, and it is very likely that people assign different weights to different types of humour based on aspects of their personal identity: their religion, their gender, their age, their immediate circumstances, their mood and so on. A hilarious joke may no longer be funny when told in the presence of respected elders, or in a religious space, or around children, or when feeling depressed. Presumably things were no different in the time of Aristophanes.[36]

Any discussion of Aristophanic humour must address two major interpretive questions: to what extent is this network of incongruities distinctive to Aristophanes as opposed to other comic playwrights; and to what extent is it distinctive to Old Comedy as opposed to other dramatic genres such as satyr drama and tragedy? We know that other poets of Old Comedy used the same incongruity techniques as Aristophanes: jokes that utilize linguistic incongruities,[37] choruses that exploit human/animal incongruities,[38] paratragedy that relies on generic incongruities,[39] and costume changes that manifest clothing incongruities.[40] We can also detect complex incongruities of gender; in his play *Cities*, Eupolis depicted his chorus of Athenian allied cities as female (unlike in *Demes*, where he followed tradition by making his chorus of Athenian demes male).[41] This gendered representation establishes Frame 1 where the cities are cities and Frame 2 in which the cities are women, allowing for a complex political metaphor where Chios is both a city that can contribute warships to Athens and a woman who is subservient to the authority of Athens:

αὕτη Χίος, καλὴ πόλις <>
πέμπει γὰρ ὑμῖν ναῦς μακρὰς ἄνδρας θ' ὅταν δεήσῃ,
καὶ τἄλλα πειθαρχεῖ καλῶς, ἄπληκτος ὥσπερ ἵππος.

She is Chios, a fine city, for she sends you warships and men whenever there is need, and the rest of the time she is nicely obedient, like a horse that does not need a whip.

Eupolis fr. 246[42]

While we can observe these types of incongruity in comic poets other than Aristophanes, the lack of complete plays from these comedians inhibits our ability to truly determine how distinctive Aristophanes was, particularly with regard to his synthesis of multiple types of incongruity throughout a whole scene or play for maximum comic effect.

Unlike comedy, satyr drama employs incongruity through the chorus of satyrs, which naturally produces incongruities through the human/animal dimension. As Lissarrague states, 'the recipe is as follows: Take one myth, add satyrs, observe the result . . . the joke is one of incongruity, which generates a series of surprises.'[43] I think it is noteworthy that Lissarrague states that '*the* joke is one of incongruity', because the inclusion of satyrs is the single overwhelming incongruity in satyr drama. The choice to include a chorus of satyrs generates secondary incongruities of sexuality and vulgarity as well, since the satyrs are by nature sexualized and vulgar. If we contrast this with a case where comedy co-opts satyr drama, such as Cratinus' *Dionysalexandros*, we see satyr drama's single incongruity transformed into a more complex comic incongruity.[44] While the chorus of satyrs in satyr drama is already inherently incongruous, a chorus of satyrs in comedy is additionally incongruous due to the generic collision between satyr drama and comedy and the violation of the expectation that the satyr chorus belongs to satyr drama, not comedy. Even more so, comedy's version of the satyr chorus tacks on an extra level of visual incongruity, since it is very likely that comedy's version of the satyr chorus somehow made the satyrs wear comic costuming in addition to their satyric costuming, thereby converting the chorus of satyrs to the conventions of comedy.[45] The complexities of the comic presentation of the satyr chorus are further embedded within broader incongruity strategies, since *Dionysalexandros* also featured clothing incongruities where Dionysus got dressed up as Paris and a ram.[46] While this is but a single example, it gestures towards a division between comedy's use of incongruity and that of satyr drama, both in their extent and their nature.

As for tragedy, there are numerous examples of incongruities and violations of BCP. As critics of incongruity theory point out, it is certainly incongruous and a violation of one's expectations to come home from work to find one's family murdered, but we would not call this humorous – maybe something more like horrific.[47] Linguistic incongruities in tragedy often produce dark irony, not humour. For example, much of the language Clytemnestra uses in *Agamemnon* can be interpreted in terms of two competing frames or scripts. When Clytemnestra says that Agamemnon will find his wife just as faithful as when he left her, and that she knows no more of the pleasure of another man than she does of tempering of bronze (606–12), two frames emerge: Frame 1 suggests that Clytemnestra is faithful, has not taken a lover, and would never plunge a bronze weapon into anything (let alone her husband), whereas Frame 2 implies the opposite. Gender norms are violated by Clytemnestra in *Agamemnon* and Medea in *Medea*, but we do not laugh at their transgressions. Clothing incongruities in tragedy produce a sense of discomfort, not humour. For example, consider Pentheus' reaction to seeing Tiresias and Cadmus dressed like maenads in *Bacchae*:

Pentheus ἀτὰρ τόδ' ἄλλο θαῦμα· τὸν τερασκόπον
ἐν ποικίλαισι νεβρίσι Τειρεσίαν ὁρῶ
πατέρα τε μητρὸς τῆς ἐμῆς, πολὺν γέλων,
νάρθηκι βακχεύοντ'·

Pentheus But this is another wonder; I see the diviner
Tiresias in dappled fawnskin,
And my mother's father – it's very ridiculous –
Acting like a maenad with a wand.

Euripides, Bacchae *248–51*

What is notable is how similar Pentheus' reaction is to Heracles' reaction to Dionysus or the Kinsman's reaction to Agathon. A lengthy debate has raged on this scene, and while some think that the presence of an incongruity means that it must be funny,[48] I submit that the context of the scene follows the norms of tragedy and that the effect of the incongruity is more unsettling than humorous. While some see Pentheus' laughter as confirmation that Tiresias and Cadmus dressing transgressively is funny, Pentheus' reaction appears long after the audience has had their own reactions to the sight of them dressed as maenads (whatever they might have been). Therefore, the audience is primed not to blindly follow along with Pentheus' aesthetic evaluations, but rather to evaluate Pentheus himself as correct or incorrect in light of their own previous responses.

The contrast between tragic, comic and satyric incongruities leads to the question of why certain violations are funny while others are not. One path forward into untangling this thorny question comes from another theory of humour, benign violation theory, which suggests that humour happens when we recognize a violation whose context renders it benign.[49] This insight can help us differentiate comic incongruities from tragic ones. Edith Hall has suggested that tragedy involves the contemplation of suffering,[50] and therefore if the tragedy is effective, the audience inhabits the mental spaces of the characters onstage. The audience feels what the characters feel – pity for the characters and fear for themselves.[51] Through this tight link between character and audience, tragedy provokes a deep emotional response in the audience such that the violations in the tragedy feel real, not benign. In comedy, however, the audience never leaves their own mental space – they do not identify with the emotional states of the characters onstage. The comic audience remains safe, the violations in the comedy remain benign, and the comedy produces humour.[52] Thus the differences between comic and tragic incongruities, at least in part, are a function of the types of emotional connections the audience feels towards the theatrical characters in their respective genres.

This chapter has proposed a new approach to Aristophanic humour based on a broadened cooperative principle that operates through cultural norms instead of solely operating through linguistic norms, and it has explored the implications of this theory in terms of genre and culture. The differences between the theatrical genres can be summed up as follows: satyr drama contains a single structural incongruity provided by the obligatory chorus of satyrs; comedy utilizes manifold incongruity strategies and blends them to create complex forms of humour; and tragedy employs many kinds of incongruities to engender a sense of horror and discomfort. Different cultures, including modern audiences, find Aristophanes funny only to the extent that their cultural standards align with those of fifth- and early fourth-century Athens. This theory can explain much about Aristophanic humour, accounting for multiple types of humour and why people in different time periods, cultures and sub-groups find different aspects of Aristophanic comedy humorous.

CHAPTER 5
LAUGHTER, OR ARISTOPHANES' JOY IN THE FACE OF DEATH
Mario Telò

In his poem '*Rire*', Georges Bataille links laughter with the frightening domains of repetition, bodily dissolution and death:

Laugh and Laugh
at the sun
at the nettles
at the stones
at the ducks
at the rain
at the pee pee of the pope
at mummy
at a coffin full of shit[1]

'Pee pee' and 'a coffin full of shit' are not just the classic objects of scatological laughter; as we can infer from some of his other works, they also allude to the momentary encounter with death and the experience of bodily decomposition that laughter, in his view, affords. In this perspective, laughter seems an expression of the Freudian death drive, the instinct – repetitious by definition – that unceasingly pushes the subject toward non-existence, haunting it with the fantasy of non-birth and the inanimate.[2] In this chapter, I want to consider implicit theorizations of laughter in Aristophanes' plays – and a couple of post-Aristophanic texts – in light of Bataille's notion of laughter as an encounter of sorts with death, a dissipation of the subject. As Nick Land observes in light of Bataille, 'it is death itself that finds a voice when we laugh'.[3] In particular, I will look at laughter as the disappearance of the face in chasms – the human throat, but also a well and a house on fire. Identifying laughter with gagging throats and the convulsions of splitting apart, I connect it with the *jouissance*, or pleasure-in-pain, of self-wounding. In this way, I show how we can locate a tragic kernel in ancient Greek comic aesthetics. Laughter enacts the subject's fall into the abyss. The gaping or gagging conjured by some of Aristophanes' figurations of laughter swallows the subject, plunging it into the flux of elemental life and of its suppressed animality.

Aristophanic Humour

(E)sc(h)atology and *faire l'amourir*

I will start by discussing laughter as scatology in the prologue of *Frogs* from an anti-Bakhtinian perspective. That is to say, I will make a case for laughter as a kind of excremental death of the subject. After briefly taking up the comic mask, whose ostensibly 'painless' expression Aristotle famously registers (*Poet.* 1449a34-6), I will move on to laughter as gaping in the *parabasis* of *Clouds*.

In the opening number of Steven Sondheim's ill-starred Broadway production of *The Frogs* in 2004, Dionysus admonishes the audience: 'Please don't cough, .../If you see flaws, please,/don't drop your jaws, please./No loud guffaws .../Please don't fart – there is very little air, and this is art.'[4] Sondheim here substitutes 'cough', 'guffaws' and 'fart' for the oft-repeated vulgar jokes of Old Comedy that Dionysus, affecting disgust, insinuates in the prologue of the original *Frogs*, aided and abetted by the slave Xanthias. In Aristophanes' unexpurgated version, we find a sequence of scatological sensations:

X   Εἴπω τι τῶν εἰωθότων, ὦ δέσποτα,
     ἐφ᾽ οἷς ἀεὶ γελῶσιν οἱ θεώμενοι;
D   Νὴ τὸν Δί᾽ ὅ τι βούλει γε, πλὴν 'Πιέζομαι.'
     Τοῦτο δὲ φύλαξαι· πάνυ γάρ ἐστ᾽ ἤδη χολή.
X   Μηδ᾽ ἕτερον ἀστεῖόν τι;
D   Πλήν γ᾽ ' Ὡς θλίβομαι.'
X   Τί δαί; Τὸ πάνυ γέλοιον εἴπω;
D   Νὴ Δία
     θαρρῶν γε· μόνον ἐκεῖν᾽ ὅπως μὴ 'ρεῖς –
X   Τὸ τί;
D   μεταβαλλόμενος τἀνάφορον ὅτι χεζητιᾷς.
X   Μηδ᾽ ὅτι τοσοῦτον ἄχθος ἐπ᾽ ἐμαυτῷ φέρων,
     εἰ μὴ καθαιρήσει τις, ἀποπαρδήσομαι;
D   Μὴ δῆθ᾽, ἱκετεύω, πλήν γ᾽ ὅταν μέλλω 'ξεμεῖν.

X   Shall I make one of the usual jokes, master, that the audience always laugh at?
D   Sure, any one you want, except *'I'm hard-pressed!'* Watch out for that one; by now it's a groaner.
X   Then some other urbanity?
D   Anything but *'I'm crushed!'*
X   Well then, how about the really funny one?
D   Go right ahead, only make sure it's not the one where –
X   You mean –
D   Where you shift your baggage and say *you want to shit*.
X   Can't I even say that I've got such a load on me, if someone doesn't relieve me *I'll break wind*?
D   Please don't! Wait till I need to *puke*.[5]

Aristophanes, Frogs *1–11*

Sondheim's introduction of the word 'guffaws' in his take on Aristophanes' scatological litany invites us to see laughter as an analogue of the strained or painful openings of the lower orifices mentioned by Aristophanes' two characters, who present us with a classic rendering of what we know from Mikhail Bakhtin as the grotesque body.[6] But in the Aristophanes passage, scatological laughter goes beyond Bakhtin's grotesque realism. It encodes a different dimension of laughter, which I will illustrate through Bataille's notion of 'joy in the face of death'.[7]

Bataille views laughter as the manifestation of an eroticized death, a moment of pleasure in pain where life seems to reach its limit. Death, of course, figures prominently in Bakhtin's theory of laughter, his grotesque realism offering a pathway for absorbing death into life, into an atmosphere of carnivalesque regeneration.[8] But when Bakhtin distinguishes between 'a joyful, open, festive laugh' and a 'closed, purely negative satirical laugh' – 'not a laughing laugh' – he also contemplates the reverse perspective of a grotesque body that turns life into death, joyous openness into stasis.[9] Embodying this alternative model of the Bakhtinian grotesque, Roman satire, as Paul Allen Miller puts it, 'brings forth not a new generation of laughing giants' – such as Rabelais' Gargantua and Pantagruel – 'but sterility, decline, and ultimately death'.[10] Bakhtin's notion of a 'non-laughing laugh' draws upon an implicit opposition between laughter and death, as though, in the generic tradition of satire, the former became something other than itself. For Bataille, laughter – whether carnivalesque or satiric – produces, in its phenomenology, an instant, a burst of death.[11] It is joy 'connected with the work of death', an 'anguished joy' that 'tears apart' and causes '"absolute dismemberment" (*déchirement*)'.[12] The 'joy in the face of death' provoked by laughter is the rapture of the abyss. This 'joy' is not the affirmation of the Heideggerian *Freiheit für den Tod* ('being-free for death'), which has been regarded as eminently tragic, but an encounter with death that shakes the subject with 'a feverish chill'.[13] It is a moment of self-wounding that, even when it conjures the fantasy of ecstatic self-loss, never simply or fully coincides with the corpse's inertness, with the terminal catharsis of human demise.[14] Bataille reproduces the serial rhythm of laughter's rapturous rupture in a poetic sequence:

> Joy before death carries me.
> Joy before death hurls me down.
> Joy before death annihilates me.
> I slowly love myself in unintelligible and bottomless space ...
> I am devoured by death.[15]

This sensation resembles 'the instant of the erotic experience',[16] the *petite mort* of sex.[17] When Jacques Lacan theorizes this concept, he highlights the kinship of death and sex through the neologism 'faire l'amourir', a play on *faire l'amour* ('to make love') in which the portmanteau word *amourir* emcompasses *rire* ('to laugh') and *mourir de rire* ('to die laughing'), an experience frequently attested in antiquity.[18] In Bataille's view, there is no substantial difference between *rire* and *mourir*, as the former *per se* implies an imaginary experience of the latter – an ebullient self-expenditure, the *jouissance* of self-shattering, a 'joyful s/laughter of subjectivity'.[19]

In the prologue of *Frogs*, Xanthias' old scatological jokes exemplify the pleasure-in-pain of laughter, locating it in momentary sundering, excretion, an instant of self-expenditure. When Dionysus disingenuously warns Xanthias not to repeat yet again the 'I am hard-pressed' ('πιέζομαι') gag – which the slave's burdened condition is precisely meant to evoke – he treats the hoary scatological joke almost as a trauma, a recursive nightmare, to which he is deeply attached. Casting this specific joke and the next one, 'I am crushed' ('θλίβομαι'), as sources of pain – ostensibly abhorred, intimately longed for – Dionysus seems to construe laughter as a kind of pleasure in pain. The physical pressure at the centre of both jokes, which brings together character and spectator in pleasurable suffering, captures less the catharsis of defecation than the excretory strain of it, which, in Bataille's view, resembles the travails of laughter – the 'spasmodic process of the oral orifice's sphincter muscles' corresponding to the contractions 'of the sphincter muscles of the anal orifice'.[20] The old scatological jokes that Dionysus pretends to shun may be the funniest because they are, in a sense, meta-jokes, figuring the quasi-excremental dynamics of laughter, the way it allows us to experience the thrill of splitting apart, to be overcome by death, to become detritus. What is barely repressed by Dionysus is an eschatological impulse, the search for laughter's *petite mort*. His sadistic treatment of Xanthias, an instance of the comic master's cruel *Schadenfreude*, slips into the masochistic lust for the excremental, the strain of 'joy in the face of death'.[21] Being 'hard-pressed' or 'crushed', mimetically enjoying the pleasure-in-pain of scatological jokes, Dionysus seems to pursue the wounding of laughter, a kind of literal *trauma* ('wound').

From this perspective, the highly programmatic Aristophanic passage problematizes Aristotle's definition of the comic mask as 'an ugly face, distorted without pain' ('διεστραμμένον ἄνευ ὀδύνης') and the 'comic' ('γελοῖον') itself, as 'non-painful and non-destructive' ('ἀνώδυνον καὶ οὐ φθαρτικόν').[22] This emphatic denial of tragic 'pain' ('ὀδύνη') on masks seems more prescriptive than descriptive, an attempt to maintain a firm binary of tragic and comic, and repress its instability.[23] The impression that Aristotle's declaration amounts almost to a Freudian negation emerges from the South Italian vases depicting scenes from Old Comedy. In the *Choregoi* vase (Fig. 5.1), the old, twisted body in the centre depicts more emphatically the pressure ('πιέζομαι') and crushing ('θλίβομαι') lamented by Xanthias. The character's mask does not seem 'ἀνώδυνον' ('non-painful') either. When these comic masks are in profile (Fig. 5.2, central figure), their wide mouths turn into gaps that resemble facial wounds. Although the mask is 'an *object* not an expression of laughter' for Aristotle, as Stephen Halliwell notes,[24] these gaps recall laughing grins, modelling laughter as a lack symbolic of pain, repetition and death. The masks, I argue, mimetically break us open in the dehiscence of laughter; they represent and generate the wounding that constitutes laughter.

The contours of gaping laughter come into relief in another programmatic Aristophanic passage, which can be read as an allegory of comic spectatorship. The prologue of *Frogs* resumes the *parabasis* of *Clouds*, where Aristophanes lambasts his competitors for their misdeeds, especially recycling the same old vulgar jokes.[25] Phrynichus, who, in *Frogs*, is named as one of the scatological offenders (13–14), is accused of having cooked up a gag, which Eupolis, Aristophanes' chief rival, has shamefully appropriated: 'προσθεὶς αὐτῷ

Figure 5.1 Paul Getty Crater, inv. 248778, Museo Archeologico Nazionale di Napoli.

Figure 5.2 Ghiottoni Crater, inv. A 0.9. 2841. Civico Museo Archeologico, Milano. Copyright Milan Municipal Authority, all legal rights reserved.

γραῦν μεθύσην τοῦ κόρδακος οὕνεχ', ἣν/Φρύνιχος πάλαι πεποίηχ', ἣν τὸ κῆτος ἤσθιεν' ('[Eupolis] tacked onto [his play] a drunken old woman for the sake of the *kordax*, the woman whom Phrynichus long ago put onstage, whom the sea monster wanted to eat', *Clouds* 555f.). The lasciviously dancing old woman whom Phrynichus brought onstage parodied the mythical Andromeda, an ecphrastic heroine, the victim *par excellence* of the devouring gaze.[26] The syntactical parallelism between 'Φρύνιχος' and 'κῆτος', which the repetition of the relative pronoun 'ἣν' emphasizes, makes us look at Phrynichus as a monstrous comedian, a grotesque Pygmalion no less erotically voracious than the sea monster itself. Yet the more striking parallelism suggested by the scene is between the monster and the comic audience, voyeuristically directing its ravenous gaze to a chained Andromeda, albeit one who is comically transformed. In a comic play, looking leads to a sea monster-like gaping of the oral chasm, a kind of laughter, as we see in compounds of 'χάσκω' ('gape') that mean 'to laugh at' such as 'ἐγχάσκω' and 'καταχάσκω', which appear throughout the Aristophanic corpus.[27]

The act of laughing in Phrynichus' scene conjures not just the monster's devouring maw, but a void that 'transport[s]' the subject 'to the level of death', as Bataille would put it.[28] In one of the autobiographical accounts in his book *Inner Experience*, he recalls a nocturnal stroll:

> A space constellated with laughter opened its dark abyss before me. Crossing the rue du Four, I became in this unknown 'nothingness', suddenly . . . I negated these gray walls that enclosed me, I rushed into a sort of rapture . . . I laughed as perhaps one had never laughed, the final depth of each thing opened, laid bare, as if I were dead.[29]

This passage marks the dissolution of the subject into a void, in an instant of death coinciding with an eruption of laughter. In this moment, identity abolishes itself, undergoing an experience comparable to sex, Lacan's *faire l'amourir*. Bataille's personal account makes us see the gaping hole provoked by laughter beyond the Bakhtinian grotesque body, as an abyss or a wound that undoes the face itself, placing the subject in contact with the darkness of non-being.[30] In Paolo Veronese's painting of the Andromeda scene (Fig. 5.3), based on Ovid's account of the mythical episode, both gazers' faces disappear – Perseus', covered almost entirely by a cap, and the monster's, devoured by the widest oral aperture, the materialization of a raging lack, of appetite and desire that almost swallow it, assimilating it to the marine chasm. The abyss in the monster's face can be compared with the scary laughing chasms serially painted and sculpted by the Chinese artist Yue Minjun (Fig. 5.4). This jaw-breaking laughter tragically hollows out the face, wrinkles it, and freezes it into a grin. Yue's art shows not only how laughter can express despair and melancholy, supplying a means of resistance against political and emotional oppression – satire's 'non-laughing laugh' – but also how it entails, phenomenologically, a wounding of the face, regardless of the feelings it conceals. Together, the two modern comparanda help us imagine how the laughing spectator, like Phrynichus' monster, is swallowed up by the gaping hole in the face just as,

Laughter, or Aristophanes' Joy in the Face of Death

in the Veronese painting, the monster appears to be swallowed up by the sea, in a kind of *mise en abyme*. Lucian tells the story of a tragic actor who scared off the spectators with 'his mouth gaping all the way' ('στόμα κεχηνὸς πάμμεγα', *De Salt.* 27), making them believe that he 'would swallow them up' ('ὡς καταπιόμενος τοὺς θεατάς', ibid.).[31] But in this image we could also see the gaping of the comic actor's laughing mask, which is an equally terrifying mirror of the spectators' own laughing, self-hollowing faces. The annihilation threatening the comic Andromeda, which the audience experiences as sadistic pleasure or vicarious intercourse, bounces back on them, as their faces mimetically wrinkle and are swallowed by their own laughing maws. While laughing, the face joyfully tears itself apart through a kind of perverse acquisition; it absorbs, and is absorbed into, crypts of nothingness, archiving pockets of death within its own inside.

As I will suggest next, laughter does not just *tear* the face *apart*, but it also *tears* the subject *apart from* the community, enacting a particular expression of the fantasy of non-existence fuelled by the death drive – what Gilles Deleuze calls 'the world without others'.[32]

Figure 5.3 Paolo Veronese, *Perseus Freeing Andromeda*, originally in the antichamber at Vaux-le-Vicomte, Musee de Beaux-Arts, Rennes.

Figure 5.4 Yue Minjun, *Expression in Eyes*, No. 168, Xiao Bao Cun, Songzhuang Township, Tongzhou District, Beijing.

The joy of chasmic laughter: 'The world without others'

One would think there is nothing more communal, nothing that gathers us together more than laughter, even though we may laugh for different reasons. But, as I will argue, laughter has a 'chasmic' dimension that can be conceptualized as a fall into the abyss, a retreat from the human world, something like the Deleuzian 'life without others'. This life, as Eleanor Kaufman puts it, 'open[s] onto an impersonal and inhuman perceptual space'.[33] According to Deleuze, it corresponds to the 'eternal present', never motionless, of the natural elements.[34] In the examples that follow, I will consider laughter's undoing of the subject as a plunge into the elements – fire or water.

In the 'tragic' finale of *Clouds*, Socrates' fiery collapse may constitute his last laugh. This collapse is captured by the prefix *kata-* in 'κατακαυθήσομαι' ('I will be burned down', 1505), which we hear from one of Socrates' pupils while the *phrontistērion* goes down in flames at the vengeful hands of Strepsiades. In the same scene, Socrates' own 'ἀποπνιγήσομαι' ('I will be choked', 1504) brings us back to the beginning of the play, where Strepsiades laid out for his son the tenets of the natural philosophy taught in the *phrontistērion* – among them, the assimilation of the sky to a 'πνιγεύς' ('barbecue lid', 96).

This resonance turns Socrates' violent death into a self-annihilating encounter with smoke and fire. Such an elemental encounter is the punchline of various ancient narratives of philosophers' deaths – in particular, Empedocles' leap into Etna, which was apparently motivated by a desire to prove his immortality to sceptics by disappearing mysteriously.[35] If we consider that fire has strong associations with laughter – as shown, for example, by the Homeric phrase 'ἄσβεστος γέλως' ('unquenchable laughter'), which, in two occurrences out of three (*Il.* 1.599, *Od.* 8.326; cf. *Od.* 20.346), refers to hilarity aroused by Hephaestus – we can see Empedocles' plunge as the very materialization of laughter.[36] In the finale of *Clouds*, then, Strepsiades sets up Socrates to re-enact this philosopher's death. During the second *agōn*, Pheidippides had raised the possibility that, as a final act of parental hubris, his father would 'die laughing at him' ('σὺ δ'ἐγχανὼν τεθνήξεις', 1436), bringing to mind, with the participle 'ἐγχανών', the gaping mouth of the monster mentioned in the *parabasis*. But in the finale it is perhaps Socrates who laughs last, not Strepsiades. Strepsiades has unwittingly granted him 'joy in the face of death', a chance to laugh *at* the world and tear himself apart from it by *becoming* fire, conjuring a laughing maw in the act of merging into the fire's maw.

Thales' fall into a well, as recounted in Plato's *Theaetetus*, offers another image of laughter as a drop into the abyss, in this case in an effort to become water.[37] In *Theaetetus* 174a6–8, Socrates speaks of how Thales, wrapped up in cosmological investigation (not unlike Socrates in *Clouds*), tumbled into a well only to be laughed at by a Thracian maid because 'he was eager to know the things in the sky, but what was in front of him and before his feet escaped his attention' ('τὰ μὲν ἐν οὐρανῷ προθυμοῖτο εἰδέναι, τὰ δ' ἔμπροσθεν αὐτοῦ καὶ παρὰ πόδας λανθάνοι αὐτόν'). According to Socrates' interpretation, the story depicts philosophers as passionate searchers for truth who are misunderstood and abused by simple-minded people. Reading against the grain, Adriana Cavarero invites us to sympathize, instead, with the rebellious wit of the Thracian woman and laugh along with her at Thales – and at a misogynistic narrative that Cavarero sees as mistakenly valorizing detachment from the world, from sensory experience.[38] As she sees it, in Plato's anecdote laughter is precisely the enactment of a resistant female embodiedness that reinscribes sensation against Plato's attempted erasure of it, his devaluation of 'what is before one's feet' as 'merely superficial appearance'.[39] But there is perhaps another pathway for reading the episode. Considering that, in what follows (174d2), Socrates portrays the philosopher that Thales typifies as 'laughing' ('γελῶν') at human self-congratulation, we might view the philosopher's fall as a kind of laughter in its own right. In that sense, he would be similar to Democritus, the 'laugher' ('Γελασῖνος') – so called for having laughed at the follies of the world (Ael. *VH* 4.20).[40] What if Thales' tumble fulfilled an intimate desire for withdrawal, for 'a life without others'? The well's void, where he disappears, would thus correspond to the chasm swallowing his face as his mouth, like that of Phrynichus' sea monster, gaped in laughter at those remaining in the world. His self-estrangement from social life and life itself evinces a defiant 'joy in the face of death', in the face of a literal abyss corresponding to the self-swallowing, the self-annihilation, of laughter. Plunging not into a dry pit, but into a well, a source of water, Thales, the 'originator' (ἀρχηγός) of natural philosophy, is immersed in, even merges with, the element that he considered the origin of everything.⁴¹ But in the laughter that leads to becoming water, we could see a drifting toward fusion with the female principle that Socrates marginalizes. Estranging the philosopher from the world, swallowing him in the abyss, laughter places him in a mobile liquid state between inorganic life and the blissful wholeness of foetal existence.⁴² Thales' fall is, in a sense, a reflection of the Thracian woman's own laughter, a spatial extension of her facial dehiscence tending toward female fluidity. A return to water, laughter submerges the subject in the 'time out of joint' of an 'eternal present'.⁴³

Like Thales, the old misanthrope in Menander's *Duskolos* falls into a well in a burst of chasmic laughter that immerses him in an eternal watery present. The turning point in the plot, Knemon's fall raises the question of who is laughing at whom. While some characters are anxious to rescue him, Sostratus, the upper-crust young man, is ostentatiously indifferent, and Sicon, the brash cook, imagines taunting Knemon, *laughing* at him: 'Fall in and drink the well dry – you won't have a dribble then of water left to share with anyone!' ('μεταδοῦναι μηδενί!', 641f.). But could we see this fall, in fact, as what the misanthrope secretly wishes for? Entombing himself away from human contact seems the fulfilment of his antisocial, misanthropic dream. Although Knemon's 'catabatic' fall need not be construed as suicidal, it does allow him to extricate himself from other characters' control and, in a sense, to *laugh* defiantly at them. The chasm of the well that serendipitously absorbs Knemon can serve as an image of the facial aperture opened by laughter in a kind of self-swallowing by which one seeks to escape from oneself while escaping from the Other. Knemon may laugh at the other characters and at us as we sadistically laugh at him,⁴⁴ but we might also be in his position, laughing, from the abyss, at the neurotic havoc that his fall has caused onstage. That the laughter binding us to Knemon may correspond to a momentary experience of pre-Symbolic life is indicated by his apparent behavioural 'rebirth' after he exits it.⁴⁵ The rope that eventually brings Knemon up evokes an umbilical cord, a suggestion reinforced by Sicon's preview of the old man's baby-like return: 'And his appearance [once he's been fished out]? Can you imagine, by the gods, what it'll be like? He'll be soaked, shivering' ('βεβ[αμ]μένου/ τρέμοντος', 656–8⁴⁶). 'Soaked' assimilates Knemon's chasmic laughter to a 'joy in the face of death' that provisionally satisfies a pull toward foetal existence, re-immersion, becoming water.

The image of the 'shivering' Knemon connects laughter with a type of experience beyond the human subject – not just living without others, but living like a broken object.⁴⁷ When Simiche speaks of the 'rotten little rope' ('καλῳδίῳ σαπρῷ', 580) that 'broke' ('διερράγη', 580) when Knemon tried to extract a bucket stuck in the well, she anticipates an assimilation that his impending tumble will bring about. Old Knemon is as 'rotten' as the rope, which, in 'breaking', offers an image of laughter – a sundering, a transformation of the face into a splitting object. Knemon's 'shivering' can be read as an after-effect of this rupture, the laughter repaired by the new rope that has hauled him back into human life.

From another perspective, Knemon's fall has made him 'drown' or 'suffocate' ('ἀποπεπνιγμένον', 668), as Sostratus puts it. This observation invites us to see laughter as suffocation or gagging. To expand on this point, I will now return to Aristophanes, exploring how laughter, 'joy in the face of death', causes the human subject to exit itself in another sense – not by joining the elemental life of water or fire, but by becoming *the animal that it intimately is*.

Laughing as gagging and becoming animal

Reflecting on the theoretical implications of the Shakespearean phrase 'laughter in the throat of death', Jean-Luc Nancy conceptualized a convulsion that defies representation and meaning.[48] Before him, Bataille defined laughter as an 'intimate overturning' with the quality of 'suffocating surprise'.[49] The void in the throat is where the 'suffocating' experience of 'joy in the face of death' arises; this void violently drops the human subject into a self-oblivion that, as Lucio Angelo Privitello suggests, can be defined as *animalêthê* ('soul-forgetting', a pun on 'animality').[50] With this self-oblivion, 'the inhuman depths of the human animal'[51] – what Bataille calls 'the obscure intimacy of the animal'[52] – break open. In his words, 'the animal opens before me a depth that attracts me and is familiar to me ... I know this depth: it is my own.'[53] In what follows, I want to look for laughter as a strain in the throat that uncovers this depth, and for laughter's 'experiential sundering',[54] the corporeal splitting it quasi-tragically effects, as tantamount to becoming animal.

In the parody of Euripides' *Andromeda* in *Thesmophoriazusae*, Phrynichus' old-woman-as-sea-monster-chow gag – the target of Aristophanes' scorn in *Clouds* – returns with another, more direct image of the laughing spectator. Facing a Scythian archer instead of the sea monster and awaiting the intervention of Euripides-as-Perseus, the Kinsman, in the guise of the tragic Andromeda, is relieved to have survived the assault of 'a rotten old woman' ('γραῖαν ... σαπράν', 1024f.), one of the ostensibly misogynist tragedian's enemies. The label is unwittingly self-referential, as the paratragic disguise turns the Kinsman, a 'γέρων' ('old man', 585; 941), into a 'γραῖα σαπρά', Phrynichus' comic stock character. Here is the beginning of the comic Andromeda's monodic lamentation, addressed to the chorus of her tragic companions, but implicating the audience:

μόλις δὲ γραῖαν ἀποφυγὼν
   σαπρὰν ἀπωλόμην ὅμως.
ὅδε γὰρ ὁ Σκύθης φύλαξ
   πάλαι ἐφεστὼς ὀλοὸν ἄφιλον
   ἐκρέμασέ <με> κόρακι δεῖπνον.
ὁρᾷς, οὐ χοροῖσιν ...

...

γοᾶσθέ μ', ὦ γυναῖκες, ὡς
   μέλεα μὲν πέπονθα μέλε-
   ος – ὦ τάλας ἐγώ, τάλας, –

...
    – αἰαῖ αἰαῖ ἒ ἔ –
ὅς ἔμ' ἀπεξύρησε πρῶτον,
ὅς ἐμὲ κροκόεντ' ἀμφέδυσεν·
...
                ...ἐκρεμάσθην,
λαιμότμητ' ἄχη δαιμόνι, αἰόλαν
    νέκυσιν ἐπὶ πορείαν.

I got free of a rotten old woman only to die anyway! For this Scythian guard, long posted over me, has hung me up, doomed and friendless, as supper for crows! See, [I am not standing] with choruses . . . Mourn me, ladies, with a hymn not of marriage but of jail, for wretched do I suffer wretchedly – alas alack, woe is me! . . . oh oh! – the one who first shaved me, the one who put these saffron things on me . . . I am hung up, damned by the gods to cut-throat grief, bound for a quicksilver trip to the grave.
            Thesmophoriazusae 1024–9, 1036–8, 1042–4, 1053–5

Just as the Scythian archer has kept the Kinsman/Andromeda under surveillance for 'a long time' and served him up as supper for crows ('κόραξι'), the comic poets – Phrynichus, Eupolis, and now Aristophanes too – have repeatedly made an elderly Andromeda the prey of their spectators' laughing maws. Earlier, while demanding to be stripped naked out of fear that as an old man in women's clothing he might provoke laughter among the crows destined to eat him, the Kinsman had implicity assimilated the devouring birds to laughing spectators – 'μὴ ... γέλωτα παρέχω τοῖς κόραξιν ἐστιῶν' ('lest ... I provide laughter to the crows, feeding them', 942).

From the hoarse, lamenting crows' voices, disseminated through the monodic texture, laughter emerges as suffocation, or a gash in the throat.[55] In the Kinsman's parody, the second-person plural imperative 'γοᾶσθε' ('mourn me'), which the tragic Andromeda addressed to her female companions, interpellates the comic spectators as crow-like laughers.[56] 'Tragic choruses' ('χοροῖσιν', 1029) are blurred with 'crows' ('κόραξι', 1028), and lamentation with laughter, as the harsh guttural and aspirated sounds of 'κόραξι', evocations of the crows' sounds, contagiously circulate in the Kinsman's words. Drawing attention to her current condition, 'hung up' ('ἐκρεμάσθην', 1053) on the rock, apparently bound by the neck,[57] the comic Andromeda is gagging, but also cawing, with the *kr* sound in 'ἐκρεμάσθην', lamenting and laughing at the same time – that is, modelling for the chorus and the audience, with her very lament, the throaty pain of laughter, like the painful constriction of the throat inflicted by the archer – a tragically coloured 'cut-throat grief' ('λαιμότμητ' ἄχη', 1054). A few lines earlier, the phonetics of 'crow' ('κόραξ') is reflected in the 'crocus' ('κροκόεντα', 1044) of the Kinsman's garments as though he were bearing on his skin, through his crocus-dyed clothes, the suffocating sound of laughter. With its aspirated, guttural, sibilant sounds, which diffuse the cawing, 'ἀποξύρω' ('shaving') is another indication of the 'cutting' force of laughter. It is as though, by becoming crows in the process of laughing, spectators did not just emit cutting sounds, but, in a sense, also had their throats cut with the arrows of the Scythian archer, the weapon whose blade is materialized in the crow-like sounds (again, aspirated, sibilant, guttural) of the words 'Σκύθης' and 'φύλαξ'.⁵⁸ Laughter is a wound in the throat – a tragic opening expressed by the Kinsman/Andromeda's interjections 'αἰαῖ αἰαῖ' (1042) – that is inflicted on the laughing spectator, who both suffers and enjoys the 'trauma' of old jokes, but also, in a sense, groans while laughing.⁵⁹ The wound opens a pathway for the human subject to animality, that is, a domain of 'obscure intimacy'⁶⁰ with the flux of the world – close yet customarily closed to the human,⁶¹ located at the edge of consciousness and discourse. While bringing us closer to the animal, the wound opened by the cawing sounds of throaty laughter is also a 'reintensification of anguish, dread, and utter loss'⁶² – the loss of the animality that we have to separate ourselves from in order (to pretend) to be human.

The animality opened up by laughter is captured by echo, in itself a figure of laughter personified in this scene. Disguised as Echo, who, in the tragic hypotext, responded to Andromeda's laments from within her cave – the spatial abyss with which the comic *skēnē* is temporarily identified⁶³ – Euripides introduces himself and his mask as an 'ἐπικοκκάστρια', which the scholiast glosses as 'a woman used to laughing'.⁶⁴ Mimicking throaty avian sounds, as suggested by its etymological link with κοκκύζω, 'to cry like a cuckoo', or as *LSJ* also puts it, 'to crow', the word invites us to consider the homology between echo and laughter, to see the latter as sound produced in a cavernous abyss of the human body, the throat or the chest. Euripides/Echo reduces the Kinsman/Andromeda's wailing sentences to their final portions, as indicated self-reflexively by 'μέρος' ('part'), in lines 1070f.:

K   τί ποτ' Ἀνδρομέδα περίαλλα κακῶν
    μέρος ἐξέλαχον;
E   μέρος ἐξέλαχον;

K   Why oh why have I, Andromeda, had so much more than my portion of ills?
E   Portion of ills?

This is a version of the customary interruption and distortion of the 'straight man's' words, each of Euripides' interventions marking comic tempo, the cadence of laughter. But the verbal decomposition also dramatizes the echoey nature of laughter as an outburst of serial sound progressively vanishing into the void – a sensory experience of repetition projected toward death.⁶⁵ In the act of laughing, the human subject has the feeling of vanishing or dissolving into the air together with the sound, becoming imperceptible, joining, in the terms of Deleuze and Guattari, 'a world of pure intensities' or the 'unformed matter of deterritorialized flux'.⁶⁶ While the harsh, repetitive phonetic intensities of laughter shake the human subject into an encounter with its repressed animality, the echo of laughter is in itself an image of this animality, which, for Bataille, is a 'steadily dilating abyss staring back into the heart of the human'.⁶⁷

I now want to consider laughter as a painful and spasmodic stretching of upper and lower orifices in the excremental landscape of the Underworld in *Frogs*. As Dionysus traverses the river Styx, the chorus of frogs sings; the god laments the pain caused by his repetitive rowing in an incommodious boat, conflating it with the aural discomfort inflicted by the persistent amphibian song, the famous *brekekekex koax koax*. As he puts it, 'my butt's getting sore, you koax koax' ('ἐγὼ δέ γ' ἀλγεῖν ἄρχομαι/τὸν ὄρρον, ὦ κοὰξ κοάξ', 221f.) – a refrain we could see precisely as a vocalization of laughter.[68] Indeed, only a *rho* separates κοάξ from κόραξ, the crow, which, as I have suggested, evokes the gaping mouths of laughing spectators in *Thesmophoriazusae*. However, the riotous croaking of the frogs is a flatulent rumbling as much as an oral explosion. When Dionysus announces 'my butt ... pretty soon will poke out – and say ...' ('χὠ πρωκτὸς ... /κᾆτ' αὐτίκ' ἐκκύψας ἐρεῖ', 237f.), the frogs complete the sentence with *brekekex koax koax* (239). Breaking out in the scatological landscape of the infernal marsh, which Heracles had previously described as 'ever-flowing excrement' ('σκῶρ ἀείνων', 146), the frogs' refrain dramatizes the relation between laughter 'as a spasmodic process of the oral orifice's sphincter muscles' (in Bataille's words) and defecation.[69] When Dionysus joins the chorus in singing *brekekex koax koax*, his lower 'ἄλγος' ('pain') loosens into the rapturous opening of the upper orifice, but this laughing explosion has a painful dimension; the verb used by the frogs, 'κεκραξόμεσθα' ('we'll bellow', 258), echoes 'κοάξ' and, in a sense, glosses it as the product of amphibian vocal stretching, with strained throat and wide-open mouth.

In *Frogs*, animality, we can say, echoes as 'laughter in the throat of death'. The vocal stretching expressed by 'κεκραξόμεσθα' is in line with Dionysus' own physical hardship, the painful bifurcation of his buttocks expressed, a few lines earlier, by 'διαρραγήσομαι' ('I will burst apart', 255). The verbs' shared phonemic sequence of rho-alpha-velar ('-ραγ/ξ-') bespeaks a rasping correspondence between the frogs' gelastic outburst and a bodily rupture, a correspondence captured in the English phrase *to crack up*, which presents the same phonestheme (|rak|). The literal *cracking up* portended by the frogs' sounds is intimated by the wheezing sesquipedalian compound 'πομφολυγοφλάσμασιν' ('bubbly ploppifications'), followed by the heavy tripartite dropping of 'βρεκεκεκὲξ κοὰξ κοάξ' (249f.), suggesting, respectively, flatulence and defecation, and thus an assimilation to the muddy faecal matter of the Underworld. The repetitious, scatological croaking of the frogs and Dionysus' eventual participation in their throaty song dramatize laughter's furtherance of an uncanny desire for self-dissolution – the self-shattering of 'joy in the face of death'. The laughter concomitant with the refrain *brekekekex koax koax* tears up upper and lower orifices, causing a self-wounding *jouissance*, which masochistically transcends the Bakhtinian grotesque body. The vertiginously ruptured rhythm of incessant guttural sounds conjures a laughing subject not just becoming a frog, an animal swallowed by its own oral abyss, but also dissolving into bubbling infernal mud, matter that is both organic and inorganic, animate and inanimate. Through Dionysus' throaty cracking up, his splitting apart, laughter becomes the 's/laughter of the self', 'the sound of how the individual loses itself in an earthly debauchery', in an 'animality ... bursting forth from subterranean and swampy regions', which resemble 'wounds and ruptures'.[70]

In *Ecclesiazusae*, we see the masochistic delight of laughter emerge through splitting, gaping, and even the sadistic thrill of posthumous revenge. In one of the last scenes of the play, the prey of three old women – the personified parts of a classic tripartite joke – is the young man Epigenes, a figure of the comic spectator, reminiscent of Dionysus in *Frogs*.[71] The sight of the second woman as Empousa (1056) – the ridiculous yet terrifying monster sporting, in *Frogs*, one brazen leg and another made of dung – terrifies the young man with scatological consequences (1059–62). In the face of a quasi-Empousa, his announced defecation could code something like Dionysus' pleased sense of disgust at a scatological joke – or the eruption of laughter itself. This impression becomes stronger with the intervention of the third woman, who is presented as equally frightening but also compared to a monkey (1072) – an animal cast, in antiquity, as riotously funny, almost a proto-comedian, and a great laugher itself. When the young man, pulled in opposite directions by the three women, laments, 'you're going to rip me in half' ('διασπάσεσθε μ', 1076), he seems to be describing the convulsions, the spasms caused by laughter, the same bodily discomfort and dissolution expressed, in *Frogs*, by the convergence of the frogs' throaty outbursts with Dionysus' splitting pain ('διαρραγήσομαι', 'I will burst apart', *Frogs* 255). The participle 'διαλελημμένον' ('split apart', 1090), modifying Epigenes a few lines later, continues this image, which is also formally visualized by the many *antilabai*, ripping the lines in half (see esp. 1083–5). Bataille characterizes laughter's 'joy in the face of death' as an experience that 'tears apart' the body as well as language.[72] What we witness here is a kind of gelastic *sparagmos* orchestrated by three bacchants at the expense (or for the perverse pleasure) of a Pentheus-like spectator. In his final speech, Epigenes envisions his impending night in the company of one of the three women as a preview of death, or death itself. He compares her to 'Phryne with a *lēkuthos* on her jaws' ('Φρύνην ἔχουσαν λήκυθον πρὸς ταῖς γνάθοις', 1101), punning on the ambiguity of Phryne, a classic prostitute name but also the Greek word for toad, a kin of the frog chorus. While Epigenes abhors the sexual horror that awaits him, he relishes the thought of revenge, imagining that another old woman will be covered with pitch and permanently installed on his tomb instead of a *lēkuthos*:[73]

θάψαι μ' ἐπ' αὐτῷ τῷ στόματι τῆς ἐσβολῆς,
καὶ τήνδ' ἄνωθεν ἐπιπολῆς τοῦ σήματος
ζῶσαν καταπιττώσαντες εἶτα τὼ πόδε
μολυβδοχοήσαντες κύκλῳ περὶ τὰ σφυρὰ
ἄνω 'πιθεῖναι πρόφασιν ἀντὶ ληκύθου.

... bury me right at the mouth of the strait. As for her, while she's still alive, cover her with pitch all over and put her feet in molten lead up to her ankles, then stick her over my grave instead of an urn!

Ecclesiazusae 1107–11

The 'covering' fantasized here by Epigenes is a kind of mimetic swallowing, first in pitch, then in molten lead, a swallowing that we may graphically detect in line 1109, where the participle 'καταπιττώσαντες' ('having covered in pitch') contains or, we can say, gulps *down* (*kata*) the letters of the preceding participle 'ζῶσαν' ('alive'), modifying the 'γραῦς' ('old woman'). The swallowing image seems to speak to the young man's hope to take revenge on the female predator by becoming another gaping mouth – something like Empousa,[74] Andromeda's would-be swallower, or, even Phryne the 'toad'. We can thus see the contours of another laughing maw emerging from Epigenes' death fantasies. Once again, descent into the pit of death coincides with laughter and an encounter with animality. The laughing maw that connects Epigenes with the gaping, in his apparently vengeful, dominating, act of *laughing at*, turns sadistic intention[75] into the *jouissance* of self-swallowing – a kind of death drive that reinscribes the *petite mort* he shuns.[76]

Concerning a line from Baudelaire's 'The Desire to Paint' ('Le Désir de peindre'), Jean-Luc Nancy observes: 'desire, tear, inspiration, and death, these are first heard in a laugh.'[77] The phrase 'Le désir déchire', Nancy says, 'lends the poem its cadence as well as its theme, and this desire ... finds its note of truth in *le rire*'.[78] I have argued that in Aristophanes laughter seems to occupy the same porous experiential space between pleasure and agony as desire. What emerges from my readings is the notion of laughter as a quintessentially masochistic experience.[79] Old Comedy – from Phrynichus to Aristophanes – seems to regard the laughter it engenders as itself a form of dissipation, a moment that turns the face into a gash, a void; the body, into the matter of elemental life, part of the flux of the world, which, for Bataille, is intimately proximate to animality. In enjoying the gags of Aristophanes and the other comedians, we are throats that are laughing and gagging at the same time. This gagging, which makes us similar to crows, is the death-driven *jouissance* making us want to laugh again and again, never tired of falling, for an instant, into the void within our human subjectivity.

CHAPTER 6
LAUGHTER AND COLLECTIVE TRAUMA IN ARISTOPHANIC COMEDY
Pavlos Sfyroeras

Among the different yet often overlapping types of Aristophanic laughter (aggressive, subversive, bond-building, celebratory, to name a few), there is one category, not necessarily incompatible with those others, that seems to have gone largely unnoticed: the laughter of suffering. By this I do not mean the hostile mockery directed at a character who is suffering on- or offstage, like Lamachus in *Acharnians* or a host of other antagonists defeated by the Aristophanic hero. Nor do I point to the joyful reminiscence of past and overcome troubles, as will be later envisioned in Aeneas' famous 'forsan et haec olim meminisse iuvabit' (*Aeneid* 1.203). Rather, I refer to the laughter of the audience as it is prompted to recall the still painful memory of a collective trauma. To be fully understood and appreciated, this historically specific laughter which springs from simultaneous or very recent grief presupposes some knowledge of, or at least speculation about, the mental state of the original audience. It also shares certain affinities, to which I shall return, with Demeter's laughing response to Iambe's obscene antics in the *Homeric Hymn to Demeter* (202f.) or with the therapeutic prescription of mirth and hilarity in the Hippocratic corpus, or even with the philosopher's laughter at our existential absurdity.[1] Yet its distinct character, ethnographically attested, may also be fruitfully approached from a psychological or neurological angle. One might correlate it, for instance, with the laughter arising, in Freud's famous account, from the discharge of the surplus psychical energy that would have been expended at the prospect of breaking a taboo, or the laughter that, in Ramachandran's theory, signals false alarm; both describe situations that create the anticipation of discomfort or danger, only to thwart the expectation.[2] For reasons that will emerge below, I prefer to invoke and draw on Helmuth Plessner's philosophical anthropology of laughing and crying and, especially, on the findings of neuroscience that social laughter has analgesic properties, as it elevates the threshold of even physical pain, but also that laughing and crying are subject to analogous neurological pathologies.[3]

Frogs and Arginusae

Frogs provides a prototype for this kind of laughter by boldly thematizing the link between jokes and suffering in the very opening of the play, a scene that has been analysed frequently and perceptively.[4] It shows us a character, Dionysus' slave Xanthias, repeatedly frustrated in his urge to tell jokes that connect the pressure of bowel movements with the weight of the luggage he carries on his shoulders (1–11), until it becomes clear that he bears this burden ('ἄχθος φέρων', 'bearing a burden', 9; 'ταῦτα τὰ σκεύη φέρειν', 'carrying this luggage', 12[5]) precisely for the sole purpose of telling such jokes (12–15). Why would his 'thrice-miserable neck' ('τρισκακοδαίμων … ὁ τράχηλος') endure the weight if not for the opportunity to say something funny (19f.)? Yet even the very fact of 'carrying' is questioned by Dionysus, who points out that the weight cannot be said to be carried by Xanthias, since it is carried by the donkey carrying Xanthias. Dionysus' quibbling hinges on semantics and logic; who bears the weight of luggage carried by a slave riding on a donkey?[6] The implied concomitant paradox of a weight carried by both slave and donkey and therefore redoubled seems to stump Xanthias, who cannot answer ('οὐκ οἶδ᾽', 'I don't know', 30), yet he knows that he bears the luggage 'weightily' ('βαρέως', 26), that is, with difficulty. The broken verse (note the *antilabē* of 26) calls attention to the expression 'βαρέως φέρω', which holds the key, as it blurs the boundary between the literal 'to carry the weight' of 'τὰ σκεύη/ἄχθος φέρειν' (9, 12) and the metaphorical 'to bear a misfortune'.

This wordplay, with its fusion of literal and metaphorical burdens, is of course part of the joke, which, as we will see, functions to acknowledge and ease trauma. It is also at the heart of this opening scene – and of the whole play to a certain extent – especially if we consider the history of the phrases 'συμφορὰς φέρειν', 'βαρέως' or 'χαλεπῶς φέρειν' and the like. Such expressions are not as established, generic, and common as their gnomic status might lead one to assume. Indeed, they turn out to be fairly novel, at any rate not going further back than the middle of the fifth century at the earliest. Briefly, 'βαρέως φέρειν' first appears in Herodotus (3.155.2, 5.19.5, 5.42.11), then returns in Aristophanic comedy, including our passage (*Wasps* 114, 158; *Thesmophoriazousae* 385, 474; *Frogs* 26, 803; *Ecclesiazousae* 174f.). The semantic cognate 'χαλεπῶς φέρειν', 'to bear with difficulty', first occurs in the late fifth century, mostly in Thucydides (1.77, 2.16, 2.62, 6.56, 8.54), who also uses 'συμφορὰς/συμφορὰν φέρειν' ('to bear misfortune(s)', 2.60).[7] Some of these Thucydidean passages, especially 2.16 and 2.60–2, are concerned with the psychological effect of the Periclean strategy of abandoning the Attic countryside in the early years of the Peloponnesian War. It is therefore possible that this trope became current with Pericles, whether or not it originated with him, and that it was a familiar marker of his rhetoric, perhaps even of the collective discourse against his plan. Moreover, the frequency of the phrase 'συμφορὰς/συμφορὰν φέρειν' in Plato's *Menexenus* (247c-d, 248c, 249c) would also inscribe the idiom within the rhetorical tradition of the funeral oration.[8] We can thus correlate the Periclean and the funerary associations; since this phrase is first used by Euripides in the 430s (*Alc.* 416, *Med.* 1018, also *TrGF* 5 F 98), we might even dare pinpoint the occasion of its birth – Pericles' funeral speech after the Samian War.[9]

But whether these phrases are part of the Periclean vocabulary or not – we shall return to this question shortly – they certainly belong in a specific thematic area within public discourse; they convey the political connotations of carrying a burden of civic import, not simply individual suffering. More than that, Pericles' speech to quell Athenian resentment, as recorded by Thucydides (2.60), is especially relevant to the opening of *Frogs*; in a reformulation of the 'ship of state' metaphor, Pericles implies a kind of

Laughter and Collective Trauma in Aristophanic Comedy

redoubling similar to that suggested by the comic Dionysus – a citizen is said to be upheld ('φερόμενος') by a sailing *polis* which is able to bear that citizen's private misfortunes ('πόλις μὲν τὰς ἰδίας ξυμφορὰς οἷά τε φέρειν').[10] The same burden appears therefore to be carried twice, both by the citizen and the *polis*! We can imagine how a clever poet would be eager to run with the comic, even seemingly absurdist, potential of this idea.

The background of the humour in the opening scene is thus partly nautical, and so is the civic context for Xanthias' 'theorizing' about jokes and suffering, as is revealed right away; the slave's rhetorical and almost incidental question, 'why didn't I take part in the naval battle?' ('τί γὰρ ἐγὼ οὐκ ἐναυμάχουν;', 33), points to Arginusae, a very recent and doubly painful memory, resulting both from the indignity that the dead had suffered and from the precipitate execution of the generals, which was instantly regretted. This first allusion is followed by more references in the comedy, not only to the sea-battle itself (49, 190–2, 693–9) but also to the subsequent trial and the prominent role of Theramenes (534–41, 968–70).[11] Even Dionysus' inept rowing keeps the naval atmosphere in the forefront of our consciousness. But, more significantly, the battle of Arginusae is really what generates the very plot of *Frogs*, since it is on board a ship (52) in connection to the battle (49) that Dionysus reads *Andromeda* and conceives his longing for Euripides.[12] The allusions to Arginusae that, subtly but persistently, punctuate the entire play are thus invested with metadramatic meaning by Xanthias' programmatic remark; suffering is futile unless one can joke about it (19–32). This is, I argue, the real point of the prologue – the pressure of carrying the symbolic burden and its inevitable explosion into laughter, not the initial scatological jokes, which can be described as simply a fake attempt to procrastinate, a type of prevarication that skirts the issue and pretends to distract, until we citizens become suddenly aware that we are made to laugh about our own trauma.

Dicaeopolis and Spartan raids

While *Frogs* can be viewed as an extended joke about death, earlier comedies also provide instances of laughter born from traumatic experiences that may vary in intensity and temporal proximity to the first staging. The opening of *Acharnians* is a good example. Dicaeopolis' enumeration of paltry joys and countless sorrows, evocative and poignant as it is in itself, serves a parallel function that is analogous to the attempts at scatological humour and logical puzzles in *Frogs*; what can be described (in dramatic terms) as delay tactics create the pretence of a mock denial (in psychological terms) – when will he finally say what we're expecting him to, bringing this mental tickling to an end? It takes Dicaeopolis about thirty lines, which culminate in the pathetic exclamation 'ὦ πόλις πόλις' (27) and explodes in an unparalleled string of eight unconnected verbs ('στένω κέχηνα σκορδινῶμαι πέρδομαι/ἀπορῶ γράφω παρατίλλομαι λογίζομαι', 'I groan, gape, yawn, fart,/am at a loss, scribble, pull my hair out, consider', 30f.), mixing high and low, to spell out what *truly* vexes the Athenians: the 'longing' for his deme ('ποθῶν', 33), rendered inaccessible by the repeated (and by now routine) ravaging of the Attic countryside (32f.).[13]

To be sure, this historical background does not sound as traumatic as the Arginusae affair. Yet if we listen to Thucydides' account of the initial impact of the Spartan raids in 431 (2.21f.), but also, a little earlier, of the Periclean strategy to abandon the countryside (2.16), we can appreciate more fully the emotional toll on the Athenians. We can even discern a progression in the intensity of emotion, starting with the two verbal phrases 'ἐβαρύνοντο δὲ καὶ χαλεπῶς ἔφερον' ('they were weighed down and bore with difficulty', 2.16.2), near synonyms that convey the quiet distress of being uprooted (cf. 2.14.1f.).[14] From the burden of the evacuation, oppressive yet tolerated, we move to the no longer bearable experience of seeing the enemy around Acharnae ('οὐκέτι ἀνασχετὸν ἐποιοῦντο ... δεινὸν ἐφαίνετο', 'they no longer considered it endurable ... it seemed terrible', 2.21.2). What strikes the Athenians as a terrible sight leads to further escalation of emotion, with violent disagreement, arousal of tempers, and rage against Pericles ('ἐν πολλῇ ἔριδι', 'in much strife', 2.21.3; 'ἀνηρέθιστο ἡ πόλις, καὶ τὸν Περικλέα ἐν ὀργῇ εἶχον', 'the city had been stirred up, and was angry at Pericles', 2.21.3).[15] His effort to quell those reactions ('χαλεπαίνοντας', 'aggrieved'; 'ὀργῇ', 'in anger', 2.22.1) is intensified after the second invasion ('χαλεπαίνοντας'; 'τὸ ὀργιζόμενον τῆς γνώμης', 'the anger of their minds', 2.59.3), judged the harshest by Thucydides (3.26). That provides the occasion for Pericles' speech (2.60-4) that will prove to be his last one; it includes, in addition to the familiar diction of emotional trauma (e.g. 'ὀργῆς', 'χαλεπαίνετε', 2.60.1; 'ὀργίζεσθε', 2.60.5; 'δι' ὀργῆς', 2.64.1; 'βαρυνόμενοι', 2.64.6), the disquisition on civic burden that, as we discussed above, must have left a memorable imprint.[16] The concentration of such vocabulary in Thucydides has a cumulative effect and offers undeniable testimony to the real Athenian trauma that is communicated through Dicaeopolis.

We should observe, however, that *Acharnians* is not exactly contemporaneous with the time of 'raw' suffering. By 425, Athenians must have become used to the almost annual raids (there was not one in 429 or in 426), so they can even laugh a bit about it, especially since there was no invasion in the summer preceding *Acharnians*. Overall, as some modern scholars have now recognized, the damage may not have been as severe as the Athenians feared.[17] In other words, the repetition develops into a certain routine to become, almost in anticipation of Bergson's concept of mechanized behaviour, rather comic in itself; it thus stands in sharp contrast to the tragic events preceding *Frogs* (52-4). Even so, there is an underlying analogy between the two plays; just as the experience of Arginusae inspires Dionysus and generates the plot of *Frogs*, so it is the trauma itself that motivates the main character and gives birth to the storyline of *Acharnians*. As a result, every subsequent instance of laughing in the play carries in itself the reminiscence of the wound that is evoked early on.

This analogy between the two comedies manifests itself in a formal element. In both *Frogs* and *Acharnians*, the reference to the underlying trauma is delayed until lines 32f., after some superficially extraneous material. This may be accidental, of course, but it is equally plausible that the comic poet had worked out a formula of comic psychology; it takes just over thirty lines of seemingly innocuous wit to put the spectators at ease before hitting them with the painful memory. Those thirty lines are intended to relax them and make them receptive to the poignant grief-tinged statement, so that it would elicit the audience's laughter, or at the very least neutralize the possible discomfort at the mention of their grief.[18] The lines that could be described in retrospect as the poet's intentional hesitation create the conditions, especially with their misplaced anxiety, to absorb the shock, if not with hilarity, at least without excessive vexation.

Cleonymus and Delium

We may now move on to the rather different case of Cleonymus the 'shield-thrower'. He is a butt of jokes in every single extant play until *Birds*. Already in *Acharnians* (88, 844) and *Knights* (956–8, 1290–9, 1369–72) he is ridiculed for his obesity, gluttony and aversion to military service; his host of flaws expands to include effeminacy, perjury and suspect political activity. Yet what made him notorious was, beyond any doubt, the act of discarding his shield. The jokes about Cleonymus' 'shield-throwing' are inaugurated in *Clouds* (353–4) and proliferate in *Wasps* (15–27, 592, 821–3), *Peace* (446, 677f., 1295–1304) and *Birds* (290, 1473–81).[19]

What is it that changes with *Clouds* and results in indelibly attaching to Cleonymus the charge of *rhipsaspia*? Some scholars have discerned the impact of the battle of Delium (424/3), and I concur.[20] Especially given its absence from the two plays that precede the battle (*Acharnians* and *Knights*) and its sudden appearance in *Clouds*, shield-throwing poignantly evokes the resounding defeat and chaotic retreat of the Athenians at Delium, as described in Thucydides (4.96.6–9, 101.2) but also in Plato's *Symposium* (220e–221b; cf. *Laches* 181b).[21]

It is worth following the timeline and sequence of some of these jokes. The events at Delium took place in the beginning of winter (Thuc. 4.89.1, 'τοῦ δ᾽ ἐπιγιγνομένου χειμῶνος εὐθὺς ἀρχομένου', 'with the coming winter just starting'), only a few months before the Dionysiac festival.[22] Therefore, while I acknowledge the complications arising from the revision of *Clouds*, I suspect that the two-line joke about Cleonymus was inserted in the description of the shape-shifting Clouds shortly before the production. In fact, the phrasing of 353f. is telling; when Socrates explains that his deities single out an objectionable quality of an individual and imitate it in order to mock him, Strepsiades interjects, 'Ah, that's why, when they saw Cleonymus the shield-thrower yesterday, since they were looking at a most cowardly man, they turned into deer' ('ταῦτ᾽ ἄρα ταῦτα Κλεώνυμον αὗται τὸν ῥίψασπιν χθὲς ἰδοῦσαι,/ὅτι δειλότατον τοῦτον ἑώρων, ἔλαφοι διὰ τοῦτ᾽ ἐγένοντο'). Strepsiades' 'yesterday' (χθές) is certainly not to be taken literally, but it is clearly meant to convey something from the recent past. The hypothesis that Strepsiades' two-liner was a last-minute addition might explain why Cleonymus' other two appearances in the comedy (*Clouds* 399f., 672–6) make no mention of his hoplitic mishap.

By contrast, after *Clouds*, Cleonymus' name never comes up without his shield-throwing, which becomes, we might say, a sort of expected leitmotif. At the same time, there is a new element, which is adumbrated in *Clouds*, with the need to interpret the allusive appearance of its chorus, but it is only spelled out in the opening of *Wasps*. The first of the dreams that the two slaves of Bdelycleon relate and decipher (15–27) features a dizzying sequence: an eagle snatches an 'ἀσπίς', which changes from 'asp' to its homonym 'shield' through the adjective 'ἐπίχαλκον', in turn transforming the bird of prey into Cleonymus, who then becomes synonymous to a riddle ('γρῖφος')! And a riddle is in fact formulated – 'the same beast on land, in the air and at sea drops its shield' ('τί ταὐτὸν ἐν γῇ τ' ἀπέβαλεν κἀν οὐρανῷ/κἀν τῇ θαλάττῃ θηρίον τὴν ἀσπίδα', 22f.) – that, like the initial dream, produces a bad feeling.[23]

A similarly cryptic method shapes Aristophanes' final reference to Cleonymus near the end of *Birds*; the exotic marvels that the birds have seen in their travels include a deciduous tree called Cleonymus (1473–81). They describe it in a series of riddling puns and puzzles; it is outlandish and out of the way, 'far from ... Heart' ('ἔκτοπόν τι Καρδίας', 1474); it is useless but 'huge and trem ... ulous' ('δειλὸν καὶ μέγα', 1477).[24] In the spring, it sprouts and brings forth figs – i.e. denunciations ('συκοφαντεῖ', 1479). And the climax – in the winter, i.e. the time of the Delium battle, this tree sheds its foliage of shields ('ἀσπίδας φυλλορροεῖ', 1481)! This extended fantasy is of course separated from the traumatic events of Delium by a decade, but it is evident that the temporal distance hardly diminishes the potency of the joke, which acquires, we might say, its own autonomy, at least for as long as Cleonymus is alive. What, then, makes it so psychologically compelling?

We may first observe that, from the deer-shaped clouds in need of interpretation, through the dream-and-riddle combination in *Wasps*, to the *Birds*' allegorical tree, the references to Cleonymus tend to be wrapped in enigmas. This persistent talk in riddles, in fact, points to the disguised function of the often repeated and ever renewed joke. On the surface, it may poke fun at one individual whose conduct, although fairly typical in the circumstances, might have perhaps stood out for several reasons.[25] Yet it has a deeper meaning – a *huponoia* – something allegorical underneath, which may explain its theatrical potential and fruitfulness on the comic stage. By enabling the citizens to project their own traumatic recollection and attendant shame onto one particularly embarrassing or otherwise prominent example, the comic poet elicits, time and again, therapeutic laughter about the disastrous routing in Delium, which resulted in the loss of close to one thousand Athenian hoplites but also in disgrace.[26] With a wink to his audience, whose collective psyche he gently massages, Aristophanes cryptically alludes also to the very fact of the allusion, the hidden trauma at the root of laughter.

Lysistrata and Sicily

Last but by no means least, *Lysistrata* is notoriously reticent about the Sicilian expedition, which it acknowledges explicitly only once (387–98). When the Magistrate storms the stage in response to the women's occupation of the Acropolis, he begins his tirade by recalling another salient example of female mischief from the past – the excessive ritual cries of the women for Sabazios and Adonis. Apart from a certain anxiety engendered, as is often the case in our sources, by exclusively female cults, these particular instances coincided with the assembly voting on the campaign and happened to disrupt it.²⁷ The mention of Sicily here is only incidental; it simply illustrates the women's inappropriate but involuntary involvement. Moreover, the focus is not on the ending of the expedition, but on its launching, so that what is not spoken casts a pall on what is. The Magistrate, in other words, makes the insinuation that the ceremonial wailing, perceived as an ill-omened sound, created the inauspicious beginning that condemned the final outcome, which is however glossed over.²⁸ If this passage were our only source for the Sicilian campaign, we would have had no idea about the disaster, especially as it is quickly overshadowed by other types of female mischief that are sexual in nature, hence trivial by comparison.

We find the same pattern later, at the encounter of the Spartan and Athenian ambassadors, both in a state of visible erection. The recently unified chorus (1042) recommends that they cover up their *phalloi*, in case 'one of the herm-cutters' ('τῶν ἑρμοκοπιδῶν … τις') might catch sight of them (1093f.). This jokingly evokes the mutilation of the herms on the eve of the departure for Sicily (Thuc. 6.27), one of the inauspicious events that marred the beginning of the expedition.²⁹ Although Sicily looms in the background, the occasion keeps our attention elsewhere; the distended figures on stage are playfully warned to avoid the fate of the mutilated herms, whose visual memory they inadvertently suggest. The word 'ἑρμοκοπίδαι', possibly an Aristophanic coinage that is however based on pre-existing diction, functions as an unexpected trigger that evokes the Sicilian adventure – its anxious beginning rather than its traumatic end – only to deflate the attendant tension; before the painful memory is given time to take shape, it already vanishes amidst the sexual banter.

The silence about Sicily becomes even more deafening when Lysistrata, concluding her wool-working analogy, rejects the Magistrate's objection that women should have no part in the war (587f.), by claiming that, in fact, their share is double, since they give birth and send their children to be hoplites ('τεκοῦσαι/κἀκπέμψασαι παῖδας ὁπλίτας …', 589f.). She does not manage to complete her sentence – 'send their sons … to war' from which they will presumably not return alive – because she is interrupted by the Magistrate: 'silence, do not remind me of evils' ('σίγα, μὴ μνησικακήσῃς', 590).³⁰ This is a moment of explosive tension, reinforced by the *antilabē* – the show-stopping broken verse. In what I would term 'psychological slapstick', the comedy rushes to suppress even the slightest hint of a memory of the disastrous defeat before it is even brought up. Yet the Magistrate is not the only one prone to censoring unsettling thoughts; Lysistrata herself anticipates this attitude when she invites Calonice, along with the spectators, to supply ('ἀλλ' ὑπονόησον σύ μοι', 'but you can imagine', 38) the terrifying and unmentionable notion that Athens itself may perish.³¹

Would then the audience laugh at the Magistrate's crude attempt to block unpleasant speech, just as they are bound to do both earlier and later, when he is symbolically reduced first to a matron (532–8), then a corpse (599–613)?³² We cannot be sure, of course, but Lysistrata herself seems to offer a model for such a reaction to an emotionally fraught moment. A little earlier, recalling the wives' subtle efforts to influence their husbands' political decisions, she described their forced smile that accompanies inner grief ('ἀλγοῦσαι τἄνδοθεν ... γελάσασαι', 'grieving inwardly, [but] smiling/laughing', 512).[33] Could this combination of simulated laughter and dissimulated pain also be taken as an allusion to the delicate task confronting the comic poet? At any rate, we may discern, in the interaction between Lysistrata and the Magistrate, the staging of Aristophanes' own anxiety in attempting to determine what is appropriate speech in a highly charged atmosphere.[34] At the same time, we may read this moment of orchestrated tension also as the playwright's recognition of the different views that created deep divisions in the citizen body, and by extension in the audience, in the aftermath of the Sicilian disaster but especially in the build-up to and in the course of the oligarchic coup.[35]

Theoretical reflections, ancient and modern

These four cases illustrate different strategies that Aristophanes employs as he negotiates the slippery boundary between eliciting laughter and reopening an old but still tender wound. Especially erring in the latter direction, i.e. recalling a traumatic experience, would be fatal for the comedy as a whole, as it would seem to replicate, in front of the assembled citizen body, the inappropriate behaviour captured in the proverbial 'jesting among mourners' ('τὸ ἐν τοῖς πενθοῦσι παίζειν'), as reported by Demetrius (*On Style* 28).[36] We should, however, keep in mind an important difference; the 'mixture of mirth with tears' ('κλαυσίγελως') that Demetrius condemns reverses fully the process which we observe in comedy. What Aristophanes attempts, in other words, is diametrically opposed to the proverb, as he brings mourning into comedy, not comedy into mourning. In that light, the advantages of using the past trauma to deepen the spectators' sense of collective belonging, thereby strengthening his own connection with them and winning them over, must have been too tempting to pass up and certainly worth the attendant risk.[37]

Aristophanes' psychological insight is also akin to that of the *Homeric Hymn to Demeter* and of the Hippocratic corpus. The former provides a mythical aetiology for ritual obscenity in the cult of Demeter, as the old servant Iambe, with her mocking and joking ('χλεύης .../... παρασκώπτουσα', 'teasing with jokes', 202f.), makes the grieving goddess 'smile and laugh and have a gracious spirit' ('μειδῆσαι γελάσαι τε καὶ ἵλαον σχεῖν θυμόν', 204).[38] In a comparable manner, the author of the medical writings prescribes, as a cure for the disturbed and anguished psyche, a short period of rest spent on sights that bring about laughter ('καὶ τὴν ψυχὴν τραπῆναι πρὸς θεωρίας, μάλιστα μὲν πρὸς τὰς φερούσας γέλωτας', 'and turn the soul towards spectacles, especially towards those that bring laughter', *On Regimen* 4.89).[39] Yet there is a crucial distinction between those two instances and Aristophanic comedy; in those texts, the object eliciting the laughter of either the bereaved mother in need of comfort or of the ailing patient in need of healing may not necessarily be the suffering itself. Indeed, in all probability, it is something entirely different: Iambe's mocking jests in the former case, the reflections that induce laughter in the latter. By contrast, the comic poet does not intend to distract. He rather finds material for laughter by drawing precisely on the very source of pain.

Along similar lines, but moving to modern exegetical frames, what we observe in Aristophanes cannot be fully captured in the terms of Freud's 'release of the pent-up energy' or Ramachandran's 'false alarm theory'.[40] Despite their different starting points – psychological for Freud, ethological and evolutionary for Ramachandran – both theories see in laughter the same basic pattern of an unrealized menace; for both, humour results from a process whereby the expectation of discomfort or danger is raised, only to be thwarted. To be sure, it would be impossible to deny completely a certain affinity of Aristophanes' jokes with the relief theory of laughter, especially if we consider the use of trauma in *Lysistrata*, which seems to come closest to Freud's understanding of jokes; the painful memory of the Sicilian disaster is like a taboo that threatens to come to the surface before it is pushed back again. Yet even here, and of course in the other examples that we discussed, Aristophanes appears more daring than the Freudian type of humour might allow; the poet does not elicit laughter by fully thwarting the expectation that trauma will be mentioned or, at the very least, conjured up in memory – on the contrary, he fulfils that very expectation, however subtly and obliquely.

A final reflection on this type of laughter concerns the interplay between its universal and culturally specific elements. Unsurprisingly, some of the universal aspects are rooted in the physiology of the brain. Neuroscientists have found that laughter, especially social laughter, elevates the threshold of pain, even physical pain, and that the analgesic properties of humour are associated with an increased release of endorphins. It is also suggested that endorphins play a critical role in alleviating the effects of physiological and psychological stress on the organism. At the same time, because social laughter is a synchronized physical exertion, the endorphins that it releases promote in turn social bonding and collaboration.[41] This very nexus seems to be at work in the Aristophanic examples that we analysed. The psychological stress that springs from a collective trauma is made the focus and source of a laughter that is by definition social, as it is shared by the assembled citizens in the theatre. This laughter, moreover, is also synchronized behaviour, fused with and enhanced by the singing and dancing of the dramatic performance surrounding it. It thus becomes the ideal mechanism to shield the citizen body from the potentially divisive effects of that stress and perhaps even to enhance the social cohesion of the traumatized community.

But in addition to the universal characteristics of this type of laughter that are neurologically based, there are historically specific dimensions, which encompass more than the mindframe of a particular audience at a given moment. Let me illustrate by invoking Woody Allen's formula; in his masterful *Crimes and Misdemeanors* (1989), a not particularly sympathetic character, who however makes some insightful pronouncements about comedy, memorably declares that 'comedy equals tragedy plus time'.[42] The equation may be universal, but different cultures or even different groups within each culture will calibrate it differently: what and how much constitutes tragedy? What part of that tragedy may be made into comedy? And, perhaps most significantly, what is the culturally acceptable length of time following a tragedy that makes public laughter possible or even desirable? In his attempt to solve that conundrum, Aristophanes may have appreciated, for instance, the reported concerns of stand-up comedians in the

Aristophanic Humour

United States wondering in the aftermath of 9/11: how long do you have to wait before you are allowed to make jokes about such a tragic event? Or, to extrapolate from Aristophanes' own method, the right question might not even be about time, but about purpose: what exactly does it take to convert trauma into laughter so as to soothe pain and bring about healing?[43]

CHAPTER 7
THE SATIRIST AS TROLL? SOCIOPATHIC STRAINS IN ARISTOPHANES
Ralph M. Rosen

The Roman satirist Horace certainly knew well what his own *Satires* owed to Aristophanes and other Greek comedic poets, as the opening of his *Satires* 1.4 famously makes clear.[1] In these five succinct lines (1.4.1–5), Horace sums up the purpose of satire as the censure of socially unacceptable behaviour. His examples are classic and generic, almost cliché; anyone who is 'bad' ('malus'), a 'thief' ('fur'), an 'adulterer' ('moechus'), or a 'murderer' ('sicarius') can be considered a legitimate target for satirists, and the Greek comic poets, whom Horace idealizes here as his models, were noteworthy in his mind for the fact that they could attack such individuals with little constraint.[2] In another programmatic satire, 2.1, Horace captures brilliantly in just a few lines the complexity of satire in any era – its shifting ironic voice, its pretence of righteous aggression and its desire to expose targets to public shame. He claims to be 'desirous of peace' ('nec quisquam noceat *cupido mihi pacis*', *Sat.* 2.1.44),[3] yet as a satirist his writing *demands* he pick a fight somehow, despite his mock-solemn prayer in the same passage that his sword – a metaphor for his pen – rust away from disuse. Moreover, as Horace states several times elsewhere in his *Satires* (1.4.138–40, 1.10.36–9), he does all this for the sake of amusement – a 'ludus', first and foremost for his own pleasure, but also for anyone who cares to listen.

Horace is a useful starting point for our topic because he was more explicit than Aristophanes in articulating what he thought satire was supposed to 'do', and since he situates his own satire in direct line with Aristophanes – or, at least, he *aspires* to write satire that displays Aristophanic affinities – his own take on satire allows us clearer entry into the dynamics of Greek comic satire.[4] Aristophanic satire, too, is a dizzying mix of ironic self-righteousness, *Schadenfreude*, free-floating revelry and aggressive play. The chorus in the *parodos* of *Frogs*, for example, offers a programmatic prayer to Demeter (384–93) that they may 'utter much that's funny' ('πολλὰ μὲν γέλοιά', 389) and 'much that's serious' ('πολλὰ δὲ σπουδαῖα', 390), and that they 'play and mock' ('παίζω', 'σκώπτω', 392). They proceed then to ask Dionysus to sanction their scattershot mockery of various Athenians: 'So should we get together and mock Archedemus …?' ('βούλεσθε δῆτα κοινῇ/σκώψωμεν Ἀρχέδημον;', 416), asks the chorus, introducing the final section of the *parodos*, which singles out two more Athenians for merciless and obscene ridicule.[5] This opening question distills the basic structure of satire in its three key words; the satirist strives to cajole an audience ('βούλεσθε') to join forces with him in a act of communal ('κοινῇ') derision ('σκώψωμεν').[6] In ordinary life, in Graeco-Roman antiquity as much as today, such an act – mean-spirited, cruel ridicule of another person for the sake of a laugh – if not actually illicit, might be considered anything from merely indecorous to deeply sociopathic.

This particular aspect of satire raises a number of often intractable questions, chief among which is why have cultural mechanisms evolved that allow humans to represent with relative impunity behaviour which in other social contexts would be repudiated? Scholars have developed various ways to account for the inherent 'incivility' of Aristophanic (and other Greek) satire, all familiar to any literary critic sensitive to the mediating effects of genre, language, and performance occasion, among other things. All of these elements have an ontologically distancing effect: a performance, for example, is not the real world anymore; the aggressor is not a 'real person'; the ritual, festive context in which a Greek comic play was produced is held to provide licence, if not sanction, for otherwise undesirable behaviours. Within these frameworks, poets themselves have recourse to their own rhetoric of self-justification – as Horace himself defensively claimed in so many words, 'my targets *deserve* abuse; they bring trouble on themselves with their own behaviour' and 'I'm performing a public service'[7] – a stance that works well for the satirical arts as long as targets are not allowed to speak in their own defence, and except for the fact that just as often the same satirists like to complicate, if not undermine entirely, any self-righteousness or moral rectitude they want to claim for themselves.[8]

In my previous work on ancient satire and comedy I have myself often deployed the range of scholarly explanations to account for what Greek and Roman satirists seem to be doing – in a sense, attempting to 'excuse' the various pathologies that make satire at once alluring and discomfiting. I would still maintain that, as a mimetic form, satirical poetry operates in a very different zone from 'real life', despite frequent claims by satirists to the contrary.[9] But in recent years it has become difficult to ignore a phenomenon evolving right under our eyes, which, at the very least, reveals that the distinction between a fictional, constructed comedic realm and the reality which it purports to represent can be blurry at best, if not entirely impossible to pin down.

I refer here to internet trolling, a *bona fide* subculture, as scholars have come to characterize it, of aggressive play, *Schadenfreude* and other disruptive behaviours, all with the primary goal of amusing its practitioners, their fellow trolls and others in a networked community which constitutes an audience of sympathizers – all of whom derive their amusement specifically from the indignation of those who respond to a troll's outrageous provocations.[10]

Internet trolling may seem to be an idiosyncratic byproduct of our particular digital age, but technology has simply organized and magnified human behaviours which have already long found expression in satirical literary forms cross-culturally and trans-historically. The perennial problem in all cases where such behaviour is represented as a kind of performance (whether a literary satire, a satirical drama, an ancient or modern stand-up performance) is to determine the effect its performativity has on such questions as sincerity, meaning, or efficacy.[11] In other words, if a work that contains mockery, invective and other forms of derisive humour is tolerated and admired by savvy audiences and literary scholars because its aggressive aspects are supposed to be detoxified by aesthetic form and an understanding that the comic world is not 'real life',[12] what are we to do when such sophistication fails to persuade? Are those who remain offended by such humour – whether or not they are themselves the actual targets of a work's mockery – blameworthy for failing to appreciate the subtleties of the work, its comic intentions, its ironies and display of formal and technical bravado? Is it, in short, wrong for people to be offended by a satirical work that claims to exist in a realm of non-seriousness ('it's only a joke') when that claim is supposed, at the very least, to qualify or complicate any surface offensiveness?

Such questions become glaringly real and problematic in our own time in the context of internet trolling, which thrives on the expectation that most people will in fact take offence at their provocations, but the same questions were also posed and problematized in antiquity in responses to satirical literature. Indeed, the connections between internet trolling and Graeco-Roman satire have struck me as startlingly close, despite their obvious differences as well,[13] and I will argue in this chapter that juxtaposing them deepens our understanding of their respective social and literary dynamics.

When I speak of connections between these ancient and modern satirical productions, I have in mind structures (e.g. performer–audience relationships), mimetic behaviours such as role-playing, persona-construction and masking, rather than 'influence' or connective 'history'. Although, as I will discuss in more detail below, the trolling subculture has adopted (or rather, misappropriated) at least one classical model for its own mischievous purposes, the through-lines from Aristophanes, for example, to contemporary trolling are more evident in their shared social and psychological dynamics, and their stylistic tropes, than in any sustained and self-conscious engagement with a long tradition of satirical performance. Indeed, the further I drilled down into the stated aims and methods of trolling, the more I felt drawn to reconsider many of the traditional questions that have guided my own work on Aristophanes and other ancient satirists, and to reassess some of my own thinking about the social function of satire and the very nature of its generically indicated disruptiveness.

To begin with some foundational questions: if we, as scholars, or members of an audience 'in the know' – who would claim to 'get' satire – explain away its transgressive, malicious thrust with recourse to the distancing effects that come with satirical performance, what are the consequences of such special pleading? What effect does it have, for example, on how we view such behaviours in a 'real world' unprotected by mediating factors such as genre, ritual or irony? The stakes will seem lower, perhaps, with ancient texts, given our cultural and historical distance from them, but satire in our own time continues to provoke very real controversy and sometimes retaliation, and the common defence that something was only meant as a joke, 'not seriously', does little to mollify the outrage of someone not already in on the joke, or who happens to be the joke's target.[14] Classicists will easily think of Socrates' complaint in Plato's *Apology* that Aristophanes' *Clouds* contributed – unfairly – to the negative public opinion that led to his trial and execution.[15] The story is familiar, but it is still worth remembering that ancient satirists such as Aristophanes had more disruptive *potential* than some modern scholars, including myself, have sometimes wanted to allow.[16]

The *nature* of such 'disruptivity' for Aristophanes is, of course, always the problem; we want to know how Aristophanes *intended* his mockery, and in particular how a simple desire to make his audience laugh interacts with something else – we call it 'seriousness', 'ideology', or other forms of satirical 'meaning' – and then what he thought was the point of being provocative or disruptive; and further, whether he even had any *intention* of making his intentions clear or consistent. Even Socrates, after all, seems to blame not so much *Aristophanes* for his demise, as those who 'misread' Aristophanic satire when they mistook ridicule on the stage for real life. Internet trolling constantly raises the same questions about the motivations and meaning of its own forms of satire. Internet trolls may seem to us more vicious and gratuitous in satirical attacks than their ancient forebears, especially because they operate anonymously in the shadows of cyberspace rather than in public view, but as we will see, at root, their motivations are little different.[17] After providing background about the world of internet trolling – who these trolls are, how they operate, and what their purported aims are – we will consider how they might be useful for thinking about Aristophanes.

Anyone who spends time on the internet will be familiar with the more casual, less organized and ideological forms of mockery that have grown up around all manner of online discourse. Whether in the realm of journalism, reviews of restaurants, the arts, commercial products, etc., unmoderated public commentary has become customary at the 'bottom of the page'. Participants in listserv discussions will have also experienced flame wars, sparked by certain kinds of comments, and fed with alarming speed by others eager for as great a metaphorical conflagration as possible. In all these cases the provocative mode of discourse is sarcasm and ridicule – all of them modes that presuppose, sometimes literally, sometimes figuratively, some person or group who will find their comments humorous.[18] In the anonymous or semi-anonymous world of online commentary, it does not take much to elicit obscenity, intolerance and other antisocial sentiments. Opinions remain divided about such social interaction, with some deeply troubled by the incivility, ignorance and cruelty of such discourse, and others maintaining that the social benefits of unfettered free speech outweigh the negative aspects of its forms that occasionally appear to be antisocial.

I mention these online attempts at mocking, satirical humour as a preamble to lay out the *kind* of humour we are investigating. With these random examples of aggressive humour, we are not yet talking about actual 'trolling', and their utility for Aristophanes is minimal at best. But with actual trolling we move from occasional, unsystematic examples of this kind of humour to an organized, intentional and ideological community which – though it is not entirely monolithic – is unified by a common goal of laughter. Recent scholars such as Coleman and Phillips have aligned trolls with traditional folkloric tricksters, that is to say figures across cultures and literatures who are playful and mischievous,[19] but more destructive than constructive, difficult to pin down morally (often wavering between amoral and highly self-righteous postures) and narcissistic. Phillips has summed up the internet troll-as-trickster succinctly:

> Specifically, trolls are agents of *cultural digestion*; they scavenge the landscape for scraps of usable content, make a meal of the most pungent bits, then hurl their waste onto an unsuspecting populace – after which they disappear, their Cheshire

cat grins trailing after them like puffs of smoke. They may not know it, they may not intend to, but deliberately or not, these grotesque displays reveal a great deal about the surrounding cultural terrain.[20]

Wikipedia – for once an appropriate place to look for an accurate discussion of a topic! – offers the following definition of an internet troll:

> In Internet slang, a **troll** is a person who sows discord on the Internet by starting arguments or upsetting people, by posting inflammatory, extraneous, or off-topic messages in an online community (such as a newsgroup, forum, chat room, or blog) with the intent of provoking readers into an emotional response or of otherwise disrupting normal, on-topic discussion, often for the troll's amusement.[21]

The only emendation I would make to this definition is to change 'often ... for the troll's amusement' to 'always'. For there has evolved over the past twenty years (the approximate age of the phenomenon as of this writing) a self-generated technical term for what trolls are after; it is called 'lulz', a term many will recognize as deriving from the acronym 'lol', for 'laughing out loud'. In the age of texting, lol has become a simple shorthand for acknowledging that one is laughing (often figuratively) at the moment of writing. But 'lulz' with its different spelling indicates a specialized version of 'lol' – it is often a troll punchline, and always an excuse for any given post; 'I did it for the "lulz"'.[22] Lulz is essentially an updated, specialized version of *Schadenfreude*, 'amusement at someone else's distress', although how a troll uses it, or defines its nuances, will vary – as it will with all satirists. As Phillips puts it, 'lulz functions both as punishment and as reward, sometimes simultaneously. Lulz operates as a nexus of social cohesion and social constraint. It does not distinguish between friend and foe, and is as much enjoyed by the trolling spectator as by the active trolling agent.'[23] Lest we think that this malevolent form of laughter is idiosyncratic to the internet age, we might remind ourselves of Athena's wheedling of Odysseus at Sophocles *Ajax* 79, where she asks him, 'Is not laughing at one's enemies the sweetest kind of laughter?' ('οὔκουν γέλως ἥδιστος εἰς ἐχθροὺς γελᾶν;'), a sentiment that recalls Homeric battleground 'flyting' and Archilochean *psogoi*, among other examples.[24] Among conspicuous examples of malicious, satirical activities that give trolls this 'sweetest laughter', we might note their practice of infiltrating Facebook memorial pages to mock the deceased, of abusing grieving families of suicide victims, or attacking celebrities whom they feel need to be taken down.[25]

Trolls attack a variety of very disparate targets – truly, nothing is sacred – but Phillips sees a 'through-line [in their] targeting practices: the concept of *exploitability*. Trolls believe that nothing should be taken seriously, and therefore regard public displays of sentimentality, political conviction, and/or ideological rigidity as a call to trolling arms ...'[26] 'Emotions are seen as a trap, something to exploit in others and ignore or switch off in yourself.'[27] Further, the more intense a target's reaction to a troll's provocation, the 'lulzier' things become for the troll, encouraging trolling behaviour in others, and further circumscribing trolling as a distinct rhetorical community.

One aspect of trolls that recalls a perennially delicate set of issues in Aristophanic studies is the relationship between their performative (online) personality and their personalities in 'real life'. Scholars who have worked with trolls report that 'the vast majority... insist that their troll selves and their offline ('real') selves are subject to totally different sets of rules'.[28] Invoking Goffman's work on social framing, they speak of the 'front' that trolls create to establish an 'emotional or spatial distance between a performer and that which is performed'.[29] Trolls create 'masks', in short, as a kind of firewall between some notional actual self and some other, constructed self that operates according to a logic and a symbolic framework dedicated to extracting laughter from an in-group.[30] Trying to locate any sort of moral stance is particularly frustrating, since trolls typically *claim*, on the one hand, to be uninterested in 'truth' as such. They are more interested in dominance and victory, and yet they are often quick to adopt positions of moral self-righteousness – just as any good satirist – if it affords them opportunity for 'lulzy play'.[31] Just having a celebrity complain about a trolling attack, for example, often serves the purpose of exposing, and offering a critique of, the media's desire for sensationalism and spectacle.[32]

Finally, to offer one very tangible link between internet trolls and antiquity, it is striking to find that Socrates is considered something of a culture hero to the trolling community. The parodic anti-Wikipedia of trolling culture, *Encyclopedia Dramatica*, has an entry for Socrates that reads as follows:

> Socrates was a famous IRL troll of pre-internets [*sic*] Greece credited with inventing the first recorded trolling technique and otherwise laying the foundation of the science of lulz. He is widely considered to be the most irritating man in history. Accounts of his successful trolls are in the form of tl;dr ['too long, didn't read'] copypasta [an inflammatory post, posted and reposted, again and again] on Plato's LiveJournal.[33]

While in prison, awaiting his execution, the entry concludes,

> He then proved with logic that his soul is immortal and heaven is way better anyway. Socrates drank the poison and died. His last words were, '*I did it for the lulz*'.[34]

Indeed, the authors state, 'The lulz started when Socrates went to the city to ask people a bunch of stupid questions about justice and virtue'.[35] It is impossible to know how seriously to take any of this, and the final words attributed of Socrates are an obvious comic punchline. But it is surely significant that this community saw something in Socrates' biography and works that led them to regard him as the actual *founder* of trolling. The article quotes Jowett's translation of *Apol.* 30e–31a:

> I am that gadfly which God has attached to the state, and all day long and in all places am always fastening upon you, arousing and persuading and reproaching

you. You will not easily find another like me, and therefore I would advise you to spare me.

οἷον δή μοι δοκεῖ ὁ θεὸς ἐμὲ τῇ πόλει προστεθηκέναι – τοιοῦτόν τινα ὃς ὑμᾶς ἐγείρων καὶ πείθων καὶ ὀνειδίζων ἕνα ἕκαστον οὐδὲν παύομαι τὴν ἡμέραν ὅλην πανταχοῦ προσκαθίζων. τοιοῦτος οὖν ἄλλος οὐ ῥᾳδίως ὑμῖν γενήσεται, ὦ ἄνδρες, ἀλλ᾽ ἐὰν ἐμοὶ πείθησθε, φείσεσθέ μου.

They might well have also quoted the text a few lines earlier where Socrates notes that the image of the gadfly itself is 'rather laughable': 'for if you kill me, you won't easily find another one like me, who, in fact – if I might use a rather laughable expression – has been offered to the city by god as a gadfly to a great and noble horse' ('ἐὰν γάρ με ἀποκτείνητε, οὐ ῥᾳδίως ἄλλον τοιοῦτον εὑρήσετε, ἀτεχνῶς, εἰ καὶ γελοιότερον εἰπεῖν, προσκείμενον τῇ πόλει ὑπὸ τοῦ θεοῦ ὥσπερ ἵππῳ μεγάλῳ μὲν καὶ γενναίῳ', 30e). All readers of Plato will quickly recognize the Socratic humour of this troll-version of Socrates – ironic, provocative, contrarian – and even in the scholarship, he has often been likened to a kind of satirist, often in the Aesopic tradition.[36] But was he in fact 'doing it for the lulz'? To most of us, certainly to staid classicists, this seems a willfully perverse and inaccurate reading, but this implicit critique of the standard assumptions about the character and motivations of Socrates is not uninteresting or completely unwarranted. It would hardly be the first time, in any case, that someone questioned Socrates' rhetorical methods and motivations as presented by Plato. Indeed, the long tradition of aligning Socrates with satirists was inspired by Plato's own portraits of the man as a canny ironist, whose gentle and open comportment with his interlocutors often served to mock them at the same time.[37] It is no surprise, then, that a direct link could also be drawn in antiquity between Socratism and the followers of the Cynic philosopher Diogenes, whose contrarian, unorthodox and socially deviant attitudes have also been compared to internet trolling.[38]

Like Socrates or Diogenes and their followers, then, internet trolls form a community of people positioning themselves in opposition to a wide variety of things. Like their ancient counterparts, trolls are particularly sensitive to hypocrisy among the powerful and celebrated, to sentimentality, the blind rule-following of the 'real world', unexamined social decorum and traditional norms of what is fair and good. Their ultimate mission is to elicit a specific form of laughter (lulz) and there is little that they will let stand in the way of that. They emphasize their own commitment to 'play', but get the most playful pleasure by exploiting those who are unlikely to join in the play. Crucial, too, is the fact that trolls operate in a different rhetorical and symbolic space from that of their offline lives, assuming masks and postures online that they would often regard as reprehensible offline.

As a comic poet Aristophanes was also after laughs, as he often tells us in various ways[39] – but one may ask of him as well, was he also mostly after the 'lulz', that programmatically freighted form of malicious laughter? Does it make any sense to think of him as a troll *avant la lettre*? The short answer to this question is certainly 'sometimes', even if identifying Aristophanes as a *bona fide* troll in our sense of the word might risk some degree of anachronism.[40] But, as our discussion below will suggest, in many respects the performative dynamics of trolling *do* seem analogous to the dynamics of Aristophanic satire, and it is illuminating to reconsider some classic Aristophanic conundrums in the light of what we can learn from analysing certain trolling practices.

Let us return, then, to Aristophanes' portrayal of Socrates in *Clouds*. The topic is the standard fare of commentaries; it seems noteworthy to us that Aristophanes' unscrupulous, sophistic Socrates is so out of step with Plato's deeply moral version of him, which we tend to assume is the 'more correct' one. Is Aristophanes trying to make a real point about Socrates, or is it all just skylarking – and are these terms mutually exclusive, anyway? Should we be indignant at the fact that his portrait is so 'inaccurate'?[41] Is Aristophanes trolling Socrates, his audience and ourselves? – that is, is he deliberately baiting him simply to get the negative reaction of the sort a troll would thrive on, and if so, is this an example of Aristophanes seeking 'lulz'? It is worth remembering that a troll's quest for 'lulz' does not mean that an attack is not tendentious – trolls, at least, like satirists of all ages, will claim to be against *something*, even if that 'something' seems more the means to an end (laughter) than the end in itself. But this also means that *our* tendency to worry about the truth or falsehood of a comic portrait is rather beside the point, when the authors themselves have no concern for such things.[42] Indeed, what Aristophanes was doing with Socrates in *Clouds* seems very much like what the *Encyclopedia Dramatica* is doing in its mock-hagiographic entry about him – both of which rely on a brash distortion of easily recognizable biographical features. Aristophanes probably knew well enough that Socrates was not really a sophist, or at least not a sophist of the sort he ridicules in *Clouds*, but this just makes his distortion all the more disruptive; it separates those 'in the know' – those who can see it as a device for getting a laugh without any concern for its 'truth' – from others, that is, outsiders fixated on the inaccuracy or unfairness of such a portrait. The predictable reaction from such outsiders – indignation, offence – is precisely what trolls are seeking from their targets and from those who defend their targets.

Such an analysis helps us understand such longstanding problem scenes as the ending of *Clouds*, which has Strepsiades and Xanthias burning down Socrates' *phrontistērion* along with its residents (1476–511). Scholars are often troubled by the violent, apparently merciless ending which seems out of place in a comedy. Revermann, however,[43] has argued persuasively for what he calls the 'genre-typical *Schadenfreude* and unified laughter' of the ending,[44] counterbalanced by the paratragic touch of the Clouds' *theomachy*. The takeaway from the final scene, as Revermann argues, is disapproval of the 'Socratism' that encourages father-beating, but whether, and in what sense, we can consider this 'serious' or not is hardly a simple question: the charge that Socrates would teach people to argue for father-beating is an obvious comic distortion itself, and seems designed expressly to set up the final scene. If Aristophanes *was* aware that his portrait of Socrates was not realistic – not 'fair', really, from the perspective of anyone who cares about veridical accuracy and who is not particularly interested in laughing at its distortion – then the ending does not so much ridicule actual 'Socratism' as it does those who (a) are incapable of, or unwilling to, get the joke of the Aristophanic Socrates, and (b) wrongly conflate Socratism with behaviour such as father-beating. Trolling often operates like this, where malicious humour directed at a specific individual is just as intent on ridiculing anyone as humourless who rallies to a target's defence, indignant at the injustice of an attack.[45] The *parodos* of *Frogs*, alluded to earlier,[46] essentially makes the same point; the chorus urges anyone, as we might say, not with the programme ('whoever is unfamiliar with such utterances as this [or has never] been initiated in the Bacchic rites of bull-eating Cratinus' language', 355) to 'stand aside' ('ἐξίσθασθαι') before the mockery begins.

Just as there are sometimes very real consequences to trolling in our own time – people suffer real-world humiliation, careers can be ruined, in some truly awful cases people have been driven to suicide – the same can happen even in the publicly sanctioned milieu of Old Comedy. Whatever the exact nature of Cleon's prosecution of Aristophanes, Cleon did not appreciate the Aristophanic 'lulz' of *Bablyonians* in 426 – a reaction that Aristophanes was quick to thematize in subsequent plays, and especially in *Knights*, which was likely inspired specifically by Aristophanes' understanding of just how *much* a new play, explicitly and relentlessly targeting Cleon, would have rankled him.[47] The rambunctious vitriol that characterizes so much of *Knights*, then, relies both on a knowing audience who are there for the 'lulz' (whether or not they agree with anything they might perceive as the poet's implicit agenda) and an assumption (or at least the conceit, true or not) that there will always be humourless people who will take offence.[48] *Knights* in particular features whole passages of pure invective dialogue that serve no other discernible purpose than to fire up an audience with laughter. One thinks, for example, of *Knights* 344–74, where the Sausage-Seller and the Paphlagonian (Cleon) trade ludicrous threats and insults with each other, with extended exchanges of this sort (370–3):

Sausage-Seller	I'll skin you and a make a thief's purse out of you!
Paphlagonian	You'll be pegged on the ground!
Sausage-Seller	I'll make you into mincemeat!
Paphlagonian	I'll pluck out your eyebrows!

Α. δερῶ σε θύλακον κλοπῆς.
Π. διαπατταλευθήσει χαμαί.
Α. περικόμματ' ἔκ σου σκευάσω.
Π. τὰς βλεφαρίδας σου παρατιλῶ.[49]

These passages (and there are many others across other plays) read like a versified flame war between internet trolls, or between trolls and unsuspecting targets who are drawn into the fray by a troll's relentless and outrageous provocations. Anyone who has used the internet will have experienced such flame wars in one context or another and will know the range of possible responses as a spectator – from guilty amusement at examples of clever insult to genuine alarm that human beings can treat each other with such incivility and cruelty.

Our collocation of Aristophanic comedy and internet trolling highlights among other things that context, occasion and genre are everything in satirical performances. But that much is hardly news; it is clear enough that Aristophanes can get away with what he does in his more aggressive moments because of the sanction of festival and genre.[50] We also know well enough from Aristophanes, and other ancient satirists, how susceptible their work was to being misjudged by audiences or individuals ignorant of genre and performative cueing, *and* how essential this looming threat of misconstrual was for their ultimate success. Internet trolling, however, offers a stark reminder that satire can sometimes transgress even the limits of audiences who *do* know when a joke is supposed to be a joke. Even in their most anarchic extremity, trolls defend themselves as comedians looking for laughs. If pressed, one can extract, or at least infer, from them a kind of perverse moralizing which has a direct lineage to more traditional forms of satire – opposition to hypocrisy and a suspicion of traditional power structures, especially – and they thrive precisely on the pushback they elicit.[51] The more outraged the reaction, the more laughter is generated for themselves and their sympathizers, who are also tracking the level of (counter-)anger and indignation that the trolling is receiving. Pushback is good for the business of satire, after all, since it means that the satirist can claim to be having an 'effect' of some sort; that notional effect adds to the satirists' 'lulz'-factor and affirms their dominance over their targets.[52]

Tracking the various reactions people have to the derisive satire of internet trolls encourages us, I would argue, to re-examine the complexity of Aristophanic satire – a medium which, as we have seen, is fuelled by similar social and aesthetic dynamics despite obvious differences in historical and performance context. Internet trolling encourages us to remember that when Aristophanes mocked the likes of Socrates, Cleon, Euripides, Aeschylus, the general Lamachus, or Orestes the cloak-stealer, for example, the relationship we infer that he had with each of them was not monochromatic – his mockery may imply that he 'disapproves' of them all in one sense or another, but in the end we cannot determine what that sense is, nor can we decide, for example, whether one attack is more ironic or sincere than another, or when it is appropriate to imagine Aristophanes winking or saying 'just kidding'. We may really want to know if Aristophanes actually *hated* Cleon, while rather 'liking' Euripides, but this will never be possible. In the end Aristophanes can only present us with his 'satirical self', and that presentation can have as much sociopathic as communitarian potential, depending on an individual's perception. In the case of Aristophanes' portrait of Socrates, it seems likely enough that he was fully aware it was an unfair caricature, and that he expected his audience to understand the humour in his mockery of Socrates' well-known idiosyncrasies – that he was just doing it for the ancient equivalent of 'lulz'. But Aristophanes could not himself control who would take it in precisely the spirit he had intended. When the *ultimate* goal of a comedy is laughter, and a laughter created within (and for) a performative world well demarcated from the real world, audiences may well laugh without ever quite knowing where their satirist actually stands on the targets of his mockery. And it is in this space where, paradoxically, the potential for social disruption and fragmentation coexists with the promise of communal aesthetic gratification.

CHAPTER 8
THE HILARIOUS POLITICS OF THE SUPERNATURAL IN ARISTOPHANIC COMEDY
Edith Hall

Introduction

In the opening scene of *Wasps*, one of Philocleon's slaves, Sosias, narrates a dream he has just had to another slave, Xanthias. They then try their hand at dream interpretation (31–51). In Old Comedy, low-class individuals suddenly have access to experiences from which other literary genres had traditionally excluded them. Only aristocrats discuss their dreams in epic and tragedy.[1] But this is not the only feature of this scene relevant to the analysis of the outlook specific to Old Comedy. The slaves go on to describe the supernatural and unlikely occurrences of their dream-world, occurrences which are scientifically impossible or socially improbable in real life, and interpret them allegorically in ways that relate to the real, contemporary experience of the political scene in Athens.

Sosias saw sheep, attired like men, meet in assembly on the Pnyx Hill, where a whale was haranguing them and weighing out units of ox-fat. Xanthias' first joke in response – that the dream stinks of rotting leather (39) – shows that he 'reads' the whale as Cleon; his second response (41) explicitly identifies the sheep as the Athenian people, who are suffering at Cleon's hands in ways symbolized by the cutting up of the fat. Sosias then adds that he saw Theorus with the head of a crow (42–5). With the help of an interjection by a dream-Alcibiades, whose speech impediment confuses the letters rho and lambda, the image plays on the similarity of the Greek words *korax* (crow) and *kolax* (flatterer).[2]

The scene provides the audience with a lesson in decoding symbols which have been produced by what we now call the subconscious, the symbols of the dream-world which are not subject to the laws of nature. In our waking lives, real sheep do not wear clothes and attend the Assembly. Whales do not deliver harangues or use scales. Humans can't have the heads of crows. And although it is not impossible, it is unlikely that a celebrated aristocrat like Alcibiades would make a remark to a slave at the Assembly. The vocabulary of Sosias' dream resembles the theatrical semantics of Old Comedy, where humans can be represented by animals, culinary equipment and tasks can represent political actions and policies, and lower-class individuals often enjoy a far greater level of freedom than their real-world counterparts to transcend social and even cosmic boundaries; a sausage-seller can become leader of Athens and a regular citizen can become king not only of the birds but of the universe.[3]

The supernatural elements during the remainder of *Wasps* include the hybrid insect-humans who form the chorus, and whose costumes must have included a sharp protuberance representing their stings (406f., 420–7). The dog trial requires at least one of the actors costumed as a dog to deliver speeches (907–31). But even more interesting is Philocleon's self-identification with Zeus. Philocleon, after describing the pleasures of jury service and the power it has given to ordinary Athenians like him, asks, 'ἆρ' οὐ μεγάλην ἀρχὴν ἄρχω καὶ τοῦ Διὸς οὐδὲν ἐλάττω;' ('as to power, am I not equal to Zeus?', 620).[4] He extends the analogy. When he and the other men of his class create the loud noise or *thorubos* associated with lawcourts or the Assembly, people liken the sound to Zeus's thunder; he uses the metaphor of discharging the lightning, which is traditionally Zeus's prerogative, to indicate how much power he, Philocleon, wields over 'rich and august men' (622–7).

Old Comedy began in the fifth century BCE in city-states where democratic constitutions were installed (Megara, Athens and in Sicily) and was inseparable from the open, egalitarian and litigious atmosphere of such radical polities. It was first introduced into the programme of the drama competitions of the classical Athenian state in 486 BCE,[5] when the Athenians had consolidated their democracy in the wake of the first Persian invasion. This chapter examines the comic possibilities created by the supernatural powers with which Aristophanes invests several of his comic heroes, most of whom are non-elite Athenian citizen males. They are otherwise relatively humble mortals, but, in the innovative presentation of these 'ordinary men in the street' as 'superheroes', they are also aesthetic projections of the new freedoms and rights of the citizen-spectator in the democratic city-state. Their supernatural powers offer numerous opportunities for the instigation of laughter through absurd conjunctions of real and impossible actions and the subversion of the authority of gods and powerful humans.

The plays are set in the 'here-and-now' of classical Athens, with recognizable topography, buildings and civic personnel, as well as highly topical jokes and comically colloquial language. But a surreal dimension is grafted onto this realist base, incorporating theriomorphic hybrids, journeys to the (in reality) unseen gods or the Underworld, and the ability to move vast distances in a split second without apparent scene change. The plays feature citizen-class heroes, some of whom possess paranormal, supernatural powers in other literature confined to the most revered heroes and divinities. But the actual gods impersonated in the plays are ineffectual and usually outwitted by their human antagonist. The form of Old Comedy's deeply democratic humour is not inherently shameful as Halliwell has argued, although it is certainly linked to a license for free speech;[6] nor is Old Comedy societally destructive by nature, as Rosen explored in the preceding chapter of this volume. Instead, humour imbues Old Comedy's protagonists with fantastic, democratic power.

Theorists of the supernatural and of alternative communities, domains and civilizations in literature often use the word *heterocosm* to denote the distinct world which a poet, novelist or dramatist creates, especially in certain sub-genres like science fiction or certain idioms such as magical realism. The word was first coined as a derogatory term by the German philosopher Alexander Gottlieb Baumgartem in his *Aesthetica* (1750). He believed that artists who could not represent faithfully, that is *realistically*, the primary world of creation, in its most advantageous light, were to be deplored. A rather beautified narrative realism was the aesthetic ideal of the day.[7] But the word *heterocosm* is useful for thinking with in reference to Aristophanes, whose comedies create a world that is similar to his contemporary Athens, while incorporating the whole panoply of non-realist elements that are to be surveyed in this chapter. This heterocosm allows his citizen heroes supernatural powers and experiences, which are a continuous source of humour.

Heterocosm theorists have also divided 'fantasy texts', a category to which Aristophanic comedies must belong, into subcategories, depending on the interface in them between 'reality' and the 'heterocosm'. Immersive fantasies are set entirely within a non-realist heterocosm from start to finish; this does not apply to any of Aristophanes' comedies. Intrusive fantasies begin in the real world into which the heterocosm intrudes, but from which it disappears again before the end; this definition might illuminate *Frogs*, which begins and *almost* ends in the land of the living, even if that land contains Heracles and is about to contain Dionysus and the ghost of Aeschylus. Portal fantasies also begin in the real world, but then move into a heterocosm by means of some device that functions as a portal. This definition might apply to *Birds*, which starts with realistic enough travellers who, arriving in northern Greece, gain admission to the world of the birds via Tereus' home in a Thracian thicket, never to return.[8] But in Aristophanic comedy there is far more complexity, as well as seamlessness, in the relationship between the heterocosm, where the supernatural may be possible, and the 'real world' of the here-and-now. There are always at least two 'real worlds', as well, both the one internal to the play (somebody's front door, or the Thesmophorion, for example) and the world external to the mimetic fiction at the Athenian festival of Dionysus.

Another way of thinking about the fantastic in heterocosms is that it is fundamentally not a generic descriptor but an epistemological stance.[9] The ontological status of any object – a piece of cheese, a dog, a wasp – can never be absolute; to a certain extent it depends on context, and the context of the theatre of Dionysus during the comic competitions was very specific. The idea of restraint and liberation is crucial here; a realist epistemology, such as that of Thucydides, must always be one of constraint and exclusion. Only certain kinds of explanation, causation, and even witnessed phenomena are acceptable. A genre like Old Comedy, by admitting the supernatural into its world, relinquishes the constraints of realist epistemology. But again, this perception needs to be informed by democratic Athenian class politics; who is now being represented as free of those constraints of realist epistemology in a way which had been reserved in earlier literature for aristocrats and divinities alone?[10]

The surreal or supernatural elements are important components in Old Comedy's use of what Ruffell calls its 'art of the impossible', through which it can 'interrogate Athenian politics, culture, and society'; the genre uses 'the naïve, implausible, impractical, utopian and downright silly', which 'can certainly change our perception' of the real world.[11] But this definition, though necessary, is not sufficient. Ruffell's art of the impossible also has a class component in that the impossible is achieved now by lower-class men.

Some cultural historians might object to the distinction I am drawing between realistic and supernatural elements in Aristophanes. Epistemology must have been different in the world of classical Greek religion, which, like the Christian Middle Ages, resonated with magical forces and in which some people believed that signs of the divine could be apprehended everywhere in nature.[12] Yet I do not think it is correct that Aristophanes' audiences had no sense whatsoever of a separation between the empirically discernible physical world and the spiritual world, nor that it is a product of only a much later progress towards modernity.[13] The remarkable lack of any theological explanations in Thucydides, the sophistication of the distinctions between theological, physical and philosophical reasoning in *Clouds*, and Theophrastus' mocking caricature of the overly superstitious man in his *Characters* (no. 16) are all important evidence that many Greeks could distinguish between a phenomenon perceptible empirically to the senses, or a law of nature, on the one hand, and on the other, the type of supernatural phenomenon that is to be discussed in the remainder of this chapter.

The supernatural in the comedies

In *Acharnians*, the first sign of Dicaeopolis' supernatural abilities is the deal he is able to cut with the mysterious divinity Amphitheus. This already makes him the equivalent of an epic hero, who, like Achilles or Odysseus, can talk directly to gods and expect special treatment from them. Immediately after Dicaeopolis' prologue, the herald of the Assembly asks who wishes to speak (45). The first volunteer is Amphitheus, who presents himself as a god when the herald asks whether he is a human or not, a pun illuminated by the fact that 'Anthrōpos', rather oddly, is an attested ancient Greek name (46–54):[14]

> οὔ,
> ἀλλ' ἀθάνατος. ὁ γὰρ Ἀμφίθεος Δήμητρος ἦν
> καὶ Τριπτολέμου· τούτου δὲ Κελεὸς γίγνεται·
> γαμεῖ δὲ Κελεὸς Φαιναρέτην τήθην ἐμήν,
> ἐξ ἧς Λυκῖνος ἐγένε᾿· ἐκ τούτου δ᾿ ἐγὼ
> ἀθάνατός εἰμ᾿· ἐμοὶ δ᾿ ἐπέτρεψαν οἱ θεοὶ
> σπονδὰς ποιεῖσθαι πρὸς Λακεδαιμονίους μόνῳ.
> ἀλλ' ἀθάνατος ὢν ὤνδρες ἐφόδι᾿ οὐκ ἔχω·
> οὐ γὰρ διδόασιν οἱ πρυτάνεις.

> No! I am an immortal. For Amphitheus was the son of Ceres and Triptolemus; he had a son, Celeus. Celeus married Phaenerete, my grandmother, whose son was Lucinus. Since I am born of him, I am immortal. The gods have vouchsafed to me alone the responsibility of making treaties with the Lacedaemonians. Yet, citizens, although I am immortal, I have no provisions to travel with; the Prytanes gave me nothing.

When the herald summons the guards to remove him from the rostrum, Amphitheus calls on the gods from whom he is descended, Triptolemus and Ceres, to lend him aid (55).

The Hilarious Politics of the Supernatural in Aristophanic Comedy

The scene with the visitors from Persia leaves Dicaeopolis so frustrated that he decides to do something 'great and marvellous' ('ἐργάσομαί τι δεινὸν ἔργον καὶ μέγα', 128), recalling Hector in the *Iliad* declaring, as he turns to face Achilles for the last time, that he wants to be remembered as 'having done something big' ('ἀλλὰ μέγα ῥέξας τι', 22.305). Dicaeopolis calls for Amphitheus, who immediately comes to him. Now he seals his bargain with the god. He gives him eight drachmas and asks him to conclude a treaty with the Lacedaemonians solely for him, his children and his wife (130–2). Amphitheus takes the money and disappears.

Soon he returns. Within the forty-one lines taken up by the episode of Theorus, the ambassador who has returned from Thrace, Amphitheus has been to Sparta and acquired treaties. He is now pursued by a chorus of angry old Marathonomachs from Acharnae, who want to stone him in reprisal for making any kind of peace with the enemy (175–85). But he does indeed have treaties for Dicaeopolis, three in fact, which Aristophanes represents by three samples ('γεύματα', 187) of wine for the hero to taste. This involves a play on the double meaning of 'σπονδαί', which denotes both 'treaties' and the drink-offerings made on the occasions that they were concluded. The first two samples are old short-term 'σπονδαί', which Dicaeopolis rejects. But the third is a new one, which will last for thirty years, both on sea and land (194f.), and Dicaeopolis accepts it with delight. It smells of the divine foods, nectar and ambrosia; it offers him the formulaic freedom of peace treaties, permitting him to go where he will; he drinks it down and announces that he has done with war and suffering. He will instead celebrate the rural Dionysia (196–203).

Some critics have seen in Amphitheus not a god but a reference to a real historical figure, perhaps a priest of that name from Aristophanes' own deme of Cydathenaeum.[15] Another candidate is the Hermogenes who was a well-known member of Socrates' circle (Plato, *Phaed.* 59B; Xen. *Mem.* 4.8.4), and an interlocutor in Plato's *Cratylus*. His family was connected with the Kerykes, who held the hereditary office of torchbearers in the Eleusinian mysteries. He could also claim divine descent on both sides of the family, one side from Nestor as an Alcmaeonid and one from Triptolemus, which meant his family held the office of being hereditary *proxenoi* of Sparta at Athens (Xen. *Hell.* 6.3.4–6).[16] A third alternative is Callias himself, Hermogenes' more notorious brother. The poverty the god claims could be connected with Callias' vast inheritance, which he was not to come into until about a year later.[17] But the identity of the mysterious figure is not solved, and he has genuine superpowers; he can travel instantaneously and make it possible for a single ordinary peasant farmer to negotiate unilaterally with the Spartan Foreign Office. In having Amphitheus as an accomplice, Dicaeopolis shows that he is by no means constrained by the physical laws of the universe or the inflexible protocols of inter-state diplomacy. He behaves like a mythical hero.

His special powers are confirmed immediately after the *parodos*, when he is found to have travelled instantaneously himself, to his rural farm in the deme of Cholleidae, several miles south-east of the city at the southern end of Mt. Hymettus. Here he inaugurates his private Dionysiac festival and thirty-year truce with Sparta (247–52). After the speech he makes with his head on the block outside his door, he travels instantaneously, again, to Euripides' house, and is knocking on the door in the line immediately after he conceives the plan (393–5):

ὥρα 'στὶν ἤδη καρτερὰν ψυχὴν λαβεῖν,
καί μοι βαδιστέ᾽ ἐστὶν ὡς Εὐριπίδην.
παῖ παῖ.

It's time I proved how brave I am, so I need to walk to Euripides. Hey, slave, slave!

It is not clear whether we are to imagine Euripides living in central Athens, in his ancestral estate on Salamis or in his parental deme of Phlya, north of the Hymettus mountains. Any of these alternatives means travelling for several hours from Dicaeopolis' farm in Cholleidae; Aristophanes seems to draw attention to the absurd speed of Dicaeopolis' arrival in saying that he needs to *walk* there ('βαδιστέ᾽').

Knights contains few supernatural features, no gods and no instantaneous travel over large distances. But both *parabaseis*, delivered by the chorus of upper-class knights, contain fantasies of paranormal occurrences – talking steeds and warships respectively. In the first, the chorus-men recall a day when their beloved warhorses sat on the benches to row the warships and were able to speak Greek like Achilles' horses in the *Iliad* (19.404–17), calling out to encourage one another (600–3); in the second, the chorus recalls a day when the Athenian war-triremes held a council, and discussed how to foil Hyperbolus' plan to take a fleet of them to Carthage (1300–15). This perhaps recalls the sentient ships of the Phaeacians, who need no man to steer them, in the *Odyssey* (8.557f.), or the speaking plank of the Argo, if that tradition had already emerged by Aristophanes' day.[18] In his lost play *Holkades, Merchant-Ships*, produced the following year in 423 BCE, everyday Athenian citizens may have been able to listen to the voices of another kind of seagoing vessel. But in *Knights*, the real supernatural work is done by that most low-class of all Aristophanic heroes, and the one with the most vertiginous social rise in Athenian society – the Sausage-Seller eventually renamed Agoracritus, 'Pick of the Agora'. He is invited by Demos to join him as special counsellor and fellow diner in the Prytaneum.

The Sausage-Seller performs a magical feat reminiscent of the miraculous rejuvenation of the aged hero Iolaus in Euripides' *Children of Heracles*, who prays to Hebe and Zeus to be made young again for a single day in order to avenge himself on Eurystheus (849–66). In *Knights*, the proletarian superhero proudly announces: 'τὸν Δῆμον ἀφεψήσας ὑμῖν καλὸν ἐξ αἰσχροῦ πεποίηκα' ('I have purified Demos by boiling him down and made him beautiful instead of ugly', 1321). The verb *aphepsein* (see also 1336) comes from food preparation (see e.g. Herodotus 2.94), and means 'boiling off' unwanted residues. It is suitable for a man whose career has involved preparing sausages. But it may well also suggest the cauldron of rejuvenation in which the sorceress Medea boiled Aeson and Pelias. And the rejuvenation has been complete; Demos, having shed more than fifty years, now looks exactly as he did in the days of Aristides and Miltiades (1325f.). He is able to respond with enthusiasm when a young female personification of a Thirty Years' Peace Treaty is presented to him (1388–95). For the Sausage-Seller, it turns out, possesses the same power to produce truces with Sparta as the god Amphitheus had in *Acharnians*.

The Hilarious Politics of the Supernatural in Aristophanic Comedy

Besides the personifications of the Right and Wrong Arguments, who do not interact directly with humans, the only significant supernatural feature of *Clouds* is the chorus itself. Strepsiades, the middle-aged protagonist, is granted a special relationship with them. His first response on hearing them approach, accompanied by thunderclaps, may allow us to see one of the comic effects Aristophanes could produce by combining demotic heroes with supernatural epiphanies. For Strepsiades at first uses reverent language, but quickly weaves bathetic scatology into the ceremonial address (293–5):

καὶ σέβομαί γ᾽ ὦ πολυτίμητοι καὶ βούλομαι ἀνταποπαρδεῖν
πρὸς τὰς βροντάς: οὕτως αὐτὰς τετρεμαίνω καὶ πεφόβημαι:
κεἰ θέμις ἐστίν, νυνί γ᾽ ἤδη, κεἰ μὴ θέμις ἐστί, χεσείω.

I too worship you, honoured ones, and want to fart back at the thunder; this is how they fill me with trembling and fear. If it is lawful, or not lawful, I need to shit *right now!*

By the end of the comedy, however, he is able to summon the Cloud-goddesses and hold a quite sombre dialogue with them after they have taught him his moral lesson (1452–66).

The hero of *Peace*, a peasant farmer specializing in vine growing (190f.), on the other hand, is invested with more superpowers than any other figure in Old Comedy, and more than most mythical heroes. Trygaeus, who combines his humble real-world identity with a suggestion that he is somehow an agent or representative of the Dionysiac spirit of Old Comedy,[19] can imitate the heroes Perseus and Bellerophon by acquiring a giant dung-beetle and riding it into the sky to heaven (as wonderfully staged by Peter Hacks in his celebrated production of *Der Frieden*, Fig. 8.1). There he converses with the god Hermes. He personally witnesses the personification of War toss foodstuffs representing different Greek states into an enormous mortar and give orders to his slave, the personification of Tumult familiar from the *Iliad* (5.593, 18.535). Trygaeus summons a congress of Panhellenic farmers who arrive instantaneously (292–300). Alongside Hermes himself, he supervises their riotous hauling of the personification of Peace herself from the cave into which she has been cast (459–519). He can even receive communications from the silent statue of Peace because Hermes does him the honour of translating her whispered messages (670–705). He can marry the personification of Harvest, Opōra, and outrageously break the fourth wall when he hands over her companion Theōria, the right to attend festivals, to the Councillors sitting in the front row of the theatre (715, 871–909). He can return to the earth within the space of a chorus even without his dung-beetle, which has been sequestered for the use of Zeus (728–819). He can see the flitting, floating souls of deceased poets as he descends through the air (829–32).

The versatile superhero Trygaeus rises from vine-dresser to be the acknowledged 'saviour' of Greece (914), an epithet primarily used of Zeus (see 1035f.). The protagonist of the next surviving play by Aristophanes, *Birds*, makes a far more vertiginous ascent in terms of status. He not only instals himself as tyrant of the birds' newly built city-state, but wrests the very power over the universe from Zeus. This spectacular denouement

Figure 8.1 Fred Düren as Trygaios in *Der Frieden*. Written and directed by Peter Hacks after Aristophanes.

follows a plot which has been conducted in the supernatural realm from fairly near the outset. Peisetaerus and Euelpides can visit a mythical king, Tereus, who has been transformed into a bird, talk to him and the other birds, and eat a magic root which turns them at least partially into birds themselves. Peisetaerus can supervise the building of a city in the air and converse with gods – Iris, Poseidon and the Triballian deity, the Titan Prometheus and the hero Heracles.

But it is in Peisetaerus' personal ascent of the cosmic status ladder that his characterization as a comic citizen hero with superpowers – even if a sinister one who rejects the democratic politics of Athens – is most enthralling. He wants to leave behind him Athenian *polupragmosunē* (44); the 'quiet' life he desires is one in which he is unaccountable to democratic laws and procedures. Peisetaerus, who does not seem to have been of a particularly high social class at Athens, is already defying social likelihoods as well as laws of nature when he becomes tyrant of Cloudcuckooland, and becomes increasingly autocratic and arbitrary in his behaviour. He puts pressure on Zeus by threatening him with a replay of the battle of the giants, but with one difference – despite being avatars of the giants, the birds will nevertheless be victorious (1248–52). But he then consolidates his power by marrying the daughter of the pre-existing local tyrant; in his case she is Basileia, the divine principle of Sovereignty, and along with her Peisetaerus acquires access to his father-in-law Zeus's powers, in particular his thunder.[20]

This scene is remarkable in that Peisetaerus, apparently an unremarkable if disgruntled Athenian citizen, exhibits behaviour associated by his audience historically with aspiring tyrants from aristocratic families and mythically with an infamous king. Public play-acting of intimate relations with divinity was of course a longstanding tradition among tyrants; Peisistratus of Athens himself was said to have been equipped by his allies with a tall woman costumed as Athena, beside whom he entered Athens on a chariot and drove to the Acropolis (Hdt. 1.60). Clearchus I of Heraclea Pontica, after studying in Athens, set himself up as tyrant, and, according to local historian Memnon,

> Turned out to be truly savage and bloodthirsty towards his subjects, and reached the peak of arrogance, so that he called himself the son of Zeus, and tinged his face with unnatural dyes, adorning it in all kinds of different ways to make it appear glistening or ruddy to those who saw him; and varied his clothing to appear fearsome or elegant. This was not his only vice; he showed no gratitude to his benefactors, was extremely violent, and ventured to carry out the most appalling deeds. He ruthlessly destroyed those he attacked, not only amongst his own people but whenever he perceived a threat elsewhere.
>
> *Memnon of Heraclea*, FGrHist 434 F 1[21]

There is a mythical counterpart to Clearchus' conduct in the story of Sisyphus' brother Salmoneus, who also wanted to display publicly his claim to Zeus-like cosmic authority. After becoming king of Elis, Salmoneus demanded that his subjects call him Zeus. To add to the insult, Salmoneus mocked Zeus by driving his chariot through the city dragging bronze kettles to simulate thunder and throwing torches to simulate lightning.[22] Peisetaerus is, hilariously, arrogating to himself not only the sovereignty of the universe, but the rights of the upper classes of myth and history to outrageous, hubristic misbehaviour.

The katabasis plot of *Frogs* is of course inherently supernatural; Aristophanes also used it in his *Gerytades*, an important drama about poetry and aesthetics, of a not dissimilar date to *Birds*, in which a delegation of poets descended to the Underworld. Great heroes had been able to visit the Underworld in myth and archaic literature – Odysseus, Heracles, Theseus – but in *Frogs* Aristophanes offers us the striking combination of a katabasis performed by a fully fledged Olympian divinity, Dionysus, attended by an intelligent, brave, resourceful, human slave. This impressive slave character may well be Aristophanes' dramaturgical response to a new sector in his audience: the citizens who had only recently been released from slavery as a reward for rowing in the battle of Arginusae – men likely to be gratified by the prospect of a slave with superpowers and the ability to endure being flogged better than a god.[23]

After leaving Heracles' house, and before the human Xanthias' role ends when he decides to enter the Underworld proper and stay there, both Dionysus and Xanthias encounter many further figures whom the laws of nature would prevent any member of Aristophanes' audience from seeing or talking to in reality: the monster Empousa, a talking corpse, Charon, frogs singing in Greek, Aeacus, and the (presumably human but deceased) maid.

The plot formula combining a divinity with a human local hero is repeated in *Wealth*, where Chremylus, a poor citizen, not only consorts with Ploutos but holds a debate with Poverty. His slave Cario reports seeing Asclepius, Iason and Panacea in the Asclepeion (696–709); he also reports the fantasy utopian Phaeacia-like state in which the household suddenly finds itself after Ploutos is cured of blindness – the flour bins, wine jars, treasure chests, oil tank, perfume bottles and fig store are all full to overflowing. Old wooden kitchen and dining wares have turned into fine metals, and the slaves can play games all day; they even get to wipe their bottoms with soft garlic stalks instead of hard stones (802–22). The happy return to prosperity is clinched when the god Hermes begs Cario to let him come and join this human household; the gods are now poor, having lost Wealth to mankind (1099–1170). Aristophanes' response to the decline in living standards in the Athenian democracy is to create his most exaggerated plot in terms of ordinary humans, citizens and slaves, exchanging situations with gods altogether; the humour in the scenes from the moment when Ploutos recovers his sight is almost entirely produced by gleefully acting out a series of detailed repercussions of the new utopia.

I have left the three plays with female choruses until last, because they do form a distinct category in terms of the supernatural elements as well as their interest in gender issues. The women comedies do not take us to heaven, down into the Underworld, or to join communities of fauna. *Thesmophoriazusae*, despite its wildly inventive play with Euripidean tragedy, contains not one miraculous, paranormal or supernatural element; no divinities, talking animals, instantaneous travel, unreal locations or magical powers. The premise of *Assemblywomen* may have seemed almost as improbable, to ancient Athenian male audiences, as talking birds or farmers flying on dung-beetles, but it contains no more supernatural elements than *Thesmophoriazusae*. *Lysistrata* resembles the plays with male citizen protagonists marginally more. Unnaturally swift movement between cities seems possible. Lysistrata herself, though apparently a regular Athenian housewife, is (if only lightly) associated through some symbolism not only with Lysimache, the historical Priestess of Athena Polias, but with the goddess of the Acropolis herself.[24] She is also able to summon a personification of Reconciliation, towards the end of the play (1114). But the women plays do not significantly confound the laws of nature.

Women competent enough to take over the Acropolis or the Assembly may well have been seen as preternatural – going in some sense *beyond* what was deemed natural for people of their sex – but they were not supernatural. Thucydides' term for this was *para phusin*. During the civil war in 427 BCE, there was a street battle in Corfu's main town. Thucydides describes how women on the democratic side joined in the actual fighting: 'the women also entered the fray with great daring, hurling down tiles from the rooftops and standing up to the din with a courage that went *further* than what was natural (*para phusin*) to their sex' ('αἵ τε γυναῖκες αὐτοῖς τολμηρῶς ξυνεπελάβοντο βάλλουσαι ἀπὸ τῶν οἰκιῶν τῷ κεράμῳ καὶ παρὰ φύσιν ὑπομένουσαι τὸν θόρυβον', 3.74). But the women of Aristophanes, except Lysistrata, come nowhere near arrogating to themselves the powers of gods or mythical heroes. In my view this is because Aristophanes did not regard the women of classical Athens as participating in the thrilling project of citizen self-refashioning as agents of sovereignty in the democratic city. This was a prerogative of the men. They could not be granted the superpowers which were within the imaginative grasp of their fathers, sons and husbands. They might even be within the imaginative grasp of male slaves who could fantasize, because of events like those after Arginusae, that they might be citizens themselves one day, and wield their power over the Assembly and courts, like Philocleon dispensing his lightning.

Conclusion

The hero with superpowers of democratic comedy was an avatar and ludic emanation of the consciousness shared by the mass of poor, male free citizens of Athens. They had acquired sovereign power with the democratic revolutions, and their worldview and attitude to religious and political authority had been revolutionized as a result, opening up, for the playwrights of the new comic genre which the Athenians had grafted onto their festivals, a rich seam of hilarity. Freedom to run their own city brought the freedom not only to imagine the impossible, but to fantasize collectively about acquiring powers to reject established authorities hilariously and to override the laws of nature absurdly. It is no coincidence that the supernatural powers of the heroes in Athenian comedy disappeared, to be replaced by Menandrean ethical naturalism and heroes with no superpowers at all, at the precise moment in the fourth century BCE when the democracy was etiolated in the wake of the Macedonian conquest.

Philip Sidney was inspired by the example of the poets of ancient Greece when he wrote, in 1595:

> Only the Poet, disdaining to be tied to any such subjection, lifted up with the vigour of his own invention, doeth grow in effect, another nature, in making things either better then Nature bringeth forth, or quite new form such as never were in Nature, as the *Heroes, Demigods, Cyclops, Chimeras, Furies,* & such like: so as he goeth hand in hand with Nature, not enclosed within the narrow warrant of her gifts, but freely ranging only within the Zodiac of his own wit.[25]

But it is not just the poet Aristophanes who can do things 'such as never were in Nature'. His heroes, the men he dreamed up and incorporated into his dramatic poems, the new protagonists of Old Comedy, were liberated, 'freely ranging' democratic citizens, laughing incessantly as they consorted with '*Heroes, Demigods, Cyclops, Chimeras, Furies* & such like'. When the democracy gave ordinary men rights to rule their richer peers in the Assembly and lawcourts, it gave them the right to comic theatre, and to laugh as they ranged everywhere in the ludicrous democratic new universe of comic (im)possibility as well.

CHAPTER 9
ARISTOTLE ON ARISTOPHANIC HUMOUR
Pierre Destrée

Aristophanes' style is coarse in words, vulgar, and only good for the mob ('τὸ φορτικὸν ἐν λόγοις καὶ θυμελικὸν καὶ βάναυσον'), which is not at all the case with Menander's. The uneducated, ordinary person is captivated by what the former says, but the educated man will be displeased ('ὁ δὲ πεπαιδευμένος δυσχερανεῖ') ... Respectable people find his lack of restraint and bad manners repugnant ('οἵ τε σεμνοὶ βδελύττονται τὸ ἀκόλαστον καὶ κακόηθες'). As for Menander, he has proved unique in displaying his charms in theatres, at lectures, at banquets ... Why is it truly worthwhile for an educated man ('ἄνδρα πεπαιδευμένον') to go to the theatre, except to enjoy Menander?[1]

Obviously those words cannot be Aristotle's. He died when Menander was about to begin his career as playwright. They are Plutarch's, from (a summary of) his *Comparison between Aristophanes and Menander* (*Mor.* 853a–b and 854a–b).[2] But would not Aristotle have made a similar judgement? In a famous chapter on the virtue of wittiness, *eutrapelia* (*NE* 4.8), he seems to recommend the humour we find in 'new comedy' (i.e. what we call Middle Comedy) against 'Old Comedy', which is full of *aischrologia* ('shameful speech'). Also, since Menander went on to study with Aristotle's younger associate and successor as head of the Lyceum, Theophrastus, it would be plausible to see an affiliation between what the philosopher may have defended in the (lost) second book of his *Poetics*, and the most emblematic author of New Comedy. Aristophanes was much praised and admired by ancient critics and authors; Aristotle would have been an exception (before Plutarch) to that trend, yet this view seems, if indirectly and implicitly, to be largely accepted among interpreters nowadays.[3] In this chapter, I want tentatively to challenge that view.

Aristotle evaluating Aristophanes: An idle question?

How did Aristotle rate Aristophanes? Even if we may never be able to answer this question satisfactorily, it is not an idle one. When discussing tragic authors in his *Poetics*, Aristotle almost always adopts an evaluative mode. Sometimes he does it implicitly, but even in those cases his judgement is clear; when, in *Poetics* 14, he cites *OT* as a play that produces 'shuddering' ('φρίττειν'), even when it is only read aloud and not performed, he is clearly taking that play to be outstanding, even paradigmatic (14.1453b3–7). Alternatively, when he mentions that Agathon first introduced 'choral interludes' ('ἐμβόλιμα'), it embodies a reproach to Agathon (18.1456a29–31). But Aristotle's judgements are usually explicit. For positive evaluation, recall the enthusiastic way he presents Homer as being 'simply divine and peerless' ('θεσπέσιος... παρὰ τοὺς ἄλλους', 1459a30–1). On the critical side, the tragic author Aristotle criticizes most vigorously is Euripides. Aristotle admires Euripides' *Iphigenia in Tauris*, which he mentions on several occasions, especially in the famous, and famously controversial, Chapter 14, where the play, or (depending on your interpretation) one of its scenes, seems to be given first place in Aristotle's evaluative hierarchy (1454a4–9). But Aristotle also chides Euripides for creating the *ad hoc* recognition of Orestes by Iphigenia, where Orestes just states his name; bafflingly, Aristotle even stresses that the way Polyides (an author who has left no other trace in the history of tragedy) wrote his own *Iphigenia* was, in that regard, much better (16.1455a6–8, 17.1455b9–11). This is not the only case; almost every time Aristotle mentions Euripides or one of his plays, it is to illustrate a device a poet should not use if he wants to succeed.[4] If one takes the *Poetics* as primarily addressed to citizens who want to learn how to appreciate plays when they go to the theatre, all those critiques would be meant to help them in critically judging new plays they may go see (or read).[5] In other words, the evaluative judgements Aristotle utters each time he mentions a well-known, 'classical' playwright are central to his project in the *Poetics*. Since Aristophanes was considered a classic in Aristotle's time, the question of how Aristotle really evaluated Aristophanes is of crucial importance if we want to understand his recommendations about citizens' correct judgement of comic plays.

Comedic *muthos*: Aristophanes in the *Poetics*

The first place to look is in Chapter 3 of the *Poetics*, where Aristophanes is explicitly named:

> So representation has these three distinct aspects to it as we said from the start; the means by which it comes about, the people it represents and how it represents them. Thus, from one perspective, Sophocles would be the same kind of representational poet as Homer, for both represent people of great worth. From another perspective, he would be the same as Aristophanes, given that both represent people in action, that is to say people who act (*dran*). This is certainly, as some claim, the origin for what we call '*drama*', because it is people who act who are represented there.
>
> 3.1448a24–9

When commenting on this passage, interpreters are content to say that Aristophanes is named because his was the most evident name in comedy; naming him should not imply anything like value judgement.[6] Yet if it is true that Aristophanes was probably the most obvious name when talking about comedy, that was certainly not the case with Sophocles. Naming Sophocles in this context sounds rather unexpected, since Euripides had become the most famous tragedian by Aristotle's time; many of his plays were performed regularly in Athens and elsewhere. The reason why Sophocles is named here, therefore, must be that in Aristotle's eyes he is deemed a paradigmatic author of tragedy. While in the *Poetics* Euripides is criticized repeatedly, that is not the case with Sophocles who is only once criticized.[7] Thus, since comedy represents, as Aristotle had just said, people who are 'of less value', who are opposed to people of 'great value', it is difficult not to draw the conclusion that Aristophanes is named here not only as the best-known name in comedy, but also as a paradigmatic comic poet, in the normative sense of the term.

The analogy's focus is not on the worth of the people represented in tragedy and comedy, but on how they are represented. Aristotle only says explicitly that, from this perspective, Sophocles is comparable with Aristophanes; both playwrights represent people in action. But saying that implies an important value judgement. Representing people in action throughout the play, which entails all actors performing on stage and no narrative elements, not only differentiates theatrical plays from epic poems; it also makes them a much more valuable genre than epic (and of course, lyric) poetry.[8]

Being entirely 'dramatic' is of highest value in Aristotle's conception of poetry. And Sophocles is especially praised for this in at least two other instances. In reviewing the history of tragedy, Aeschylus is credited with introducing a second actor, while Sophocles is credited with having added a third actor; having two actors allows for dialogues, but three allows for triangular, truly dramatic action between several protagonists.[9] Later, at the end of Chapter 18, Aristotle recommends that the chorus 'should be considered as one of the actors' (1456a25–6). Back in Chapter 4, Aeschylus was credited with 'inventing' such a concept of the chorus ('Aeschylus reduced the parts of the chorus and gave dialogue the leading role', 1449a18–19) – but in Chapter 18 it is Sophocles who is presented as the paradigm to follow when it comes to implementing that conception; the chorus 'should be part of the whole and of the action on stage, not as in Euripides but rather like Sophocles' (1456a26–7). This is an odd remark which no modern interpreter can fully explain, but it is interesting for my purposes; here again, it is Sophocles who is said to have completed the achievement of tragedy as a representation.

There is another feature for which Sophocles is highly praised. As every reader of the *Poetics* knows, the key feature in Aristotle's view on poetry is *muthos*, 'plot'. In the Aristotelian characterization of the term, plot is a representation of people acting, that is, a representation where everyone involved acts, and where, correlatively of course, all the actors on stage, including the chorus, are acting. When he defines *muthos*, it is action that is underlined: 'The plot is the representation of the action – when I say 'plot', what I mean is the structured sequence of events' (6.1450a3–5). To be sure, *praxis*, 'action', here means the ensemble of all *pragmata*, which includes the actions of the heroes, as well as, more generally, the events that take place in the story. On this criterion, too, even if Aristotle may not say it explicitly, Sophocles is taken to be paradigmatic. As I recalled earlier, when at the beginning of Chapter 14 he recommends that 'the plot should be constructed such that, even without seeing it on stage, but merely by listening to someone reading out how the events unfold, one shudders and is moved to pity because of what happens' (1453b3–6), Aristotle cites *OT*, a huge mark of appreciation. For if by merely reading the play, you are moved into the genuine emotions that tragedy is supposed to evoke, your plot must be extremely well composed.

Aristophanes is not mentioned again in the *Poetics* (as we have it, i.e. its first book). Aristotle recognizes properly, not without some regret, that in the case of comedy he has no information to report about 'who introduced the usage of masks, prologues, a group of actors and other such features' (5.1449b4–5). But there is one feature he can report:

> As to the creation of plotlines, that comes originally from Sicily [Epicharmus and Phormis]. From amongst the Athenian poets, it is Crates who is the first to have dropped writing satire in iambic metre and to have written stories with a general structure, that is to say, plots ('Κράτης πρῶτος ἦρξεν ἀφέμενος τῆς ἰαμβικῆς ἰδέας καθόλου ποιεῖν λόγους καὶ μύθους').
>
> 1449b6–9

It would be a mistake, I believe, to read this as if Aristotle were making an opposition between iambic poetry where one character (or actual person) would be blamed, while a plot would be 'general', with 'general characters'. For there is no reason to believe that Aristotle would have denied that iambic poetry would be incapable of telling a story; iambic poetry may have a story, but that story, centred on one person or character, does not make a plot, that is, a story where all the events are interconnected. This is in substance what he will repeat in Chapter 9, where being *katholou* is presented as a crucial feature of plot, namely the fact of being constructed 'with a general structure', or rather 'with a comprehensive structure' (1451b8). This statement has often been taken as an opposition between particulars and generals, but how could we say that Oedipus or Thyestes are 'general' characters? The opposition lies rather in how the poet writes his story. The historian must tell his story with all the possible deeds and sufferings Alcibiades has done or suffered, whether or not all his deeds and sufferings were related to one another. By contrast, the poet, whether tragic or comic, must write a story wherein all the deeds and sufferings must be related to one another, and that is mainly done with a view to enabling his audience to follow the plotline. The historian must report what happened for the purpose of informing his audience; the poet must tell his audience a story they can enjoy following – an audience that could not follow a story because all its events were totally unconnected would not be able to 'get into the story'. Also, in a poetic plot, in contradistinction to a historical report, the emphasis is on actions, or rather the series of actions making the dramatic action. In the case of history, what mostly counts is the accurate account of what exactly such and such a person did or what was done to them; when he says 'a particular case study, that is what Alcibiades did or what happened to him' (1451b10–11), Aristotle emphasizes that it was that particular person who did it, or suffered from it. It is from this perspective, I suggest, that we should read Aristotle's remark about names:

> That is what poetry aims at, though it assigns proper names to individuals . . . This much is obvious from the start with comedy; it is only once the plotline is set up from a series of likely events that the poets assign fictional names, unlike the satirists who write about a particular person.
>
> 1451b9–15

Here, the emphasis is perhaps more on the opposition between fictional characters and real persons. But a few lines further down, Aristotle does not hesitate to say that a tragic poet could also perfectly well write a tragedy involving persons who really existed – provided that he follow the rule that a plot must be a story where the events are causally linked (1451b27–9). Thus, the contrast is between the story an iambic poet tells, where one (real or fictive) person and their deeds are mocked, and comedy where plot is essential and where names of characters can therefore be whatever one wants.

This is what Aristotle credits Crates with; he is the first Athenian poet who has written a 'true' comedy, with a *muthos* as Aristotle defines it. But, as we have seen in the case of Aeschylus, being first should not mean that he must be taken as a paradigmatic author of comedy. In the case of tragedy, Aeschylus is outdone by his 'follower' Sophocles, who perfected what Aeschylus 'invented' and should be considered paradigmatic. What about comedy? Admittedly, Aristotle never explicitly states whom he would name as his paradigmatic comic playwright. But since he names Aristophanes together with Sophocles as, apparently, the eminent cases of dramatic poetry, and plot is what fulfils the key requirement of dramatic poetry, what would prevent Aristophanes too being Aristotle's paradigmatic author of comic plot, and hence of comedy more generally speaking? Aeschylus, as we saw, is systematically presented by Aristotle as the 'inventor' of something that Sophocles perfected; when it comes to comedy, Crates is named as the 'inventor' of plot (at least in Athens), while Aristophanes is presented as a counterpart to Sophocles from the perspective of dramatic poetry. Why not see the affiliation between Crates and Aristophanes in the same way as the affiliation between Aeschylus and Sophocles?

If the logic of all the passages I have reviewed tends towards this picture, scholars would raise in objection the way we usually view Aristophanes and most of his plays, where the so-called *onomasti kōmōidein* is central. Aristotle may well consider Crates the Athenian inventor of plot; there is nothing proving that Aristophanes should be seen by Aristotle as Crates' follower, perfecting his 'invention'. Here is what Ian Storey writes: 'Aristotle with the advantage of hindsight saw in Crates the ancestor of the structured comedy of wit and manners prevalent in his own day. In his view Aristophanes and the great days of Old Comedy may have been a detour on the straight course to New Comedy.'[10] But nothing in the *Poetics* indicates a link between plot as it is defined there, and the 'comedy of wit and manners' that would define New Comedy. For this to be true, Aristotle should have drawn a strong and clear-cut contrast between *onomasti kōmōidein* and its direct ancestor, iambic poetry, and comedy as he normatively conceives it. As I have argued, this is what he does from the perspective of the series of events. But there is no such contrast between their respective contents. When Aristotle famously writes that Homer 'τὸ τῆς κωμῳδίας σχῆμα πρῶτος ὑπέδειξεν, οὐ ψόγον ἀλλὰ τὸ γελοῖον δραματοποιήσας' (1449a36–8), we must understand that Homer 'was also the first to mark out the contours of the comic genre, not by writing a satire but by giving a dramatic form to the laughable', instead of, as it is often mistranslated, 'by dramatizing not invective but the laughable'. The difference is crucial; according to the latter reading, we would have a difference between two sorts of humour: the 'bad', offensive humour of invective, and the 'good', I guess not offensive, humour of comedy. Perhaps, from a philological perspective, nothing prevents the latter translation. But a few lines before, Aristotle had just presented Homer's comic epic *Margites* as 'a poem of the same sort as' satire ('ψόγους ... τῶν μὲν οὖν πρὸ Ὁμήρου οὐδενὸς ἔχομεν εἰπεῖν τοιοῦτον ποίημα, εἰκὸς δὲ εἶναι πολλούς, ἀπὸ δὲ Ὁμήρου ἀρξαμένοις ἔστιν, οἷον ἐκείνου ὁ Μαργίτης', 1448b27–30). Thus, it would be odd to suppose that he would now make a difference between satire and the laughable from the perspective of their content. Again, it is dramatic poetry that Aristotle credits Homer with adumbrating against lyric poetry which is entirely narrative; nothing indicates that Homer would have invented a new sort of 'laughable', or humour. And more generally, the context of all this is an 'historical' reconstruction of birth of tragedy and comedy, with Homer as the *Ur*-Father, as it were, of both genres; would it not be strange to suppose that Homer adumbrated New (or Middle) Comedy while bypassing Old Comedy, except for Crates?

Comedic *lexis*: Aristophanes in the *Rhetoric*

In the *Poetics*, plot is the central and most important constituent of dramatic poetry, which is why Aristotle devotes a detailed analysis to it. In the case of tragedy, things are straightforward. As Aristotle recommends, tragic emotions should 'arise from the structure of events itself' which is 'the sign of a first-rate poet' (1453b3). As we have seen, it is the *muthos* of *OT* that excels at evoking such emotions. The way words are written is, of course, important, but they cannot be as crucial as *muthos*. As Aristotle says, *lexis* is like music: it should be considered a 'condiment' to 'spice' the 'taste' of the play, to augment the audience's emotional reaction, but not to create it.[11] In brief, *lexis*, like music, is at the service of the plot and the emotions the plot is supposed to produce; it is certainly not a *sine qua non* of tragedy, and the pleasure it is expected to afford.

In the case of comedy, things appear more complicated. In the *Poetics*, Aristotle seems to put tragedy and comedy on the same footing. But we do not get exactly the same picture when Aristotle discusses comedy in his *Rhetoric*:

> And similarly, since games are among pleasurable things, all relaxation is, too; and since laughter is among pleasurable things, necessarily laughable things – human beings and words and deeds ('ἀνθρώπους καὶ λόγους καὶ ἔργα') – are also pleasurable. The laughable has been defined elsewhere in the books *On Poetics*.
>
> 1.11.1371b34–72a2

Whether or not Aristotle is referring to the definition of comedy we find in the *Poetics* here, the difference between this presentation and that definition is striking; while in *Poetics* 5, what is laughable refers only to human beings (probably their corporal clumsiness) and their deeds ('τὸ γὰρ γελοῖόν ἐστιν ἁμάρτημά τι καὶ αἶσχος', 1449a34–5), the presentation given in this *Rhetoric* passage adds words or jokes as integral to a comedy. We find this in at least one other passage of the *Rhetoric* where Aristotle refers his readers to his *Poetics* (here presumably its second book), saying that there 'the number of forms of humour' or 'jokes' ('εἴδη γελοίων') have been stated (3.18.1419b6).

This difference is not insignificant. *Lexis* has a much bigger role in comedy:

> If poets do not do this well, they fail most seriously with the public; and if they do it well, they are popular. I mean when they make terms correspond: 'Hey, here he comes, with his hairy legs like curly parsley.'
>
> 3.11.1413a10–13

As this example indicates, the poets Aristotle has in mind here are comic playwrights; these are successful when they invent good comparisons. A good comparison (which is a kind of metaphor) is one that vividly makes you 'see' such-and-such in such-and-such a light. The comparison between hairy legs and parsley makes us 'see' the legs of the character as being as curly-haired and in the way that parsley is curly; as Aristotle adds, 'you would think he had parsley for legs, they're so hairy' (1413a29), which causes amusement. (Perhaps the joke may not sound especially funny to us, but imagine the butt of the joke being an arrogant, self-important snob; in that case the joke would have got a good laugh from the audience.) In other words, creating jokes, of which metaphors and comparisons are an important device, makes a comic poet succeed. He succeeds because he makes his audience laugh because of the description's incongruity. Since making his audience laugh is the comic poet's very aim, we can readily see why these figures are so important for him, and why he should be good at creating them if he wants to excel (and presumably win contests at the Dionysia and other festivals). This is not to say that plot is unimportant in comedy, but humorous *lexis* is certainly a crucial element without which a play would fail.

In this presentation of *lexis* in the third book of his *Rhetoric*, Aristotle gives us examples of jokes, *bons mots*, puns etc., of which I shall cite a few more examples. But first, let me emphasize one point crucial for my purposes. He here refers to Aristophanes again, mentioning his play *Babylonians* and its repeated use of diminutives:

> Diminutives have the same effect – the use of diminutives being to make something bad less bad or something good less good. So, in *Babylonians* Aristophanes makes sarcastic use of 'moneykins' for 'money', 'cloakette' for 'cloak', 'gibelet' for 'gibe', and 'ill-ish health'.
>
> Rhet. 3.2.1405b29–33, trans. Waterfield

Aristotle also quotes two of Aristophanes' verses without mentioning his name when exemplifying a wordplay in what he calls *paromoiōsis*, i.e. when we have two verses with resemblance between words ('ἀγρὸν γὰρ ἔλαβεν/ἀργὸν παρ' αὐτοῦ', 1410a29–30). True, this may not sound like many quotations, especially if we compare Aristophanes to the Middle Comedy poet Anaxandrides, who is named and quoted four times in that book (11a19–21, 12b17–18, 13b26–8 and b28–9). But there is no indication that Aristotle preferred the latter, who is most probably referred to more often because he was on everyone's mind; one evident case is 1413b25–9, where Aristotle quotes two examples of Anaxandrides' 'repeated words' as they were vividly spoken by the actor Philemon at performances Aristotle himself and his readership probably attended. Other quotations from unnamed authors are probably from Middle Comedy poets too, but again Aristotle may well have chosen them because they were fresh in his audience's minds. Thus, arguing from the paucity of Aristophanes' references versus numerous quotations from Middle Comedy will not do as an argument for Aristotle's preferences.[12] Quite the contrary, I would say; it is striking that Aristotle does not hesitate to quote verses from Aristophanes twice in the midst of quotations from Middle Comedy.

It would be dishonest though, I readily admit, to claim that Aristotle chose his examples of jokes for the sole reason that his audience knew them well. As many ancient sources testify, Aristotle was a witty joke-teller himself.[13] For this reason alone, we would find it hard to believe that he did not like the jokes he reports. And actually, in many instances, the jokes he quotes are meant to illustrate what we might perhaps label his own 'theory of humour'.[14] But if so, why not try to imagine how he might have reacted upon reading (or perhaps watching a reperformance) of Aristophanes' plays? If for Aristotle humour mainly consists in incongruity and unexpectedness, where puns, wordplays and parody are the most important devices, and as ancient and modern scholars alike have stressed, Aristophanes was a master of such devices, how could Aristotle not have valued Aristophanes very highly?[15] Let's read a few jokes we find in the *Rhetoric*, and compare them to similar jokes in Aristophanes to see whether that purely logical inference might find some corroboration.

Let me first get back to the 'parsley joke', which illustrates a funny comparison. Do we find similar jokes in Aristophanes? Of course! One that I find quite funny is *Ecclesiazusae* 126f., when Second Woman looks at herself in a mirror with her fake beard and laughs: 'It's just as though you fastened beards on cuttlefish that had a light brown grilling!' (trans. Halliwell), where the women's pale faces with a brown beard are compared to white cuttlefish with grilled tentacles.

Another joke Aristotle seems to find quite funny is meant to illustrate unexpectedness: 'There he was walking around with ... blisters (χίμεθλα) on his feet', whereas the hearer thought he would have said 'slippers' ('πέδιλα') (*Rhet.* 3.11.1412a31–2). Several features contribute to making the joke funny. There is of course the incongruity of the word in this context, enhanced by its unexpectedness. Secondly, the word that is actually uttered refers to something rather vulgar, or even repugnant.[16] Finally, at least for a sophisticated audience, the amusement comes not only from this unexpected word as such, but also from the awareness that this is a parody of Homeric verses, where the description 'walking with fine sandals' normally applies to gods or goddesses. Especially if you think of the verse where the sandals are described as being 'in gold', the incongruity is blatant!derivative[17]

Similar instances abound in Aristophanes' work. One is at *Frogs* 190, where Charon refuses to take a slave on board: 'No slaves! Not unless he took part in the seafight to save ... our bacon' ('δοῦλον οὐκ ἄγω, εἰ μὴ νεναυμάχηκε τὴν περὶ ... τῶν κρεῶν', trans. Halliwell). The word every hearer would have expected is 'περὶ ψυχῆς' (see e.g. Hdt. 9.37, or Hom. *Il.* 22.161). The use of a rather vulgar word in an unexpected way must have sounded quite funny (especially if at the première, the actor said it in a solemn tone, parodying that of tragedy). Another one is at *Wasps* 440: 'Lord Hero Cecrops, Dracontides below the waist, will you simply look on when I'm being manhandled this way by barbarians, the very ones I myself taught how to weep ... their full measure of bread (κλάειν τέτταρ' ἐς τὴν χοίνικα)?' As Taillardat has (I think) rightly explained, the verb that is expected here is to 'knead', 'μάττειν', the 'τέτταρ' ἐς τὴν χοίνικα' referring to the four measures of *kotulai* that make one *choinix*, which corresponds to a slave's daily allowance.[18]

As far as we know, these two examples do not directly parody Homer or any tragic poet. But as any reader of Aristophanes would expect, we also find similar jokes where parody is at stake. One example is from *Ecclesiazusae* (391–3): 'O my, what a blow! Antilochus, raise the dirge for me – not for my ... three obols; for all I had is gone' ('Ἀντίλοχ', ἀποίμωξόν με τοῦ <u>τριωβόλου</u> τὸν ζῶντα μᾶλλον· τἀμὰ γὰρ διοίχεται', trans. mod. Henderson), which parodies Aeschylus' *Myrmidons*: 'O my, what a blow! Antilochus, raise the dirge for me – not for the dead; all I had is gone!' ('Ἀντίλοχ', ἀποίμωξόν με τοῦ <u>τεθνηκότος</u> τὸν ζῶντα μᾶλλον· τἀμὰ γὰρ διοίχεται', fr. 138).

Another example, one where Aristophanes is perhaps at his best, comes at the end of the hilarious exchange between Lamachus and Dicaeopolis, both ordering their slaves to prepare everything for their armament and their dinner respectively:

Λ.	φέρε δεῦρο γοργόνωτον ἀσπίδος κύκλον.
Δ.	κἀμοὶ πλακοῦντος τυρόνωτον δὸς κύκλον.
Λ.	ταῦτ' οὐ κατάγελώς ἐστιν ἀνθρώποις πλατύς;
Δ.	ταῦτ' οὐ πλακοῦς δῆτ' ἐστὶν ἀνθρώποις γλυκύς;

Lamachus	Bring hither my buckler round and Gorgon-bossed.
Dicaeopolis	Give me a pizza round and cheese-bossed.
Lamachus	Isn't this what men call explicit insolence?
Dicaeopolis	Isn't this what men call exquisite pizza?

Acharnians 1124–7, trans. mod. Henderson

The two last verses need no explanation; Dicaeopolis parodies what Lamachus just said, with an extraordinary consonantal wordplay on 'οὐ κατάγελώς πλατύς/οὐ πλακοῦς γλυκύς'. But before we get to the fireworks as it were, the first two verses light the fuse with a formidable parody of solemn words Euripides invented, while 'γοργόνωτον ἀσπίδος κύκλον' is a sort of (humorously) hieratic reminder of 'χαλκόνωτον ἀσπίδα' (*Troades* 1136), 'σιδηρονώτοις δ' ἀσπίδος κύκλοις' (*Phoenissae* 1130) and 'χρυσεόνωτος ἀσπίδα' (fr. 159), against which 'πλακοῦντος τυρόνωτον δὸς κύκλον' resounds with a formidably deflationary effect.

It is thanks to jokes such as these that so many ancient writers admired Aristophanes for being an exceptionally witty comedian. Since the jokes Aristotle quotes are of a similar vein, why would he not have admired Aristophanes' as well? Or to put it more philosophically, if for Aristotle a good joke is one that plays on incongruity and unexpectedness, offers its audience novelty, and also (in many cases) hilariously parodies other (serious) literary work, why would he not have considered Aristophanes a great master of comedy?

Being truly witty: Aristophanes in the *Nicomachean Ethics*

In the second part of the chapter, I argued that the unique mention of the name of Aristophanes in the *Poetics* should be best interpreted as a laudatory evaluation on Aristotle's part. In the third part, I have suggested that if humour for Aristotle consists in incongruity and unexpectedness, where puns, wordplays and parody are the most important devices, there is no reason why Aristotle would not have valued Aristophanes, who is a great master of these devices. But there is an (in)famous passage in the *Nicomachean Ethics* that seems to jeopardize my proposals. In that chapter on *eutrapelia*, 'wittiness', or the 'sense of humour', I mentioned at the beginning, Aristotle seems to recommend the humour we find in comedy that was written and performed at his time, which he calls 'the modern comedy', rather than what he calls 'Old Comedy'. His main argument bears on *aischrologia*, and runs like this; while Old Comedy mostly uses obscene speech to make its audience laugh, 'new comedy' uses more innuendo. Since obscene speech aims at 'slavish people' while innuendo aims at 'free people', it goes without saying that obscene speech, and therefore Old Comedy, cannot be recommended for the leisure of these 'free people'. And if Aristophanes is considered an author of 'Old Comedy', as no one would deny, Aristotle cannot possibly be taking him to be paradigmatic in his normative conception of comedy, and humour more generally.

At first sight, this logic seems to be devastating, but one way of defusing it consists in reading the argument in its immediate context. According to Heath, all that this reference to comedy provides is an analogy that aims at illustrating the sort of humour acceptable in social gatherings; it should not be read as a value judgement on comic theatre.[19] To be sure, in his *Politics*, when describing his own ideal city, Aristotle recommends that younger people not attend spectacles of 'iambic poetry and comedy' that are full of 'obscene speech', but he immediately adds 'before they have reached the age at which they have been rendered immune to the potential noxious effect of them', which amounts to accepting spectacles of iambic poetry and Old Comedy for adults (7.17, 1336b20–3). True, this passage seems to confirm that Aristotle took obscene speech to be an important component of comedy, and he obviously shared Plato's concerns at least when it comes to the youth. But contrary to the conclusion Plato draws from this, that is, the condemnation of comedies where such obscene speech is so important, Aristotle does not condemn them. If one takes seriously what he says in *Poetics* 24 ('what is right is not the same in politics and in poetry, nor is it the same in other arts as it is in the art of poetry', 1460b13–15), there is no reason why he would condemn comedy and its *aischrologia*; just because it must be condemned in social gatherings, there is no reason why that should be the case in the theatre.

The theatre certainly need not follow the same rules as real life. After all, in the case of pity and fear, Aristotle would have disapproved of citizens crying and cowering in real life as they do in the theatre. Pity, he says in *NE*, must be moderate and follow the rule of the mean in order to qualify for being a virtuous emotion (2.5, 1105b19–28); the same goes for fear when soldier citizens are confronted with the enemy on the battlefield (3.7, 1115b10–13). In the case of poetry, this rule of the mean does not apply; it is rather the aim of the poet to arouse pity and fear in the strongest way in order to create the typical pleasure one expects from tragedy. Yet, it seems to me implausible to dismiss completely the evaluative tone of our *NE* passage, especially if one compares the passage from the *Rhetoric* I have already quoted. There Aristotle refers to his *Poetics*, where he had presented 'the different kinds of humour', adding this crucial remark:

> Some kinds of jokes are appropriate for a free man, but others are not, so the issue is to find what is appropriate for oneself. Ironic mockery suits a free man better than coarse humour; it is the difference between telling jokes for one's own amusement or, in the case of coarse humor, for the amusement of others.
>
> 3.19, 1419b5–9, trans. Waterfield

Again, Aristotle is referring to real life. But since he just referred to the 'kinds of humour' he had been treating in his *Poetics*, where comedy, not humour in the real world, was at stake, it should mean that he does not draw a clear-cut line between jokes in real life and jokes on stage. Whether it comes to social gatherings or the theatre, entertainment is for the 'free people', and it is not supposed to consist of *bōmolochia* and *aischrologia*. After all, a little further along in his description of his ideal city in the *Politics*, when it comes to music, Aristotle also proposes that there be a kind of music that would be enjoyable for uneducated labourers, while 'free people' should enjoy more elevated styles of music (8.7, 1342a18–28). And in the *Poetics* itself, a similar distinction is drawn, too, between an educated audience that enjoys real tragic plays, those that end 'tragically', that is with *pathos*, and uneducated audiences who prefer plays with a happy ending (13, 1413a33–5). Why should this not be the case when it comes to comedy?

Now what does characterize a 'good' comedy that would suit 'free', 'well-educated' people? The mistake one should not make in reading the analogy under consideration is to take the opposition between Old and Middle Comedy as what would exactly correspond to a 'bad' and a 'good' comedy. What Aristotle says is much more subtle; what should characterize 'good' uses of humour is innuendo, which one can see in a more evident manner in Middle Comedy, while obscene speech, which characterizes 'bad' uses of humour, is more visible in older comedies. Thus, the crucial difference we need to assess is that between obscene speech and innuendo. Let me give the whole passage 1128a16–25 – I quote one of the most readable, and widely used, translations, that by Roger Crisp:

> Seemliness ('ἐπιδεξιότης') is proper to the mean state. It is characteristic of a seemly person ('τοῦ δ' ἐπιδεξίου') to say and to listen to the sort of things that are

suitable for a gentleman of good character ('οἷα τῷ ἐπιεικεῖ καὶ ἐλευθερίῳ ἁρμόττει'). For there are some things that it is appropriate for such a person to say and to listen to by way of amusement, and the amusement of a gentleman differs from that of a slavish person, and that of an educated person from that of an uneducated. One can also see this from old and new comedies: to the earlier writers, bad language was what was funny, while, to the later, it was innuendo ('τοῖς μὲν γὰρ ἦν γελοῖον ἡ αἰσχρολογία, τοῖς δὲ μᾶλλον ἡ ὑπόνοια'), which is far more decent ('διαφέρει δ' οὐ μικρὸν ταῦτα πρὸς εὐσχημοσύνην').

This translation misreads what the text says. First of all, as I already mentioned, Aristotle does not say that innuendo was the only method newer comic authors use, but only that for these newer playwrights, innuendo is more what constitutes funniness, which of course implies that obscene language was more in use in older comedies. More importantly, I doubt that 'seemliness' and 'decency' genuinely capture what Aristotle wants to convey.

A little earlier (1128a6–7), he used the phrase 'λέγειν εὐσχήμονα' to characterize the 'good' way of joking that suits 'the good and free citizens', which Crisp translates as 'speaking decently'. It is true that in the passage from *Politics* 7.17 I have just referred to, comedies and iambic poetry full of *aischrologia* are described as providing 'indecent stories' ('λόγους ἀσχήμονας', 1336b14). But in our passage, how would saying things that are described as 'decent' evoke laughter, especially when it comes to comedy? Actually, in another passage of the *Politics*, Aristotle uses 'εὐσχημοσύνη' in connection with 'περιουσία', where it obviously means refinement (1329b28). Since the opposition in this passage is between 'slavishness', which goes with 'uneducatedness', and 'educatedness', would not 'refinement' be a more natural rendering?

As to 'ἐπιδεξιότης', the meaning 'seemliness' is not apparently found anywhere else in classical Greek. As some interpreters render it here, it may refer to tactfulness, especially if one considers the theme of aggressiveness that Aristotle is also evoking in this context (a 'good' joke is the one that should not hurt its target). But it does not seem that when using 'ἐπιδεξιότης' or 'ἐπιδέξιος' in our passage (1128a17, 33), Aristotle is directly referring to that theme. As other interpreters have (I think) rightly claimed, it seems much more likely that Aristotle means something like dexterousness, especially when it comes to both making and taking a joke (cf. *Rhet*. 1381a34–5: 'οἱ ἐπιδέξιοι καὶ τῷ τωθάσαι καὶ τῷ ὑπομεῖναι', 'able to be kidded and kidding in good sport', as Kennedy translates). And, more specifically, it must also refer to the cleverness that allows one to make and enjoy a good joke, especially since Aristotle, a little later on, concludes his analysis in saying that 'ὁ δὴ χαρίεις καὶ ἐλευθέριος' (which Crisp here accurately translates as 'the sophisticated gentleman') who has the virtue of *eutrapelia* can be called either *epidexios* or *eutrapelos* ('εἴτ' ἐπιδέξιος εἴτ' εὐτράπελος λέγεται', 1128a31–3) where 'clever', not 'decent', is quite obviously the right rendering.[20] In brief, I propose that we understand this passage to be claiming that the funniness that is appropriate to 'free' people amounts, among other things, to innuendo that requires dexterousness and cleverness, which 'makes a great difference when it comes to refinement' ('διαφέρει δ' οὐ μικρὸν ταῦτα πρὸς εὐσχημοσύνην', 1128a22).

This understanding is perfectly aligned with the distinction between 'αἰσχρολογία' and 'ὑπόνοια'. It is slavish persons, Aristotle forcefully says, who enjoy 'αἰσχρολογία'. And for Aristotle, what fundamentally defines slavishness (of course in the metaphorical sense) is the importance one gives to bodily pleasures. There is, among others, a famous passage at the beginning of the *NE* where Aristotle quickly dismisses pleasure as a viable candidate for happiness, saying that 'for the masses and the most vulgar people (οἱ μὲν πολλοὶ καὶ φορτικώτατοι), happiness consists in pleasure', and that 'ordinary people do seem wholly slavish (οἱ μὲν οὖν πολλοὶ παντελῶς ἀνδραποδώδεις), because the life they choose is one that is characteristic of grazing cattle' (1.5, 1095b16–20). That is, those people live for the sake of purely bodily pleasures such as those obtained from food, drink and sex. In our passage on *eutrapelia*, it should come as no surprise that the buffoon is also called a *phortikos*, a vulgar person. For 'αἰσχρολογία' is typical of uneducated and slavish people, those who have no idea of 'εὐσχημοσύνη', 'refinement' – in other words, they are the people lacking all sophisticated taste.

Now, what exactly is 'innuendo', 'ὑπόνοια', and why does it make 'a great difference when it comes to refinement'? Unfortunately, 'ὑπόνοια' is a hapax in Aristotle, so direct comparison is impossible. But when using it in reference to myth, Plato refers to what we call symbolic or allegorical meaning (*Rep.* 378d); and in his commentary on that passage, Aspasius says it means 'to hint at something by way of a riddle' ('τὸ μεθ' ὑπονοίας σκώπτειν, τουτέστιν μετὰ τοῦ αἰνίττεσθαι', 125.33-4). Thus 'ὑπόνοια' implies some sort of cognitive search for a meaning. In other words, what the witty person is supposed to activate, and help activate in his audience, is cognitive powers, understanding. What most significantly differentiates 'αἰσχρολογία' and 'ὑπόνοια' is that 'ὑπόνοια' refers to the use of intelligence. It is true that in our context, the objects of the jokes that are meant to require 'ὑπόνοια' are exactly those intended in the obscene language. So it is only the way these objects, or features, are meant that makes the whole difference, and it is presumably these two ways that differentiate the pleasure the buffoon and the free person can enjoy from such features. Clearly, the buffoon is the one who takes pleasure in talking 'αἰσχρολογία', and the uneducated are those who enjoy hearing such jokes, which presumably amounts to enjoying a pleasure that is directly linked to the body (and indeed buffoons and vulgar people are normally described as people who laugh very loudly – a laughter the body plays a great part in). What the 'free person' is meant to enjoy, one may suppose, is rather the witty way such objects or features are alluded to.

This normative view on humour as I understand it goes hand in hand with Aristotle's views on humour as we find them in his *Rhetoric*. As I said earlier, incongruity and unexpectedness are the two main features he says prompt our laughter when it comes to verbal humour. And there he highlights the importance of wordplay, puns and other such devices as metaphor and comparison. As we have seen, Aristotle says it is when comic playwrights present comparison (a kind of metaphor) and 'make them well that they are popular' and are considered truly funny and entertaining. But creating metaphor or comparison, Aristotle repeatedly says, is crucially a matter of intelligence and cleverness: 'Metaphors should be drawn from things that are closely related but not evidently so, exactly as in philosophy it takes a sharp mind to observe similarities between things that are very far apart' (*Rhet.* 3.11.1412a11–13). Aristotle does not mean that poets or orators should be philosophers, but that they need to have a sharp mind, and see similarities where people usually do not see them, to produce fine metaphors and comparisons. As we have seen, Aristotle very much emphasizes the importance of jokes that allow a poet to be successful. The poet of course succeeds because he makes his audience laugh. And they laugh because of the incongruity of the description, which, for a demanding and sophisticated audience, requires finding new and fresh ways of dealing with language, that is, cleverness. Thus, we may suppose that a good, refined audience is one that can appreciate the cleverness of the jokes they enjoy. Αἰσχρολογία-based jokes only produce a pleasure that is directly linked to the body, while innuendo implies much more demanding jokes, intellectually speaking. And it also implies a much more refined use of incongruity and unexpectedness. Since 'material for humour is always near at hand' ('ἐπιπολάζοντος δὲ τοῦ γελοίου'), the buffoon, Aristotle adds, is always quick in uttering a joke, and uneducated people readily 'call him a witty person' (1128a12–15). But his jokes are not witty, just flat; in his jokes, incongruity and unexpectedness are rather poor. Thus, the conclusion one can draw from this is that if you define a joke as based on incongruity and unexpectedness, αἰσχρολογία-based jokes are not what best answers to that definition.

Before I get back to Aristophanes and how he may fit into this story, let me give an example of what Aristotle presumably would have described as a good example of 'ὑπόνοια'. This is a joke reported by the fifth-century BCE rhetorician Theodorus of Byzantium, thus a joke that presumably comes from Old Comedy.[21] We must imagine a character named Nicon, a cithara player from Thrace, who is readying himself to play; instead of saying 'θράττεις σύ', 'you are going to playing the cithara', as the audience would have expected, his protagonist on stage unexpectedly says 'Θρᾷττ' εἶ σύ', 'you are a Thracian girl' (*Rhet.* 3.11.1412a33-b1).[22]

Probably no one nowadays would find this joke particularly clever and witty, since it is based on homophobia, misogyny and racism taken together, as the poor Nicon is called a female slave prostitute from Thrace (a region Athenians commonly despised and from which many slaves came). But it would be a mistake, I submit, to think that this joke was not a good example of a witty innuendo in the eyes of Aristotle (and his contemporaries). Calling some male citizen a Thracian prostitute would not have been far from *aischrologia*, not very far indeed from calling him an 'εὐρύπρωκτος', 'wide-arse', *vel sim*. But Nicon is a cithara player who actually comes from Thrace, as Aristotle emphasizes: 'if the audience did not take Nicon to be Thracian, it would not seem witty' ('εἰ μὴ ὑπολαμβάνει Θρᾷκα εἶναι, οὐ δόξει ἀστεῖον εἶναι'). And, if Thracian people were usually despised by Athenians, it also remains true that cithara playing was intimately linked to Thrace; according to Pindar, the paradigmatic player of the cithara (and 'the father of song', *Pythian Odes* 4.4.315), Orpheus, was Thracian by origin (fr.128c) and it was therefore common to speak of a Thracian cithara too.[23] If one takes this into consideration, which of course educated minds in Athens did, the joke sounds much more like a clever witticism, indeed an 'ἀστεῖον'.

Needless to say, in Aristophanes' plays we find quite a few puns that rely on changing one letter. But many of them are not exactly innuendos, and most of them are actually rather innocent and not as offensive as the Thracian joke.[24] Perhaps the most similar joke is this:

> And if any of them clowned around … by showing himself harmonically playing the Chian or the Siphnian
>
> <εἰ> δέ τις αὐτῶν βωμολοχεύσαιτο, αὐτὸς δείξας ἐναρμονίως χιάζων ἢ σιφνιάζων
>
> fr. 930 Kassel and Austin/912 Kock, trans. Henderson

This text has produced much comment. We do not know where exactly the quotation is supposed to begin, and since '<εἰ> δέ τις αὐτῶν βωμολοχεύσαιτο' is a literal quotation from *Clouds* 969, whether it might come from another version of that play, or whether it might not be from Aristophanes at all.[25] At first sight there is nothing especially humorous, as 'χιάζων ἢ σιφνιάζων' may just refer to the islands of Chios and Siphnos. But according to lexicographers, the verb 'σιφνιάζων' was also apparently used to mean 'to poke someone's bum with the finger' ('τὸ ἄπτεσθαι τῆς πυγῆς δακτύλωι'), and 'χιάζων' may have had a similar meaning, or connotation (see the phrase 'χιαστὶ τίλλειν' at CA 919: 'to pluck in the Chian manner').[26] If this *double entendre* is not a pun based on a one-letter change, it almost exactly parallels the tone of our Thracian joke; in both case, musicians are quite offensively mocked through sexual innuendo.

In the case of Aristophanes, one might say, this comes as no surprise; are not even real people such as Cleon and Cleophon regularily insulted in such a way? And this is of course the second main reason why interpreters reject the idea that Aristotle would have particularily praised Aristophanes. If we rely on the *NE* chapter on wittiness, where the buffoon is not only condemned for his flat jokes, but also for the way he offends his targets, how could Aristotle possibly have considered Aristophanes as a paradigmatic author of comedy? But as the Thracian joke makes obvious, on this aspect there must be quite a difference between what Aristotle recommends in a social gathering and in the theatre. That difference, I suggest, must bear on the status of the people who are mocked; in a social gathering, it is indeed crucial to avoid offending your target who is also your friend or at least your co-symposiast; in the theatre, characters are mocked, not real persons. Again, one may insist that Cleon or Cleophon were real persons, not characters. But in the Thracian joke, it may also be the case that Nicon was a real musician – otherwise Aristotle would not have added that people had to know the fact that he was from Thrace in order to get the joke. So unless Aristotle were to be proven to be in sheer contradiction with what he says in that *NE* chapter, one must conclude that in his eyes, mocking a person in the theatre should not be taken as equivalent to mocking them in real life. After all, Socrates was of course a real person too. But, as all interpreters easily agree, in the *Clouds* the character Socrates stands not only for the real Socrates but also for the sophists and other 'Presocratic' philosophers (notably Diogenes of Apollonia), and Aristophanes' mockery was addressed to odd intellectuals in general, not only Socrates, the real individual. Similarly, should it not be the case that Cleon and Cleophon were mainly chosen because they were prominent figures, and, like Socrates, easy targets?

Interpreters may of course still insist that there were political motives behind these repeated attacks against them. But even if this were true, that would not change the fact that nothing indicates that, around half a century after Aristophanes' (and those politicians') death, Aristotle himself would have attached much importance to these motives while reading his plays. For, as we have seen, Aristotle takes for granted that the aim of the comic poet is to elicit laughter and the pleasure that goes with it; he never says, or even alludes to the idea, that comedy would or should also convey any sort of political message. In the *Poetics*, where he famously states that the rules that preside over the art of writing poetry should not be the same as those that preside over the other arts, he gives the example of a painter who intentionally represents 'a horse with two right legs stretched out towards the front' (1460b18–19); this is a mistake from a biological point of view (as Aristotle actually mistakenly believes), but if painting that way allows for a better effect on the viewer, this is a perfectly acceptable mistake. Similarly, if mocking a well-known figure proves more entertaining than mocking a totally fictive character, why should a comedian refrain from doing so? If Aristotle enjoyed reporting the Thracian joke, there is no reason why he would not have enjoyed, and therefore praised, Aristophanes for his jokes, as offensive as they may have been – provided they were sophisticated.

Plutarch harshly condemned Aristophanes for his coarse and vulgar style. By contrast, Cicero praised Old Comedy for its 'refined, urbane, clever, witty' kind of jokes ('iocandi genus ... elegans, urbanum, ingeniosum, facetum', *De officiis* 1.104), and especially Aristophanes, whom he takes to be the 'wittiest poet of Old Comedy' ('facetissumus poeta veteris comoediae', *De legibus* 2.37). Judging from Aristotle's own views on humour and the kind of jokes he reports, it is difficult to see why he should not be taken as having anticipated Cicero's judgement, instead of Plutarch's.[27]

PART TWO
PRACTICE

CHAPTER 10
SURFACE AND DEEP ARISTOPHANIC PARODY
Athina Papachrysostomou

In 1994, Carey noted that 'the question of the precise evaluation of comic criticism remains a live one'.[1] More than twenty years on, his remark still holds true. The complexity of the relationship between the comic stage and the real world of Athens of the fifth century BCE (and beyond) remains an intriguing and challenging research area. Accordingly, the present contribution offers an alternative hermeneutic approach to Aristophanic criticism and satire, especially the question of how parody is funny, based on modern psychological analyses.

First, the precise meaning of the term 'parody', as featuring in the title and as used throughout this contribution, needs clarification. Unlike the widely established meaning of 'parody' in relation to Greek Comedy as 'any kind of distorting representation of a (literary) original',[2] I will henceforth use 'parody' to designate *any kind of satire and all satirical techniques used in order to communicate a distorted, satirical representation of reality* (i.e. without necessarily any reference to a literary work).[3]

In two recent landmark studies, Italian psychologists Francesca D'Errico and Isabella Poggi explored the potential impact and powerful role of parody as a core parameter in politics and especially political persuasion. To this end, they identified – on the basis of a meticulous socio-cognitive process[4] – two distinct types of parody, 'surface parody' and 'deep parody',[5] using the recent political situations in Italy as exemplary cases. Surface parody is defined as simple distortion of reality by exaggeration; that is, the author/parodist reproduces – in a distorting, exaggerated and variably misleading way – the target's main traits (physical characteristics/flaws, personality attributes, behavioural patterns, etc.). Of course, reality can also be distorted in other, less anodyne ways; for example, the parodist can choose to *recategorize* the target, that is, to shift the target from its own category to another that has the target's main flaw as its most prominent feature. Distortion is at work, again; only this time distortion assumes a more drastic and more hostile form and, accordingly, it has deeper, more poignant, and potentially harmful implications for the target; and this is what D'Errico and Poggi identify as deep parody.[6] It is important to note that 'distortion' is understood in its widest sense, ranging from caricature to substitution, addition, subtraction, exaggeration, condensation, contrast and discrepancy. Understandably, deep parody requires a more complex cognitive process, control of more information and a higher level of erudition by both the recipient and the generator of parody.

The purpose of the present contribution is to apply – *mutatis mutandis* – this modern (and resourceful) psychological pattern of surface and deep parody to Aristophanic satire (hereafter referred to as parody), and thence pursue the resulting implications and issues.[7] Immediately, the present discussion becomes relevant to Halliwell's differentiation between vulgar laughter that is expressive of hostility (as in laughing someone down, 'καταγελᾶν') and playful, sophisticated laughter that involves only a pretence of ridicule.[8]

The figure of Cleon is a most apposite starting point for this twofold-parody discussion; his treatment by Aristophanes in *Ach*. 659–64 constitutes an archetypical example of deep parody. These lines (which correspond to the *pnigos* of the *parabasis*) display an abrupt change of tone[9] and constitute a harsh invective against Cleon, which swiftly climaxes from a statement of daredevil defiance ('πρὸς ταῦτα Κλέων καὶ παλαμάσθω', 'therefore, let Cleon hatch his plots', 659)[10] to an offensively obscene insult ('λακαταπύγων', 'utterly lecherous' or 'habitual pathic', 664).[11] It is interesting to closely follow how this attack escalates; after the initial defiance of 'παλαμάσθω', the chorus leader insinuates that Cleon regularly engages in intrigues and conspiracies: 'καὶ πᾶν ἐπ' ἐμοὶ τεκταινέσθω' ('let him contrive everything against me', 660). Next, he assumes all virtue and righteousness for himself (and the poet), leaving Cleon deprived of these qualities: 'τὸ γὰρ εὖ μετ' ἐμοῦ καὶ τὸ δίκαιον/ξύμμαχον ἔσται' ('for virtue and righteousness will be my allies', 661f.). Finally, he claims that Cleon acts against – even betrays – the city's interests: 'κοὐ μή ποθ' ἁλῶ/περὶ τὴν πόλιν ὢν ὥσπερ ἐκεῖνος/δειλός' ('and never will I be caught behaving toward the city as he does, a coward', 662-4) – and, on top of all that, he is also 'utterly lecherous'.

Deep parody against Cleon is at work here, since the element of exaggeration surpasses the boundaries of anodyne distortion of reality. Cleon is not superficially described as a merely incompetent politician; instead, he is portrayed as (a) a wicked outlaw, (b) a skilful conspirator who betrays his city's interests, (c) a coward who avoids the battlefield, and (d) a lecherous person. Through this culminating accumulation of accusations, Cleon is manifestly recategorized; that is, he is shifted from the category of politicians (or politically prominent figures) into a different category of individuals. What should not escape our attention is the fact that in real life Cleon enjoyed conspicuous popularity and exercised considerable influence on Athenian citizens in critical cases of political importance and military decision making, and was attacked by the elite and their sympathizers for this reason. He was 'τῷ πλήθει πιθανώτατος', as Thucydides cares to emphasize (he had 'very great influence with the multitude', 4.21).[12] What is more, Thucydides also considers him the 'most violent of the citizens' ('βιαιότατος τῶν πολιτῶν', 3.36), and there are many Athenians who shared the – controversial – view (explicitly stated by Thucydides, 5.16.1) that Cleon was a cynical warmonger, who was staunchly 'opposed to peace … because of his success and the reputation he had derived from war' ('ἠναντιοῦντο τῇ εἰρήνῃ, ὁ μὲν διὰ τὸ εὐτυχεῖν τε καὶ τιμᾶσθαι ἐκ τοῦ πολεμεῖν …').[13] Likewise, a sense of antipathy is manifest in [Aristotle]'s *Athenian Constitution*:

> τοῦ δὲ δήμου Κλέων ὁ Κλεαινέτου, ὃς δοκεῖ μάλιστα διαφθεῖραι τὸν δῆμον ταῖς ὁρμαῖς, καὶ πρῶτος ἐπὶ τοῦ βήματος ἀνέκραγε καὶ ἐλοιδορήσατο, καὶ περιζωσάμενος ἐδημηγόρησε, τῶν ἄλλων ἐν κόσμῳ λεγόντων.

Head of the People was Cleon son of Cleaenetus, who is thought to have done the most to corrupt the people by his impetuous outbursts and was the first person to use bawling and abuse on the platform, and to gird up his cloak before making a public speech, all other persons speaking in orderly fashion.

28.3[14]

The ancient sources, almost all biased against the dominance of the democracy by the least wealthy citizens who followed Cleon, claim that the real-life Cleon was impetuous and pugnacious, and entertained more adventurous and aggressive views than both his contemporaries (e.g. Nicias) and his predecessors (e.g. Pericles) on how Athens should fight the Peloponnesian War.[15] His one defining attribute (according to these sources) was his idiosyncratic personality and daring (at times even daredevil) temper. It is precisely on this distinctive personality trait of Cleon that Aristophanes builds his deep parody against him. Through a blatant distortion of Cleon's real-life trait (his impetuousness), Aristophanes manages to transfer him from the category of politicians to the category of scoundrels, rogues or even public enemies. Unlawfulness, a penchant for conspiracy plotting, betrayal of the city's interests for personal profit, cowardice;[16] all these traits make for a despicable and egocentric individual, unworthy of holding public office.

As if the *pnigos* of the *Acharnians* was the warm-up phase, the following year, in his *Knights*, Aristophanes takes the deep parody against Cleon to its ultimate extremes.[17] By the Lenaea of 424 BCE, Cleon's political influence had considerably advanced, since the military breakthrough on the island of Sphacteria the previous summer (425 BCE) had sent his popularity skyrocketing (and had further incited Aristophanes' appetite to ridicule him on stage).[18] Aristophanes, in order to be able to effectively attack such a popular politician right after a military breakthrough, needed more than a few satirical lines spoken in passing; he needed an entire play. In the *Knights*, Cleon is stripped from his political, social and economic status, and is shifted from the category of victorious generals and preeminent political figures to the category of uncouth, cunning, bootlicking and self-seeking slaves of non-Athenian, barbarian, origin. This is by far the most extended and the most radical recategorization of a parody target within surviving Greek Comedy. It is probable that comparable deep parody was also exercised by Plato the comic against the politically prominent figures of Cleophon and Hyperbolus in his two plays named after these politicians,[19] as well as by Eupolis against Hyperbolus in his *Maricas*.[20] Yet, due to the fragmentary nature of surviving evidence, we cannot confidently establish the extent and precise content of these attacks.

The vulgar Paphlagon, a slave tanner ('βυρσοδέψην', *Knights* 44), who beats up the other slaves and disgustingly flatters his master, serves as a disguise for Cleon, a disguise that becomes transparent to the audience early on in the play – if not through the term 'βυρσοδέψην',[21] then through the reference to the 'τριώβολον' (the jury-payment, recently increased from two obols to three by Cleon, 51), and definitely through the intensely compact four-line allegory of the Pylos events (54–7), which Aristophanes uses to (inaccurately) claim that Cleon had undeservedly been given credit for winning a fight that had already been over when he arrived.

Again, just like in the *pnigos* of the *Acharnians*, the one distinct trait of Cleon that Aristophanes primarily exploits in the *Knights* in order to recategorize him is his unwavering determination, his impetuousness and bold temperament – the temperament which earned him the Pylos triumph in the first place. But additionally, in the *Knights*, Aristophanes exploits a second attribute of Cleon; his non-traditional socio-economic origin. The attack against Cleon, political in its quintessence, encompasses an additional socio-economic perspective. Cleon did not belong to the old, traditional, Athenian aristocracy; he was not a '*eupatridēs*'.[22] But, still, he was wealthy (as was his father before him)[23] and belonged to a relatively new type of plutocrat. This 'new' breed of plutocrats (who had in fact been around for some time already)[24] received a huge boost as a result of the multifaceted social mobility that took place in fifth-century Athens after the Persian wars, mainly (though not exclusively) because of the emphasis on maritime development. Unlike the *eupatridai*, Cleon and this plutocracy (a) lack noble origin (although this does not mean that they are of low social provenance), and (b) derive their rapidly increasing wealth from sources other than land-owning; it comes mainly from trade, navy expeditions, mercenary services (the braggart soldier of Middle and New Comedy is not irrelevant) and craftmanship – hence the tannery theme in Cleon's family (real or imaginary), Hyperbolus' lamp-making business, and Cleophon's lyre-making profession.[25] It is not coincidental that the three main targets (Cleon, Hyperbolus, Cleophon) of Old Comedy's harsh personal invective (and deep parody) have a non-noble, albeit conspicuously wealthy, family background that is closely associated with banausic occupations.

Cleon is not exactly a *nouveau riche*, since, by the time he engaged in politics, he was not a newcomer any more, but he and his ilk had been established (at least one generation back) as a new type of aristocracy, which nonetheless was diametrically different from the old aristocracy, the *eupatridai*. Alexis fr. 94 captures the quintessence of this old, traditional, aristocratic spirit:

ἔστιν δὲ ποδαπὸς τὸ γένος οὗτος; (Β.) πλούσιος.
τούτους δὲ πάντες φασὶν εὐγενεστάτους
εἶναι· πένητας δ' εὐπάτριδας οὐδεὶς ὁρᾷ.

What sort of family is this fellow from? (B.) He is rich.
Everyone agrees that they're the noblest people there are;
no one has ever seen a pauper from a noble background.

If we reverse the last, apophthegmatic verse of Alexis' fragment ('no one has ever seen a pauper from a noble background'), another apophthegm – complementary to the first – is formulated: *no one has ever seen a rich person from a non-noble background*. This is exactly what Cleon was – a well-off individual from a non-noble background. It is against this rigid and long-established ideological/moral/social structure that we need to comprehend the multifaceted 'disturbance'[26] caused by Cleon (and other plutocrats), who manages to transcend his original, non-noble, social rank by accumulating wealth.

Accordingly, in the *Knights*, Aristophanes grossly and preposterously exaggerates this characteristic of Cleon – that is, his non-traditionally aristocratic origin and his non-landowning-based wealth. Thus, he recategorizes him and ends up visualizing him as a barbarian slave of coarse manners.

There is another conspicuous instance where Aristophanes exercises deep parody against Cleon; this is in the second *parabasis* of *Wasps*, where Cleon is memorably described as a grotesque, inhuman monster (1031–6). This is again a case of recategorization (from human to monster), which starts with an ironic allusion to Cleon's teeth (he is 'καρχαρόδους', 'jagged-toothed', 1031) and a pun with the common image of Cleon as a hard-working guard-dog (conflating 'κύων', 'dog', with Cynna the *hetaira*, 1032),[27] before swiftly escalating, rather obscenely, thanks to Aristophanes' uncontrollable imagination.

One year after the *Knights*, in the *Clouds*, Aristophanes subjects another well-known figure, Socrates, to the deep parody process and similarly dedicates an entire play to him. The caricature of the Aristophanic Socrates is an unprecedented amalgam of miscellaneous and heterogeneous characteristics; although a few appear to have been possessed by the real-life Socrates, at least as communicated to us by Plato and Xenophon (and Aristophanes probably expected his audience to recognize them as accurate), most of these characteristics are either general features of the sophists (such as teaching for payment, teaching forensic rhetoric and how to achieve worldly success by winning every argument) or conspicuous features of other contemporary intellectuals (such as asceticism, for which the Pythagoreans already had a reputation).[28] Aristophanes seems drastically to distort and purposely misrepresent Socrates' philosophical interests, religious beliefs and teaching methods, at least if we are to believe the portraits of him in Plato and Xenophon. The Socrates we see on stage is an absurd figure diametrically different from the philosopher accounts of his students. Even though there is a fair percentage of that Socrates in the Aristophanic caricature, in the *Clouds* the grotesque Aristophanic Socrates is not a philosopher, but an amoral charlatan, who rejects tradition and traditional gods (and even his atheism is not consistent),[29] takes interest in cosmology, astronomy, meteorology and geology, and teaches – upon payment – how to speak persuasively, so that one can get away with all wrongdoing.

Albeit on a smaller scale than Cleon and Socrates, Pericles also becomes a target of Aristophanes' deep parody;[30] in *Ach.* 530–2, the popular politician is assimilated to Zeus:

ἐντεῦθεν ὀργῇ Περικλέης οὑλύμπιος
ἤστραπτ', ἐβρόντα, ξυνεκύκα τὴν Ἑλλάδα,
ἐτίθει νόμους ὥσπερ σκόλια γεγραμμένους

And then in wrath Pericles the Olympian,
did lighten and thunder and stir up Greece
and started making laws worded like drinking songs

Pericles' ability to prevail over his opponents and eventually become the dominant political figure in the city is the precise trait that Aristophanes uses to recategorize him,³¹ shifting him from the category of politicians to the category of despotic tyrants. Aristophanes shares this imagery of Pericles as tyrant with Cratinus and Teleclides.³²

The deep parody targets studied so far are either political figures (Cleon and Pericles) or intellectuals (Socrates); yet, not all deep parody cases are of the same nature, extent or intensity (Aristophanes dedicates an entire play to Cleon and Socrates, but only a few lines to Pericles). In the *Thesmophoriazusae* we come across another case of deep parody, albeit of limited nature.³³ Here the target is another intellectual, the tragic poet Agathon.³⁴ Widely known for his musical innovations,³⁵ but also for his exceptionally good looks (Pl. *Smp.* 213c, *TrGF* 39 T 14), Agathon was the young lover of Pausanias of Kerameis (Pl. *Prt.* 315d–e). In the *Thesmophoriazusae*, not only is Agathon portrayed as excessively effeminate (with a list of feminine features ascribed to him: he is 'good-looking, fair-skinned, clean shaven, with a woman's voice, soft, presentable', 'εὐπρόσωπος, λευκός, ἐξυρημένος,/γυναικόφωνος, ἁπαλός, εὐπρεπὴς ἰδεῖν', 191f.), which could account for surface parody,³⁶ but he is actually recategorized (from the category of men to that of women). Upon Agathon's appearance on stage, the Kinsman sees in him not a man, but a woman, and in particular the famous *hetaira* Cyrene: 'I can't see any man there at all, only Cyrene' ("ἐγὼ γὰρ οὐχ ὁρῶ/ἄνδρ' οὐδέν' ἐνθάδ' ὄντα, Κυρήνην δ' ὁρῶ", 97f.). Shortly after, Euripides claims that Agathon could safely attend the women's meeting covertly, because he passes for a woman (184f.). Other scattered references to his effeminacy complement the picture, such as his possession of razors, an article of exclusively female toiletry (218–20). Agathon's pale complexion, conspicuously good looks, and his overall effeminate bearing constituted adequate grounds for Aristophanes to base his parody on and build his comically exaggerated, female portrait of him.³⁷

As far as surface parody is concerned, this is practically omnipresent in Aristophanes. For example, the politically prominent Cleisthenes is regularly ridiculed by Aristophanes simply for being beardless and effeminate; such passages are to be found in most Aristophanic comedies, e.g. *Acharnians* 117–21, *Knights* 1373f., *Clouds* 355, *Birds* 829–31, *Thesmophoriazusae* 235, 574f., 582f., *Lysistrata* 1092, and *Frogs* 57, 422–4. Cratinus also ridicules Cleisthenes' effeminacy (fr. 208).³⁸

Another example of a surface parody target is the general Lamachus in the *Acharnians*. Lamachus is preposterously portrayed as a bellicose warmonger, who treats war irresponsibly, sees it only as a means to make easy money, and hence passionately pursues its continuation. Dicaeopolis epitomizes Lamachus' opportunism with two patronymics; he accuses him of being 'σπουδαρχίδης' ('son of eager-to-work', 595) and 'μισθαρχίδης' ('son of paid-to-work', 597).³⁹ Aristophanes playfully winks to his audience and fakes ignorance regarding the way generals were designated into office (that is, by vote and not by lot; cf. [Arist.] *Ath.* 44.4⁴⁰). Hence, through distortion of reality and exaggeration, he depicts Lamachus as a money-hungry and self-interested general, who undeservingly holds this public office, depriving it from honest, poor citizens.

Other surface parody targets include the tragic poet Euripides in the *Thesmophoriazusae* (mocked *passim* for portraying women as evil creatures), the comic playwrights Magnes, Crates and Cratinus, ridiculed in the *Knights* for having their fame worn out as soon as they got old (520ff.), plus a large number of other (relatively minor) figures elsewhere, such as the citharode Phrynis for his contribution in developing the so-called 'New Music'[41] (*Clouds* 971, cf. Pherecrates fr. 155.14ff.), the tragic poet Acestor for his allegedly Asian ancestry (*Wasps* 1221, *Birds* 31; cf. Metagenes fr. 14), the politician Epicrates for his long, imposing beard (*Ecclesiazusae* 71, Plato Com. fr. 130), the three sons of Hippocrates, nephews of Pericles, for being uneducated and boorish (*Clouds* 1001, cf. Eupolis fr. 112), etc.

There are also some political figures against whom Aristophanes practises both surface and deep parody, such as Cleonymus and Alcibiades. In certain passages from the *Acharnians* (88f., 844) and the *Knights* (956–8, 1290–9) Aristophanes satirizes Cleonymus via grotesque exaggeration (surface parody), mocking his gluttony and his extra-large physique.[42] But elsewhere he deepens his parody and charges Cleonymus with 'ῥιψασπία', 'shield-abandoning',[43] thus shifting him from the category of political figures to the category of cravens and deserters. The reality upon which Aristophanes based his deep parody against him was either the disorderly Athenian retreat from Delium in 424 BCE[44] or a successful case of exemption from military service ('ἀστρατεία') that Cleonymus filed.[45]

As for Alcibiades, he is mocked simply for his lisp in *Wasps* 44–6 (surface parody), but he becomes the recipient of some serious criticism (deep parody) late in the *Frogs* (1422ff.), when Euripides describes him as a betrayer (1427–9): 'I hate the citizen who will prove to be slow to aid his country, quick to do her great harm, resourceful for himself, incompetent for the city' ('μισῶ πολίτην, ὅστις ὠφελεῖν πάτραν/βραδὺς φανεῖται, μεγάλα δὲ βλάπτειν ταχύς,/καὶ πόριμον αὑτῷ, τῇ πόλει δ' ἀμήχανον').[46]

But it is not only humans that Aristophanes subjects to deep and surface parody; gods (and demigods) can be made targets too. Dionysus in the *Frogs* is recategorized from the category of immortal gods to the category of mortals; most memorable is the interrogation scene in the Underworld, where Dionysus is being beaten and proves able to feel pain, a sense unknown to gods by nature (605ff.). As for surface parody, a typical example is the constant derision of Heracles as an insatiate glutton (*Wasps* 60, *Peace* 741, *Birds* 567); a good example is the scene towards the end of *Birds* (1583ff.), where the hungry Heracles is easily bribed with a single meal to reconcile with Peisetaerus and the humans.[47]

Having gone through a number of surface and deep parody examples, let us now turn to germane issues pertaining to the essence, aim, and impact of such parody.[48] First, let us consider the ultimate purpose of each type of parody. Surface parody was essentially meant to generate – rather straightforwardly and uncomplicatedly – pure laughter (perhaps occasionally mixed with a touch of imperceptible contempt or light irony); in other words, to borrow an expression from modern psychology studies, surface parody was meant to induce 'just a joke effect'.[49] But the cases of deep parody are far more complex to decipher, and the parameters of the audience's erudition, familiarity with, and support (political and other) of the target are fundamental in analysing and unravelling each deep parody case. It is plausible that Aristophanic deep parody aimed to derogate and/or cast discredit on the targeted individuals, arouse negative emotions and moral doubts about them, and induce bitter/cynical laughter.[50] Of course, we cannot expect a unanimous reaction to deep (or even surface) parody within Aristophanes' audience. An unknown percentage of the audience will have laughed their hearts out at Socrates teaching for payment, or at Cleon-Paphlagon boasting about being an expert in manipulating the Athenian Demos (*Knights* 710ff.), because they considered these visualizations *funny* (as in *hilariously untrue*). Some, however, may have found them funny precisely because they seemed to express a level of absurd *truth* about the targets; some will not have laughed, but instead frowned, got sceptical, perhaps nodded in agreement, and developed even further their already existing enmity, opposition against and doubts about these figures and their morals. Deep parody had an individualized impact upon every single member of the audience; and these individual reactions largely depended on the distinct personality of each spectator (idiosyncrasy, knowledge, erudition, political beliefs, social origin, level of engagements in public affairs, etc.).

It is vital to remember that fifth-century Athenian audiences were, in their majority, substantially politicized – which means that, for the most part, they had first-hand knowledge and hands-on experience of current political affairs. The same men who voted in the Assembly, participated as jurors in the lawcourts and sat as councillors in the *Boulē*, came together to watch the comedies in the Theatre of Dionysus. Within this intensely politicized climate, Aristophanic deep parody tackled controversial issues, helped raise questions about critical agendas of political and military nature, and subjected people and political behaviours to the watchful microscope of the entire city. Nevertheless, it would be absurd, if not naïve, to believe that Athenian citizens would shape their fundamental political views or radically modify their political attitude according to Aristophanes' or to any other comic poet's (sinister) deep parody.[51] The audience were both politicized to varying levels and belonged to different socio-economic strata. Certain scholars (like Sommerstein and Bowie)[52] make a case for a predominantly elite audience in fifth-century Athens, but others (like Dawson, Wilson and Revermann), with whom I am inclined to agree, argue in favour of a broadly stratified one.[53]

But the regular exposure of Athenian citizens to the experience of dramatic performances resulted in a deep, subconscious training, to the point that the spectators could prove instrumental in making a theatrical performance meaningful and catalytic in unravelling the threads of Aristophanic parody.[54] We can assume that incisive and outstanding parody would indeed have been properly appreciated and rewarded by laughter and applause, while simultaneously remaining to an extent safely confined within the ritually defined context of comic theatre.

Surface parody is a bread-and-butter comic strategy for Aristophanes and, on occasions, could even trigger positive emotions towards the target. But, considering the (political/socio-economic/intellectual) status of the deep parody targets, it appears that Aristophanes meant to 'mess with' these individuals – more or less seriously (since not all deep parody cases are of the same length or significance). Nonetheless, the generally high level of politicization and the active engagement in public affairs that characterized – for the most part – fifth-century Athenian audiences prevented Aristophanes' deep parody from functioning in ways analogous to those described by D'Errico and Poggi in relation to Italy's modern political affairs. The strong politicization of Athenian spectators nicely combined with the long-established and clear-cut demarcation between reality and the variously distorted/grotesquely exaggerated world of comedy. Arguably, the most telltale sign of this fundamental differentiation is how Athenian citizens in 424 BCE appreciated Aristophanes' creativity and originality at the performance of the *Knights* and awarded him the first prize (rightly acknowledging the ingenious allegory), but just a few weeks later, they elected Cleon as one of the Ten Generals for the following year. The ultimate impact of the (Aristophanic) comic stage upon contemporary (fifth-century) reality remains an unprecedented – and, arguably, elusive – amalgam of literary conventions, unmediated engagement with political affairs, ever-changing political climate, and varying audience tastes.

CHAPTER 11
A GRAMMAR OF *PARA PROSDOKIAN*
Dimitrios Kanellakis

Aristophanes' poetic arsenal comprises a plethora of techniques of verbal humour, but 'the comic use of figures and tropes other than metaphors and personifications is much less well studied.'[1] Despite its prominence in Aristophanic comedy – a prominence acknowledged since antiquity[2] – *para prosdokian*, or a joke which provokes laughter because it juxtaposes elements which one would normally not expect to find conjoined, is one of those understudied figures. The surprisingly scarce bibliography on it tends to follow the scholia in an uncritical manner and/or to simply compile and translate individual jokes.[3] This oversight is not only due to the figure's seeming simplicity but also (and most importantly) due to theoretical biases. It is often claimed that 'comedy is notoriously difficult to study and analyze. The creation of taxonomies of jokes or comic techniques risks destroying the very subject it studies.'[4] More emphatically, Storey rejects the theorizing of humour by saying that 'to explain a joke is to kill a joke, and I would argue that the same applies to analyses of humour on a larger scale.'[5] Ruffell discards *para prosdokian* in particular, by maintaining that 'the categories used, such as the *para prosdokian* or "surprise" joke or the classification of comic characters into quasi-Aristotelian types, have passed into the common language of Aristophanic criticism, but this approach is no longer particularly fashionable.'[6] In answer to the latter view, it should go without saying that being 'particularly fashionable' is not a *sine qua non* of scholarship, especially in a discipline called 'Classics'. The first dogma requires addressing more seriously. First, 'not killing the joke' should be the concern of the comedian rather than of the scholar of comedy. Secondly, in most cases, philology is not concerned with explaining whether a passage is funny, but rather how a passage, recognized as funny, (co)operates within a larger textual and non-textual context; in other words, to explain the system of humour, rather than its obvious expressions. At the same time, however, when engaging with temporally or spatially distant texts such as Aristophanic comedies, there are also some linguistically or culturally obscured jokes that demand explanation *per se*. For example, 'I plan nothing wicked; just what Cillicon did' ('οὐδὲν πονηρόν, ἀλλ' ὅπερ καὶ Κιλλικῶν', *Peace* 363) is funny only if we happen to know that Cillicon was a traitor of his city. On such occasions, to explain a joke is not to 'kill it' but to perceive its existence as such. To understand *para prosdokian*, we first need to know what the *prosdokia* was for the audience of classical Athens.

Tracing the historical development of *para prosdokian* as a term is necessary for a systematic study of the figure. An early formulation of the term is found in Aristotle ('*para tēn doxan*', '*paradoxon*'), with reference to oratory and tragedy (*Poet.* 1452a; *Rhet.* 2.1379a, 3.1412a).[7] However, the unexpectedness of which Aristotle speaks is primarily a situational one (i.e. referring to events) rather than a verbal one. In the same way, the historians of the Hellenistic era and late antiquity used *para prosdokian* as a set phrase, first attested in Polybius, to denote unexpected facts.[8] Contemporary rhetoricians, however, appropriated the term as a stylistic one, for poetry (Demetrius) and oratory (Hermogenes, Tiberius). Demetrius, in particular, applied the term to Aristophanes and characterized the figure as a *'charis'* (charm, witty trick).[9] The extensive discussion of the figure in Cicero's *De Oratore* and its popularity among the Hellenistic and medieval scholiasts established the term as a poetic *terminus technicus*.[10] The term now denotes 'a "straight" sequence interrupted by a sudden explosive joke',[11] or more precisely, 'a figure of speech in which the latter part of an idiom, proverb, or well-known expression or formula of words is altered to make an unexpected and humorous ending, as in "If I understand you correctly – it will be the first time ever"'.[12] Despite the technicality of *para prosdokian*, and in order to blur somehow its distinction from situational surprise, it is important to acknowledge that all figures have a morphological and a conceptual aspect, and that their classification by grammarians as either *schēmata lexeōs* (figures of speech) or *schēmata dianoias* (figures of thought) is an arbitrary convention. Irony for example, the *schēma dianoias par excellence*, does have a typology;[13] and conversely, 'hard-core' *schēmata lexeōs* do have a hermeneutic purpose.[14] *Para prosdokian*, in turn, is usually coordinated with situational surprise but it is the textual markers that make it a figure. As Berk aptly identifies, the figure emerges more as a *side effect* in episodes that contain constant change;[15] it comes to formalize a dramatic shift. For instance, when Carion announces the cure of Wealth, Chremylus's wife greets him thus: 'By Hecate, I want to drape around your neck/a string of loaves/for delivering such good news' ('νὴ τὴν Ἑκάτην, κἀγὼ δ' ἀναδῆσαι βούλομαι/εὐαγγέλιά σε κριβανιτῶν ὁρμαθῷ/τοιαῦτ' ἀπαγγείλαντα,' *Wealth* 764-6).[16] This *para prosdokian* replacement of a wreath (the typical accoutrement of bearers of good news) by a 'string of loaves' is dramatically justified in light of the preceding reassurance by Carion that from now on bread will exist in abundance (762f.).

To identify *para prosdokian* jokes within a text requires that we first know what the *prosdokia* is – what the receiver would normally expect to encounter. However, the horizon of expectations of an ancient audience is only partially retrievable. *Para prosdokian* jokes reverse oral tradition (idioms, tales, fables, proverbs and proverbial expressions, everyday gossip), literary tradition (any genre, with tragedy being the main interlocutor of Aristophanic comedy) and logical sequences. Of these sources, only the latter is fully accessible. Literary tradition is known to us insofar as the surviving texts permit; oral tradition and everyday life are known even less, indeed only to the degree that they are embodied (or assumed to be embodied) in the surviving texts. The Hellenistic and medieval scholia offer important aid in bridging this gap but are full of rhetorical biases, ostentatiousness, anachronisms and inaccuracies. Therefore, we need to content ourselves with the fact that we can only restore *some* of the jokes and mostly on the basis of logic, as in the following example. In *Wealth* 26f., Chremylus admits his preference for Carion over his other servants: 'I consider you the most trustworthy of my slaves, and the most larcenous' ('τῶν ἐμῶν γὰρ οἰκετῶν/πιστότατον ἡγοῦμαί σε καὶ κλεπτίστατον.'). The last word appears *para prosdokian* instead of a positive quality expected after 'trustworthy', which would probably be 'well-disposed' (cf. Lys. 13.18.6).[17]

Linguistically, the figure occurs when the semantic load of the second part of a structure (word, phrase, or sentence) contradicts the semantic load of the first part, motivating the reader or the listener to reinterpret the first part in the direction of the latter part. 'Because the direction of *erasure and replacement* is from the modifier to the head-word (it is the modifier that does the erasing and the replacing), readers feel an emphasis of meaning placed upon the modifier.'[18] To give an example using semantic markers (componential analysis),[19] consider what Meton says in *Birds* 995:

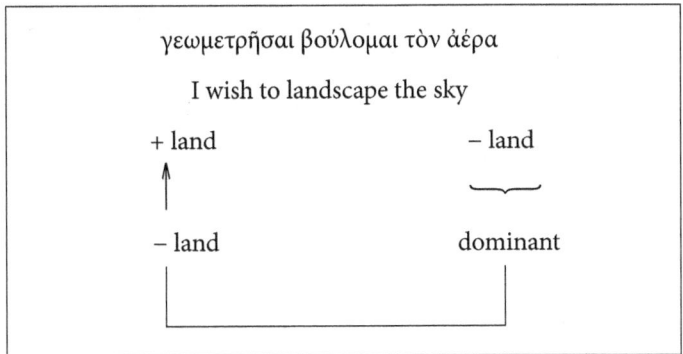

Meton's geometry is thus equated to 'airometry'. This example confirms Berk's suggestion that, for a *para prosdokian* not to be degraded into mere nonsense, it should retain some link with reality,[20] whatever the dramatic 'reality' of a play is – in this case, that Meton is a geometer, but the implication is that he is a fraudulent one.

A second, less frequent group of *para prosdokian* jokes depend on the semantic contradiction between the word given and the word expected, rather than between two given words. In *Peace* 378, for example, the invocation 'πρὸς τῶν κρεῶν' ('by the roasts!') is a *para prosdokian* for 'πρὸς τῶν θεῶν' ('by the gods!'), exploiting the phonological resemblance of the two words. But even in this case, 'πρὸς τῶν θεῶν' itself appears two lines earlier, in order for the pun to be clear. That *para prosdokian* should be sought in the last part of a structure is not a dogma, but a statistical observation. In fact, there are some exceptions in this scheme. For example, when the first part of a well-known idiom is changed, one perceives the *para prosdokian* of the whole structure in retrospect, soon after, as in 'meowing up the wrong tree'. In *Birds* 1476, the chorus mock Cleonymus as 'δειλὸν καὶ μέγα' ('timorous and great'), instead of the formulaic 'δεινόν καὶ μέγα' ('vigorous and great').[21] In most cases, however, it is a matter of common sense that in order to unexpectedly reverse something, that something, the point of reference, needs to be known in advance. Consider the following two examples:

ἔτει τετάρτῳ δ' εἰς τὰ βασίλει' ἤλθομεν·
ἀλλ' εἰς ἀπόπατον ᾤχετο στρατιὰν λαβών,
κἄχεζεν ὀκτὼ μῆνας ἐπὶ χρυσῶν ὀρῶν.

So, after three years we got to the royal palace,
but the King had gone off to a latrine with an army,
and he stayed shitting for eight months upon the Golden Hills.

Acharnians 80–2

The scholia suggest that 'a latrine' has humorously replaced 'a battle', but the latter could not have actually been expected, because 'with an army' appears afterwards. What *is* a *para prosdokian*, instead, is 'with an army'. Given that the Persian king went 'to take a shit', one would expect something like 'he took a sponge' (cf. *Frogs* 483), but he instead took his entire army. If the principle that the second part overwrites the first part is true, then instead of a 'shitty expedition', the poet rather projects the imagery of an 'epic shitting'.

In the next example, Carion mocks the chorus for their old age:

ἐν τῇ σορῷ νυνὶ λαχὸν τὸ γράμμα σου δικάζειν,
σὺ δ' οὐ βαδίζεις; ὁ δὲ Χάρων τὸ ξύμβολον δίδωσιν.

In the coffin; your turn has now come to serve there.
Won't you go? Charon is offering you a pass.

Wealth 277

The imagery comes from the judicial system, according to which the citizens registered as potential jurors by being assigned a letter from α to κ, and sat in court when their letter-class was summoned by lot, receiving a token for their service. It is clear that 'in the coffin' has replaced 'in the court' and that this replacement is intended to be funny. Technically speaking, however, the *para prosdokian* can only be perceived as such when the judicial vocabulary (coming last) interrupts the deathly imagery, rather than vice versa. After hearing 'in the coffin', one would expect something like 'Charon summons you' (cf. *Lysistrata* 606). The mixed imagery of death and the lawcourts is extended into the next line; here, Charon *gives* a token rather than *receiving* a coin as we might expect, and Charon would be expected to give a pomegranate, if anything, rather than a token.[22]

Some *para prosdokian* jokes are defined in relation to the performance. Towards the end of *Wealth*, an old woman arrives and the chorus addresses her with 'ὦ μειρακίσκη' ('hey lassie', 963), either as an ironic response to her addressing them as 'old men' four lines earlier (959),[23] or more likely, as a reference to her intonation and voice quality.[24] This address is not a verbally marked *para prosdokian*, in the sense of 'μειρακίσκη' contradicting a preceding word; that the woman is old becomes evident from the moment she enters and the audience sees her mask. The incongruity between her appearance and the chorus' address signifies the *para prosdokian* on this occasion. The meta-dramatic or extra-dramatic context is also employed in some cases. To celebrate the restoration of peace, Trygaeus asks his slave to sacrifice a sheep on stage:

O   οὐχ ἥδεται δήπουθεν Εἰρήνη σφαγαῖς,
        οὐδ' αἱματοῦται βωμός.
T   ἀλλ' εἴσω φέρων

θύσας τὰ μηρί' ἐξελὼν δεῦρ' ἔκφερε,
χοὔτω τὸ πρόβατον τῷ χορηγῷ σῴζεται.

Slave Peace takes no pleasure in slaughter, nor is her altar bloodied.
Trygaeus All right, take it inside and sacrifice it, then remove the thigh pieces and bring them out here; that way our producer gets to keep his lamb!

Peace 1019–22

The justification that Peace is not happy with sacrifices on her altar is merely poetic licence for the sake of economy (cf. *Birds* 1056f., *Lysistrata* 189f.), given that the real cult of Peace did feature sacrifices.[25] Indeed, within the fiction of the play, Trygaeus still calls for it to be sacrificed, but inside, out of sight of the audience – before breaking the 'fourth wall' and acknowledging that the sheep will be 'saved'. The thigh pieces he orders brought out by the slave will be substitutes, apparently because the *chorēgos* is a cheapskate. Even though Aristophanes compromises with this solution, he does not miss the opportunity to publicly mock his own *chorēgos* for his strict budgeting. To 'save this sheep for the funder' is a sharp, embarrassing, metatheatrical *para prosdokian*.

To draw a typology of *para prosdokian* requires gathering as many instances as possible. Here I confine myself to four plays; *Acharnians*, *Peace*, *Thesmophoriazusae* and *Wealth*. A nearly exhaustive catalogue of the *para prosdokian* jokes in these plays is presented at the end of this chapter (Tables 1–4).[26] By 'typology' I mean the morphological, semantic and pragmatic components of the figure that regularly appear. Which grammatical, syntactical and metrical forms are used, and what kind of vocabulary? In which parts of comedy does *para prosdokian* occur, and by what kind of characters is it employed?

Starting with the linguistic width of application, i.e. the linguistic structure-levels in which *para prosdokian* is observed, the vast majority of the occurrences of the figure (> 85%) are found in phrases or small sentences. Only a few cases in the material examined occur within single words. At *Acharnians* 336, when Dicaeopolis threatens that he will slay the charcoal-basket, the chorus exclaim, 'Then you'll kill this, my coeval, my coal-eague?' ('ἀπολεῖς ἄρ' ὁμήλικα τόνδε φιλανθρακέα;') instead of 'colleague' or 'beloved' ('φιλάνθρωπον'). At *Acharnians* 751, the Megarian complains about everyday life in his city; they 'have starvation-contests by the fireplace' ('διαπεινᾶμες ἀεὶ ποττὸ πῦρ') instead of 'drinking contests' ('διαπίνομεν'). In such instances of single-word *para prosdokian*, the unexpected meaning is constructed at the level of morphemes and phonemes. The poet coins words ('φιλανθρακέα', 'διαπεινᾶμες') that display a sufficient phonetic overlap with the 'expected' words ('φιλάνθρωπον', 'διαπίνομεν'). Not just any word starting with *phil-* or *dia-* would capture the pun; more phonetic overlap is needed. A single-word *para prosdokian* is too short for the mind to process – the semantic complexity of the 'acoustic image' being disproportionate to its duration – and requires an alertness which is impossible in terms of performed (oral) speech.[27] This also explains why 'φιλανθρακέα' is preceded by 'ὁμήλικα' and 'διαπεινᾶμες' is followed by 'by the fireplace'; technically, the *para prosdokian* occurs only within the coined words, but some additional interpretative hints are necessary.

At the other end, there are examples of *para prosdokian* extending over wider sentences and periods. *Acharnians* 68–75, though an underappreciated passage, constitutes the most elaborate *para prosdokian* in the play.[28] The fake ambassador describes a fictitious mission to Persia and Dicaeopolis replies in an analogous manner:

Π καὶ δῆτ' ἐτρυχόμεσθα τῶν Καϋστρίων
  πεδίων ὁδοιπλανοῦντες ἐσκηνημένοι,
  ἐφ' ἁρμαμαξῶν μαλθακῶς *κατακείμενοι*,
  ἀπολλύμενοι.
Δ   σφόδρα γὰρ ἐσῳζόμην ἐγὼ
  παρὰ τὴν ἔπαλξιν ἐν φορυτῷ *κατακείμενος*.
π ξενιζόμενοι δὲ πρὸς βίαν ἐπίνομεν
  ἐξ ὑαλίνων ἐκπωμάτων καὶ χρυσίδων
  ἄκρατον οἶνον ἡδύν.

A And we truly wore ourselves out wayfaring through Castrian plains, *reclining* on the soft canopies of a four-wheel carriage, simply perishing!
D Right... and I was safe and sound, *reclining* on the rubbish by the ramparts!
A And when they regaled us, they forced us to drink fine unmixed wine from goblets of crystal and gold.

Acharnians 68–75

The dipole 'we suffered in luxury – I rejoiced in poverty' is actually a *para prosdokian* chiasmus; properly, happy feelings should be joined to pleasurable activities, and discomfort with harsh activities. However, the surprise lies not only in the contradiction within each of the statements, but also in their sequence. Imitating the ambassador's attitude, Dicaeopolis responds with an ironic 'γάρ' ('right...', 71) as if he agreed,[29] and uses the same word as they do to describe his own condition ('κατακείμενοι', 'κατακείμενος', 70, 72), even though he means the exact opposite; they are resting, while he is standing guard. The ambassador in turn, as if he does not perceive the irony, continues his narration even more passionately (emphatic 'δέ', 73) and provocatively ('they forced us to drink', 'πρὸς βίαν ἐπίνομεν', 73), prolonging this game of 'who makes fun of whom'.

In terms of grammar and syntax, the core of the figure, i.e. the unexpected meaning, often lies in a noun (≈ 60% of the time), which in most instances operates as an object and seldom as a prepositional phrase (e.g. *Acharnians* 480, 732) or a complement (e.g. *Thesmophoriazusae* 532, *Wealth* 27). Subjects are reasonably avoided for *para prosdokian*, since they usually come at the beginning of sentences and thus have nothing preceding to contradict. Indeed, the rare times when a *para prosdokian* noun is the subject, it is always reserved for the end (e.g. *Peace* 363). Occasionally (≈ 20%), the figure lies in an adjective (e.g. *Acharnians* 909, *Peace* 823, *Thesmophoriazusae* 131f., *Wealth* 706) and equally frequently in a verb (e.g. *Wealth* 165, 372, 972). Three quarters of the identified instances are metrically highlighted, appearing either at the end of a line (e.g. *Acharnians*

464) or within an *antilabē* (e.g. *Thesmophoriazusae* 57) or before a strong internal pause (e.g. *Wealth* 963). The common feature in all these methods is pausing, which enables the mind to process the joke. Other metrical devices employed for emphasis are alliteration (e.g. *Peace* 898) and rhyme (e.g. *Acharnians* 69–71).[30]

With regard to the vocabulary preferred, three groups alone represent more than half of the *para prosdokian* instances listed. Unsurprisingly, scatology is one of them (e.g. *Acharnians* 80–2, discussed above). A second distinctive group of *para prosdokian* vocabulary conveys gluttony and wine drinking. The Megarian urges his hungry daughters to 'listen with your full starvation' instead of the formulaic 'listen with your full attention' (*Acharnians* 733, 'ἀκούετε δή, ποτέχετ' ἐμὶν τὰν γαστέρα' instead of 'τὸν νοῦν ἐμοί');[31] in reporting the cure of Wealth, Carion says to Chremylus' wife:

καὶ πρίν σε κοτύλας ἐκπιεῖν οἴνου δέκα,
ὁ Πλοῦτος, ὦ δέσποιν', ἀνειστήκει βλέπων·

And before you could even drink five pints of wine,
mistress, our Wealth stood up and could see.

Wealth 737f.

According to the scholia, the proverbial expression equivalent to 'in the blink of an eye' was 'before you could even say a word' or 'before you could even spit' (cf. Menander *Perikeiromene* 392; 'πρὶν πτύσαι'). The *para prosdokian* lies not only in the distortion of a known formula but also in the distortion of its diminutive intention; it is not just that 'a word' or 'a spit' has been replaced by 'a bottle of wine', but '*one* word' or '*one* spit' has been replaced by '*ten* bottles of wine'. Ten *kotylai* is about five pints, which is a rather extreme quantity for drinking at once (Chremylus's wife starts drinking at 645).[32]

Sexual vocabulary could hardly be left off the list. Consider the following examples from *Thesmophoriazusae*. The Kinsman expresses his sexual excitement for the chorus of maidens led by Agathon:

ὡς ἡδὺ τὸ μέλος, ὦ πότνιαι Γενετυλλίδες,
καὶ θηλυδριῶδες καὶ κατεγλωττισμένον
καὶ μανδαλωτόν, ὥστ' ἐμοῦ γ' ἀκροωμένου
ὑπὸ τὴν ἕδραν αὐτὴν ὑπῆλθε γάργαλος.

Holy Genetyllides, what a pretty song!
How breastial and tongue-gagged
and deep-kissed! Just hearing it
brought a tingle to my very butt!

Thesmophoriazusae 130–3

The first line anticipates a high-toned vocabulary to match Agathon's tragic diction (we expect words like 'μειλίχιος' ('gentle'), 'σεπτός' ('sacred'), *vel sim.*), so that all three following adjectives, and especially the striking coinage 'θηλυδριῶδες' ('breastial', 'womanly', modelled on 'θηριῶδες', 'bestial'), appear *para prosdokian*. The final line, too, must be a *para prosdokian* appropriation of Archilochus fr. 191 ('What a desire for love coiled within my heart!', 'τοῖος γὰρ φιλότητος ἔρως ὑπὸ καρδίην ἐλυσθείς'); 'love' has become 'tingle' and 'within my heart' has become 'within my butt'. Soon after, Agathon offers his robe to Kinsman to wear and the latter comments, 'By Aphrodite, it smells sweetly of a little-dick' ('νὴ τὴν Ἀφροδίτην, ἡδύ γ' ὄζει ποσθίου', 254), with the last word standing *para prosdokian* for 'μύρου' ('perfume'). Even though 'ἡδύ' is occasionally used for sex,[33] its principal meaning is for a sweet smell or taste, appropriate enough for the expected perfume. In light of Ar. fr. 613 ('wine sweet to drink, the milk of Aphrodite'), this could be the smell of mellow wine. Instead, Agathon's robe smells of 'a little-dick', i.e. his own penis – probably an allusion to masturbation.[34] Here 'ποσθίου' must be an affectionate diminutive of 'πόσθη' ('sweetie penis'), rather than a mocking one ('small penis') – the idea being that by wearing Agathon's clothes, the Kinsman again acquires Agathon's queerness and yearns for male genitals.[35]

In terms of structure, the figure usually occurs in the prologue and the episodes, occasionally in the *parodos* (in its spoken portion), and rarely in the *parabasis* (only twice, with chanted anapaests) or the lyric parts (*Peace* 864, *Thesmophoriazusae* 529–30). This observation supports Berk's theory that *para prosdokian* is connected to dramatic developments, rather than an irrelevant interpolation. Given that the progression of the plot happens precisely in these parts – the prologue introduces a surprising 'great idea' and the episodes feature surprising arguments between the characters – it seems legitimate to say that *para prosdokian* is coordinated with dramatic surprise, and that they go together emphasizing one another. As for the general avoidance of *para prosdokian* in the lyric parts, this can be attributed to the music and the dancing, which would distract the audience from focusing carefully on language. Moreover, with regards to the dispersion of *para prosdokian* jokes, there is a tendency for them to gather in the first half of the play (prologue and first episode) and progressively reduce towards the end. This tendency can be attributed to the audience's ability more easily to notice details (linguistic, scenic, or others) at the beginning of a play. After some point, mental alertness naturally falls and attention is paid to the plot itself; this is a reason why the *exodus* is conventionally a formulaic, unrefined carnival – so that little thinking is required. Being a challenging task to decode, *para prosdokian* towards the end of a play would go to waste. Of course, this is not to say that Aristophanes read cognitive theories before composing his plays, but that he was poetically perspicacious. Finally, a noticeable feature is the occasional accumulation of the figure, i.e. consecutive *para prosdokian* jokes (*Acharnians* 68–75, 119f., 255f., 732f., *Thesmophoriazusae* 130–3, 935–7) aiming at inducing non-stop laughter.

Turning to the characters who use *para prosdokian*, we notice that more than half of these jokes are said by the protagonists (Dicaeopolis, Trygaeus, the Kinsman and Chremylus). Even though these characters are not equally or exclusively *eirōnes* – in fact, their plans for private treaties, neglecting the orders of Zeus, and invading secret rituals rather signify *alazōneia* – the employment of the figure is clearly ironic.[36] First, the protagonist is often 'ψευδόμενος μὴ ἀγνοῶν' ('pretending ignorance', Aristotle *Eth. Eud.* 1234a). For example, when listening to the fake ambassadors' story, Dicaeopolis pretends not to understand that these men are lying, as discussed earlier. Secondly, *para prosdokian* is used ironically in the sense of *prospoiēsis epi to elatton* ('pretence in the form of understatement').[37] For instance, in the parodic 'my heart will go on, even without chervil' ('ὦ θύμ', ἄνευ σκάνδικος ἐμπορευτέα', *Acharnians* 480), suffering has been degraded into not having vegetables. Similarly, Dicaeopolis pretends to have been scared by Lamachus' shield, which in reality bears a Gorgon, i.e. a typical symbol of ferocity and means of intimidating the enemy,[38] but Dicaeopolis calls it a *Mormōn*, i.e. a female bogey-monster evoked by nurses to frighten the children (*Acharnians* 582).[39] Some further examples of minimizing *para prosdokian* are the coarse homophobic addresses by Dicaeopolis and the Kinsman to Cleisthenes and Agathon respectively (*Acharnians* 119-20, *Thesmophoriazusae* 50, 57). As for the *alazōn* function, the attribution of *para prosdokian* jokes to such characters could only be argued for the case of the fake ambassadors in *Acharnians*. These men are certainly 'impostors' (62f., 87, 109, 135), and do employ the figure as we saw earlier (68-71, 7-75, 81f.). Even in that case, however, the figure is explicitly described as an ironic manner of speaking – it is 'κατάγελων' (76). At any rate, *para prosdokian* usually remains the protagonists' bailiwick, over and above any Aristotelian character types.

To sum up, a typical *para prosdokian* joke occurs within a phrase or short sentence. It is a semantically distinct noun, adjective or verb, often with gastronomic, sexual or scatological meaning, and is metrically highlighted. It occurs almost exclusively in the spoken parts of a comedy, it is often said by the protagonist and serves a wide range of ironic and buffoonish functions.

Let us lastly examine how Aristophanes' use of *para prosdokian* changed over the course of his career. The first observation is quantitative; slightly more instances of the figure exist in *Acharnians*, but the plays otherwise display almost the same number of *para prosdokian* jokes – a striking coincidence.[40] Since there is no substantial change in numbers, we shall focus on the qualitative differences. In fact, not a single *para prosdokian* in *Wealth* is of the type that prevails in *Acharnians*. In terms of form, the poet moves from mainly employing noun-based *para prosdokian* to mainly employing verb-based *para prosdokian*. I would argue that noun-based *para prosdokian* are more imaginative and 'redemptive' than verb-based *para prosdokian*, in the sense that the former *adorn* the world of comic fantasy by importing into it some familiar *objects* (pots, vegetables, animals), whereas the latter *undermine* the world of comic fantasy by projecting into it familiar *behaviours* (to be corrupt, to steal, to judge). Other factors also suggest a weakening of the figure. The majority of *para prosdokian* jokes in *Acharnians* are (a) metrically highlighted, (b) often accumulated in consecutive lines, (c) placed early in the play in view of the audience's readiness to decode them, (d) serving political, social, or literal criticism, (e) said by the protagonist, thus gaining authority. In *Wealth*, on the other hand, (a) emphasis with internal pauses and alliterations is rare, while a fair amount of *para prosdokian* jokes do not even appear at the end of the line, (b) consecutive *para prosdokian* jokes appear only once (*Wealth* 277-8), (c) there is a reasonable

Aristophanic Humour

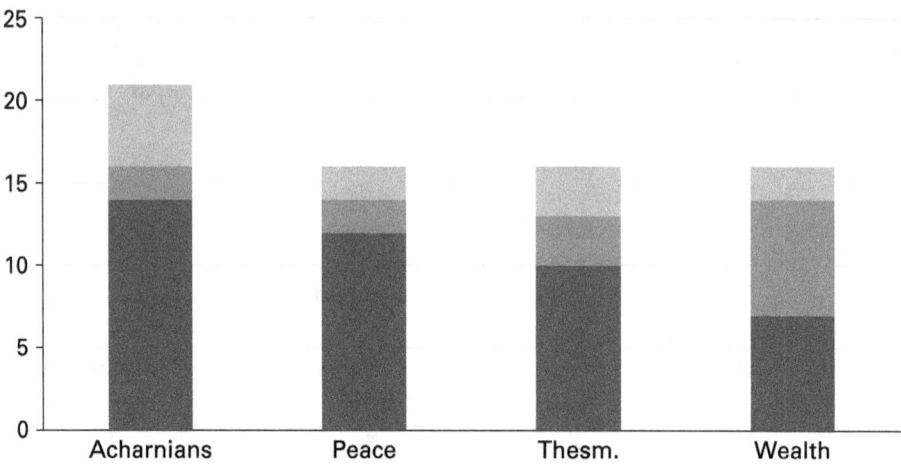

Figure 11.1 Distribution of *para prosdokian* across the four plays (according to Tables 1–4 below).

dispersion of the jokes across several parts of the play, but this does not facilitate the audience's comprehension, (d) there are no *para prosdokian* jokes serving political criticism, and social criticism is restricted to a single case (*Wealth* 165); the figure is used almost exclusively for personal abuse, (e) the slave Carion says as many *para prosdokian* jokes as his master, challenging (and rather conquering) his comic primacy.

While it might be tempting to explain, say, that *Wealth* proves exceptional in this respect since it is our sole example of Aristophanic Middle Comedy, we need to remind ourselves that Aristophanes' later period is poorly represented through the extant comedies, and any late developments probably arose gradually; in fact, *Thesmophoriazusae* already attests to some of the changes in the use of the figure. Less political, less emphasized, less imaginative, less dramatically needed, *para prosdokian* seems to become less *para prosdokian* over time. This is not some symptom of the wider decay of Old Comedy; it should rather be viewed, from a synchronic perspective, as a symptom of Aristophanes' never-ending poetic experimentation and persistence in having a stylistic signature of his own.

A Grammar of *Para Prosdokian*

Tables 1–4 *Para prosdokian* jokes in *Acharnians, Peace, Thesmophoriazusae* and *Wealth*.[41] What the expectation would be for each case, according to various commentators or myself, appears parallel to the original text.

Line	Acharnians	Expected
68–75	ΠΡ: **καὶ δῆτ' ἐτρυχόμεσθα διὰ Καϋστρίων πεδίων ὁδοιπλανοῦντες ἐσκηνημένοι,** ἐφ' ἁρμαμαξῶν μαλθακῶς κατακείμενοι, **ἀπολλύμενοι.** ΔΙΚ: σφόδρα γὰρ ἐσῳζόμην ἐγὼ **παρὰ τὴν ἔπαλξιν ἐν φορυτῷ κατακείμενος.** ΠΡ: ξενιζόμενοι δὲ **πρὸς βίαν** ἐπίνομεν ἐξ ὑαλίνων ἐκπωμάτων καὶ χρυσίδων ἄκρατον οἶνον ἡδύν. A: **And we truly wore ourselves out a-wayfaring through Castrian plains,** under canopies, reclining softly on litters, simply **perishing!** D: I must have been on easy street, then – reclining **in the garbage by the ramparts!** A: And when they regaled us **they forced us** to drink fine unmixed wine from goblets of crystal and gold.	[Elements in bold (sufferings) should be together; non-bold elements (pleasures) should be together.] (For the last sentence, see Rogers 1910: *ad loc.*)
81f.	ἀλλ' εἰς ἀπόπατον ᾤχετο **στρατιὰν** λαβών, κἄχεζεν ὀκτὼ μῆνας ἐπὶ χρυσῶν ὀρῶν. The King had gone off with **an army** to a latrine, and he stayed shitting for eight months upon the Golden Hills.	'σπογγιάν' (*Frogs* 483) 'a sponge'
119	ὦ θερμόβουλον **πρωκτὸν ἐξυρημένε** O **shaver** of a hot **and horny arsehole**	'σπλάγχνον' (Eur. fr.585) 'spirit…soul' (See scholia and Starkie 1909: *ad loc.*)
120	τοιόνδε γ' ὦ πίθηκε τὸν **πώγων'** ἔχων With such **a beard,** you monkey	'τὴν πυγήν' (Archil. 187, Aesop 81 Perry) 'an arse'
255	κἀκποιήσεται **γαλᾶς** [He will] get upon you a litter of **kittens**	'παῖδας/θυγατέρας' 'kids/daughters' (See scholia, Starkie 1909, Rogers 1910, and Olson 2002: *ad loc.*)
256	σοῦ μηδὲν ἥττους **βδεῖν** As good as you are **at farting**	(anything graceful)
336	ὁμήλικα τόνδε **φιλανθρακέα** My coeval, my **coal-eague?**	'φιλάνθρωπον' 'colleague' (See Olson 2002: *ad loc.*)

Line	Acharnians	Expected
464	ἀφαιρήσει με τὴν **τραγῳδίαν** You'll make off with my whole **tragedy**!	'τὴν οὐσίαν' 'property'
480	ὦ θύμ' **ἄνευ σκάνδικος** ἐμπορευτέα My soul, **without chervil** must you venture forth.	'κακοῖσιν ὅμως ἄτλητα πεπονθώς' (Thgn. 1029) *vel sim.* 'though you have suffered unendurable ills'
582	ἀπένεγκέ μου τὴν **μορμόνα** Please, take that **scare**-face away from me!	'Γοργόνα' 'Gorgon' (See Olson 2002: *ad loc.*)
732	ἄμβατε ποττὰν **μᾶδδαν** Go up the steps there **for bread**	'θύραν' 'towards the door' (See Olson 2002: *ad loc.*)
733	ἀκούετε δή, ποτέχετ' ἐμὶν **τὰν γαστέρα** Now listen, give me your undivided **bellies**	'τὸν νοῦν' 'attention' (See scholia, Starkie 1909 and Olson 2002: *ad loc.*)
751	**διαπεινᾶμες** ἀεὶ ποττὸ πῦρ We're always in front of the fire, **fasting**.	'διαπίνομεν' 'feasting' (See scholia *ad loc.*)
904	**συκοφάντην** ἔξαγε **An informer** ... export him.	(any commercial product)
909	ΒΟΙ.: μικκός γα μᾶκος οὗτος. ΔΙΚ.: ἀλλ' ἅπαν **κακόν**. B: He's not very big. D: But every inch of him's **bad**!	'καλόν' (cf. Eur. *El.* 1003) 'fine' (See Olson 2002: *ad loc.*)

Line	Peace	Expected
7	μὰ τὸν Δί', ἀλλ' ἐξαρπάσας ὅλην **ἐνέκαψε** περικυλίσας τοῖν ποδοῖν. Oh no; it only grabbed it, trundled it with its feet, and **scoffed** it whole!	'ἀπέρριψεν' *vel sim.* 'threw away'
123	κολλύραν μεγάλην καὶ **κόνδυλον** ὄψον ἐπ' αὐτῇ. A great big bun, topped off with a nice **knuckle sandwich**.	'κάνδυλον'/'κάνδαυλον' 'dessert' (See Sharpley 1905 and Platnauer 1964: *ad loc.*)
300	ἡμῖν αὖ σπάσαι πάρεστιν **ἀγαθοῦ δαίμονος** Now is our chance to hoist **one for the Good Spirit**!	'τοὺς λίθους'/'τὴν Εἰρήνην' 'the rocks'/'Peace' (See Sharpley 1905: *ad loc.*)

A Grammar of *Para Prosdokian*

Line	Peace	Expected
308	τὴν θεῶν πασῶν μεγίστην καὶ φιλα**μπελωτάτην**. The greatest of all goddesses, and the one most friendly to **vines**.	'φιλανθρωποτάτην' 'the people' (See Paley 1873 and Platnauer 1964: *ad loc.*)
363	οὐδὲν πονηρόν, ἀλλ' **ὅπερ καὶ Κιλλικῶν**. Nothing wrong, just **the same as Cillicon**.	'πᾶν ἀγαθὸν'/'ὅπερ καὶ [name of a true benefactor]' 'the best'/'the same as Mr [benefactor]' (See scholia *ad loc.*)
378	ναί, πρὸς τῶν **κρεῶν** Please do, by the **meat**	'θεῶν' 'gods' (See scholia *ad loc.*)
425	οἴμ', ὡς ἐλεήμων εἴμ' ἀεὶ **τῶν χρυσίδων**. Uh oh, I've always had such a soft spot for **gold plate!**	'ἀνθρώπων'/'ἱκετῶν'/'πόλεως' *vel sim.* 'humans'/'prayers'/'the city' (See scholia, Paley 1873, Platnauer 1964 and Olson 1998: *ad loc.*)
474	οὐδὲν δεόμεθ', ὤνθρωπε, τῆς σῆς **μορμόνος**. We want none of your **bogy**-blazon, sir!	'γοργόνος' 'Gorgon' (See Olson 1998: *ad loc.*)
708	ταύτῃ ξυνοικῶν ἐκποιοῦ σαυτῷ **βότρυς** Set up house with her in the countryside and beget yourself a brood of **grapes**	'παῖδας', 'τέκνα' 'babies' (See Paley 1873, Sharpley 1905 and Olson 1998: *ad loc.*)
756f.	ἑκατὸν δὲ κύκλῳ κεφαλαὶ **κολάκων** οἰμωξομένων ἐλιχμῶντο And all around his pate licked a hundred heads of damned **flatterers**	'ὀφέων' 'snakes' (See Sharpley 1905 and Olson 1998: *ad loc.*)
821–3	ἀπὸ τοὐρανοῦ 'φαίνεσθε κακοήθεις πάνυ, ἐντευθενὶ δὲ πολύ τι **κακοηθέστεροι**. From my heavenly vantage you seemed a very bad lot, but from down here you seem a far sight **worse!**	'καλοήθεις' 'better'
864	εὐδαιμονέστερος φανεῖ τῶν **Καρκίνου στροβίλων** You'll seem luckier than **Carcinus' whirligigs!**	'ἀνθρώπων πάντων' *vel sim.* 'every other man' (See Sommerstein 1985: *ad loc.*)
898	παίειν, ὀρύττειν, πὺξ ὁμοῦ καὶ τῷ **πέει** Bang and gouge with fist and **prick**	'σκέλει' 'kick' (See scholia and Platnauer 1964: *ad loc.*)

Aristophanic Humour

Line	Peace	Expected
1022	χοὔτω τὸ πρόβατον **τῷ χορηγῷ** σῴζεται That way **our producer** gets to keep his lamb!	'τῷ πένητι' *vel sim.* 'a poor man' (See Rogers 1913 and Starkie 1909: lxvii f.)
1065	συνθήκας πεποίησθ' ἄνδρες χαροποῖσι **πιθήκοις** You have struck a pact with glaring-eyed **monkeys**	'λέουσι' 'lions' (See Platnauer 1964: *ad loc.*)
1116	τὴν Σίβυλλαν **ἔσθιε** Go **eat** your Sibyl!	'αἰτοῦ' 'ask' (See Starkie 1909: lxvii–lxviii)

Line	Thesmophoriazusae	Expected
50	ΘΕ. μέλλει γὰρ ὁ καλλιεπὴς Ἀγάθων πρόμος ἡμέτερος – ΚΗ. μῶν **βινεῖσθαι**; S. For that mellifluous Agathon, our champion, prepares— K. To **get fucked**?	'ᾄδειν'/'χορεύειν' *vel sim.* 'to sing'/'dance'
57	ΘΕ. καὶ χοανεύει. – ΚΗ. καὶ **λαικάζει** S. Funnelling metal—K. And **sucking cocks**.	(any craft-term)
130–3	ὡς ἡδὺ τὸ μέλος, ὦ πότνιαι Γενετυλλίδες, καὶ **θηλυδριῶδες** καὶ **κατεγλωττισμένον** καὶ **μανδαλωτόν**, ὥστ' ἐμοῦ γ' ἀκροωμένου ὑπὸ τὴν **ἕδραν** αὐτὴν ὑπῆλθε **γάργαλος**. Holy Genetyllides, what a pretty song! How **feministic** and **tongue-gagged** and **deep-kissed**! Just hearing it brought a **tingle** to my very **butt**!	'καὶ ἱερὸν καὶ μειλίχιον καὶ σεπτόν' *vel sim.* 'holy, gentle and venerable' 'ἔρως – καρδίην' (Archil. 191) 'passion – soul'
254	νὴ τὴν Ἀφροδίτην, ἡδύ γ' ὄζει **ποσθίου**. By Aphrodite, it has a nice scent of **weenie**.	'μύρου'/'οἴνου' *vel sim.* 'perfume'/'wine' (See scholia, Rogers 1904, Prato 2001 and Austin and Olson 2004: *ad loc.*)
290	καὶ τὴν θυγατέρα Χοιρίον ἀνδρός μοι τυχεῖν **πλουτοῦντος**, ἄλλως δ' **ἠλιθίου κἀβελτέρου** And may my daughter Pussy meet a man who's **rich** but also **childishly stupid**	'πενιχρὸν μέν, ἄλλως δ' εὐπρόσωπον καὶ καλὸν καὶ χρηστόν' (*Wealth* 976f.) 'Penniless but very good looking, fine and honest'
509	τὸ γὰρ ἦτρον **τῆς χύτρας** ἐλάκτισεν Yes, the baby had kicked the **pot's** belly!	'τῆς μητρός'/'τῆς μήτρας' 'mother's' (See Austin and Olson 2004: *ad loc.*)

A Grammar of *Para Prosdokian*

Line	Thesmophoriazusae	Expected
529f.	ὑπὸ λίθῳ γὰρ παντί που χρὴ μὴ δάκῃ **ῥήτωρ** ἀθρεῖν. You've got to look under every rock, or a **politician** may bite you.	'σκορπίος' 'scorpion' (See Prato 2001 and Austin and Olson 2004: *ad loc.*)
531f.	ἀλλ' οὐ γάρ ἐστι τῶν ἀναισχύντων φύσει γυναικῶν οὐδὲν κάκιον εἰς ἅπαντα—πλὴν ἄρ' εἰ **γυναῖκες**. No, there's nothing worse in every way than women born shameless – except for **the rest of women**!	(any other creature) (See Rogers 1904, Prato 2001 and Austin and Olson 2004: *ad loc.*)
829	ἔρριπται **τὸ σκιάδειον**. Others have cast . . . their **parasols**!	'ἡ ἀσπίς' 'shields' (See Prato 2001 and Austin and Olson 2004: *ad loc.*)
857	λευκῆς **νοτίζει μελανοσυρμαῖον λεών**. Bright Egypt [is flooded] for **a people much given to laxatives**.	'τακείσης χιόνος ὑγραίνει γύας' (Eur. *Hel.* 3) 'pale snow drenches the fields with moisture'
935	ὀλίγου μ' ἀφείλετ' αὐτὸν **ἱστιορράφος**. Just a minute ago a man did try to make off with him – a **sail-stitcher**!	'μηχανορράφος' 'schemer' (See Austin and Olson 2004: *ad loc.*)
937	ὦ πρύτανι, πρὸς τῆς δεξιᾶς, ἥνπερ φιλεῖς κοίλην προτείνειν, **ἀργύριον** ἤν τις **διδῷ**, Marshal, by this right hand of yours—which you're so fond of cupping in the direction of anyone who might **put silver in it**,	'βοήθειαν αἰτῆται' *vel sim.* 'ask you for help'
1201	μεμνῇσι τοίνυν τοὔνομ'· **Ἀρταμουξία**. Remember that name: **Artamuxia**.	'Ἀρτεμισία' 'Artemisia'

Line	Wealth	Expected
27	πιστότατον ἡγοῦμαί σε καὶ **κλεπτίστατον** I consider you the most trustworthy of my slaves, and the most **larcenous**	'εὐνούστατον' 'well-disposed' (See scholia and Rogers 1907: *ad loc.*)
152	οὐδὲ προσέχειν τὸν νοῦν, ἐὰν δὲ πλούσιος, **τὸν πρωκτὸν** αὐτὰς εὐθὺς ὡς τοῦτον τρέπειν [They] pay him no mind, but if he's rich, they right away offer him their **arse**	'τὸν νοῦν' 'attention'

Line	Wealth	Expected
165	ΧΡ. ὁ δὲ χρυσοχοεῖ γε χρυσίον παρὰ σοῦ λαβών – ΚΑ. ὁ δὲ **λωποδυτεῖ** γε νὴ Δί', ὁ δὲ **τοιχωρυχεῖ** – CHR. [Some craftsmen] smelt gold that they obtain from you – CA. Or **mug people**, by heaven, or **break into houses** –	(any proper professions)
180	ΚΑ. ὁ Τιμοθέου δὲ πύργος – ΧΡ. **ἐμπέσοι γέ σοι**. CA. And Timotheus' tower – CHR. May it fall on your head!	'οὐχὶ διὰ τοῦτον ἐγένετο;' 'wasn't it built thanks to him?' (See scholia and Sommerstein 2001: *ad loc*.)
277f.	ἐν τῇ σορῷ νυνὶ **λαχὸν τὸ γράμμα σου δικάζει**, σὺ δ' οὐ βαδίζεις, ὁ δὲ Χάρων **τὸ ξύμβολον** δίδωσιν. In the coffin; **your turn has now come to serve there**. Won't you go? Charon is offering you a **pass**.	'ὁ Χάρων σε καλεῖ' 'you've been called by Charon' 'σίδῃ'/'ῥοΐδιον' 'pomegranate'
372	μῶν οὐ κέκλοφας ἀλλ' **ἥρπακας**; Maybe you aren't a thief, but **a robber**.	'εὕρηκας' *vel sim*. 'you randomly found them'
706	μὰ Δί' οὐκ ἔγωγ', ἀλλὰ **σκατοφάγον**. Certainly not; he's just a **shit eater**.	(any religious adjective)
737	καὶ πρίν σε **κοτύλας ἐκπιεῖν οἴνου δέκα** And sooner than you could **drink five pints of wine**	'εἰπεῖν λόγον ἕνα'/'πτύσαι' 'say a word'/'spit' (See scholia *ad loc*.)
765	νὴ τὴν Ἑκάτην, κἀγὼ δ' ἀναδῆσαι βούλομαι εὐαγγέλιά σε **κριβανωτῶν ὁρμαθῷ** By Hecate, I'd also like to drape **a string of loaves** around your neck for delivering such good news	'στεφάνῳ' 'a wreath' (See scholia *ad loc*.)
818	ἀποψώμεσθα δ' οὐ λίθοις ἔτι, ἀλλὰ **σκοροδίοις** ὑπὸ τρυφῆς ἑκάστοτε We no longer use stones to wipe our bottoms, but **cloves of garlic** every time	'σπογγίοις' 'sponge'
963	**ὦ μειρακίσκη**· πυνθάνει γὰρ ὡρικῶς My **girl** (since you ask so girlishly)	'ὦ γραῖα' (cf. Eur. *Hel*. 441) 'my hag'
972	ἀλλ' οὐ λαχοῦσ' **ἔπινες** ἐν τῷ γράμματι; Then maybe you showed up **for drinking** service without a valid token?	'ἐδίκαζες' 'for judging' (See scholia *ad loc*.)

CHAPTER 12
LAUGHING AGAINST THE MACHINE
Maria Gerolemou

Introduction

This chapter attempts to show how Aristophanes, in experimenting with the borders between mimesis and artificiality, plays with his characters' automated movements and gestures.[1] Specifically, it examines the idea, first introduced in a systematic way by Henri Bergson in his work *Le Rire*,[2] that to have a codified, non-spontaneous, inelastic behaviour when the audience expects to see behavioural adaptability to a changing environment, produces incongruity, and this tends to provoke laughter (see Arist. *Rhetoric* 3.2).[3] It should be noted that though we cannot be certain how enthusiastically the audience of Aristophanes might have laughed at a character who lacks an *élan vital* and functions like an automaton, we can look to comparative examples outside of Aristophanes; stories of Daedalus' mobile and talking statues, for example, seem to form a recipe for laughter.[4]

Prior to discussing the 'automatic' and its effect on Aristophanic characters, it is important to draw briefly its basic parameters. Let us start by defining natural automatic behaviour and, consequently, non-natural automatic behaviour. According to the results of the recent University of Paderborn research project 'Automatismen', natural behaviour is comprised of bodily and mental automatisms which elude conscious control, and, as habits rooted in repetition, stand very close to mechanized procedures and their main feature, reiteration.[5] The notion of natural automatism is important for the understanding of the body in classical antiquity as well. The pre-Hellenistic (pre-mechanical) notion of the *automaton* is often attested in the Hippocratic corpus and defines unchosen bodily activities (for instance, the unpredictable recovery of health in *Nature of Man* 12), which, however, enjoy a certain degree of repetition as they occur *kata physin* (see e.g. *Superfetation* 7).[6] Whereas, however, the body is signified through random, natural automatisms, it still responds to the guidance of the Hippocratic physicians who try to facilitate its return to its natural track. Moreover, bodily functions are visualized through material and technological analogies which makes their function graspable and their manipulation feasible. To give one example, the Hippocratic author of the text *Ancient Medicine* 22 explains that organs such as the bladder, the head and the womb are shaped like medical 'cupping glasses' ('σικύαι'), which allows them to attract bodily humours.[7] The analogy between bodily functions and technological devices is also known from the works of Presocratics such as Empedocles, who describes the analogy between respiration and the *klepsudra* (B100 D–K).

Recognizing technological tools and devices as visual analogies to the physical behaviour of the body opens up the possibility not merely of imitating the seen part of the human body (i.e. its outer form, as a sculptor or a painter does), but also its internal workings along with its automatisms.[8] Hence – like the natural, automatic body – the artificial body, which is the product of artisanship and not nature, could also be imagined as directed by unpredictable but potentially repeatable automatic action (see e.g. Arist. *Metaphysics* Z 7–9).

According to Aristotle in *Physics* 2.8, there are two types of *technē*; a first type merely imitates the natural world, while a second type of art completes and improves nature through its artificial products.[9] This latter *technē* is what is being described as the discipline of mechanics at [Arist.] *Mechanical Problems* 847a in the face of difficulty (*aporia*) towards nature's workings.[10] As I have argued elsewhere, this ability not merely to mimic but also to challenge the boundaries of the natural generates questions about the potential harmful effect of its artificial reproduction.[11]

Attic drama seems to reflect the notion of the natural, automatic body as described by Hippocratic physicians as well as the aspiration for its technical reproduction and the risk and anxiety that this procedure might entail. On Euripides' stage, for instance, 'stony' or 'ethereal' bodies,[12] by reproducing physicality, deconstruct the distinction between naturalness and artfulness. Helen's moving *eidōlon* in Euripides' *Helen*, which is described as a living breathing body ('ἔμπνουν', 34) perplexes Teucer and Menelaus after they have seen the true Helen; Teucer is impressed by the copy which is identical with Helen in the face but not in mind (71–7, 160–3). Menelaus also seems confused with the spectacle of the second, true Helen and he doubts her physical presence (as the 'true' Helen was with him in Troy). Hence, his confusion carries great weight; 'what kind of craftsman can fashion a living body?', he asks ('καὶ τίς βλέποντα σώματ' ἐξεργάζεται;', 583).[13]

On the other hand, a technical reproduction of the human body could also refer to a procedure that opposes its natural character only partly, such as prosthesis;[14] this could refer both to artificial limbs that serve to replace a missing part and to non-natural parts that are intended to artificially augment the body, for instance its strength and, in effect, expand human skills. Such a mechanism might also render the difference between the natural and artificial body or body-parts thoroughly ambiguous. The bow in Euripides' *Heracles* is an example which illuminates the notion of artificial enhancement of bodily limbs as well the danger that this procedure may involve. The bow in this play gives the impression of being attached to the hero's body, as an extension of his hand; as a result, if Heracles is deprived of his bow, he can no longer be considered the bravest man (157–64). Moreover, during Heracles' madness, this powerful extra limb kills his wife and children; ultimately separated from his body, the bow clashes against his ribs and acquires a voice that warns Heracles that, if he keeps it, it would be like saving his children's murderer (1379–81; cf. 1098–100). Shortly before the end of the play, Heracles decides to keep his bow and arrows and thus learn to cohabit within his mortal, fragile and, simultaneously, heroic enhanced self. The bow elevates him to a higher plane of fulfilment, towards an ideal conception of himself, but it also reminds him that without it, he is just a mortal man.

Aristophanes reacts to the possibility of a non-natural, mechanized body on stage and considers artificial physicality to be a threatening force not merely towards the human body, but, most importantly, towards the human intellect and consciousness, and consequently the unique and unpredictable that Aristophanic comedy propagates as its distinctive feature (cf. e.g. *Wasps* 1016f., 1044f., *Clouds* 545–59). Artificial, non-natural and thus inelastic behaviour tends to nullify this force.[15] As already noted at the outset, gestures and movement produced through *technē* seem to challenge naturally produced activity, one of the two constituent parts of delivery or *hupokrisis* (the second is naturally produced voice). It appears that Euripidean theatre, with its abundance of cases of artificial life, probably unwittingly and in a preliminary form, opens a window into a wider discussion that will be fully developed in later centuries about what can be defined as a natural performance with regard to the art of oratory. The key question is: if delivery and performance should be the outcome of natural faculty, or if the performer (actor or orator) is allowed to reach perfection unnaturally, i.e. with the assistance of *technē*. The latter could mean, for instance, the ability to repeat stereotypical movements (cf. Quintilian, *Inst.* 11.3. esp. 788–91; Cicero, *De oratore* 213–27)[16] or memorize a script (cf. Alcidamas, *On Sophists*),[17] which, as Aristophanic plays argue, has little to do with the notion of natural, laborious performance or with an alert audience who will supplement through imagination any missing physical evidences; at *Frogs* 1109–14 the chorus says that the Athenian audience is now equipped with books that prepare them in a technical way for every 'clever stuff'. The non-natural reaction to a play, character or general situation is the danger Aristophanes claims to confront when he causes his audience to laugh against the 'machine'.

Laughing at the *mēchanē*

Aristophanes praises the *automatos bios*, which stands for the natural and opposes the technological, automatized way of life. This is a *topos* not only in Aristophanes but in Old Comedy generally; Athenaeus in his *Deipnosophistae*, referring to natural life, cites a number of comic plays to show how in ancient times, probably during the Hesiodic age of Cronos, goods were provided automatically and there was no need for slaves or other intermediaries between natural production and human consumption (6.267e–270a).[18]

Praise of natural automatisms is translated in Aristophanes' plays into mockery of technical automation. His first victim is the most obvious enemy; theatrical devices and their users. Evidence about theatrical devices helps us to understand both the aesthetic value of stage machinery in the theatrical setting and how they might have been conceptualized by spectators. They could lift weights in the air or move them back and forth, thus simulating bodily action (motion).[19] As such, theatrical devices were able to provide humans and humanized gods with superhuman abilities and were used by tragedians as a means of overcoming theatrical difficulties. Specifically, by its ability to extend physical movement, the solution of the *mēchanē* operating above the stage and theatre roof enables the performer and character to rise in the air (cf. e.g. the Dioscuri in Euripides' *Electra* 1349; see further Pollux on the crane which grabs the body of Memnon in Aeschylus and raises it above the earth, 4.131);[20] on the other hand, the *ekkuklēma* plays with the necessity of visual appearance on stage.[21] Hence, the new technology used in theatre can be said to have applied a new force to the performer's and character's body, thus suggesting that the natural body is deficient and need to be enhanced.

The need to constrain this kind of *technē* is extensively depicted in Aristophanes' metatheatrical comments. To this end, he gives a face to the operator of the *mēchanē*, the *mēchanopoios*, and reveals, in contrast to Euripidean theatre, 'mechanical' workings to be the work of a labourer.[22] At the same time, he mocks users who take advantage of the effects produced by machines in order to impress the public. *Peace*, in a scene that, according to the ancient scholia (*ad* ll.76 and 136), serves as a parody of the use of the flying Pegasus in Euripides' *Bellerophon*,[23] depicts the protagonist using a giant dung beetle with outstretched wings to rush up to Olympus (154); the operator of the monstrous beetle is called a *mēchanopoios*, 'crane-maker', and Trygaeus breaks the fourth wall to caution him to pay attention (174). At *Thesmophoriazusae* 1098–102, Aristophanes parodies Euripides' frequent use of the crane by bringing him onstage by way of a flying machine, dressed as Perseus. Aristophanes' *Clouds* provides another example; Socrates appears on a *mēchanē*, from which he looks down upon Strepsiades and asks: 'Why do you summon me, ephemeral creature?' ('τί με καλεῖς, ὦ 'φήμερε', *Clouds* 223). He then explains: 'I am walking in the air and investigating the sun' ('ἀεροβατῶ καὶ περιφρονῶ τὸν ἥλιον', *Clouds* 225). Here, Aristophanes does not make fun of performance technology as such but, by further correlating machines with philosophical elites, lampoons the distinction made by people like Socrates between those who have access and use machines, and the technologically naïve people who don't, i.e. between the wise and the foolish.

The case of the *ekkuklēma* is more complicated, as it does not merely generate motion, but, more importantly, physical presence. Tragedy used the *ekkuklēma* or 'out-roller', probably a shallow platform on wheels, to bring out interior tableaux, usually corpses, through the central doors of the *skēnē*. In *Thesmophoriazusae*, Agathon's entrance and exit on the *ekkuklēma* (97, 265) is intended, according to Austin and Olson, to 'parody the use of a theatrical trolley to represent interior scenes in contemporary tragedy'.[24] In the same vein, Euripides, in *Ach*. 407–9, uses the *ekkuklēma* to hasten his entrance into the scene and save time for his poetic composition; again, what is being laughed at is not so much the *ekkuklēma* itself but its users, the tragic poets who tend to use theatrical machines to make a grand entrance or have a spectacular finale, probably in the absence of an innovative, intelligent script.[25]

Lys. 430–2 is even more indicative of this point; here Aristophanes again parodies or bemoans the tragic use of the *mēchanē* when Lysistrata proudly claims that she is coming out of the Acropolis on her own, *automatē*, without needing any crowbars but only by using her brain and intellect ('μηδὲν ἐκμοχλεύετε·/ἐξέρχομαι γὰρ αὐτομάτη τί δεῖ μοχλῶν;/οὐ γὰρ μοχλῶν δεῖ μᾶλλον ἢ νοῦ καὶ φρενῶν', 'Don't be doing any jimmying; I'm coming out on my very own. Why do you need crowbars? It's not crowbars you need, but rather brains and sense').[26] The *mochloi* in the play, at first iron bolts (i.e. defensive means), are, up to this point, in the hands of the women who have shut themselves within the Acropolis (246, 263f., 310, 487); nevertheless, as soon as the *mochloi* fall into the hands of men, transforming into 'levers' or 'crowbars' (424–8), Lysistrata decides to come out without any technical equipment, defensive or offensive, only by using her mind.[27] Here, the automaton is re-established in its connection with physicality (natural automatism) and the mind, *nous* and *phrenes*, marking, in a similar way to Anaxagoras (see esp. fr. 13 D–K), intelligence and cunning as the governing agent for the production of human action in general and dramatic composition in particular.[28]

Embodied mechanisms

The idea that a living body could be replaced by an artificial one raises certain issues in Greek drama, particularly with regards to the limits of mimesis or *technē* and the authority that the latter exerts on the human body and actions. Two kinds of mimesis appear to be employed in Attic drama:

a. mimesis may refer to the production of a simple copy of something that exists in nature, and;

b. mimesis can designate the procedure by which someone actively tries to be similar to someone different to them.[29]

In *Thesmophoriazusae* 155f., the latter is clearly suggested by Agathon. According to him, one can supplement the natural body and behaviour through the imitation of opposite manners (149–52; cf. *Frogs* 590–606). No purpose seems to be served by imitating something of your own nature, since such imitation is unnecessary and ineffective (167; cf. *Frogs* 109f., *Wealth* 290–2, *Ecclesiazusae* 278, 545). On the other hand, imprints, *mimēmata*, can refer to simple copies of nature as well (reminiscent of the first case of *technē* discussed by Aristotle in *Physics* 2.8 seen above). This kind of *mimēmata* could fall victim to manipulation by their consumers. With this in mind, the Right Argument in *Clouds* 975f. advises young boys not to leave imprints of their penises in the sand because they could stimulate prospective lovers.

Before drawing more extensively on Aristophanes, I would like to refer briefly further to the focus of Euripides' drama on the non-natural, mechanized behaviour of some of his characters, especially due to devious directives. Dionysus in the *Bacchae* is represented not only as an inspiring religious leader but also as a theatre *didaskalos* ('director') who gives instructions to his followers (cf. e.g. 847–61; cf. also the role of Athena in S. *Aj*.).[30] For instance, Cadmus and Teiresias, equipped with new moving legs which have replaced their old, rigid legs, are part of the Dionysian plan to gain control over the body and mind of non-believers, as seen earlier in the play with regards to the women of Thebes. 'Where shall our dance steps take us, where shall we set our feet and shake our aged heads?' ('ποῖ δεῖ χορεύειν, ποῖ καθιστάναι πόδα/καὶ κρᾶτα σεῖσαι πολιόν', 184f.),[31] Cadmus asks the seer Teiresias, who, as the wiser man, is in charge of the expedition to Cithaeron and the Bacchic feasts (178–98). The scene with the two old men moving their newly acquired young limbs while trying to imitate Dionysian dance steps raises the suspicion that a 'hidden mechanism' implanted by Dionysus might be behind their bodily movement (187–9);[32] this charges the episode with a comic effect, as Seidensticker notes (1982: 116–23). In the same spirit, Pentheus is unwittingly urged by the humanized Dionysus to change his mind and approach the maenads, whom he had previously pursued, in order to secretly observe them and learn their practices (850f.: 'πρῶτα δ' ἔκστησον φρενῶν,/ἐνεὶς ἐλαφρὰν λύσσαν', 'first drive him from his senses, put giddy madness in his breast', cf. also *Ba.* 999);[33] he allows Dionysus to dress him ('ἰδού, σὺ κόσμει· σοὶ γὰρ ἀνακείμεσθα δή', 'There. You must be my hairdresser, for I am entirely given over to you', 934), to instruct him on how to hold the thyrsus (941–4) and, essentially, to transform him into a maenad ('σκευὴν γυναικὸς μαινάδος βάκχης ἔχων', 'wearing the kit of a female bacchant', 915; cf. also 828, 830). He is now concerned with hair dressing (831, 928), which used to annoy him (235, 455f., 493), and asks Dionysus how he looks in his maenadic dress ('τί φαίνομαι δῆτ''; 'what do I look like?', 925; see also 914). Ultimately, he is sent to Cithaeron, where, even though he hides in a tree, the maenads discover him, rip off his limbs, tear off his head and cut his body into pieces; shortly before his death, Pentheus impulsively throws away the maenadic headband, hoping that this gesture will restore his inborn male identity (1115–21). However, it is too late, as Agave, Pentheus' mother, maddened by Dionysus, cannot recognize her son, even after he removes his female insignia. By the time of his death, he is actually left without a body ('κεῖται δὲ χωρὶς σῶμα', 'his body lies scattered', 1137). In the final scene of the play, what was once Pentheus' body has become butchered limbs; Cadmus, his grandfather, finds first the head, then the hands and, finally, the limbs, which he sticks together as Agave asks; 'πᾶν ἐν ἄρθροις συγκεκλημένον καλῶς;' ('has it been properly fitted together, limb with limb?', 1300). Thus, non-natural activity is taken from its comic expression in Cadmus and Teiresias to its sinister, tragic expression in Pentheus, before his artificial maenadic body is finally and fatally ripped apart – alongside the integrity of the natural body it has been grafted onto.

Such experience of artificial and mechanized behaviour as the outcome of manipulative instruction on the Euripidean stage finds its comic parallel in *Thesmophoriazusae*, where the Kinsman offers to help Euripides ('ἐμοὶ δ' ὅ τι βούλει χρῶ λαβών', 'put me to use however you want', 212). The plan is to transform the Kinsman into a woman who, by sneaking into the Thesmophoria, will be able to defend Euripides to the women who hate him. The Kinsman is cut in pieces ('τεμνόμενος', 226) in order to be manufactured anew, and he subsequently feels puppet-like, that is, under someone else's control. The Kinsman must take off his over-cloak (214), shave his beard and remove all other hair (215f.). Furthermore, he must talk like a woman (266–9). After he patiently follows all the instructions provided by Euripides, he looks at himself in the mirror, which reflects his transformation; i.e. from Kinsman to a womanish man (233–6).[34] In this guise, he calls an imaginary slave girl, Thratta, to accompany him to the festival, where he mimics actions normally undertaken by women festival-goers, such as lighting the torches, taking cakes from a box, putting them on the altar, etc. (279–94). Later, in front of the women, he attempts to reproduce a female pose, though he seems incapable of holding his body in quite the same way (643–6). Earlier in the play, a more schematic approach to mechanization is outlined, though here nature is the crafter; Euripides describes to the Kinsman an ancient type of person – a recollection of a proto-human (14–18).[35] Under the influences of new philosophical trends, a new cosmogony is imagined. Ether fabricates parts for living creatures whose eyes are manufactured as an 'ἀντίμιμον', a counter image, to the wheel of the sun, and whose ears are perforated as a funnel for hearing (17f.).

Hence, this technical mode of creation is associated with the use or production of an artificial body that promises to correct the shortcomings of the natural body. Such a body resists decay and is easily repaired, its old or damaged body parts substituted or upgraded. On the other hand, Aristophanic theatre, by mocking a character or plot inspired and engineered by technology, actually reflects a kind of nostalgia for the 'pure' human body and mind. Let us study a final case which profoundly demonstrates this. The protagonist of Aristophanes' *Clouds*, Strepsiades, offers both his body and mind to Socrates, who is in charge of the *phrontistērion*, allowing him to manipulate it as it pleases him, in the hope of learning how to deceive his enemies (439–41). More precisely, in ll.478–80, Socrates asks Strepsiades to enlighten him on the ways of his mind – for instance, if he has a good memory or a natural gift for speaking – in order that he may design new components for him and replace the old ones (he will prepare 'μηχανὰς/... καινὰς', 'new mechanisms', 479f.;[36] cf. *Acharnians* 445, 'πυκνῇ γὰρ λεπτὰ μηχανᾷ φρενί', 'you contrive [mechanize] finely with your dense mind'). Strepsiades has already offered himself up to Socrates as an anvil 'for hammering into shape' ('ἐπιχαλκεύειν', 422). By accepting these new artificial parts, Strepsiades will become enhanced beyond his inborn characteristics; he will look like Chaerephon (502f.). Strepsiades, however, ultimately emphatically reacts against this enhancement procedure, which will turn him into something resembling a half-dead person ('ἡμιθνὴς', 504).[37] Once more, as in the case of the Kinsman in *Thesmophoriazusae* examined above, the technical procedure fails, or, rather, is never completed; Socrates pursues more lessons with Strepsiades, including a form of meditative incubation in which the old man lies under a blanket while thoughts are supposed to arise in his mind naturally. The incubation brings no results and, finally, Socrates refuses to be further acquainted with him.

So in Euripides' plays, the mechanization of body and mind – the ability of art to produce copies that imitate and/or enhance nature – is welcomed, while the perplexity of these mechanizations is acknowledged. Aristophanes, on the other hand, presents artificial physicality as a threatening force not merely towards the human body, human intellect, emotions and consciousness but, most importantly, towards the creative, flexible and unpredictable that Aristophanic comedy propagates as its distinctive feature. Moreover, in contrast to the Euripidean abstract use of the machine, the Aristophanic machine functions only with the direct human agency of a worker's labour; thus, by introducing the *mēchanopoios* along with the machine, Aristophanes tries to naturalize the mechanical effect. Socrates and Euripides, who forget or conceal the natural physicality at work behind their artificial machines in their zeal to impress the public with advanced technology, are simply left to be laughed at.

CHAPTER 13
NO LAUGHING MATTER? THE COMIC POTENTIAL OF MADNESS IN ARISTOPHANES
Natalia Tsoumpra

Madness has been most commonly considered tragedy's literary territory; the loss of reason, distorted perception, the actions of a deluded mind, and the consequences of a frenzied fit all feature prominently in many tragic plays. Whenever insanity appears in a comic environment, it has most often been associated with a tragic intertext. To name but a few examples: Philocleon's *mania* with the law courts has been compared to Phaedra's or Stheneboea's obsessive *pathos*,[1] and Heracles' fit of madness in Euripides' *Heracles*;[2] Trygaeus' insane wish to reach Olympus finds role models in Euripides' *Bellerophon* and *Aeolus*;[3] and Strepsiades' loss of reason at the end of *Clouds* has been likened to the delusion of Euripides' *Ixion*.[4] Although these are all sound observations, I wish to argue that there is more to comic madness than its association with tragic intertexts allows us to see. Cases of madness in Aristophanes show that madness could be appreciated as a purely comic phenomenon despite any affinities with tragedy, and that, indeed, its humorous effect makes it more suitable for comedy than tragedy. In this sense, cases of madness which arouse laughter in tragedy are not just an exception, a temporary lapse of the horrendous to the ridiculous.[5] The prevalent model according to which tragedy occupies a privileged poetic authority over comedy when it comes to madness must be revisited; not all cases of madness in comedy are parodic challenges to tragic decorum, while tragedy often borrows manifestations of madness from comedy. We should thus move away from readings of madness in comedy as funny because they are merely paratragic. In the case of madness, the gags of comedy come prior to the world of tragedy.

I will begin with some general remarks about the comic potential of absurdity and physical violence that accompany manifestations of madness. I will then focus on specific literary instances of madness in comedy versus tragedy which exemplify the connection between visual humour, incongruity, violence and madness. I will finish with some thoughts about the function of laughter in cases of madness. Disengaging madness from tragedy and viewing it as a comic phenomenon has implications about the way we think about laughter and the comic. The model which distinguishes between laughing at (tragic) and with (comic) madness and the madman needs to be adjusted.[6] Although the question of whether humour is a domain where morality has no purchase is open for debate, the categories of 'positive' and 'negative' portrayals of madness in comedy and tragedy respectively are hardly helpful or accurate. Laughter with madness need not be motivated by feelings of power and superiority; it is the laughter of absurdity. We laugh both at others and ourselves in unhappy, distressing, and embarrassing situations. In this sense, laughter takes on aspects of Ionesco's 'comic improbability' about the 'unendurable

Aristophanic Humour

absurdity of existence'[7] or Beckett's '*risus purus*', the laughter directed 'at the laugh itself';[8] it represents the continuous effort to laugh in a world that often turns absurd.

Madness and absurdity

One of the most plausible theories about laughter is the incongruity theory.[9] According to this view, humour springs from a clash of incongruous aspects; 'a sudden shift of perspective, an unexpected slippage of meaning, an arresting dissonance or discrepancy, a momentary defamiliarizing of the familiar and so on'.[10] Psychological studies also reveal that laughter in infants may occur as a response to something unusual performed by the mother.[11] According to psychological accounts of incongruity theory, laughter seems to depend on two factors:

> First, the occurrence of something unsettling, abnormal, new or frightening (something that might otherwise provoke tears, such as being chucked up and down in the air); second, the fact that this abnormality takes place within a safe context, a play situation which neutralizes the threat.[12]

There are two important observations here; first, just as in infants, adult laughter may also be a response to a socially deviant behaviour, a conduct regarded as mad, when there is no awareness of personal threat in sight.[13] Thus, laughter naturally arises through what we would now classify as mental disturbances, such as delusions, hallucinations and delirious speech. In theatre, the tension which is created between the 'nonsense' of the insane character and the 'sense' of the other dramatic characters and the audience is one of the more fundamental incongruities claimed as a mechanism of humour. As Eagleton notes, the 'catastrophic collapse of the reality principle, one which pressed far enough ends up in madness, is prototypically comic'.[14]

Comedy is therefore better placed than tragedy to offer a rich and elaborate portrayal of madness due to its focus on the very acts of insanity and the inexplicable behaviour of the mentally ill.[15] Tragedy focuses on the 'before' and 'after' of madness, while the whole repertoire of *mania* is not represented on the tragic stage but only symptoms involving distorted vision, delusion or hallucination.[16] The fits of madness occur offstage and are reported to the audience via a messenger: the fit of Sophocles' Ajax or Euripides' Heracles is not performed on stage; Heracles' burst of madness in *Trachiniae* after he dons the poisonous robe is reported; Agave's disparaging of Pentheus' body is again related, and the same goes for Orestes' attack of frenzy in *Iphigenia in Tauris*.[17] The account of madness in tragedy focuses more on the sufferer's demise and their self-damage – or the damage to the community. By contrast, comedy displays the acts of madness as devoid of meaning, and there lies its comic potential. Madness can have a comic effect in tragedy (or, indeed, other literary habitats) only when there is no imminent danger and no catastrophic outcomes result; the laughter stops when the symptoms of madness lead to a lethal outcome.[18]

The exaggeration of the merely stupid or perplexing into the genuinely pathological is a very common comic device. Madness in the guise of comic absurdity occupies a central role in Aristophanic comedy, as it is inextricably linked to the 'great idea' of the comic hero. Comic heroes appear insane because they make plans and statements which are perceived to be very distant from reality; Trygaeus in *Peace* comes up with the idea of riding a beetle to get to Zeus, Peisetaerus in *Birds* wants to build a city in the sky and make birds the absolute rulers, and Chremylus in *Wealth* follows what appears to be a blind man because an oracle told him to. The comic heroes' odd conduct is every time charged with madness.[19] In contrast to tragedy, where madness is a temporary state of mind, a single seizure, which is imposed on the tragic hero by outside forces, and is always followed by a painful and shameful recovery, in comedy madness afflicts the hero permanently and often results in a relapse instead of recovery. The comic hero remains narcissistic throughout and suffers from grandiose identifications and the illusion of omnipotence. Significantly, the supposed madman triumphs in the end and his insanity prevails.[20] While in political discourse insanity is a common form of ridicule against a public speaker with the intention of compromising their status and effectively eliminating them as an opponent,[21] Aristophanic comedy appropriates the vocabulary of madness and turns it from an insult to a celebration of absurdity. It could be said that comedy advocates and celebrates madness, that it becomes a sort of institutionalized madness itself.

Madness and violence

Singer rightly notes that tragedy avoids the dramatization of physical symptoms of madness,[22] such as violent activity, wild eyes, shaking and foaming, and tentatively suggests that the reason for this selective representation, apart from genre conventions and practical problems of dramatization, may be that frenzied, violent activity on stage could have a humorous effect. To avoid this out-of-place humour, such actions were relayed rather than enacted on stage. In contrast, the overtly physical symptoms of madness make a frequent appearance on the comic stage. Violence and aggressiveness as by-products of insanity fit right into – and sometimes are hardly distinguishable – from comedy's slapstick routine. Stage violence and aggression are powerful forms of visual humour in which Aristophanic comedy often engages,[23] despite Aristophanes' mendacious claims (*Wasps* 58–61, *Clouds* 537–44). The comic potential of abuse and violence, which is amply displayed in Old, New (and modern) Comedy, is further accentuated by the violent acts of the madman.

Scenes of comic violence have most commonly been associated with superiority humour.[24] According to this theory, the audience focalizes through the speaker or actor, and their laughter is directed at the target or victim. Laughter slides into ridicule and becomes 'consequential' laughter.[25] In this sense, insane characters in comedy, who perform acts of violence, may often become the directors of laughter.[26] However, as has been rightly noted by Ruffell,[27] with visual humour in stage violence the butt of the joke

Aristophanic Humour

is not always straightforward or stable. Violence in comedy may be funny, but this does not mean that the humour is aggressively directed against the receptor of violence (at least, not always).[28] Madmen themselves may also become the objects of humour because of their hyperbolic and inexplicably violent reactions.[29] A good example is the stock comic character of the misanthrope, such as Knemon in Menander's *Duskolos*, whose behaviour is very close to that of a madman. Knemon is considered insane ('μαινόμενος', 'going mad', 82, 116; 'μελαγχολῶν', 'overcome with black bile', 89)[30] because he repeatedly chases away and acts violently against all people who attempt to approach him. The laughter arises from the visual humour of physical violence on stage, but also from the exaggerated reactions and statements of Knemon, which do not match the dramatic reality.[31]

Madness, performance and breach of illusion

One of the ways in which comedy generates humour is through its self-referential nature and its deployment of moments of disillusion; it draws attention to its theatrical nature and its capacity as a play. Comedy often breaks the fourth wall and operates simultaneously on two plains, that of ontological reality and that of dramatic reality. In that way, it establishes a complicity between actors and spectators, then returns to the illusion as if nothing has happened.[32] For a moment, a well-ordered world of meaning, which has been carefully built, is disrupted, and the grip onto the reality principle is loosened. This is a purely comedic mechanism which never occurs in tragedy.

This movement is paralleled in the acts of the madman. The performance of madness reinforces the playful diversifying of sense and the breach of illusion. Just as the spectators are caught between their reality and dramatic reality, maddened characters also occupy simultaneously two different levels. Madness almost becomes another performance, a play within the play, and the victim of madness becomes an actor in their own extra-dramatic reality. Maddened characters who move freely in and out of dramatic reality are perhaps more suitable for comedy than tragedy.[33] Acts of madness draw attention to the problematic interaction between spectator, illusion and reality. Insofar as the element of play is reinforced, the audience can laugh at the vicissitudes of the character with the detachment of a spectator.[34]

I will now proceed to demonstrate the above remarks about the close link between visual humour, incongruity, violence and madness, by focusing on the role of madness in specific literary instances in comedy and tragedy.

Setting the tone: Madness in *Wasps* as literary competition

Philocleon's madness in *Wasps* has been compared to Heracles' madness in Euripides' *Heracles*.[35] *Wasps* was performed in 422, while Euripides' *Heracles* is thought to have been composed around 415.[36] The assumption that madness is a purely tragic topos and that, therefore, any similarities between the two plays should be attributed to comedy's loans from tragedy, and not vice versa, has led scholars to assign the tragedy an earlier date. However, as the case of *Thesmophoriazusae* and *Bacchae* shows,[37] it should not be deemed unthinkable that tragedy has drawn from a comic topos. As I argue, in *Wasps* madness features as a purely comic spectacle and signals comedy's triumph over tragedy.

In the opening scene of *Wasps*, the two slaves provide a string of jokes to get the audience warmed up and set the tone for what will follow. Aristophanes goes out of his way to convey that this will be a middlebrow play that will appeal to a broad audience – nothing too intellectual but nothing too low either (56f., 64–6). He also seemingly refutes his ties with tragedy, as he ascertains that Euripides will not feature in the play ('οὐδ' αὖθις ἀνασελγαινόμενος Εὐριπίδης', 'no Euripides once again taking outrageous abuse', 61). Although Aristophanes does not stick to his programmatic claims – tragedy and paratragedy feature prominently in *Wasps*[38] – it may be important that after the abuse of tragedy is dismissed, it is revealed that the plot will revolve around an old man's incurable sickness ('νόσον γὰρ ὁ πατὴρ ἀλλόκοτον αὐτοῦ νοσεῖ', 'his father, you see, suffers from a bizarre sickness', 71). The story pattern where a disease is contracted by the main character and is later cured or, having not been cured, leads to disaster is a *tragic* sequence of events[39] – or is it? Could it be that Aristophanes is claiming back the ground from tragedy and wishes to demonstrate that madness can be comic territory?

After several attempts to cure his father's obsessive behaviour, Bdelycleon and the rest of the comic entourage give in. They pretend that Philocleon's mad behaviour is acceptable as long as it is limited within the domestic space and indulge his obsession by setting up a domestic court where he can try cases. An important dichotomy is created between the internal and the external audience; the external audience acknowledges the absurdity of the situation and suspects it will not work, whereas the internal audience plays along and behaves as if the idea were perfectly sensible. When the plan fails, Bdelycleon undertakes Philocleon's education, but Philocleon's madness now takes on a new turn.[40] Repetition here adds to the comic force;[41] whereas in tragedy madness comes as one finite episode, comic madness comes in repeated pangs and changed forms. As Xanthias reports, in his first symposium Philocleon breaks decorum and engages in all sorts of inappropriate behaviour (insulting the other symposiasts, narrating inappropriate stories, farting and being violent; 1299–325). Finally, he abducts the flute-girl and sets off drunkenly on his rowdy solo *komos*. Up to this point, his behaviour is characterized as 'drunk' ('παροινικώτατος', 1300; '(ἐ)μέθυεν', 1322) and 'outrageous' ('ὑβριστότατος', 1302) but when he appears on stage to perform his dance, the vocabulary shifts to that of madness ('μανίας ἀρχή', 'the start of madness', 1485; 'μανικὰ πράγματα', 'mad acts' 1496).

Xanthias advises Philocleon to drink hellebore (1489), which according to contemporary medical opinion and popular imagination was used to cure madness,[42] and warns him that he will be pelted with stones, a common way to treat madmen who represented a danger to the community. Dance is a common accompaniment of madness – gods affect their victims through music and dance (the Furies in *Eumenides*, Dionysus in the *Bacchae*, Lyssa (personified Madness) in *Heracles*), while the violent shaking of the body when in the grips of insanity resembles dancing; in this way, seizures and dancing may become indistinguishable.[43]

Most importantly, the scene of Philocleon's manic dance (1474–537) represents the culmination of Aristophanes' preoccupation with tragedy.[44] Philocleon is not simply dancing wildly but proposing a contest between tragedy and comedy through a manic dance-off (1498–500), in which comedy is the winner. We have now come full circle; at the beginning of the play Aristophanes disavows any ties with tragedy and proceeds to announce Philocleon's madness as the main subject of the play. At the end, he establishes comedy's superiority over tragedy through Philocleon's manic dance. Madness is reappropriated as comic material.

Visibility, concealment and insanity: Trygaeus versus Ajax

The difference in portrayal of Trygaeus' madness in *Peace* and Ajax's madness in Sophocles' *Ajax* (and elsewhere) shows that visual humour is inherent in physical representations of madness on stage, and while its comic potential is fully exploited in comedy, it is carefully avoided in tragedy.

The connection between insanity, visibility and the comic is clearly displayed in *Peace*. At the beginning of the play, Trygaeus' delusions are reported by the slave, while his 'delirious' speech is heard from behind the stage:

ὁ δεσπότης μου μαίνεται καινὸν τρόπον

My master's mad in a novel way

Peace 54

τὸ γὰρ παράδειγμα τῶν μανιῶν ἀκούετε·
ἃ δ' εἶπε πρῶτον ἡνίκ' ἤρχεθ' ἡ χολὴ
πεύσεσθ'.

You're hearing the typical symptom of his delusions. I'll tell you what he said when the bile first came over him.

Peace 65–7

However, the full extent of Trygaeus' madness, namely the realization of his plan with the riding of the beetle, is shown on stage in all its graphic detail; Trygaeus is thrashing around while trying to keep his balance on the beetle. The accusation of madness comes back now in full force, repeated three times by the slave:

O	ὦ δέσποτ' ἄναξ, ὡς *παραπαίεις*.
T	σίγα σίγα.
O	ποῖ δῆτ' ἄλλως *μετεωροκοπεῖς*;[45]

T	ὑπὲρ Ἑλλήνων πάντων πέτομαι τόλμημα νέον παλαμησάμενος.
O	τί πέτει; τί μάτην *οὐχ ὑγιαίνεις*;

Second Slave	Ah master, lord, you're so *deranged*!
Trygaeus	Be quiet, be quiet!
Second Slave	Well why are you *vainly beating the air*?
Trygaeus	I'm flying for the sake of all Greeks, trying my hand at a novel adventure.
Second Slave	Why do you fly? Why *act crazy* for nothing?

Peace 90–95

The undeniably comic sight of Trygaeus mounting a beetle with bridle and reins is described as pure insanity, and the absurdness of the act is shown – rather than reported – on stage.[46] This is at odds with the prevalent notion (in tragedy, and elsewhere) that madness is something that should be concealed and not displayed in public.[47] In this respect, Sophocles' *Ajax* offers a good counter-example to the case of Trygaeus, as questions of exposure and visibility become important; Ajax in his maddened state is kept offstage with an almost obsessive attentiveness. This is particularly obvious in a scene similar to the Aristophanic passage above. Tecmessa relates to the chorus Ajax's acts of madness, while Ajax is heard screaming backstage (333, 336, 339), which is acknowledged by Tecmessa and the chorus as a sign of his madness and confirmation of her narrative (334f., 337f.). These are all similar movements to the interaction between the slave (on stage) and Trygaeus (offstage). Yet, in contrast to the comic play, in the tragic environ, the door of the hut opens to reveal Ajax only when it is ascertained that he is sane:

X	ἀνὴρ φρονεῖν ἔοικεν. ἀλλ' ἀνοίγετε.
	τάχ' ἄν τιν' αἰδῶ κἀπ' ἐμοὶ βλέψας λάβοι.
T	ἰδού, διοίγω· προσβλέπειν δ' ἔξεστί σοι
	τὰ τοῦδε πράγη, καὐτὸς ὡς ἔχων κυρεῖ.

Chorus	The man seems to be sane! Come, open the door! Perhaps the sight of me will make him feel some shame.
Tecmessa	Look, I am opening the door, and you can see what he has done, and his own condition.

Ajax 344–7

Ajax is not allowed to come on stage while insane, because – I suggest – this spectacle may be laughable, as is the case with Trygaeus' majestic entrance. A similar case is presented in Euripides' *Medea*; the nurse describes Medea's agitated state (91, 94, 99, 103f.) while Medea sings and laments from within the house. When she finally shows up on stage (214ff.), she is fully composed and displays no signs of insanity. In the light of her constant preoccupation with not appearing laughable to her enemies, it may not be accidental that any signs of agitation and insanity are reserved for backstage.

Ajax does make one appearance on stage while in the grip of madness, when Athena calls him out in order to expose him to ridicule before Odysseus (90ff.), who will remain invisible. Odysseus is made an unwilling spectator in Athena's production of *Ajax Furens* ('μένοιμ' ἄν· ἤθελον δ' ἂν ἐκτὸς ὢν τυχεῖν', 'I shall remain; but I wish I were not here', 88), and is explicitly invited to laugh at his enemy's madness (Athena asks, 'οὔκουν γέλως ἥδιστος εἰς ἐχθροὺς γελᾶν;', 'is not laughing at one's enemies the most delightful kind of laughter?', 79). Odysseus, for his part, offers a counter-approach to madness, that of pity ('ἐποικτίρω', 121). This raises unanswerable questions about the audience's response. It is true, however, that the only symptoms of madness that we are allowed to see on stage are not the distinctly physical ones – Ajax does not appear to be gesturing wildly, as Trygaeus does – but just an altered perception of reality. When it comes to the physical symptoms and his violent activity, Ajax withdraws from stage to finish off his deed ('χωρῶ πρὸς ἔργον', 'I go to work', 116). Hence, laughter is suspended.

Singer notes that the laughter of Athena may represent the higher, distanced level of the gods, but at the same time he suggests that laughter at madness may be encouraged and engaged in by the actual audience.[48] I believe a mediating approach is possible here; instead of choosing either pole, pity or mockery, 'pure laughter' before the absurdity of the human condition may be another viable response. Odysseus' comments are important; he is moved by Ajax's misery because it is a reminder of his own (and every mortal's) predicament ('οὐδὲν τὸ τούτου μᾶλλον ἢ τοὐμὸν σκοπῶν', 'not thinking of his fate, but my own', 124). So laughter with (not at) madness may be a response to the helplessness of the human condition – and this may be another possibility suggested to the audience.

The connection between visibility, comicality and the performance of madness becomes evident in a passage from Lucian's *On Dancing*, in which the character Lycinus offers praise (as sincere as Lucianic praise can be)[49] of pantomime. In the extract Lycinus recalls a performance of Ajax's madness ruined by the dancer's 'over-imitation'. The dancer goes over-the-top in his performance, so much that the insanity of the actor becomes indistinguishable from the insanity of the character:

> ὀρχούμενος γὰρ τὸν Αἴαντα μετὰ τὴν ἧτταν εὐθὺς μαινόμενον, εἰς τοσοῦτον ὑπερεξέπεσεν ὥστε οὐχ ὑποκρίνασθαι μανίαν ἀλλὰ μαίνεσθαι αὐτὸς εἰκότως ἄν τινι ἔδοξεν. ἑνὸς γὰρ τῶν τῷ σιδηρῷ ὑποδήματι κτυπούντων τὴν ἐσθῆτα κατέρρηξεν, ἑνὸς δὲ τῶν ὑπαυλούντων τὸν αὐλὸν ἁρπάσας τοῦ Ὀδυσσέως πλησίον ἑστῶτος καὶ ἐπὶ τῇ νίκῃ μέγα φρονοῦντος διεῖλε τὴν κεφαλὴν κατενεγκών, καὶ εἴ γε μὴ ὁ πῖλος ἀντέσχεν καὶ τὸ πολὺ τῆς πληγῆς ἀπεδέξατο, ἀπωλώλει ἂν ὁ κακοδαίμων Ὀδυσσεύς, ὀρχηστῇ παραπαίοντι περιπεσών.

> In presenting Ajax going mad immediately after his defeat, he so overleaped himself that it might well have been thought that instead of feigning madness he was himself insane; for he tore the clothes of one of the men that beat time with the

iron shoe, and snatching a flute from one of the accompanists, with a vigorous blow he cracked the crown of Odysseus, who was standing near and exulting in his victory; indeed, if his watch-cap had not offered resistance and borne the brunt of the blow, poor Odysseus would have lost his life through falling in the way of a crazy dancer.

The Dance 83[50]

The exaggeration, which is reproached by Lycinus, consists in the mimesis of violent actions (tearing and hitting) which, as we know, were not enacted in the original tragic play. The performance provokes two kinds of laughter; for Lycinus and the 'learned' ('ἀστειότεροι', 83) among the audience, the spectacle was ridiculous ('γελοιότερον', 84) because it was unnecessarily exaggerated and hence inartistic. By contrast, a rival's performance is praised for enacting the madness 'discreetly and prudently' ('κοσμίως καὶ σωφρόνως', 84). It would be interesting to know what exactly a 'discreet' and 'prudent' performance of madness entailed, and the grounds on which it was praised. Yet what is important is that the dancer's manic gestures had a different effect on the wider, less cultured audience; they thought this was a supreme piece of acting, a 'consummate imitation of [Ajax's] suffering' ('ἄκραν δε μίμησιν τοῦ πάθους', 83) – they responded with laughter and wondered whether the actor had indeed gone mad ('καὶ τὸ πρᾶγμα οἱ μὲν ἐθαύμαζον, οἱ δὲ ἐγέλων, οἱ δὲ ὑπώπτευον μὴ ἄρα ἐκ τῆς ἄγαν μιμήσεως εἰς τὴν τοῦ πάθους ἀλήθειαν ὑπηνέχθη', 'the thing caused some to marvel, some to laugh, and some to suspect that perhaps in consequence of his overdone mimicry he had fallen into the real ailment', 83). For the wider audience, the representation of Ajax's full-on madness was funny but not ridiculous. In fact, they proceeded to imitate the actor's actions ('ἀλλὰ τό γε θέατρον ἅπαν συνεμεμήνει τῷ Αἴαντι καὶ ἐπήδων καὶ ἐβόων καὶ τὰς ἐσθῆτας ἀνερρίπτουν', 'the pit, however, all went mad with Ajax, leaping and shouting and flinging up their garments', 83). Madness, just as laughter, is contagious; it is riotous and convulsive, and involves the disintegration of sense.

A similar story is reported in Macrobius' *Saturnalia* 2.7.16, where the dancer Pylades performs the part of mad Hercules. His performance amused the crowd ('ridentes', they begin 'laughing') because the actor did not keep his dancing to the right step and threw arrows at the audience.[51] The actor then broke character and reprimanded the audience for not appreciating a realistic representation of madness ('μωροί, μαινόμενον ὀρχοῦμαι', 'Idiots! I'm dancing a madman!'[52]). Of course, the audience might have done exactly that; contrary to the actor's (mis)perception, laughter may arise due to the realistic performance of madness, and not the supposed bad acting.

Both stories invite the possibility that enactment of madness is a dangerous business, as it may result in the blending of actor and character, performance and reality.[53] Most importantly, they show that when madness is performed in its full splendour, it is comic, but not necessarily mockingly comic; the laughter aroused need not be the laughter of ridicule, but laughter in the face of a bizarre and unanticipated conduct.

Incongruity, violence and madness: The case of Heracles in Aristophanes' *Frogs* and Euripides' *Heracles*

Aristophanes' *Frogs*

I now move on to another prominent example of insanity, that of Heracles. The story of Heracles' insanity lurks at the background of *Frogs* and substantiates the comic potential of the incongruity and violence that accompany acts of madness. In the opening scene of *Frogs*, Dionysus shows up at Heracles' doorstep in his incongruous mix of Dionysian/Heraclean costume, which makes Heracles burst into laughter (42f.). Xanthias' comment offers an interpretation to Heracles' amusement at the sight of Dionysus; he thinks he is mad.

Δ	ὁ παῖς.
Ξ	τί ἐστιν;
Δ	οὐκ ἐνεθυμήθης;
Ξ	τὸ τί;
Δ	ὡς σφόδρα μ' ἔδεισε.
Ξ	νὴ Δία, μὴ μαίνοιό γε.

Dionysus	Boy?
Xanthias	What is it?
Dionysus	Did you see that?
Xanthias	See what?
Dionysus	How extremely scared of me he was!
Xanthias	Sure, scared that you've lost your mind.

Frogs 40f.

Heracles' inability to make sense out of Dionysus' costume is an indication of madness which provokes laughter. Heracles' laughter is quite telling, since just a few lines above, in the opening scene (1–20), Xanthias and Dionysus engage in a conversation about what constitutes a good joke and what should arouse laughter among the audience. Just like in the case of *Wasps*, Aristophanes may be instructing the audience about what constitutes comic material; through Heracles' uncontrollable laughter, he is giving them the cue to laugh with Dionysus' insanity.

The reference to Dionysus-as-Heracles' madness may be a nod to the story of Heracles' own insanity, which is again alluded to later on in the play. Plathane, the innkeeper in Hades, complains of the outrageous conduct of Heracles when he had visited the underworld. A good part of the satire refers to the proverbial gluttony of Heracles (550f., 553, 555, 558–60), but the Innkeeper goes on to remark that, when she demanded payment, Heracles gave her a fierce look, and bellowed and drew out his sword as if he were mad ('μαίνεσθαι δοκῶν', 'seeming to go crazy', 564). Heracles' violent acts due to his insatiable hunger are here linked to the famous story of his madness.

A more direct link between symptoms of hunger and symptoms of madness in Heracles is established in a fragment from Epicharmus' *Busiris*. The subject of the play was probably the mythological encounter between Busiris, the fearsome king of Egypt, and Heracles.⁵⁴ In the surviving fragments Heracles' voracious appetite is derided. In fr. 21 (PCG = Athen. 10.1) a speaker reports to Busiris the terrifying experience of watching Heracles eat:

πρᾶτον μὲν αἴ κ' ἔσθοντ' ἴδοις νιν, ἀποθάνοις·
βρέμει μὲν ὁ φάρυγξ ἔνδοθ', ἀραβεῖ δ' ἁ γνάθος,
ψοφεῖ δ' ὁ γομφίος, τέτριγε δ' ὁ κυνόδων,
σίζει δὲ ταῖς ῥίνεσσι, κινεῖ δ' οὔατα.

If you saw him eating, first of all, you'd die. His throat emits a roar, his jaw rattles, his molars resound, his canine teeth squeak, he snorts loudly, and he wiggles his ears.⁵⁵

Rattling jaws, loud teeth squeaking and snorting are vaguely reminiscent of Heracles' onset of madness in Euripides, when Heracles spurts foams from the mouth onto his beard ('ἐκβαλὼν ἀφρὸν καθέσταζ' εὔτριχος γενειάδος', 'while foam came out of his mouth and dripped onto his handsome beard', 934), and he is 'not himself anymore' ('ὁ δ' οὐκέθ' αὑτὸς ἦν', 931).⁵⁶

The insanity displayed by Heracles 'cheated of his dinner' may be the subject of a scene on an Apulian red-figure *oinochoē* which has been associated with the Dionysus/Heracles episode in *Frogs*.⁵⁷ A comic actor attired as Heracles chases after a woman who carries an *oinochoē*. There are no obvious indications of madness in this scene, but if indeed the female figure is meant to recall the maenads, the crazed women who accompany Dionysus,⁵⁸ there may be a hint at Heracles' madness, once more exploited here for comic effect.⁵⁹ In general, depictions of Heracles' various comic exploits of eating and drinking on pottery (Heracles stealing food, having his food stolen, consuming large quantities of food, burlesque banquet scenes) may also be inscribed in the wider context of madness; the food-crazed Heracles may be a reminder of Heracles 'μαινόμενος', and it is his acts of madness that invite the laughter of the onlooker.

Euripides' Heracles

The manifestation of Heracles' insanity in a tragic context, Euripides' *Heracles*, shows that non-cruel laughter is an expected reaction in the face of madness.⁶⁰ The messenger relays Heracles' onset of madness, which comprises the full range of symptoms; delirious speech, maniacal laughter, frothing, hallucinations and violent activity. He then reports the slaves' reaction:

διπλοῦς δ' ὀπαδοῖς ἦν γέλως φόβος θ' ὁμοῦ,
καί τις τόδ' εἶπεν, ἄλλος εἰς ἄλλον δρακών·
Παίζει πρὸς ἡμᾶς δεσπότης ἢ μαίνεται;

> The servants' feelings were torn between mirth and fear, and one of them, looking at his fellows, would say, 'Is our master playing a game with us, or is he insane?'
>
> Heracles 950–2 [61]

This is an important passage because it showcases a reaction to madness which involves laughter but not mockery. The slaves find Heracles' behaviour funny or amusing due to its absurdity and because it completely defies any logical explanation. Heracles' insanity is perceived as a 'game', as if Heracles were putting on a performance and was pretending to be someone else. Heracles, in the grip of madness, moves in and out of the dramatic reality of the play, which causes confusion and mirth in his (internal) audience. If the scene were enacted on stage, the confusion of the slaves would probably add to the amusement of the external audience. As it is, there is a clash between the perception of the external audience, who realize what the situation is, and the *aporia* of the characters in the dramatic reality of the play.

A depiction of Heracles in his grip of madness on a Paestan vase by Asteas, associated with the theatrical stage, supports the idea that madness arouses the laughter of the onlooker (Fig. 13.1). This is the only painting of the narrative to survive, and, although it has some correspondences with Euripides' tragedy, it also diverges from it in some details. I quote here Taplin's description:

> To the left of Herakles is a heap of domestic furniture and utensils piled up and already on fire … His wife, Megara, flies with a gesture of horror toward the doorway. Herakles, wearing greaves and an ornate helmet with feathers – but no lion skin, bow or club – is carrying a small child toward the fire, and is clearly, despite the boy's pleading, about to immolate him.[62]

The vase has divided scholars between those who believe this is a depiction of straight tragedy and those who view it as a local form of tragicomedy.[63] Heracles' feminine dress beneath his armour and the ridiculous feathers on his helmet, along with the absurd inclusion of non-flammable metal objects in the bonfire have been thought to produce a comic effect. Taplin is quick to refute this view and maintains that these details are merely the result of Heracles' delusions and part of his macabre fantasy rather than a sign of comedy. Taplin seems to miss the point; these details are comic *because* they are part of Heracles' delusions. We don't have to give a definite answer to the question about the origin of the scene but even the division in the scholarship is telling. We are presented with an instance in Heracles' madness which oscillates between the horrific and the comic. Just before the tragic outcomes occur, we, like the slaves in Euripides' play, may hesitate between laughter and horror.

There is one more instance in Euripides' *Heracles* which harks back to Heracles' manic moment and reiterates its potential comicality. Towards the end of the play, Euripides imagines his weapons coming to life and reproaching him for the murder of his wife and children (1378–81). The strange occurrence has been explained as an attempt at exonerating Heracles of direct responsibility and representing his weapons as morally

No Laughing Matter?

Figure 13.1 Heracles in the grip of madness. Red-figure krater from Paestum by Asteas. 350–320 BCE. Museo Arqueolólogico Nacional, Madrid.

responsible;[64] it has also been suggested that, since the weapons are now Heracles' only companions, it is not uncommon for the hero to converse with them. Nevertheless, we may also consider the possibility that Heracles is tormented by grief and guilt, which instigate these hallucinations. In this sense, the weapons occupy a similar role to that of the Furies in the case of Orestes; they function as the physical manifestation of the hero's guilt, but at the same time are a tangible symptom of his madness. Heracles does not go through with his plan to commit suicide nor is he expiated for the murders he committed in any other way. The hallucination of the talking weapons is caused by his guilty conscience and could indicate a momentary lapse into madness. Significantly, while the attribution of speech to inanimate objects is unpreceded in tragedy, it is not at all uncommon in comedy. Although the scene need not be associated with a specific comic

165

instance, the passage is indeed 'negatively "marked" for its audience as unusual and out of place'.[65] My suggestion is that the talking weapons are meant to produce a comic effect for the audience, who are invited to laugh in the face of Heracles' delusion, just as earlier Heracles' slaves were torn between laughter and dread when they witnessed Heracles lashing imaginary horses and wrestling invisible opponents. This is not the laughter of ridicule, which is suggested in the case of Ajax by Athena; it is the uneasy laughter of awkwardness and hopelessness.

Conclusion

I have argued that madness, with its absurdity, its blurring of illusion and reality, its occasional playfulness, and its onstage violence as a source of visual humour, can be appreciated as a comic rather than tragic spectacle. Due to these characteristics, madness stirs a sort of aporetic laughter, laughter as a reaction to helplessness in the face of (a spectacle of) irrationality and farce. When events exceed our capability to grasp, comprehend and explain them, the 'unendurable' quality of humour can be the only answer. We are accustomed to thinking that madness in comedy is 'tragic', in the sense that instances of comic madness are parodic takes or derivative citations from tragedy. Perhaps we should acknowledge the inherent comicality of madness, even as it is performed in tragedy, which invites laughter as an expression of the futility of the human condition and existence. Perhaps if we take a moment to experience the world as detached spectators, it will also seem to us 'comic in its improbability'.[66]

Acknowledgement

I wish to thank the editors of the volume for their comments, patience and support. Many thanks also go to my friend, Myrto Aloumpi, whose moments of pure comic madness during the writing-up of the paper were a source of great inspiration.

CHAPTER 14
SEXUAL VIOLENCE AND ARISTOPHANIC HUMOUR
Peter Swallow

In the run-up to the 2016 US Presidential Election, a hot-mic tape from 2005 was released by the *Washington Post* of the Republican candidate, Donald Trump, graphically discussing the sexual assault of women. The reaction against the tape was instant and sustained, particularly focusing on one harrowing line: 'When you're a star, they let you do it. You can do anything... Grab them by the pussy. You can do anything.'[1]

What for me made the so-called *Access Hollywood* tape even more disturbing was hearing the reaction of Trump's interlocutor, Billy Bush – himself closely connected to Republican politics through his family. On the tape, as Trump describes in ever greater detail his behaviour towards women, Bush can be heard laughing.[2] While I hope nobody reading this article would find what Donald Trump was saying on the tape funny, it is clear, then, that some people – among them Billy Bush – *might* find it funny. Humour is, like beauty, in the eyes of the beholder, and while some people would find it anathema to try and *joke* about sexual violence, some people obviously do not. Anyone who has ever been on social media will know this to be true. For the sake of clarity, I am going to refer to this as humour *potential*, which is in a sense tautological because, to reiterate, *all* humour is subjective, but which I hope will underline the fact that I do not myself find sexual violence an appropriate or effective topic for humour.

Why, then, we may ask, is Trump talking about sexually assaulting women a site for humour potential? As this volume has heretofore demonstrated, it is a misconception that humour is not capable of sustaining theoretical models to explain it, although the field of humour theory remains nascent and complex. The most widely accepted theory is incongruity theory, although other brands are very much still available. As this article is intended not as a discussion of theory as a whole but an examination of humour *practice*, however, I do not want to get waylaid with outlining the various models (for which one can refer to the Introduction of this volume). I *will* briefly explain an incongruity theory, before applying it specifically to the *Access Hollywood* tape. Then we will apply it to five scenes from Aristophanes, from *Ecclesiazusae*, *Birds*, *Thesmophoriazusae*, *Peace* and *Acharnians*, to explore how sexual violence interacts with humour in Old Comedy.

There are numerous variants of incongruity theory, but, in short, it argues that amusement is derived from two conflicting ideas, and the act of reconciling these two incongruities. Therefore we might laugh at a clown's funny walk because of the incongruity between their bumbling and our concept of how to walk properly. Essentially, if there is a tension between the 'script' set up by a joke and a juxtaposed script more concordant to reality, there is humour potential. Of course, not every incongruity is funny – for example, as Martin notes, 'the ironies present in the plot of *Oedipus Rex* can be aesthetically enjoyed, although they are anything but funny'.[3]

Veatch has usefully set this up as a tension between 'a predominating view of the situation as being normal' (N) and 'a violation of a "subjective moral principal"' (V).[4] The N-script sets off no alarm bells; in the V-script, something feels wrong. Specifically, 'V' may constitute not only a violation of logic (clowns walking funnily) but also *a moral violation*. (Veatch in fact exclusively talks about moral violation, but in a far broader sense of the term.) This is the model I propose to adopt here, and in particular I want to carry forth his conceptions of an incongruity set up between N-script and V-script. We can set out the formula for this like so:

N + V = H

    Where N is the 'predominating view' of a 'normal' situation

    V is a (moral) violation of the N-script

    H is humour (potential)

Though of course, it is not enough for both an N-script and a V-script to be merely present; they must interact with one another. The use of an addition sign is therefore somewhat misleading. And an interaction of N and V does not automatically generate H – the equals sign is also an approximation. Likewise, even very basic jokes can self-evidently sustain multiple N- and V-script interactions to create humour and can therefore work on multiple levels. An excellent example of this is the opening scene of *Frogs*, in which the slave Xanthias is working overtime to produce slapstick prop comedy complete with repeated scatological quips while Dionysus chides his 'lowbrow' comedy:

    X τὸ πάνυ γέλοιον εἴπω;
    D   νὴ Δία
        θαρρῶν γε· μόνον ἐκεῖν' ὅπως μὴ 'ρεῖς—
    X   τὸ τί;
    D μεταβαλλόμενος τἀνάφορον ὅτι χεζητιᾷς.
        …
    X τί δῆτ' ἔδει με ταῦτα τὰ σκεύη φέρειν,
        εἴπερ ποήσω μηδὲν ὧνπερ Φρυνίχοις
        εἴωθε ποιεῖν καὶ Λύκις κἀμειψίαις

    X Can I say the really funny one?
    D   Yes, by Zeus,
        By all means; just don't say this.
    X   What?

D That you're moving the pole around to take a shit.
...

X So why do I have to carry all this stuff, if I can't do what Phrynichus and Lycis and Ameipsias were always doing?

Aristophanes, Frogs *6-8; 12-15*[5]

This is (potentially) funny because they are talking about defecating, one of the surest topics for a certain kind of humour:

Scatology is a taboo

+

Xanthias and Dionysus are talking about defecation

=

H

It is also funny because, in his appeal to Dionysus, Xanthias inadvertently – and therefore Aristophanes consciously – sets other comic playwrights who make such jokes up for Dionysus the god of theatre to knock down. Phrynichus, Lycis and Ameipsias are the sorts of poets who *do* resort to this dreaded lowbrow comedy.[6] And on another level altogether, it is funny because by refusing to let Xanthias talk about pooing himself, Dionysus actually *facilitates* and *participates* in the dialogue, undermining his own reticence by becoming part of the shit skit after all. The 'two elements (the prohibition of cliché and the enactment of cliché) rub against each other to produce an unstated but implied inference for the audience, namely that the play or its author are in some sense being "hypocritical".'[7] Or to plug the variables into our formula:

Dionysus (and thus perhaps Aristophanes) criticizes scatological humour

+

Dionysus (and thus certainly Aristophanes) is hypocritically participating in a scene dependent on scatological humour

=

H

An audience member may laugh at any combination of these different scripts, which is to say that any given script, or all three, may produce humour potential. This is rather the point of the scene – it can appeal to those with a 'lowbrow' *and* those with a more 'refined' sense of humour equally well. We could no doubt list a number of other incongruities in the scene besides the three outlined here.[8] But what is important is that we have a basic model with which to test humour potential. Our formula (Veatch's) is a shorthand, but is nevertheless still productive.

Veatch also notes that for humour potential to be generated, the perceiver must be able to overcome their concern for the N-script. Equally, they must value the N-script to some extent.[9] That is to say, if Aristophanes performed the opening scene of *Frogs* to an audience who all regarded the taboo of discussing defecation as paramount, something not to be transgressed on any account, a V-script violation of that taboo would not generate humour potential but other, less positive emotions. Likewise, if Aristophanes' audience already regularly discussed their stools with passing strangers, they would scarcely be excited by the V-script violation because it would not, in fact, *be* a violation. The gap between N and V must be wide enough to be productive, but small enough to be bridgeable.

What is going on in the *Access Hollywood* tape, I would argue, is a tension between an N-script acknowledging that sexual assault is wrong, and a V-script of masculinity which is able to over-ride that N-script:

The sanctity of (women's) bodily autonomy

+

Imposition of masculinity onto and against a feminized victim

=

H

In Bush's and Trump's appreciation of the joke, the N-script is valued more highly than the moral transgression inherent in sexual assault – that is to say, because Donald Trump is hypermasculine and also a celebrity, he is in his view *allowed* to transcend the N-script without consequence. It is telling that Trump later defended his joking by calling it 'locker-room banter';[10] however real the acts described happened to be, for both interlocutors, the V-script is not a significant moral violation at all. 'They let you do it' as a celebrity. It *is* still a violation – if it were not, it would not be funny.

Many people more ethically decent than Billy Bush do not find the *Access Hollywood* tape funny, on the other hand, because in our perception of their dialogue the N-script is so subdued by the moral violation of sexual assault that we cannot reconcile the two competing N- and V-scripts. Our focalization is fundamentally different – unsurprisingly, Trump is only concerned with himself, whereas we are concerned with the victims of his masculine attentions. There is a fundamental difference in our internal moralities, which means that we have 'important differences of attachment to various moral principles';[11] we are more attached to the N-script and are incapable of resolving the violation.

This is all underpinned by the fundamental nature of sexual violence as 'the ultimate translation of phallicism into action . . . [enacting] the principle of domination by means of sex'.[12] It is the assertion of the perpetrator's masculinity against and onto the victim, who is usually (but not exclusively) female. Therefore it serves a double function: it degrades and dehumanizes the victim, acting to feminize them still further, but it also reinforces the gender identity of the assaulter as masculine. It is, in short, a performance of gender dynamics at their most troubling. This is the basis of the V-script moral violation set up by rape jokes. What is important to remember – and this is why I have spent so long talking about Donald Trump – is that it *is* possible to create humour potential through rape jokes – which is to say, some people do unfortunately find the idea of a man asserting his masculinity and sexually assaulting a woman genuinely funny, at least in certain defined social situations, specifically because of the gendered dynamics at play in the construction of the joke's N- and V-scripts.

There are two important qualifiers here, one general and one specific to the performance context of Old Comedy. First, it is important to note that rape jokes are rarely accompanied by actual sexual violence. To be sure, a far larger number of people may find rape jokes funny than find the actual act of rape funny, because there is less moral commitment to reconciling the V-script when the act described is in some way a fantasy. Even in the case of the *Access Hollywood* tape, Trump is bragging about types of behaviour rather than referring to a particular past event when unambiguously describing assault. And sexual violence in Old Comedy is almost always dependent upon 'fantasies or threats about rape in the *future*', to use Robson's words;[13] that is, it sets up sexual violence that is never actually performed and has no realistic chance of being performed.[14] Secondly, when talking about Old Comedy, it is important to remember that the performers, including those playing the roles of female victim, were all male-bodied.[15] Again, therefore, there is no possibility of actualized violence against women. This narrows that N–V gap, particularly for those able to tolerate such fantasies, though may do little to placate those of us who maintain that rape jokes are always inappropriate.

And so we come to Aristophanes. In New Comedy, sexual violence is frequently a plot feature;[16] in Old Comedy, it is given less weight, but is used as a repeated source of humour potential. Even so, Aristophanes' jokes tend to be built around a very different V-script to Trump's. Rather than asserting the masculinity of the perpetrator, Aristophanes in fact sets up a social tension – an incongruity – between the status of the perpetrator and their intended victim. I concede the same may not be true of shorter (and therefore inherently less developed) jokes, which perhaps do rely more on a similar masculinity V-script to the *Access Hollywood* tape. I am not trying to refute that Aristophanes told 'rape jokes'; I am merely trying to demonstrate that in extended scenes of sexual violence, that is usually not all that is happening.

'In Greek there is no single word for rape.'[17] True, words such as *bia*, *helkein* and *hubris*, as well as their cognates, may appear in the context of sexual assault,[18] but none perfectly maps onto our own concepts.[19] It seems that the ancient perspective on these issues was somewhat less defined than our own.[20] We cannot necessarily expect to see clear given consent in sex scenes. This is not the same as saying the ancient Greeks had no *concept* of rape – they evidently did, as we will see later. But in choosing examples for this article, I have selected scenes that seem to me to be unarguably sexually violent; I have avoided the merely questionable, uncomfortable or overcharged with misplaced eagerness. In an article on 'Rape and Young Manhood in Athenian Comedy', Sommerstein has identified ten moments where sexual violence is threatened or fantasized about.[21] Space precludes me from commenting on each item in his list, and many of the items do not fall within the strict parameters I have set for this article, namely that they are extended scenes and not lyrical passages or isolated jokes with sexual assault as the punchline. It is, however, interesting to note that he passes over two of the scenes I discuss here in what is, I think, supposed to be an exhaustive list.²² There is nothing surprising in this; as he himself remarks, 'it is not always easy to draw a line distinguishing rape from non-rape in Old Comedy',²³ and we must therefore expect two readers to interpret problematic scenes in different ways. Likewise, in his 2015 article on 'Sexual Assault in Aristophanes', Robson analyses two scenes from *Peace* (894–904) and *Birds* (1253–6), which I do discuss here, but also includes two phallic songs from *Acharnians* (263–79) and *Lysistrata* (973–80), which fall outside my scope because they are lyric passages and not a scene.²⁴

That said, let us start with a scene from *Ecclesiazusae*. Over the course of the play, women seize control of Athens and set up a proto-socialist state in which everything must be shared equally. Unfortunately for one young man, that includes him – although he wants to have sex with an attractive young girl, the law clearly states he must have sex with an old woman first. In fact, the law explicitly states that older women have the right 'τὸν νέον/ἕλκειν ἀνατεί' (1019f.), to '*drag off* the young man with impunity'. The verb *helkein* implicitly suggests sexual assault, and it is no coincidence that it appears *seven more times* over the next eighty lines in various lexical forms, always as a *double entendre* (*Ecclesiazusae* 1037, 1050, 1055f., 1066, 1087, 1094).²⁵ Three women, each older and uglier than the last, try and claim the young man, before eventually he is dragged off by two of the women, crying out in 'paratragic tone':²⁶

> ὦ τρισκακοδαίμων, εἰ γυναῖκα δεῖ σαπρὰν
> βινεῖν ὅλην τὴν νύκτα καὶ τὴν ἡμέραν,
> κἄπειτ' ἐπειδὰν τῆσδ' ἀπαλλαγῶ, πάλιν
> φρύνην ἔχουσαν λήκυθον πρὸς ταῖς γνάθοις.

> I'm three times damned if I have to fuck a rotten woman all day and night, then, when I'm free of her, next fuck a toad who has a funeral urn by her jaw.
>
> Ecclesiazusae *1098–1101*

The joke here is obviously dependent on sexual assault – the voracious older women are compelling their victim to sleep with him. But what is unusual is that the victim here is a young, virile man, while the perpetrators are old and ugly women. There is a different N-script and V-script here. Our N-script is that in the common conception of sexual assault, the perpetrator is invariably a male inflicting his masculinity on a (young) female victim. The V-script violation is that here, the traditional roles of masculine perpetrator and feminine victim have been reversed so that it is a man at prey to women:

Men commit sexual assault against women
+
Here, women are committing sexual assault against a man
=
H

Sexual Violence and Aristophanic Humour

Indeed, apart from the fact that it is such a masculine act, the sexual violence is almost beside the point of the joke – it creates humour potential of the simplest kind, by setting up an incongruity between expected and presented realities. This is not to say that women cannot commit serious sexual assault and men cannot be victims, because both statements are demonstrably false, but the joke's N-script is dealing in generalizations. The age and ugliness of the grotesque women provide a further layer of humour potential. At the same time, of course, this is *also* a joke about sexual assault, so that there is also another N-script and V-script working on that level as well, but they are modified by the specific dynamics of the scene in question.[27]

Our next scene is from *Birds*, in which the winged god Iris attempts to fly through the airspace of our protagonist Peisetaerus' new bird city Cloudcuckooland. After hurling general innuendo at her and threatening her with execution (that is to say, more generalized expressions of his masculinity against her), Peisetaerus makes an explicit sexual threat:

σὺ δ' εἴ με λυπήσεις τι, τῆς διακόνου
πρώτης ἀνατείνας τὼ σκέλει διαμηριῶ
τὴν Ἶριν αὐτήν, ὥστε θαυμάζειν ὅπως
οὕτω γέρων ὢν στύομαι τριέμβολον.

But you – if you annoy me at all, I'll spread the servant's legs first and fuck Iris herself, so that you'll be amazed at how, although I am an old man, I stay hard like three ship's beaks.

Birds 1253–6

Here, we do have a masculine perpetrator attempting to perpetrate sexual violence against a female, and on an initial, textual reading the scene is deeply disturbing. Peisetaerus does not use any of the vocabulary we have identified as rape vocabulary, although the threat is transparent and Iris hopes that Zeus will stop Peisetaerus' 'ὕβρεως' (his 'outrage', *Birds* 1259). She must mean the *hubris* of making the threat, not carrying it out. What is at stake is Peisetaerus' virility, as he demonstrates by expressing concerns over his old age with a concessive participle (I will commit sexual assault 'although I am an old man', 'γέρων ὤν') before assuring us that he does not in fact suffer from impotence. His allusion to naval warfare – he can stay hard 'like three ship's beaks' – recalls the specific context of this threat against an enemy at war with his new city. This is a threat to use rape as a weapon of war. We can therefore apply a simple N–V script opposition to this scene and see the humour potential here as being explicitly tied to sexual violence and masculinity. However, the scene also sets up two other competing N–V script oppositions, both of which modify Peisetaerus' violent language. First, he is threatening to assault not some helpless woman, but a god. This is important characterization for Peisetaerus, who over the course of the play increasingly appropriates divine prerogatives; per Robson, 'were it to take place, Peisetaerus' rape of Iris would help to establish a new world order and symbolize his dominance over the gods'.[28] On the other hand, the attempted sexual assault of Iris may have been a common theme of satyr plays,[29] so that this scene perhaps associates Peisetaerus' character less positively with satyrs. But it also sets up an incongruity between the status of the victim and perpetrator similar to that seen in *Ecclesiazusae*. A man may very well impose his masculinity on a woman through sexual violence (our N-script), but he should not against a she-god (our V-script):

Men commit sexual assault against (physically weaker) women
+
Here, a man is attempting sexual assault against a she-god
=
H

Second, and more visually, Peisetaerus' attempts to commit sexual assault against Iris are undermined by the spatial distance between threatener and intended victim. Peisetaerus is on the stage, throwing sexual language at Iris as she hangs from a crane above his head. The crane is a comic *topos* of its own, and what in tragedy is the agent of the *deus ex machina* is used by Aristophanes to fly characters into a scene to engage in slapstick physical comedy dependent on them being suspended awkwardly in the air.[30] This underlines the emptiness of Peisetaerus' threats, because Iris is out of his reach and therefore cannot be the recipient of his violence. True, Peisetaerus has actually had wings of his own since line 801, but we never see him use them (and on a practical note, the crane is already being used by the actor playing Iris). So there is another incongruity between proposed action and the realistic probability of achieving it:

Peisetaerus has made a serious threat of sexual violence
+
He is physically unable to fulfil his threat because of the staging
=
H

Our third scene is from the *Thesmophoriazusae*. Euripides has sent his Kinsman, in female dress, to spy on Athens' women during their celebration of the Thesmophoria, but the Kinsman has been captured and tied to a board, and is now watched over by a Scythian archer. Euripides, ever the tragedian, concocts a cunning plan to dress up as Perseus and go to rescue the Kinsman, who is to play the part of Andromeda. The Scythian, however, fails to play his part, and continues to see the Kinsman as an old man dressed in women's clothing. 'By his rejection of fiction, his "rational" insistence on the difference between appearance and reality, his dispersal of the tragic illusion, the archer reveals that he is going to be much harder to deceive than his [captor] counterparts in satyr play or tragedy'.[31] He is willing, however, to allow pseudo-Perseus to have sex with pseudo-Andromeda – as long as he does not untie her to do so:

E φέρε δεῦρό μοι τὴν χεῖρ', ἵν' ἅψωμαι, κόρη.
   φέρε, Σκύθ'· ἀνθρώποισι γὰρ νοσήματα
   ἅπασίν ἐστιν· ἐμὲ δὲ καὐτὸν τῆς κόρης
   ταύτης ἔρως εἴληφεν.
T   οὐ ζηλῶσί σε.
   ἀτὰρ εἰ τὸ πρωκτὸ δεῦρο περιεστραμμένον,
   οὐκ ἐπτόνησά σ' αὐτὸ πυγίζεις ἄγων.
E τί δ' οὐκ ἐᾷς λύσαντά μ' αὐτήν, ὦ Σκύθα,
   πεσεῖν ἐς εὐνὴν καὶ γαμήλιον λέχος;
T εἰ σπόδρ' ἐπιτυμεῖς τῇ γέροντο πυγίσο,
   τῇ σανίδο τρήσας ἐξόπιστο πρώκτισον.

E Bring me her hand, so I can grasp the girl. Bring me it, Scythian. For all men are passionate. And for me too, love for this girl has seized me.
S I don't envy you. But if he turns his arsehole this way, I won't begrudge you taking him and bumming him.[32]
E Why don't you let me release her, Scythian, and fall on the bed and marital couch?
S If you're really eager to bum the old man, drill through the plank and bugger him from behind.

Aristophanes, Thesmophoriazusae 1115–24

This is not so much a scene depicting perpetrator and victim, since Euripides obviously does not intend to act upon the Scythian's proposal. But the Scythian is *suggesting* that Euripides undertake sexual violence, as the consent of the Kinsman is not sought. Indeed, the sexual abuse of a bound prisoner with the willing participation of his or her captor must surely strike us as particularly disturbing because of the multiple layers of power abuse at play. But the Scythian's consent also sets us up against other potential sexual violations of male queerness and incest. Although male queerness was largely accepted in ancient Athens within certain social parameters, it 'rarely appears in comedy without some pejorative coloration'.[33] That is not necessarily what is happening here, although there is tension between the Scythian's assertion that the Kinsman is a 'wicked old man' ('ἁμαρτωλὴ γέρων', 1111) and Euripides' pretence that she is Andromeda. There was no such moral ambiguity around incest, also implicit in this scene.[34] In one sense, these incongruities are little more than humorous examples of dramatic irony; Euripides, the Kinsman, and the audience all know that the Scythian's encouragement is inappropriate, but the Scythian does not. In another sense, I think, they also undercut the proposed sexual violence, which might nevertheless be said to characterize the Scythian in broad ethnographic and xenophobic terms as barbaric and ignorant. Thus we have (at least) two interacting N–V scripts something like this:

Aristophanic Humour

> The Scythian is encouraging Euripides to commit sexual assault against a male-bodied prisoner
> +
> To commit this sex act would be inappropriately queer and incestuous, which the Scythian does not realize
> =
> H

> Euripides is pretending to be Perseus rescuing Andromeda
> +
> The Scythian, unable to engage with such a fantasy, transparently rejects this play-acting
> =
> H

This is on top of a range of other incongruities being set up by this scene, in particular the intertextual parody of a tragedy, which is often a source for humour potential in Aristophanes on its own but is here coupled with a simultaneous deconstruction of the parody by the vulgar Scythian. Hall has persuasively argued that the Scythian himself acts as a parody of 'the villainous barbarian monarch' common in Euripides' escape tragedies,[35] so that he both reinforces and deconstructs the paratragedy. If nothing else in this chapter has demonstrated that a joke can work on multiple competing or complementary levels at the same time, setting up a series of simultaneous incongruities to be noticed, resolved and reacted to, this scene surely does.

My fourth example is more of a liminal case, because here there does seem to be less complexity to the joke to help displace its sexually violent theme. In *Acharnians*, Dicaeopolis has set up a private market when a starving Megarian arrives to sell his two daughters. He dresses them up as piglets, which is suggestive of cannibalism but also of sex, because in ancient Greek piglet, or *choiros*, is slang for a hairless (prepubescent?) vagina.[36] The daughters in fact express a desire to be sold at line 735, though not consent for other activities and with the threat of starvation hanging over them. Dicaeopolis expresses some scepticism, but is invited by the girls' father to examine the piglets in degrading detail. We also learn during this encounter that they must be *young* girls (too young to consent). The scene is quite long, but I quote a gobbet to give the sense of it:

M   αὕτα 'στὶ χοῖρος;
D   νῦν γε χοῖρος φαίνεται.
    ἀτὰρ ἐκτραφεὶς γε κύσθος ἔσται.
M   πέντ' ἐτῶν,
    σάφ' ἴσθι, ποττὰν ματέρ' εἰκασθήσεται.

D	ἀλλ' οὐχὶ θύσιμός ἐστιν αὑτηγί.
M	σά μάν; πᾶ δ' οὐκὶ θύσιμός ἐστι;
D	κέρκον οὐκ ἔχει.
M	νεαρὰ γάρ ἐστιν· ἀλλὰ δελφακουμένα ἑξεῖ μεγάλαν τε καὶ παχεῖαν κἠρυθράν.

M Is this a piglet or what?
D It looks like a piglet now, but it will be a cunt once it's grown up.
M In five years, you know, she'll be like her mother.
D But she's not fit for sacrifice.
M What? How is she not fit for sacrifice?
D She hasn't got any tail.
M Well, she's young. But once she's a big pig, she'll get a great, thick, red one.

Aristophanes, Acharnians *781-7*

They go on to discuss sacrificing the piglets to Aphrodite, an obvious euphemism.

To understand the various incongruities at work within this joke, we must recall the original performance context of *Acharnians*, which was first staged in 425 during the Peloponnesian War. Megara was on the Spartan side against Athens in this conflict, and as such would invade rural Attic villages such as Acharnae, burning farms and forcing the rural citizens into the city.[37] If we want to interpret this scene as a simplistic rape joke, with Dicaeopolis imposing his masculinity on the defenceless and starving girls dressed as embodiments not only of their sexuality but also of sacrificial victims, we might see why an Athenian audience would be more willing to accept that moral violation as conducive to humour potential than in our other examples. To explicitly refer back to Veatch's model, he notes that:

> In general, dislike for those who are discomfited in a joke makes it more humorous. Why? Evidently, dislike for another creates a detachment from violations of their dignity or comfort, so that the strong attachment that gives rise to offended interpretations is absent. Further, a violation of the dignity, comfort, etc., of a disliked character seems to be acceptable, gratifying, and positively pleasurable to humans.[38]

Trump and Bush are more liable to find rape jokes funny because they are misogynists; an Athenian audience is more liable to find rape jokes against Megarians funny because they were at war with the Megarians (and were obviously misogynistic by any modern standards as well).

At the same time, *Acharnians* seems to represent the Megarians pathetically – they are physically starving, the father is so desperate he is selling his own daughters into sex slavery, and they are hardly set up as a credible threat to peace. The overzealous prosecution of Megara before the war through the Megarian Decree may have been the trigger cause for the Peloponnesian War.[39] Indeed, Dicaeopolis is more than happy to trade with them, and the only party accused of invasion in the scene is *Athens* – the Megarian explicitly accuses Athens of constantly invading his country at l.762. So we cannot entirely dismiss this scene as being vindictive against an enemy of the state.

One potentially mitigating incongruity is the girls' costume – they are dressed as sacrificial pigs. Dicaeopolis therefore acts not only as sexual assaulter, a man asserting his masculinity against girls, but also (in the play-acting all parties appear to be engaging in) as a cautious buyer inspecting the goods before purchase. The V-script here is that he is not, in point of fact, buying piglets for sacrifice but human beings. This might seem to us an equally horrible V-script, but it does, if nothing else, increase the complexity of the interplaying incongruities.

I have described this scene as a liminal case, because it is clearly not a simple joke about sexual violence. As with my other examples, Aristophanes has introduced additional incongruities into the scene. However, the power dynamics at play in this joke closely match up to a standard model of sexual violence perpetrated by men against women, and if anything, additional details – the presence of the victims' complicit father, their age, their costume – make the V-script worse and not better. We come back to a simple fact: Aristophanes sometimes *did* use unmediated rape jokes to generate humour potential.[40]

A comparative scene is set up in *Peace*. Trygaeus has won possession of (an abstract representation of) 'Festival' ('Θεωρία'), whom he intends to give to the Athenian council (*Peace* 713f.), but before he hands her over he imagines how the councillors will use her:

ἔπειτ' ἀγῶνά γ' εὐθὺς ἐξέσται ποιεῖν
ταύτην ἔχουσιν αὔριον καλὸν πάνυ,
ἐπὶ γῆς παλαίειν, τετραποδηδὸν ἱστάναι,
[πλαγίαν καταβάλλειν, εἰς γόνατα κῦβδ' ἱστάναι,]
καὶ παγκράτιόν γ' ὑπαλειψαμένοις νεανικῶς
παίειν, ὀρύττειν, πὺξ ὁμοῦ καὶ τῷ πέει·
...
ἀλλ', ὦ πρυτάνεις, δέχεσθε τὴν Θεωρίαν.
θέασ' ὡς προθύμως ὁ πρύτανις παρεδέξατο.

Then you can hold a very fine contest straight away, tomorrow, now you have her, to wrestle her to the ground, stand her on all fours, [throw her onto her side, get her on her knees headfirst,] and fuck her with oiled-up members in the *pankration* like young men, gouge her with fist and dick combined;
...
Prutaneis, receive Festival. See how eagerly the *prutanis* welcomed her!

Peace 894–8; 905f.[41]

Festival has already disrobed (886).[42] This is similar to Dicaeopolis' discussion of what he will do with the Megarian daughters, though strikingly Trygaeus is imagining the *council* as the sexual aggressors, and not himself – that is to say, Festival is to be sexually assaulted by 500 old Athenian men, whereas the Megarian daughters only have to endure one. Consent is scarcely at issue here; none of Trygaeus' figures talk,[43] and therefore cannot offer consent, but even discounting this, the language used is too excessively violent to be referring to anything but rape. The councillors are to hold an 'ἀγῶνά', a 'contest' or even 'struggle', where they will engage in the violent sports of wrestling, boxing and *pankration*, all in order to use 'fist and dick combined' on Festival.[44] They are not going to compete with each other in this *agōn*; it is Festival they are going to 'wrestle to the ground'.

Even this scene is not, however, without competing N- and V-scripts. The sporting *double entendres*, while adding to the violence of the sexual assault, are also fitting for the personification of Festival, who with her return to Athens might be expected to engender athletic games. This mitigates some of their violent force:

Festival might be expected to bring about sports events

+

The sports events she is to bring about are turned into *double entendres*

=

H

Likewise, she is neither human like the young man from *Ecclesiazusae* nor fully divine like Iris; her role in this play is to stand for 'a return to normality and youthfulness', a return to peace, which is tied up with a return to sexual proclivity.[45] She is more metaphor than physical embodiment.[46] In that sense, threats of sexual violence against her are even more fantastic. Needless to say, one cannot actually have sex with the abstract concept of a festival, even if she is being performed and physically represented by an actor, and therefore does exist in physical space within the fiction of the play. Abstraction removes her from reality just as the Megarian daughters are delegitimized as concrete objects of sexual assault by their pig costumes. And the climax of this sequence is not focused on Festival at all; by breaking the fourth wall and giving her to a *prutanis* sitting in the audience (905f.),[47] Trygaeus shifts the focus of the scene away from the sexual victimization of Festival onto the sexuality of the *prutanis* who receives her. He becomes the butt of the joke and not her. Each of these elements adds to the wide array of metatheatrical, performative and linguistic N–V scripts at play in this scene, adding complexity to the humour and undermining, or perhaps overwhelming, any humour potential dependent on sexual violence.[48]

Why, then, does Aristophanes usually (but not always) feel the need in some way to mitigate his jokes about sexual violence in extended scenes? We must surely acknowledge that fifth-century BCE Athenian men obviously did not have the same moral repulsion to rape as would a twenty-first-century audience conscious of #MeToo and with (one hopes) a far wider appreciation of inequality. In fact, in ancient Athens, issues of consent do not seem to be of concern in law cases surrounding heterosexual assault, where the issue is invariably the effects of sexual misconduct on men and the state.[49] Adultery is thus a parallel offence, because to quote Omitowoju, 'a woman's consent to sex is both unrecognizable by the law as the seat of the offence, and morally untenable as a mode of justifying action'.⁵⁰ But the Greeks were nevertheless still aware that sexual violence was a moral violation. In his *Laws*, Plato proposes that 'if a man forces a free woman or a boy with regards to sex, he should die with impunity at the hands of the offended party by force and at the hands of their father or brothers or sons' ('ἐὰν ἐλευθέραν γυναῖκα βιάζηταί τις ἢ παῖδα περὶ τὰ ἀφροδίσια, νηποινὶ τεθνάτω ὑπό τε τοῦ ὑβρισθέντος βίᾳ καὶ ὑπὸ πατρὸς ἢ ἀδελφῶν ἢ ὑέων', *Laws* 874c) – although note the qualification that the woman must be 'free'. It is also coupled with a similar provision for adultery.

Tragedy presents another example where rape matters. In Aeschylus' *Suppliants*, the play's chorus are fleeing an arranged marriage to their cousins, and in a later part of the tragic trilogy murder their spouses on their wedding night; the cycle 'thematizes the contrast between consent and coercion, persuasion and force, both in the sexual sphere and in others', as Sommerstein puts it.⁵¹ 'In the theatre the myth of the Danaids becomes an event re-enacted in present time through which feminine figures, as impersonated by male actors ... are given a voice they may raise on their own behalf.'⁵² In *Trachiniae*, Sophocles presents two women, Deianeira and Iole, who have been the repeated victims of sexual violence. Deianeira talks powerfully of the emotional pain she felt at the hands of two potential abusers, Achelous and Nessus, both of whom were only fended off by the arrival of Heracles (6–21; 555–81). In turn, Iole is shocked into silence by the violence – sexual and physical – inflicted on her and her community by the same man who defended Deianeira (322–8). To be sure, portrayals of sexual violence in Greek tragedy are not always sympathetic to the victims,⁵³ but the physical and psychological effects against women were not entirely lost to Athenian men either, even if women's experiences were not always considered as important as what was happening to men. This male-centric view is on display in *Lysistrata*, when Calonice expresses concern that the sex-striking women will suffer marital rape, but Lysistrata replies that they must 'παρέχειν ... κακὰ κακῶς' ('submit to bad things badly', 162). Marital rape remains an option for the Athenian women's husbands, but 'if the [male] ideal were to make love to a woman who was frigid, passive and unfeeling, Lysistrata's ruse would not be very practical'.⁵⁴ Even in New Comedy, rape was not entirely without consequences, however menial compared to the crime; 'rapists can be compelled to marry their victims, sometimes with a reduced dowry'.⁵⁵

I have presented a very narrow discussion of a much broader topic here, so let me finish by borrowing Harris' conclusion from his more extensive exploration of sexual violence in antiquity: 'It would be both inaccurate and unfair to call ancient Greece a "rape culture" ... Men in ancient Greece often held misogynistic views and placed restrictions on women's conduct. But they did pay attention to when a woman said no and preferred it when they said yes.'⁵⁶

It is worth emphasizing that in all five Aristophanic scenes discussed above, the victims of sexual assault are not young free Athenian women – a cross-section of society which might be defined by, on the one hand, its social value (if only as the producers of legitimate male heirs) and on the other hand, its vulnerability. The assault of such a victim would create a V-script that is harder to resolve than the assault of a victim less valued by society, because the more valued victim demands higher emotional commitment. Sommerstein has demonstrated that (against the example of New Comedy) there are strict 'constraints on who may be portrayed as the victim of an Old Comic rape'.[57] Athenian citizen women are not raped or threatened with rape; men and she-gods are. When the suggestion of (marital) rape does attach itself to a group of Athenian wives, at *Lysistrata* 160–3 as discussed above, it is not a joke.

Let us return to that original script we assigned to Trump's attempt to create humour potential:

The sanctity of (women's) bodily autonomy
+
Imposition of masculinity onto and against a feminized victim
=
H

The Greeks' response to such a V-script dependent on sexual violence may indeed be closer to Trump's than to ours, but a rape joke told without sufficient context to shorten the gap between the N-script of bodily autonomy and the V-script of transgressions against femininity might nevertheless be liable to fail. So Aristophanes does not tend to *use* simplistic rape jokes, at least in extended scenes, and certainly not against Athenian citizen women. Where his humour potential does depend on in some way laughing at sexual violence, and therefore uses the above script, there is usually something more complicated going on as well – other scripts interacting with, and moderating, an *Ur*-script of sexual assault. A modern, socially conscious audience may still not find it funny because of a strong ethical and emotional aversion to any script dependent on such a topic, but we can still recognize what the scripts being offered by Aristophanes are actually violating. We do not often think of Aristophanes as a cautious joke-teller. Old Comedy is defined by its licence. But even Aristophanes had an audience, and even a Greek audience must have had its limits.

CHAPTER 15
ARISTOPHANES, PHILOSOPHER: THE COMEDY OF TRUTH IN NIETZSCHE AND FREUD

Adam Lecznar

The title of this chapter is a riff on Jean-Joseph Goux's *Oedipe, Philosophe*;[1] there, Goux traces the ways in which the memory of Oedipus haunts the idea(l) of the philosopher in fifth-century Athens and beyond, and explores the ramification of this memory in the works of Sophocles and Plato, Hegel and Nietzsche, as a means of arguing that 'Oedipus is the prototypical figure of the philosopher, the one who challenges sacred enigmas in order to establish the perspective of man and self'.[2] Taking this approach as my lead, I want to use this chapter to situate the philosophical reverberations of Aristophanes and his humour in a similar intellectual genealogy. To this end I will focus on two examples (Nietzsche and Freud) that I believe offer insight into some of the implications of the connections between comedy and the pursuit of truth.

Pursuing this angle means that I will not directly explore Aristophanic drama and will focus instead on the impact of the image of Aristophanes on understandings of philosophical praxis. As a backdrop to this, however, I want to begin by dwelling briefly on the philosophical elements of his corpus. Alongside its explicit reflection on the practice and matter of philosophy in a play like *Clouds*, Aristophanes' dramas incorporate themes and concerns (often through parody) that demonstrate his interest in philosophical issues such as the body and gender differences (*Lysistrata*), the ideal forms of political organization (*Birds*), justice (*Wasps*) and the jostling of rational and irrational faculties in human behaviour (all of the above, and beyond).[3] A further crucial theme that runs throughout the Aristophanic corpus is the dyad of comedy and tragedy (we see this especially in *Acharnians, Thesmophoriazusae* and *Frogs*), and the way in which a comic perspective can travel *beyond* the precepts of tragedy to fashion a fresh mode of considering pressing social and intellectual issues.[4]

This is illustrated particularly well in *Peace*, and the parody of Euripides' no-longer-extant tragedy *Bellerophon* that begins the drama (lines 1–179).[5] In this opening episode Aristophanes has his protagonist Trygaeus capture a giant dung-beetle that he will ride to heaven to confront them about the war in Greece, with a threat to prosecute the gods if they are unable to stop it; this is in emulation of Bellerophon's attempt to ride to the top of Mount Olympus on the flying horse Pegasus to prove his belief that there are no gods.[6] The very symbol of a human flying on an animal is ineluctably philosophical (not to mention psychoanalytical), and reminiscent of Plato's metaphor of the good and bad horse of the psyche in *Phaedrus* as well as of powerful myths like Icarus and Phaethon.

It is an expression of the different drives underpinning human experience, the element of reason embattled by the animal appetites of sexuality, aggression and destructiveness (and it is no coincidence that Goux traces these same themes in Sophocles' *Oedipus Tyrannus*, where it is the failure of the encounter between the human Oedipus and the bestial Sphinx that prefigures the former's tragic demise).[7] According to some reconstructions, the surviving fragments of Euripides' *Bellerophon* suggest that the playwright focused for internal consistency on the *hubris* of Bellerophon's journey, as he depicted his hero struck down by Zeus from the sky to a tragic death. By contrast, Trygaeus flies more or less safely to heaven, retrieves Peace and returns its benefits of Harvest and Festival to the Greek world. Aristophanes' characters seem aware of the divergence between their performance and its tragic antecedent and, at one point, Trygaeus' daughter explicitly warns her father not to become a tragedy by falling to his death (*Peace* 148). In his parody of tragedy, Aristophanes seems to suggest that, when the same events or actions are observed from a tragic or a comic perspective, the resulting parallax denotes the very different human implications of the genres, poised between life and death, peace and destruction, success and failure. Following on from this, one part of my argument in this chapter is that Aristophanes has operated as a parody of Oedipus at moments in the history of philosophy in the same way Aristophanes' Trygaeus is a parody of Euripides' Bellerophon.[8]

The relationship of tragedy to comedy was something that fascinated Plato and formed a major interest in his philosophical writing, emerging at crucial points in dialogues including *Philebus*, *Cratylus* and, most notably, the *Symposium*, and it informed his decision to incorporate Aristophanes as a character in this final text in an exploration of comedy's philosophical ramifications.[9] Throughout the dialogue, Plato is at pains to juxtapose Aristophanes the comedian and Agathon the tragedian (whose victory at the Great Dionysia is being celebrated at the symposium which forms the dialogue's setting) as participants in the debate about the nature of *erōs*. In service of this juxtaposition, Plato includes certain seemingly meaningless events (such as Aristophanes' hiccups, 185c–e) that enable their speeches to come next to one another and to dramatize the very different visions of love and desire that these two genres could produce.[10] Plato intimates the competing philosophical success of the speeches through his elaboration of Socrates' reaction. Despite the success of Agathon's speech (Aristodemus describes the ecstatic response of the audience with the Bacchic verb 'ἀναθορυβῆσαι', 'to make a loud uproar', which reappears later at 213a3 when Alcibiades has just burst in drunk), it is immediately and resoundingly criticized by Socrates for the elegant emptiness of its eulogy of love (see especially 198a4–199b5).[11] By contrast, Aristophanes conjures a mythic aetiology of desire that receives a cloaked rebuttal in Socrates' speech (see 205d10–206a1, and 212c4–6 for Aristophanes' attempt at a response).

From the very outset Aristophanes is eager to stress the comic dimension of his account, while simultaneously protesting that he does not want to be laughed at for what he has to say (189b2–7 and 193d6–8). In Aristophanes' story, humans are the descendants of Titanic creatures that had four arms, four legs, two faces and a spherical body. After these creatures tried to assault heaven (like Bellerophon and Trygaeus), their failure led them to be split asunder by Zeus as punishment and as a result each half took on human form.¹² Love is the yearning of these halves to be reunited with their own other half in prelapsarian wholeness; as Aristophanes states, 'this is the cause, that our original being was such [as I have described] and we were whole; and love is the name of the desire and pursuit of the whole' ('τοῦτο γάρ ἐστι τὸ αἴτιον, ὅτι ἡ ἀρχαία φύσις ἡμῶν ἦν αὕτη καὶ ἦμεν ὅλοι· τοῦ ὅλου οὖν τῇ ἐπιθυμίᾳ καὶ διώξει ἔρως ὄνομα', 192e9–193a1). This mythical memory from which Aristophanes derives the dynamics of *erōs* is in its very fundamentals a leap into the *beyond* of human perception, a conjecture about the 'ἀρχαία φύσις' or original form of human being; what has been termed the 'anti-philosophical' nature of Aristophanes' speech is in fact simply another way of doing philosophy.¹³

The conclusion to the *Symposium* is perhaps the most memorable example of Plato's interest in the relationship between tragedy and comedy, where our reporter of the night's events, Aristodemus, wakes up hungover while the cocks are crowing, and sleepily watches the following scene:

> ἐξεγρόμενος δὲ ἰδεῖν τοὺς μὲν ἄλλους καθεύδοντας καὶ οἰχομένους, Ἀγάθωνα δὲ καὶ Ἀριστοφάνη καὶ Σωκράτη ἔτι μόνους ἐγρηγορέναι καὶ πίνειν ἐκ φιάλης μεγάλης ἐπὶ δεξιά. τὸν οὖν Σωκράτη αὐτοῖς διαλέγεσθαι· καὶ τὰ μὲν ἄλλα ὁ Ἀριστόδημος οὐκ ἔφη μεμνῆσθαι τῶν λόγων – οὔτε γὰρ ἐξ ἀρχῆς παραγενέσθαι ὑπονυστάζειν τε – τὸ μέντοι κεφάλαιον, ἔφη, προσαναγκάζειν τὸν Σωκράτη ὁμολογεῖν αὐτοὺς τοῦ αὐτοῦ ἀνδρὸς εἶναι κωμῳδίαν καὶ τραγῳδίαν ἐπίστασθαι ποιεῖν, καὶ τὸν τέχνῃ τραγῳδοποιὸν ὄντα <καὶ> κωμῳδοποιὸν εἶναι.

> ... when he awoke he saw that the others were sleeping or setting out, and only Agathon, Aristophanes and Socrates were still awake, drinking from a large bowl that they were passing to the right. Socrates was talking to them; and Aristodemus said he couldn't remember the rest of the discussion, as he wasn't present at the beginning and he was nodding off, but he said that the main point was that Socrates was forcing them to agree that the same man could know how to write comedy and tragedy, and that the person who was a tragedian by craft could also be a comedian.

> Symposium *223c2–d6*

Understood in terms of the competing perspectives that have been ventured by Aristophanes and Agathon, this enigmatic vignette seems to suggest that a true philosophical account of love, or of any topic, has to incorporate both comic and tragic perspectives, the speeches of Aristophanes and Agathon, in order to understand its subjects both in themselves *qua* concepts and in terms of their human implications.

A second sleepless symposium, held almost two-and-a-half thousand years later in a Paris bar at 3 o'clock in the morning, evokes some of these same ideas. Here, in January 1951, the French medievalist, librarian and philosopher Georges Bataille and the British analytic philosopher A. J. Ayer, along with the phenomenologist Maurice Merleau-Ponty and the physicist Georges Ambrosino, debated a 'very strange question' – whether the sun existed before human beings.¹⁴ As Bataille describes the scene:

Ayer had uttered the very simple proposition: there was a sun before men existed. And he saw no reason to doubt it. Merleau-Ponty, Ambrosino, and I disagreed with this proposition, and Ambrosino said that the sun had certainly not existed before the world. I, for my part, do not see how one can say so. The proposition is such as to indicate the total meaninglessness that can be taken on by a rational statement. Common meaning should be totally meaningful in the sense in which any proposition one utters theoretically implies both subject and object. In the proposition, there was the sun and there are no men, we have a subject and no object.[15]

For Ayer the logician this was an uncontroversial statement of fact, based on the foundations of scientific understanding; for the others this question was at best preposterous and meaningless, and at worst, in Bataille's words, 'humanly unacceptable'; 'it is impossible to consider the sun's existence without men. When we state this we think we know, but we know nothing.'[16] What Bataille finds objectionable about Ayer's approach is that it fashions philosophy as something independent of human perception and beyond a subject–object relationship. In this connection, it is striking that Bataille's comments on the gulf between his way of thinking and that of Ayer has been understood as one of the first articulations of the split between continental and analytic philosophy.[17] Bataille goes on to describe what he is seeking from philosophy as connected to what he terms 'non-savoir', variously translated into English as 'un-knowing' or 'non-knowledge', and suggests, 'that which I feel in confronting un-knowing comes from the feeling of playing a comedy, and in a position of weakness.'[18] In another essay from the early 1950s, Bataille goes further and places laughter at the heart of this project:

> Knowledge requires a certain stability of things known. The realm of the known is, in at least one sense, a stable one, in which we recognise ourselves, whereas although the unknown may not be in motion – it may even be quite immobile – there is no certainty of its stability ... The unknown is obviously and always unforeseeable.
>
> One of the most remarkable aspects of this realm of the unforeseeable unknown is the risible, in those objects which produce in us that effect of inner upheaval, of overwhelming surprise which we call laughter.[19]

In philosophical terms, then, we might understand the difference between the tragic and the comic mode as styles of philosophy, one of which seeks insight into a stable system of meaning, and one of which pursues the surprising, the laughable and the uncertain outcomes of philosophy in the context of life.

In the following analysis I will understand these two debates as dramatizing a particular schism of philosophical thought that is not one of content, or at least not primarily so, but one of perspective; it is a question of what it means to write philosophy in the tragic or the comic mode. For Plato, this question seems to have a more literary connotation, and we can see it at play in the different accounts of desire presented by Aristophanes and

Agathon; for Bataille, it seems to be present in the idea of the tragic absurdity of a philosophy that thinks it can reflect seriously and helpfully on a world bereft of human beings, or on the sun without its human observers.[20] Indeed, it is the fact that these two debates interpellate an observer with a perspective that can incorporate two seemingly disparate understandings of the fundamental questions of philosophical inquiry that accounts for their emblematic importance. On one reading, this can be understood as a question of dialectic; the Aristophanic perspective impels philosophy to push past its tragic assumptions and to plot thought as a narrative with an ending (in this it is unsurprising that Aristophanes was one of Hegel's favourite writers).[21] To think about what this means in practice, and to trace some of its implications in the history of thought, I want to focus on *Beyond Good and Evil* by Friedrich Nietzsche, first published in 1886, and *Beyond the Pleasure Principle* by Sigmund Freud, first published in 1920. Both of these works are predicated on the idea of a 'beyond', a 'jenseits', and both think about what lies on the other side of traditional modes of thought and understanding.[22] As we will see, the symbol of Aristophanes plays a peripheral yet crucial role in both of these texts; and on this reading, what is funny about Aristophanes is the way that his writing, and his example, allows philosophy to push beyond the dominant 'tragic' mode of thinking to establish a way of thinking based on humanity rather than concepts.

To begin with, Nietzsche. *Beyond Good and Evil* (1886) is a provisional work; its subtitle is 'Prelude to the Philosophy of the Future', its first word is 'Vorausgesetzt . . .' ('supposing . . .'), and throughout we can see Nietzsche thinking through different possibilities, assumptions and hypotheses about what a future philosophy, and its future philosophers, could look like.[23] The initial appearance of a concern with the tragic and comic possibilities of this style of thought comes at the close of section 25, where Nietzsche describes 'the absurd spectacle of moral indignation, which is an unmistakable sign that a philosopher has lost his philosophical sense of humour'.[24] He continues by invoking the 'dangerous wish to see many of these philosophers in their degeneration for once', and declares:

> It's just that, with this sort of wish we have to be clear about *what* we will be seeing: – only a satyr play, only a satirical epilogue, only the continuing proof that the long, real tragedy *has come to an end* (assuming that every philosophy was originally a long tragedy –).[25]

Here we see Nietzsche referencing the longstanding notion that philosophy is a fundamentally tragic enterprise. This tradition has one of its most significant birthplaces in the confrontation between Oedipus and the Sphinx, the aftermath of which is narrated in Sophocles' *Oedipus Tyrannus*, where, at the very close, the chorus makes the following comment:

ὦ πάτρας Θήβης ἔνοικοι, λεύσσετ', Οἰδίπους ὅδε,
ὃς τὰ κλείν' αἰνίγματ' ᾔδει καὶ κράτιστος ἦν ἀνήρ,
οὗ τίς οὐ ζήλῳ πολιτῶν ἦν τύχαις ἐπιβλέπων,
εἰς ὅσον κλύδωνα δεινῆς συμφορᾶς ἐλήλυθεν,

> ὥστε θνητὸν ὄντ' ἐκείνην τὴν τελευταίαν ἰδεῖν
> ἡμέραν ἐπισκοποῦντα μηδέν' ὀλβίζειν, πρὶν ἂν
> τέρμα τοῦ βίου περάσῃ μηδὲν ἀλγεινὸν παθών.

> Dwellers in our native land of Thebes, see to what a storm of cruel disaster has come to Oedipus here, who knew the answer to the famous riddle and was a mighty man, on whose fortune everyone among the citizens used to look with envy! So that one should wait to see the final day and should call none among mortals fortunate, till he has crossed the bourne of life without suffering grief.[26]
>
> OT *1524-30*

This closing reflection on the primal scene of intellectual enquiry marks the philosopher as the figure who can solve the riddle posed by the female Sphinx, and who by doing so assumes the mantle of a specifically male, and ineluctably tragic, philosopher, who must suffer for his knowledge. In this respect, it is resonant that it was a reproduction of one of these lines that appeared as an epigram on a medallion presented to Sigmund Freud in 1906 by friends and colleagues on the occasion of his fiftieth birthday.[27]

Nietzsche has already turned to the confrontation of Oedipus and the Sphinx at the beginning of *Beyond Good and Evil* to offer his own account of its lessons to would-be philosophers:

> The will to truth that still seduces us into taking so many risks, this famous truthfulness that all philosophers so far have talked about with veneration: what questions this will to truth has already laid before us! What strange, terrible, questionable questions! That is already a long story – and yet it seems hardly to have begun? Is it any wonder if we finally become suspicious, lose patience, turn impatiently away? That *we ourselves* are also learning from this Sphinx to pose questions? *Who* is it really that questions us here? *What* in us really wills the truth? ... The problem of the value of truth came before us, – or was it we who came before the problem? Which one of us is Oedipus? Which one of us is the Sphinx? It seems we have a rendez-vous of questions and question-marks.[28]

Nietzsche suggests here that the ideal seeker of truth ought to share more qualities with the Sphinx than with Oedipus, and that there are limits to the traditional account; and we see this later in the text when Nietzsche invokes another female mythical character, Circe, the great counterpart of the Greek hero Odysseus. Here, he critiques what he calls 'the mistaken ideas about tragedy that have been nurtured by both ancient and modern philosophers'; Nietzsche's claim is that 'almost everything we call "higher culture" is based on the spiritualization and deepening of *cruelty*':

> Cruelty is what constitutes the painful sensuality of tragedy ... Consider the Roman in the arena, Christ in the rapture of the cross, the Spaniard at the sight of the stake or the bullfight, the present-day Japanese flocking to tragedies, the Parisian suburban labourer who is homesick for bloody revolutions, the

Wagnerienne who unfastens her will and lets *Tristan and Isolde* 'wash over her' – what they all enjoy and crave with a mysterious thirst to pour down their throats is 'cruelty', the spiced drink of the great Circe.²⁹

This cruelty, he concludes, is also present in the fact that 'treating something in a profound or thorough manner is a violating, a wanting-to-hurt the fundamental will of the spirit, which constantly tends towards semblances and surfaces, – there is a drop of cruelty even in every wanting-to-know'.³⁰ By prioritizing the Sphinx and Circe over Oedipus and Odysseus, Nietzsche is challenging the presuppositions of the primal scene of philosophy at the same time as he looks beyond it; and as we will now see, through the figure of Aristophanes he develops an avowedly *comic* alternative.

As early as *The Birth of Tragedy*, Nietzsche presents his philosophical attitude against the thought of Socrates, and to a lesser extent Plato, under the sign of an affinity with Aristophanes; in section 17 of this early work, he describes how 'Aristophanes' sure instinct certainly grasped things correctly' when he expressed his dislike of Socrates and Euripides and his critique of their influence on ancient Greek culture.³¹ Tracy Strong has described the philosophical implications of this emphasis on an Aristophanic point of view as follows:

> The oldest Attic comedy ... [ends] with a *komos* or marriage, in which a unity, a new beginning and grounding, is established. An end to what comes before is marked, a renewed path can be pursued. The logic of Socratism, however, is the constant pursuit of a goal that could never be satisfied. This starts the journey of the Western world to nihilism ...³²

On this reading, the turn to Aristophanes, and to comedy more generally, offers an alternative philosophical narrative to Nietzsche, which integrates him into a very ancient tradition of anti-Socratism and offers him a way of moving beyond a tragic patterning of philosophy. Two references to Aristophanes in *Beyond Good and Evil* support the development of this fresh philosophical mode; we see this first in section 28, where Nietzsche imagines an opposition between Aristophanes and Plato:

> And as for Aristophanes, that transfiguring, complementary spirit for whose sake we can *forgive* the whole Greek world for existing (as long as we have realised in full depth and profundity *what* needs to be forgiven and transfigured here): – nothing I know has given me a better vision of *Plato's* secrecy and Sphinx nature than that happily preserved *petit fait*: under the pillow of his deathbed they did not find a 'Bible' or anything Egyptian, Pythagorean, or Platonic – but instead, Aristophanes. How would even a Plato have endured life – a Greek life that he said No to – without an Aristophanes!³³

Here, Nietzsche turns a reference to a story preserved in Olympiodorus the Younger's sixth-century *Life of Plato* into a broader comment about how to understand Plato's philosophy, and the role of the philosopher more generally.³⁴ Plato, and Platonism more specifically, has been under almost constant attack throughout the whole book (it is, in the preface to *Beyond Good and Evil* that Nietzsche describes Plato's dogmatism, his particular style of philosophy, as 'the worst, most prolonged, and most dangerous of all errors to this day');[35] and here, in a vision where Plato dreams of Aristophanes, we see Nietzsche advancing the comedian as the very opposite to the Platonic approach, the very opposite to dogmatism. This makes Plato a Sphinx rather than an Oedipus, and a Sphinx whose riddle is the comic substratum of his philosophy. The second key reference comes in section 223, where Nietzsche describes how his experience of modernity might encourage such a new, undogmatic, and comic approach:

> We are the first age to be educated *in puncto* of 'costumes' . . . and prepared as no age has ever been for a carnival in the grand style, for the most spiritually carnivalesque laughter and high spirits, for the transcendental heights of the highest inanity and Aristophanean world mockery. Perhaps it's that we still discover a realm of our *invention* here, a realm where we can still be original too, as parodists of world history or buffoons of God, or something like that, – perhaps it's that, when nothing else from today has a future, our *laughter* is the one thing that does![36]

Past Oedipus and the Sphinx, past Odysseus and Circe, past Plato and Socrates, there stands Aristophanes; and in this preparatory satyr-play, this 'Vorspiele', for his philosophy of the future, it seems appropriate that Nietzsche should turn to a comic playwright as a model for how to write the laughing philosophy that he so desires; tired of rewriting tragedy, Nietzsche starts writing comedy.

Turning now to Freud, we glimpse a very different manifestation of a similar tendency in *Beyond the Pleasure Principle* (1920).[37] While Nietzsche was interested in the way that the influence of Aristophanes might complicate Plato's philosophical legacy, Freud is concerned with the way that the style of Aristophanic thought (as depicted by Plato) might shed light on some of the more enigmatic interests of psychoanalysis. This is one of Freud's most difficult essays, and one which Ernest Jones described as 'profoundly philosophic';[38] one of the reasons for this is that it sets out to explore elements of experience and existence that lie beyond the realm of the unconscious, and for which clinical material has no evidence.[39] The 'beyond' that has become most associated with this essay is the primal realm of pre-human existence, as Freud explores the idea of drives that force living organisms towards a resumption of certain archaic states; as he says, 'a drive might accordingly be seen as a *powerful tendency inherent in every living organism to restore a prior state*'.[40] In this vein, the essay is most famous for its exploration of the 'death drive', and Rodolpe Gasché explains the particular mode of speculative discussion required by such a topic as follows: 'the work of death happens in silence. In order to fill this gap, to say it in the very impossibility of saying it – for it invalidates every expression, linguistic or other, every possible signification – all analogies are good so long as they are ceaselessly replaced, unceasingly dissimilated.'[41] Consequently, the essay is famous for its analogies; it begins with Freud's description of a small boy playing a game in which he threw away a wooden reel on a length of string, while saying 'Fort', after which he would draw it back in while saying 'Da'.[42] Freud links these dynamics of disappearance and reappearance to the child's attempt to master the inchoate feelings of destructive hatred and passionate happiness that were stirred up by the disappearance and reappearance of his parental objects. Elsewhere, Freud invokes the opposition of light and dark to communicate the difficulty of the topics he wants to discuss, and at one point he uses it to conjecture about the environmental rhythms of development and evolution that could have led to the emergence of life in previously inanimate matter:

> On this view, the elementary organism did not start out with any desire to change, and given the continuance of the same circumstances would have constantly repeated the selfsame life-cycle, but in the final analysis, so the argument goes, it must be the development history of our planet and its relationship to the sun that has left its imprint for us to behold in the development of organisms . . . If we may reasonably suppose, on the basis of all our experience without exception, that every living thing dies – reverts to the inorganic – for *intrinsic* reasons, then we can only say that the *goal of all life is death*, or to express it retrospectively: *the inanimate existed before the animate*.[43]

Again, it is the sun that proves the deciding factor in the development of life; but Freud is aware that this is not the only instinct that he must account for here, and that, in contrast to this conservative instinct towards death and quiescent inanimacy, there are others 'that press for new forms and for progress'.[44] Building on this, Freud elaborates the 'life instinct', or the libido, which he at one point associates with 'the Eros evoked by poets and philosophers, the binding force within each and every living thing.'[45]

This reference to the philosophical subject matter of Plato's *Symposium*, and its exploration of *erōs*, is then made explicit when Freud explores the difficulty of understanding the very origins of these instincts. This search for origins also transgresses the limits of science, and Freud again uses the vocabulary of darkness and light to describe the value of his intuition: 'we can liken the problem to a Stygian darkness that remains unrelieved by even the faintest glimmer of a hypothesis.'[46] In this search for the origins of sexual procreation Freud is forced to invoke an unlikely model:

> We *do* come upon such a hypothesis in a very different sort of place, but one that is so fantastic – unquestionably more myth than scientific explanation – that I would not dare to mention it here but for the fact that it meets precisely that particular condition that we are so keen to see met. For it traces a drive back to *the need to restore a prior state*.[47]

He continues:

> Needless to say, I mean the theory that Plato has Aristophanes expound in the *Symposium*, and which deals with the origins not only of the sexual drive, but also of its most important variation in relation to the object.[48]

Aristophanic Humour

There are several more or less explicit mentions of Aristophanes' speech from the *Symposium* across Freud's writings, which seem to point to a basic fascination with the text and with the way that its narrative creates a possible marriage between the idea of the drives and the possibility of procreative desire.[49] Freud uses this myth as an explanation for what original state a drive towards progress might try to recapture:

> Shall we follow the poet-philosopher's hint and venture the hypothesis that when living matter *became* living matter it was sundered into tiny particles that ever since have endeavoured by means of the sexual drives to become reunited? ... That in this way the scattered fragments of living matter achieved multicellularity and ultimately transferred the reunificatory drive to the germ-cells in the most intensely concentrated form? – But this, I think, is the appropriate point at which to stop.[50]

While Nietzsche depicts Aristophanes as a checking force on Plato's tragic, life-hating philosophy, Freud uses his depiction by Plato as putting forward 'an untestable piece of mythology' that might explain the libido that co-exists with the death drive.[51] Aristophanes becomes the narrator of the 'living matter' that subtends all being, and which all creatures are trying to help return to through their sexual behaviour.[52]

These examples demonstrate the subterranean presence of the image of Aristophanes in the history of thought, and how he has come to be associated with going *beyond* traditional modes of philosophy. Whether we philosophize in the tragic or the comic mode, whether our inquiry takes place under the pale light of a world without humans, or in the lively proliferation of life that marks the world of our perception is an issue of tone, of style and, fundamentally, of choice. For both Nietzsche and Freud, the comic drive that they associate with Aristophanes focuses not on excavating some enigmatic, impossible-to-capture and ultimately destructive essence of reality, but on enabling a more human register of philosophizing that formulates fresh questions and looks beyond the tired paradigm of a tragic truth.

CHAPTER 16
MELANCHOLIA AND LAUGHTER: MODERN GREEK PRODUCTIONS OF ARISTOPHANES IN THE TWENTY-FIRST CENTURY
Magdalena Zira

At the conference from which this edited volume has developed, intended to be about what makes Aristophanes *funny*, I chose to talk about *melancholic* elements in recent productions in Greece and Cyprus. I think this *melancholia* reveals new and perhaps bolder ways to be funny when reviving this distant form of comedy. At the same time, it may help bring us closer to the original historical context, which was, for Athens near the end of the Peloponnesian War, rather tragic.

This chapter will focus mostly on the 2016 *Lysistrata* produced by the National Theatre of Greece and directed by Michael Marmarinos,[1] one of the most influential and avant-garde directors in Greece at the moment. But I will also investigate this new tonality in a few other productions, since I think melancholy in Aristophanes is definitely a phenomenon that can be observed in several recent revivals. These revivals mark a turning point aesthetically in many aspects of the *mise-en-scéne* and dramaturgy. Melancholy is only one element that contributes to these directors' overarching goal to find a new approach towards a playwright that they feel has been misunderstood, a new method of communicating his humour.

Old orthodoxies

Since these directors frame their interpretations as a challenge to orthodoxies and a diversion from what is expected, we should first look at what was considered the dominant aesthetic in Aristophanic revivals in Greece for many years. The countless examples of modern Greek 'Aristophanes-as-a-country-fair' productions by the end of the twentieth century and the beginning of the twenty-first prove that Karolos Koun's revolutionary concept of 'Folk Expressionism' was so influential that it eventually ceased to feel innovative and became the norm.[2] Gonda Van Steen describes the political roots of Koun's Folk Expressionism in the staging of Aristophanes as 'a grassroots form of modern Greek theatre and culture. From this movement, the *laikos* (popular) poet emerged as the champion of the Greek people and of the political Left.'[3] In terms of imagery and stagecraft, the folk elements in his Aristophanes productions constituted clear allusions to the Greek countryside, especially by creating the atmosphere of the country fair, which included visual references and techniques from the popular shadow theatre *Karagkiozis* and from folk carnival traditions.[4] For several decades in the first years of the Epidaurus festival, the *fustanella* (the traditional men's kilt worn in the Greek countryside) became for comedy what the *chlamus* was for tragedy.[5] Phallic processions, fertility rituals, allusions to customs from rural Greece, all first introduced by Koun, became the staples of Aristophanes productions. At the same time, a production's success was measured against Koun's legendary versions, the stress of this legacy weighing down many directorial approaches.[6]

The other big trend – which is, of course, not exclusive to Greece – has been to stage Aristophanes as a revue, with abundant references to current politics and currently famous people. For some theorists and critics in Greece and Cyprus, this is highly controversial. Dimitris Tsatsoulis writes that this approach is 'a scourge of Aristophanic comedy in our time that completely deletes the meaning and values of the original'.[7]

Most of the directors I will focus on react against both these trends in their effort to find their own visual metaphors, a new theatrical language to unlock the tone of the original and a new aesthetic. They put emphasis on the poetry of the text as well as on visual poetry and sometimes create highly stylized productions in a daring pastiche of styles. In these mercurial, sometimes truly postmodern, deconstructed attempts, the pervasive melancholy co-exists with the humour.

The cultural context

There are some aspects of the cultural context of these productions that I should mention here, as they illuminate the ideological and philosophical foundation of this new approach. The first parameter to take into account is the strong influence of *auteur* directors working with a postmodern aesthetic, who emerged on the Greek theatre scene in the 1990s. Their lasting influence is the cultural and aesthetic background for artists working with classical texts today. In recent years revivals of canonical plays began to be talked about in terms of rewriting and deconstructing, in recontextualizations that were often unsettling.[8] Theatrical trends such as non-realistic techniques and directing as an act of authorship, trends which had been a staple of European stages more widely since the 1970s, have since the 1990s become increasingly influential in Greece.[9] To these *auteur* directors we owe the introduction into Greek drama of revivals of techniques such as open-ended readings that do not follow the Aristotelean structure of conflict resolution and catharsis, site-specific staging, and the exploration of boundaries between audience and performers. Issues of what is funny, what is serious and why also come under scrutiny in this new sensibility.

The second parameter relates to the socio-economic context of these productions. In 2009 the economic crisis hit Greece, putting an end to an era of (superficial) prosperity and taking most people by surprise. It is difficult to express here the magnitude of this historical event, with effects on all sections of society, including artistic production. In the theatre world it has had noticeable effects both in terms of ideology and aesthetics. Theorists have noted the link between the new social reality and the reawakening of political theatre. The widespread civic awakening and engagement applies to audiences and artists alike.[10] Within this new framework, old methods and ideologies are rejected, or viewed with irony, especially in the field of Attic drama, a genre enduringly associated with issues of Modern Greek identity and the nation's relationship with the past. Savvas Patsalidis writes, in reference to theatre production in Depression-era Greece:

> Whether in the form of an 'alteration' or an 'imitation,' 'spinoff,' 'appropriation,' 'abridgement,' 'transformation,' 'version,' 'offshoot' or 'tradaptation,' the past, ancient and more recent, is constantly reshuffled, reterritorialized, and rehistoricized in order to suit better the situation created by the economic crash.[11]

Tragicomedy

There is one particular aesthetic choice that may be observed repeatedly in adaptations of Greek drama during this period and that is relevant to this chapter – the blurring of generic lines. This is a result of the postmodernist influence in combination with the heightened sense of theatre's political role and the challenging of old orthodoxies. The blurring of lines leads to the appearance of 'tragicomedy' as a new tonality in revivals of Attic drama.[12]

According to J. L. Styan, who coined the phrase 'dark comedy', one of the principal achievements of great modern dramatists 'is to make the audience suffer without the relief of tears and to make it mock without a true relief of laughter. The audience remains at a distance, yet within immediate call; impersonal, yet strangely involved.'[13] Helene Foley, writing about comic elements in Greek tragedy, has stressed the influence of tragicomedy and the theatre of the absurd, which are 'forms of serious modern and postmodern drama that wrestle with important metaphysical issues' on how we perceive and perform Attic drama today.[14] The blurring of lines between tragic and comic tone as a dramaturgical technique, when done well, is a complex device that ensures the audience stays intellectually alert and avoids preconceptions, while also recognizing and identifying with the world of the play.[15]

The trend of introducing a light, comic tone in tragedy, a very *new* tendency in revivals in Greece, marks a definite break with the past. It has been observed in several recent productions, such as the 2015 *Rhesus* directed by Katerina Evaggelatou and *Helen* of the same year directed by Dimitris Karatzas, both presented at the Athens and Epidaurus Festival. To an extent, the independent company Baumstrasse followed a similarly 'irreverent' approach in their productions of *Ajax* and *Bacchae*.[16] This trend is, I think, the mirror image of introducing tragic or melancholic elements in Aristophanes. In both cases pessimism is evoked, through the eschewing of easy and expected solutions; in tragedy, through the comic undermining of the seriousness of the main plot and its 'message', catharsis, justice and understanding are not guaranteed. At the same time, heroic protagonists are deconstructed with a touch of sarcasm and irony. In Aristophanes, this pessimism may take the form of the notion of dystopia instead of utopia, or of placing the main plot within a framing meta-narrative marked by nostalgia, melancholy and a sense of loss.

Michael Marmarinos' *Lysistrata*

To illustrate these points, I would like to take a closer look at a few case studies. As mentioned earlier, special emphasis will be given to the National Theatre of Greece's 2016 *Lysistrata*, performed at the Epidaurus festival and directed by Michael Marmarinos, one of the *auteur* directors who have created a theatrical tradition of their own in Greece.[17] The text was translated by renowned Greek author Dimitris Dimitriades, and the notoriously provocative playwright and actor Lena Kitsopoulou was cast in the leading role. The production has been characterized as poetic, and I would agree;[18] it was a carefully composed *mise-en-scène* of high aesthetics, with an atmospheric score played live on a grand piano, constant stylized movement and choreography, and, above all, emphasis on the language and the poetry of the text, which was delivered with great clarity and musicality, and often as a group narration. The following is an account of my own experience viewing the performance in the summer of 2016.

The ensemble

At the beginning of the performance, a statue of a man in the classical style was removed from its pedestal centre-stage. This was the cue for the ensemble of women to enter. Soon Lysistrata broke away from the group to sit on the empty pedestal, doing a series of movements denoting boredom, despair and a state of waiting. With the exception of Lysistrata and Kleoniki, and the small four-person chorus of old men, the rest of the characters were narrated or acted by more than one female actor from the ensemble of women. One male actor played the male parts, the Proboulos and Kinesias, but he was silent. Instead his lines were delivered by the female ensemble. This ensemble, always present, always narrating and commenting, was even more empowered by the fact that it consisted of several famous leading actors, in distinctive costumes and with distinctive characterization.[19] The director in an interview claimed that he cast those particular women actors in order 'to give them the opportunity to talk about the city and about their feelings, to express their personalities, because they are all so different'.[20]

This directorial and dramaturgical choice is an exploration of motifs and ideas that have been central and consistent in the work of Marmarinos throughout the years. One is his particular interest in the chorus, often mentioned in his talks and interviews but also in his online biography, in which he states his view of the chorus as 'an ancient structure that can produce forms both in theatre but also in daily life'.[21] In an interview about his *Lysistrata* he focuses on the chorus as a 'fascinating structure, absolutely contemporary even though it is ancient and mythical. It can produce characters, forms, text, poetry, a reaction against the way things are and a potential.'[22] Here the chorus, as a collective and an axis of stagecraft and dramaturgical interpretation, is also clearly viewed as a bridge between the play and the here-and-now of the performance.²³ This demands of the actor a constant duality on stage, a bifurcation but at the same time a fusing of two aspects, the actors' real-life identity and the dramatic persona – a clear influence of performance art in the work of Marmarinos, but also a manifestation of the political and activist streak in his *oeuvre*.²⁴ It also demands the complex viewership, in the Brechtian sense, of the spectator, who is constantly called to distinguish between but also reconcile the semiotics of the performance and the identity and function of the performer.

As for the play's second chorus, that of the (usually) large chorus of old men, which is often realized as a chorus of young actors disguised as old men, Marmarinos cast only four very well-known and well-loved actors from the older generation, who came on stage to try to defeat this formidable ensemble of well-known leading ladies. Casting the chorus of old men true to the characters' age, in combination with their realistic costumes, enhanced their emotional and physical fragility, thus endearing them to the audience rather than ridiculing them, as is usual in performances of this play. At the same time, the delightful rapport these actors had with the audience and their virtuoso improvisational skills created an emotional bond with the spectators that also added to the pervasive atmosphere of melancholy punctuated by nostalgia. This tonality also served to put special emphasis and emotional power on the reconciliation between the choruses. This is the moment in the text when a woman removes a bug from an old man's eye (*Lysistrata* 1025–34), a linchpin for the directorial view of the play as a story that juxtaposes discord and unity.

In an unusual choice for Aristophanes and Epidaurus, the atmospheric music by Dimitris Kamarotos was played live on a grand piano on stage, providing a constant musical score. That was all the musical accompaniment: minimalist, melancholy and without any songs, which is one of the most striking ways in which this production broke from the norm. The pivotal importance of this style of musical accompaniment to the directorial vision is obvious from the director's programme note, in which he calls the play '*Lysistrata*: a play with [accompanied by] piano' ('Λυσιστράτη: ένα έργο με πιάνο').²⁵

The device of narration

One of the most defining directorial and dramaturgical choices was the dominance of the narration of events by the ensemble of women, which often overrode the actual dialogue. The device of the narration itself is again related to the pervasive feeling of melancholy because the subtext created by this group narration of an old and universally known story (at least within Greece) was that 'there was once a woman named Lysistrata, that there was once a city called Athens'. The air of melancholy came from feeling that there was something lost forever in the past and also that this is a story that we've heard many times before but whose meaning has been obscured under many layers of contemporary revivals. For example, the opening scene, in which Lysistrata waits for the women to arrive, was presented as a montage of many things happening at once, in juxtaposition. This had the effect of forcing us to notice the dynamics of the scene afresh, as well as to consider more seriously the given circumstances of the whole play. Supertitles were projected with Lysistrata's original opening lines, while she remained silent. The chorus made some comments about her, which were additions to the text and possibly the result of improvisation. At the same time there was an improvised scene between Kleoniki and Lysistrata, about how to make *spanakopita*. Finally, the rest of the scene was recited by the chorus in two groups corresponding to each of these two characters. This structure, instead of being distracting, forced us, I think, to really notice what was going on. The leading lady's reaction as herself, as her real-life persona, to the narrated scene invited the audience to view the text critically. This invitation to examine the situation in a new light was reinforced by the comments from the chorus with regard to Lysistrata, such as 'this is a normal woman', 'this is a woman alone', 'this is a sound that a woman makes when she is alone'. Thus, from the very beginning, the central theme was clarified; this was a play about the women's loneliness as a result of the war, and on the theme of alienation and distance between the sexes.

The set design: Exposing the convention

As is often the case in Marmarinos' productions, there was no scenography in the traditional sense. The theatre space, which was the ancient amphitheatre, was used holistically, almost applying the principles of site-specific staging to a theatrical setting. The traditional conventions of theatre, even including the projected supertitles, were part of the show. For example, simple platforms were used, some of them on wheels, just to create compositions on stage or to group the actors, as well as to vaguely allude to the Acropolis hill. The scene during which the women try to escape the Acropolis under the cover of darkness, proffering various ridiculous excuses (*Lysistrata* 715–760), was done in a complete blackout, thus in the actual night. During the *parodos* of the male chorus, the old men came on stage to attack the women carrying a theatrical smoke machine, which they wheeled around the stage. They brought with them an eclectic selection of useless objects such as can be found in the props room of an old theatre; an old-fashioned table lamp, a stuffed peacock, floral-patterned pillows. Throughout the performance the supertitles continued to show the actual text as the actors improvised. Exposing the convention was part of the pervasive nostalgia and melancholy of the performance and so was Kinesias' silence and his sad smile during that famous scene with Myrrhine (*Lysistrata* 829–953). Thus, as often with Marmarinos' productions, these were elements of meta-theatre that revealed a dialectic with the ancient text – in this case, also an appreciation, nostalgia, a love for the poetry and its message.

Beauty and the gaze

Now we come to a potentially controversial aspect of the production. The chorus' costumes alluded to the boudoir; the women wore see-through shifts of pastel colours, lace underwear, embroidery, ethereal fabrics, pearls and red lips; they were voluptuous and sexy without a sign of comic sexual exaggeration or kitsch. Nudity, without the usual comic padding and exaggeration, but with emphasis on natural beauty, was central to the performance. Now, a lot can be said about this: were they presented as sexual objects, were they exposed to the male (or female) gaze? Was this meant to arouse us? Was this the usual objectification of the female form, in a play about sex? In my opinion, quite the opposite – the frame of melancholy and nostalgia, generated by the entire ensemble, the women as well as the men, prevented a sexualized reading. At the same time, a crucial element of this performance, part of what made it very moving, was that the women *returned* the gaze. They entered the space very slowly, performing their hypnotizing choreography, which was a simple repetitive movement of slight bounce by gently bending the knees, as they moved into the space, and they were always, constantly, looking at the audience, with a warm smile; their heads were always, throughout the show, turned toward us. Furthermore, this was a realistic collective representation of the female form by a group of women of many ages, from their twenties to their sixties. At various times attention was drawn to the very structure and ability of the physical body, not just as an object for our viewing pleasure but with the intention to remind us of its strength or fragility. For example, one of the chorus, a dancer, performed a very complex, acrobatic and athletic dance solo during one of the scenes that put emphasis above all else on her physical strength. One of the principles and methodology of Marmarinos is that the actor is being watched while the audience is also watched by the actor, and that, to Marmarinos, is the beginning of a relationship.[26] In his programme note, in which the director includes his directorial notes for the beginning of the performance, we read: 'Enter "*theōrēma gunaikōn*"' ('Θεώρημα γυναικών'). This is what he calls the female ensemble – meaning, in my opinion, a group of people watching while being watched.[27]

The *mise-en-scéne* thus invited us to examine the relationship between the viewer and the performer being watched in a way that corresponds to his main dramaturgical idea, that beauty needs to be appreciated. In the translator's, dramaturg's and director's programme notes, and in many interviews on this play, we read repeatedly that the production wants to remind the audience that we do not notice beauty anymore, that we forget about it, and that it is something that is easily lost.[28]

In my view the beauty emphasized in the performance was a fragile and ephemeral beauty, a beauty framed in melancholy. The music, choreography and dramaturgical emphasis were underscored by the idea that Aristophanes' beauty was going to waste because of loneliness and because of the passage of time, and that it would eventually be lost forever like the men lost in the war.

All these themes fused and reached their climax during the lines 638–57, which usually function as a *parabasis* in productions of this play.[29] In the original text, the conflict between the old men and the women leads to the famous moment where both choruses take off their clothes and stand 'naked', with just their comic padded suits, in the orchestra, as if to start fighting. Instead they argue against each other over their relative contributions to the state. As was expected in this production, the women actors removed most of their already sparse clothing and appeared completely naked to narrate the famous lines about a woman's contribution to the Athenian state through important religious ceremonies. 'And if I was born a woman, don't be indignant with me' adds the coryphaeus. 'I have a stake in the commonwealth. I contribute men to it' ('εἰ δ' ἐγὼ γυνὴ πέφυκα, τοῦτο μὴ φθονεῖτέ μοι,/ἢν ἀμείνω γ' εἰσενέγκω τῶν παρόντων πραγμάτων', *Lysistrata* 649f., trans. Sommerstein). Here is an instance in which the original, like this production, oscillates between comedy and seriousness. In its theatrical realization by Marmarinos, the nudity here was not intended to make people laugh, or to ridicule, provoke or arouse. This felt like a political act that, by echoing the sexual revolution of the 1960s, was liberating and an act of solidarity, without any fear or shame. In the description of the stages of a woman's civic life from girlhood to adulthood, this moment of theatre felt to me almost like a sacrifice; by calling attention to the power of beauty and its ephemeral nature, it brought home many of the production's more serious themes – the destruction of the fabric of society brought on by the war, the determination of the women to do everything to help the city by sacrificing their youth, their body, even their lives, the sadness at the inevitable passage of time, the urge to appreciate beauty in other human beings. This celebration of beauty and femininity was at once one of the most powerful anti-war moments of the performance.

Reconciliation

During the reconciliation scene towards the end of the play (*Lysistrata* 1114–87), instead of the usual raucous shtick in which priapic Athenian and Lacedaemonian ambassadors divide among them areas of female anatomy by comparing them to areas of Greece, there was something altogether different. The men and women of the company performed a slow, ritualistic movement piece in the orchestra. Inner peace, joy and reconciliation between human beings seemed to be the dominant theme here, with smiles of genuine happiness and calm all around. This was the moment of another theatrical coup, when the pianist, who had been playing the live accompaniment throughout the play, left the piano to enter the action and became the allegorical figure of *Sundiallagē* ('Reconciliation') herself. It became obvious then that Reconciliation had always been there, she had been the music around us, but we had not noticed. Nonetheless, when she exited the stage, Lysistrata was still sad. There was melancholy in the air, instead of an explosion of exuberance, a reminder that this was a utopia we wouldn't get to experience in reality.

Other melancholy productions

While Marmarinos' *Lysistrata* was a high-profile production that almost certainly marked a turning point in the Modern Greek approach to Aristophanes, there are other instances of melancholy Aristophanes that I would also like to look at briefly, as examples of a noticeable trend among directors.

Yiannis Kakleas' *Frogs* in 2014 for the National Theatre of Greece, which was also presented at the Epidaurus festival, was conceived as a story within a story in a dystopian world; the dramatic location was a desecrated temple, a sacred place destroyed by a highway built over it. This was an allusion to modern-day Eleusis, the ancient place of the important mystical cult of Demeter, which is now dominated by factories and pollution. The mysteries of Demeter's cult in Eleusis are of course a strong motif in the *Frogs*.[30]

The director framed Dionysus' *katabasis* as fantasy or time travel that fused the past and the present, by introducing at the beginning a very imaginative passer-by who found a theatrical mask among the ruins of Eleusis. As he put it on, the broken statues came to life and he imagined he was the god Dionysus, on his way to the underworld. Hallucination and ritual were at once evoked by the *mise-en-scène*. Furthermore, the mood of reflection, which was suggested by the juxtaposition of the Greek past and the Greek present, was reinforced by the replacement of the original *parabasis* by well-loved modern Greek poems recited by the company. This appealed, perhaps a bit heavy-handedly, to the audience's emotions. Tapping into this dynamic of the location, the director included during the tragic contest between Aeschylus and Euripides the recorded voices of famous tragedians Katina Paxinou (1900–73) and Alexis Minotis (1900–90) reciting the verses from the plays.[31] We must remember that Epidaurus is a massively attended festival, not theatre for the few and the cynical. It also carries its own history that has been to a great extent inscribed on the audience's collective memory.[32] At the end of the performance, utopia was not realized, since in this framing of the story neither of the poets could really return to the world of the living.

Lysistrata (2010) by the same director and also produced by the National Theatre of Greece, was also framed by several other layers of narrative; it included a pre-show of a heterosexual couple, very convincing as audience members, fighting in their seats and continuing their fight onstage, where they rudely interrupted a lyrical dance duet expressing Aristophanes' thoughts on love as ascribed to him in Plato's *Symposium*. The audience caught onto the fact that the fighting couple were actors only gradually and towards the end of their little scene. The point was clear; the battle between the sexes is never-ending and unsolvable.

Wealth, by the appropriately named independent group *Ftochologia* (which can be translated as 'poor people', or 'the poor'), was the surprise of the 2016 International Festival of Ancient Greek Drama in Cyprus, winning several awards and the audience's admiration. A bittersweet feeling ran through the whole performance, which was realized on a very low budget. At the end of the performance a very sympathetic *Penia* (Poverty) became best friends with *Ploutos* (Wealth) and they left the stage arm in arm as the audience, with tears in their eyes, sang along with the cast to an old popular song, whose refrain is: 'I only ask for a few breadcrumbs of your love and I will love you till the next life.' The reduced chorus of one was a purely meta-theatrical device, commenting on the fact that usually they would be required to sing and dance, but have absolutely no desire to do so. In any case, the financial constraints of the production meant that that approach was not feasible.

Finally, a production of *Frogs* that I directed in 2012, as the economic crisis was laying waste to the arts budget in Cyprus, was again meta-theatrically framed to draw a parallel with the struggles of the contemporary theatre scene. The device of a play-within-a-play

Figure 16.1 *The Frogs* (2012) at the Cyprus International Festival of Ancient Greek Drama.

was used, the whole performance a memorial for the passing of a theatre director who once imagined he was god. The performance was conceived as a love letter to theatre, with recurring melancholy elements, as we all wondered if we would be able to keep working or if the system was telling us that as theatre people we were superfluous in the new reality defined by economic crisis.

Laughing at melancholy

I want to conclude by returning to the central question of this edited volume: what makes this recent trend of melancholic performances of Aristophanes *funny*? How does Aristophanic humour operate through a more sombre tone? I feel that melancholic performances are all ultimately less prudish that the kind of Aristophanic revival we had been used to seeing in the last few decades, since they dare to include the ubiquitous sex jokes in a more serious framework. Marmarinos' *Lysistrata*, for example, put sexuality centre-stage while avoiding the grotesque or the carnivalesque atmosphere that in the past gave licence to be graphic about such things. By being more open and honest about sex and human nature, these performances are more political, even without direct references to current politics. Furthermore, the laughs are perhaps less 'cheap', and harder to achieve, since the rules of the game have changed; a different kind of arsenal in acting and dramaturgical skill needs to be used to make the audience laugh, which includes:

1. Improvisation and additions to the text that need to be new, unexpected, more sophisticated and more self-referential. Sex jokes and slapstick, even though they've worked in the past, are not the high points in these productions. When they seep through the cracks, emerging as a result of persistent theatre traditions, they may appear awkward and out of place. Contrast this with, for example, actor, performance artist and singer Lena Kitsopoulou as Lysistrata, who in her career has cultivated a provocative persona; her improvisational ability was put to great use, as she was free to elaborate on comic moments while the chorus and the surtitles stuck to the original text.

2. Acting without the grotesque 'mask' of comedy; there is an investigation of a different acting technique in these productions which includes a wide spectrum of aesthetics. For example, in *Lysistrata* we may detect elements of formalism, such as in the carefully orchestrated stagecraft of Marmarinos, coexisting with a realistic approach in the dialogue and characterization. The old men of the chorus were emotionally (and visually) very realistic and as such even funnier in their *idée fixe* to defeat the women – even though they were often very touching in their fragility. Kalonike and Lysistrata talked about making spanakopita, making casual chit-chat as two contemporary Athenian friends would, overlapping with the original text.

3. Other elements of the *mise-en-scène* such as the music and the movement explore a mosaic of stage idioms, creating a theatrical canvas of infinite variations. What is funny here can be the manipulation of a well-known convention – but as we saw in Marmarinos, this can also be bittersweet.

4. The virtuosity of actors is, as ever in Aristophanes, a decisive factor; but with smaller-budget shows – more and more frequently the norm in the last decade – the ensemble is smaller, and often each actor has to perform more than one character while taking part in a dancing and singing chorus as well.[33] This can be an effective source of humour; the almost acrobatic ability for transformation, the stamina, and the skill were part of a central metaphor in my production of *Frogs*, in which the desperate effort required to perform this multilayered play with only eight actors and a small budget was part of the point. This ability to transform was also quite delightful to watch in *Wealth*. So the emphasis shifts from a big, uniform and 'expensive' ensemble to the individual contribution of each actor and their virtuosity and, as we saw in *Lysistrata*, offstage personality. Thus the activist potential of the ancient material can be highlighted further.

Maybe in these productions we were not rolling in the aisles, as the laughter at a sex joke was often soured by the sharp emphasis on the seriousness of the situation that came up at unexpected moments. They still had the potential to be very funny. And in the end, we left the theatre with a more fulfilling experience. The artists involved wanted to bring into relief the dichotomy between dramatic poetry on the one hand and social disintegration on the other. That these two are polar opposites is the shared idea behind all the productions. Reflecting on whether poetry can ever win the battle is the source of this *melancholia*.

CHAPTER 17
SAVING CLASSICS WITH THE *CLOUDS*: A CASE STUDY IN ADAPTING ARISTOPHANES
David Bullen

I want to begin this chapter with an observation. At the conference from which this volume emerged, organized by Edith Hall and Peter Swallow at King's College London in July 2017, the question posed was 'How was/is Aristophanes funny?' The responses were uniformly fascinating in their range of approaches to the topic, as well as in the critical and theoretical resourcefulness with which they unpicked Aristophanes' comedies as material to make audiences, ancient and modern, laugh. Only one speaker, however, answered the question Hall and Swallow had posed directly and practically. This was Helen Eastman, a theatre director and writer as well as scholar, and architect of two acclaimed stagings of Aristophanes during her tenure as director of the Cambridge Greek Play (2010–16).[1] As someone who also works across both academic and theatrical territories in engaging with Greek drama, and as someone whose experience of Aristophanes is almost exclusively part of the latter, I was not surprised by Eastman's refreshingly pragmatic response; she knows how Aristophanes is funny because as a director of his plays it is her job to ensure the audience do actually laugh.

This is not a passive process, as Eastman made clear. When putting Aristophanes on stage with the threat of a live audience, there is no room for passivity; the material must be rigorously worked on, tested and tweaked, in order to clear the way for audiences to elicit laughter, a terrifyingly stark indicator of whether an audience is amused. Unlike tragedy, where the 'correct' audience response is harder to quantify (how do you measure *katharsis*, Aristotle?), comedy instantly indicates some measure of its success through laughter[2] – and for a director and the rest of their creative team, including the actors, the daunting prospect of a silent audience necessitates the total transformation of any and all academic questions about Aristophanes' comic credentials into the practical mechanics of where the jokes are, what they are, and how they can be made to work. There can be nothing sacred, nothing immutable.

At the July 2017 conference I also spoke from a practical perspective, albeit as a writer adapting Aristophanes for a performance in English rather than a director staging the original Greek, as Eastman did at Cambridge so successfully. I came at the central question in a roundabout way, reflecting on the (humorously) political dimension of an adaptation of *Clouds* I wrote in 2011. Here I want to extend that reflection. At the outset I think it important to underline the fact that, following on my observation above, my intention is *not* to make an academic intervention into the study of Aristophanes and his reception. Rather, I wish to offer an account of one discrete instance of bringing Aristophanes' *Clouds* before a very particular audience in a highly fraught political context, reflecting on what might be gleaned about adapting Aristophanes for contemporary audiences, and what that might mean for proponents of Classics (of which I count myself as one). This account therefore proceeds from a practitioner's perspective, both as the writer for the *Clouds* in question and more broadly as a theatre maker whose work is more often than not explicitly engaged with the ancient world.[3]

Clouds and saving Classics at Royal Holloway

In 2011, the senior management of Royal Holloway, part of the University of London, proposed major changes to a number of its academic departments, including Classics. The changes included the abolition of the Classics degree (while maintaining Classical Studies, Ancient History and a range of Joint Honours programmes) and the redistribution of Classics academic staff into the History, Philosophy and English departments – which would have involved at least six job losses and effectively marked the end of one of the oldest and highest ranking Classics departments in the UK.[4] The proposals were, in part, cost-cutting measures, but they emerged alongside a wider shake-up of the college's official ideology that accompanied the arrival of Paul Layzell as Principal in August 2010 and the national shift to fees of approximately £9,000 per year for undergraduates at English universities announced around the same time (they came into effect in 2012). Universities were changing, so those of us at Royal Holloway at the time were told; students wanted to study subjects that were of more direct use to them in a twenty-first-century, fast-paced, globalized job market – subjects such as management and marketing. The college would thus invest in those degrees and their departments, all of which paid for themselves in student fees (much of that income from international students), and cut back on less profitable – and, as was the palpable intimation, less valuable – areas of study.

The story made the national press.[5] Mary Beard, writing in the *Times Literary Supplement*, articulated a common response – that these changes were the fallout from the corrosive policies of the incumbent Conservative–Liberal Democrat Coalition government, and it signalled the 'slow death' of Classics in a move that would 'impoverish and devalue' all the humanities at Royal Holloway.[6] While the proposals were strategically announced in the late summer of 2011, by the time that term began, the view epitomized by Beard's comments and shared by both students and staff in Classics had generated real outrage. As a Master's student at Royal Holloway at the time, I distinctly recall how politically charged the day-to-day atmosphere became, and how a once friendly institution seemed so suddenly hostile. When Edith Hall, who was a professor across the Classics, English and Drama departments at the time, launched a campaign against the college's proposals, it gained a considerable following in a relatively short space of time, not only for the sake of saving Royal Holloway's Classics department specifically – though the threat of redundancies was galvanizing – but because, on both an affective and intellectual level, this situation seemed to be the harbinger of an existential threat to the discipline. In only a few months, the campaign had received the endorsement of many with national and international public profiles, including Stephen Fry, Steven Berkoff, Natalie Haynes, Ian Hislop, Terry Eagleton, Tony Harrison and a number of the UK's Members of Parliament.

In October 2011, Hall asked me to write an agitprop version of the *Clouds* for a day of performances on campus celebrating the value of Classics. This pop-up piece of Aristophanes would be performed against the backdrop of Royal Holloway's famous Victorian-era Founder's Building multiple times throughout the day, catching the attention of students and staff outside of the humanities who were less aware of the proposals. Eastman was recruited to direct the adaptation, and it would be performed by students and staff from the Classics, Drama and English departments; Hall herself was in the chorus. Although only fifteen minutes long, the performances were intended to satirize the situation while demonstrating the artistic legacy of the ancient world and thus the need to protect the study of that world from senior management cuts.

At this point I should return to the question I mentioned above. With this agitprop *Clouds*, I was suddenly faced with having to provide concrete answers as to how Aristophanes is funny. There was more than a little pressure to succeed; failure to make the audience laugh would undermine the whole point of the endeavour. If the adaptation showed how Aristophanes *wasn't* funny – even if the problem was my interpretations of existing jokes – I felt that I would have inadvertently proven to those casting doubt on the relevance and importance of Classics that they were right, and the cuts were justified. So, for me, the stakes were rather high (even if, in hindsight, this grandiose sense of a knife-edge seems more than a little silly). As I sat down to write the adaptation, however, I quickly discovered that trying to make what I was producing funny for its own sake was not going to be a successful strategy. Instead, I decided on three conditions to guide my work. First, I would stick as closely as possible to the concept Hall had provided me with; she had given me a detailed brief and made some astute suggestions for sections to cut (this is of course another way of saying that I would stick closely to our political aims). Second, I would need to be precise in the localization of the play to Royal Holloway; given the nature of the audience, the text needed that sense of familiarity. Carrying on logically from this was the final guideline; be as merciless in the parody of those figures familiar to the audience as I felt Aristophanes had been to those in his day. Neither the politics nor the humour of the piece would be served by being overly allusive or moderate; it needed to be polemical. The logic was, I suppose, that if nothing else, the jokes would be so close to the bone that people would laugh from sheer awkwardness.

Hall's brief was very clear. The concept was:

> To show what happens if you substitute education in how to make money for education in critical thinking. Our hero and his son go to study Entrepreneurship at the Department of Entrepreneurship, Business and Communication Skills in the University in Eghead [a pun on Egham, the Surrey town in which Royal Holloway is situated].[7]

Strepsiades and Pheidippides became Wayne and Phil Twister, with the former as a 'nouveau riche parent with an agribusiness' and the latter as a 'dreamy type who likes poetry/art/moody music and wants to read Classics and Philosophy at Eghead University'.[8] After arriving on campus, they meet our version of Socrates – a thinly veiled parody of Paul Layzell, here called Professor Getrichquick. The professor is supported by a chorus of directors of communication that:

> rephrase things in Orwellian fashion like our own Senior Management Team's spokeswoman does – so e.g. 'I am going to make ten people redundant' becomes 'Management proposes a finely judged reconfiguration of our academic portfolio'. They can correct our hero every time he says something too direct.[9]

It is important to point out that Hall's brief was responding acutely to both the actual proposed cuts and the context in which they came about. This context was marked in particular by the college's renewed focus on image, marketing and university education as more than anything being about careers (translated as: bigger salaries post-degree). Layzell was in fact quoted as remarking on the proposals to Classics as being a 'finely judged reconfiguration of our academic portfolio' – something that Charlotte Higgins in the *Guardian* described as an example of Steven Poole's 'Unspeak'.[10] But it is also important to point out that in defending Classics, the project never intended to denigrate the value of other academic subjects such as business and management, though many of the jokes came at their expense. What this unwittingly said about Classics and our attempts to defend it with Aristophanic satire is something I reflect on at the end of this chapter.

In any case, the adaptation broadly followed the line of Aristophanes' plot, though much condensed. Wayne's son Phil eventually gets sucked into Professor Getrichquick's way of thinking; the brief specified that Phil ended up 'arguing that it's right to put his parents on eBay or to sell their organs for transplant or otherwise make money out of them so he can use the capital to set up a dodgy educational services business or a new London university like A. C. Grayling's'.[11] This leads to the conclusion, in which Wayne burns down Royal Holloway, 'thus destroying ALL education in the process as British citizens will if they don't twig soon'.[12] The mapping of the situation at the college onto Aristophanes' plot clearly set out the piece's agenda, with very clear targets for mockery. Thus the task of negotiating the transposition of the original's plot and character was fairly straightforward; the key was ensuring it resonated with an audience more familiar with Royal Holloway than with Greek comedy.

Wayne Twister's decision to burn down Royal Holloway, though taken directly from Strepsiades' actions, is a helpful example of the ways in which I sought to capitalize on the geography and culture of the college. As I mentioned above, the piece was performed in front of the Founder's Building – an urban legend familiar to many Royal Holloway students, but obscure outside of the college, is that the building is one of the fastest-burning in the country. I recall being told by another student that if nearby Windsor Castle is on fire at the same time as Founder's, the fire department *have* to come to the college first; while this urban legend was only implied in the performance, the adaptation was rife with similarly contextualized jokes. In place of Socrates' entrance in a basket, Professor Getrichquick instead appeared after an offstage crash; it's revealed that he's just tripped up and destroyed one of the incredibly valuable paintings held in the collection amassed by the college's founder, Thomas Holloway. The professor enters with his head through the painting – an apt symbol for what many in the campaign felt the likes of Getrichquick's real-life counterparts were enacting. Drawing again on the incongruous architecture of the college, there were also numerous references to the stark contrast between Founder's and the then new management building – what I considered at the time a grotesque piece of work with what looks like giant strips of dried cucumber peel hanging outside. In the play, Phil describes this as being akin to having 'Hogwarts next to a posh McDonald's'.[13] Of course, Professor Getrichquick remarks that he admires McDonald's because, like him, they put money before well-being.

The professor was certainly the target of much of the piece's satirical disdain – and the goal was not to pull punches. While I refrained from naming the man who was the professor's direct inspiration, there were many jokes at Layzell's expense. When Wayne asks why the professor's office is in Eghead University's castle instead of the new management building, the professor responds, naming recognizable features of Founder's Building:

You mean, leave the comfort of my plush corridor? Not have a picture gallery to stroll through? No chapel to go to confession in? Not that I have anything to confess! *(coughs guiltily)* I couldn't contemplate a thing anywhere other than my cosy office. I'm a leader of men, I need to be paid well and looked after. As I'm the boss, I see to it that I get both.[14]

This played on the criticisms – based more on malicious rumour than fact – that were launched against Layzell at the time: that he was seeking to strip Founder's Building of academic departments to make room for offices for the senior management team, and of inflicting the rest of the campus with architectural eyesores while staying in the finery of his nineteenth-century office and corridor. In fact, throughout, the adaptation of Aristophanes' searing portrayal of Socrates as self-promoting and at odds with everyday values provided apt material to send up a man who – unfairly or otherwise – had come to embody the 'fat cat' senior management culture that was perceived to be a factor in the Classics cuts. An aspect of this culture which manifested prominently in the adaptation was contempt for ordinary academic and professional services staff. For example, in response to the professor's claims about the benefits due a leader, Wayne asks: 'With this degree of yours, can I expect to be paid well and looked after?' The professor replies: 'Of course, as long as you don't come work for me.'[15]

Another aspect of the senior management team's policies that was lampooned was their intense focus on rebranding the college as embracing the newly increased tuition fees with degrees considered much more appealing to potential students. Our *Clouds* opened with Wayne describing how he came across the prospectus for Eghead University's business degrees as reading material in the toilet of a Debtors Anonymous meeting. He tells the audience that his eye was caught by the headline 'LOOK HOW WE'VE GROWN: OUR NEW DEPARTMENT OF ENTREPRENEURSHIP, BUSINESS AND COMMUNICATION SKILLS OPENS'.[16] This directly parodied Royal Holloway's own brand slogan 'Look how we've grown', which managed to smugly cover up the jobs, departments and degrees that were being scrapped to fuel that growth.

This idea of slick communication masking ugly realities fed the adaptation's interpretation of the chorus. After their entrance, Professor Getrichquick declares:

> By these heavenly delights, these goddesses of Facebook, lazier men than myself can speak as eloquently as the oiliest politician. I owe them everything – how else would I have been able to tell those members of staff they're fired? Through the words of the directors they were bamboozled into thinking it was a fine decision. Some even thanked us.[17]

Later in the play, the *agōn* between Right and Wrong – reimagined as two lecturers – staged two opposing accounting systems, explaining to the audience the way it might be possible to adequately fund all the departments in the college (Doctor Right's view) versus how it was currently being done at Royal Holloway/Eghead University. The latter, couched as Doctor Wrong's view, aimed to expose the college's ludicrous policies by sending them up as part of a morally bankrupt and bordering-on-fraudulent approach to administering higher education. Alongside the chorus of communication directors, the *agōn* thus sought to situate the proposals to the Classics department as part of a disastrous new approach to the management of the college that was not only bad for *all* departments but downright ethically dubious. It was far from subtle – the management's mouthpiece was, after all, called Doctor Wrong – but with only fifteen minutes to grab the attention of passers-by on campus and 'convert' them to the cause, there was little room for subtlety.

The piece's finale was no less obvious. As Eghead University's castle burns, the student who had earlier acted as a guide for Wayne and Phil remarks: 'There goes history – there goes the noble, hundred-year-old institute of Eghead University, up in smoke!';[18] to which Wayne then replies: 'Along with every institute that follows suit, every university so obsessed with making money – they'll all burn, if that Professor Getrichquick and Doctor Wrong get their hands on them. Their thinking is the thinking that fuels the flames here!'[19] The chorus' final lines, and the final lines of the play, are: 'Goodbye Eghead – you used to be great' – inversing the rhetoric of growth and progress they had previously employed.[20] This sombre tone, marked by violence, underscored the grim determination of the campaign to change the college's mind about Classics. Moreover, it demonstrates the intense feeling with which Hall, myself and many others involved in the campaign believed that what was being attempted by senior management was more than it seemed. This was an egregious attempt by a coalition of institutional forces to change the cultural preoccupations of the university system and devalue the humanities, and it had to be stopped.

Did these overt, polemical politics facilitate or hinder humour? Perhaps it is telling that I recall most clearly the laughter of the actors in the rehearsal room – almost all of whom were fellow zealots for the campaign – reading the material for the first time, as well as the friends I had – also sympathetic to the cause – who turned up especially to see the performances. It must be said, I do not know for sure how effective the performances were in convincing anyone to back the campaign or to reassess their opinion of the college's management. Nevertheless, someone laughed. The answer to the question of how Aristophanes was funny, albeit on one day in November 2011, became apparent; his humour was realized through keenly re-embedding the jokes into a contemporary scenario that turned on a particularly familiar set of anxieties for at least some in the audience. A simple enough reflection, but one which merits further attention. Does this case study have any deeper implications for adapting Aristophanes? Perhaps more to the point, what are the implications for those such as Hall, Eastman and me using Aristophanes to defend the virtues of Classics?

Reflections

Adapting *Clouds* for the Save Classics campaign at Royal Holloway was my first in-depth engagement with Aristophanes; with my background in theatre, not Classics, I had only ever read translations of his plays out of interest rather than for creative or academic purposes. It may be unwise to admit this, but prior to the project I had never found his comedies especially funny. But although the 2011 agitprop version I produced was hastily written, with quality admittedly often sacrificed to blunt passion for the cause, during the process I gained a new appreciation for Aristophanes' humour. The jokes, particularly those to do with Socrates, felt perilously close to the bone – sometimes so close that I often wondered how many in the audience felt that they strayed over the line to outright attack. This was thrilling to discover; the politics behind my version fuelled the rewriting of Aristophanes' lines into a form that would hopefully make them intelligible not just as gags but as the biting satire that I felt underpinned Aristophanes' original play. It was also a relief, as recognizing that the politics and the humour of the piece were inextricably bound up together freed me from trying to otherwise make the comedy 'work'. For the humour to come across, it had to be embedded fully in the politics of the community receiving the adaptation. In turn, this depended on both my capacity to speak from a position inside that community and an audience composed of community members.

I am certain that this is not a ground-breaking discovery – the notion that Aristophanes predicated his comedy on being both a part of a relatively small community and on the social and cultural reference points of that community is fairly straightforward. In the context of this volume, however, this observation raises some important questions. If Aristophanes' humour is best appreciated by those within the community it emerges from and is written for, are those of us in the modern world ever able to fully appreciate it, given our overwhelming distance – socially and culturally – from fifth-century BCE

Athens? Does it mean that our best chance of understanding how Aristophanes is funny is through adapting it to contemporary scenarios and putting it in front of an audience? Perhaps – but where, in an increasingly globalized world, are there sufficiently discrete communities facing crises relevant enough to be able to receive an adaptation's precise satire? Even those that exist – university campus communities, for example – would still require a politics to underpin the satire, and those politics emerge from socio-cultural crises; mapping them onto Aristophanes can only go so far before it becomes reductive or simply self-serving. Theatre makers – directors and actors as well as writers – can work to establish parallels between the situations they are responding to and those of Aristophanes, but this leads to something of a paradox. For Aristophanes' comedies to be found funny, they must be transposed entirely out of the context of the fifth century BCE and into whatever context, whatever community, they are being performed into. How much of Aristophanes would be recognizably his, rather than simply Aristophanic comedy inspired by him?

These questions may be part of the reason that contemporary theatres, particularly in Britain, rarely stage Aristophanes – or, at least, stage his work much less than Greek tragedies. If staged without the work of adaptation being done, it risks not being very funny at all. And why stage a comedy that isn't funny? If adapted, however, it loses its explicit connection to Aristophanes. Why, then, stage his plays and not the work of more recent, less situational comic writers? This is not to say that Aristophanic comedy (rather than Aristophanes) is absent from the contemporary world; the US sketch show *Saturday Night Live* has a long history of generating laughs from acute political satire, and since the election of Donald Trump in 2016 it has come ever closer to the razor-sharp comic savagery I found so exciting in Aristophanes when adapting *Clouds*. Hall also recently pointed out to me the ruthless satire of the hit musical *Book of Mormon* as startlingly Aristophanic.

Perhaps this is the point. Aristophanes' humour is so brilliantly drawn from the culture and society it lampoons that it depends on being received within that culture and society. Divorced of this context, it may be possible to theorize about what makes Aristophanes funny, but it is much harder to actualize it in performance. This being the case, it is perhaps more productive for both scholars and theatre makers seeking to understand this defining function of Aristophanes' work to think *less* about Aristophanes and *more* about the Aristophanic – the typifying features of his comedy, rather than the specifics of a single play. Accordingly, when it comes to approaching the necessary process of transposing Aristophanes' plays into new contexts in order to access the laughter, the appropriate focus might be Aristophanic adaptation rather than adapting Aristophanes. In other words, the focus is on the creation of new work rather than on the material that inspired it. On reflection, this was my experience in 2011; while I was concerned about 'proving' the virtues of Aristophanes, the version of *Clouds* I produced came about by paying attention to the contemporary situation I was aiming to send up rather than trying to make funny English translations of ancient Greek jokes.

This shift marks a movement away from the original text – the traditional object of scrutiny in Classics scholarship – to the creation and realization of new performance –

the territory of theatre and performance studies. It thus demands an interdisciplinary approach. This may be in the form of an individual who combines different disciplines, such as Eastman, or a collaboration between those within disciplines, as with Hall, Eastman and me on the 2011 *Clouds*. Either way, knowledge of Aristophanes' original must be tempered by what might be called theatrical intelligence – if it is to raise some laughs.[21]

It is this matter of interdisciplinarity that proves to be the sticking point in my reflections on the *Clouds* in 2011. To conclude this chapter, then, I want to consider some of the drawbacks of our – my – satire in that piece. Famously *Clouds* is mentioned in Plato's *Apology*; it seems Aristophanes' caricature helped to stoke hostility that eventually led to the trial and execution of Socrates in 399 BCE.[22] While I think it is highly unlikely that Paul Layzell is to be brought to trial any time soon – and if he does, it certainly will have nothing to do with a small campus agitprop performance in 2011 – among the targets of our satirical ire were other academic disciplines outside of Classics (and the Humanities). The Save Classics events that *Clouds* was a part of set out to performatively demonstrate the value of continuing to study the ancient world, aiming to register the scope and weight of the loss should Royal Holloway's senior management put through their proposals and other universities follow their example. It is hard to escape the sense that *Clouds* weaponized Aristophanes for this cause – and, in trying to articulate the importance of Classics, maligned the integrity of other departments in the college, each of which contributes in its own way to the life of Royal Holloway. What kind of a subject is Classics if its credentials must be proved by asserting its superiority, humorously or otherwise? It is, I realize now, not unusual for a subject with a long association with cultural imperialism.[23] Moreover, although we were mocking entrepreneurship, not theatre studies, this kind of disciplinary chauvinism does not suggest a subject conducive to productively working with those outside of it.

The irony of this unintended dimension to the 2011 *Clouds* is that those classicists working on it, and on the campaign more generally, are among the most willing to engage in dialogue with other disciplines. Hall, for example, has a consistent record in this regard; indeed, at the time of the campaign, her position straddled three departments.[24] Furthermore, Classics as a discipline often depends on borrowing approaches and ideas from beyond its borders, as Neville Morley demonstrates so clearly in his recent *Classics: Why It Matters*.[25] He writes that 'while masquerading as a pedigree animal, [Classics] was always, in reality, a mongrel – fighting for territory with other, larger and more popular disciplines, scavenging methods and ideas from wherever it could find them ... Today, its methods and ideas are more varied than ever.'[26] Although I could not quite articulate it in 2011, it is this mongrel of a subject that I hoped our *Clouds* was standing up for; certainly, I think that piece of theatre was the product of Classics as conceived in this way. In targeting other disciplines at Royal Holloway, however, we inadvertently raised the spectre of a different conception of Classics.

The distinction between the two different kinds of Classics is helpfully demonstrated by some of the responses to Morley's book. Infamously, classicist Richard Jenkyns' review – somewhat inexplicably published by the outreach charity Classics for All – perceived the book as an 'attack on Classics'.[27] He particularly objected to what he understood as an anti-language approach to Classics. Morley rebutted this in his response to the review, also published by Classics for All: 'it's not that I wish to destroy [Jenkyns'] language-focused approach to Classics, but I do see it as just one element of a much broader, inclusive and multidisciplinary approach.'[28] It does not altogether escape me that there are parallels between Jenkyns' perception of Classics being attacked and the initial outcry at Royal Holloway's proposed changes to the department. In both cases, the responses balked at perceived criticism of the subject that emerges from the frank demands of the present. There are fundamental differences, of course: Morley's book ultimately makes a robust case for Classics, whereas it was clear that the senior management of Royal Holloway were simply looking for an easy target to help cut costs. Still, I think it important to situate this chapter's discussion in the context of ongoing debates about exactly what Classics is, or what it should be, in the twenty-first century – and to consider the possibility that in seeking to utilize the *Clouds* in the way that we did, those of us working on it may have demonstrated the vices, not virtues, of the subject.

That being said, speculating on the future of Classics as a whole, whatever form the subject takes, is beyond the remit and scope of this chapter. In 2011, Eastman, Hall and I, along with our collaborators, attempted to make the case for the preservation of the subject – and, in the process, raised a few laughs. Our *Clouds* did so not through strict adherence to Aristophanes' original, but by transposing his ideas and techniques into a modern moment and for a modern community that faced a crisis. The transposition required not just Classicists, but trained theatre makers, and depended more than a little on the goodwill of students from other disciplines to realize in performance. It is unfortunate that in the course of standing up for Classics, some aspects of our *Clouds* revealed more regressive ideas. Recognizing this, however, helps to underline the importance of an interdisciplinary approach when it comes to Aristophanic adaptation. In Jenkyns' review of Morley's book, he asks whether anybody can 'suppose that reading Virgil or Aeschylus in translation is equal to reading their own words, written in languages much unlike English?'[29] This is not the place to comment on those other ancient writers, but for Aristophanes, at least, what my experience with the 2011 *Clouds* makes clear is that without interdisciplinary intervention of some kind – whether from a director, a writer, or otherwise – one thing can be certain; his comedies won't be getting many laughs any time soon.

NOTES

Chapter 1

1. White 1941: xvii.
2. Slater 2002: 4.
3. All translations mine.
4. Morreall 2009: 79. Provocatively, he contrasts the complexity of comedy with the comparatively simple task of appreciating Greek tragedy, which relies on more basic brain functions (ibid.).
5. Boyd 2004: 6.
6. Ibid. 9.
7. For which, see Chapter 3.
8. Provine and Fischer 1989: 303.
9. Polimeni and Reiss 2006: 348.
10. McGraw and Warren 2010: 1141.
11. Morreall 1983: 1.
12. Morreall 2009: 39.
13. Vettin and Todt 2005.
14. Hobbes 1985: I.6 p.125.
15. On which see Destrée in this volume.
16. This fits with his discussion of humour as a personal characteristic which – in the right amounts and of the right type – is compatible with the virtuous mean in his *Nicomachean* and *Eudemian Ethics*; see Heath 1989.
17. Halliwell 2008: 216.
18. See Melfi 2010: 334; Halliwell 2008: 16f.
19. On the change in meaning of the words 'wit' and 'humour' from Shaftesbury to the modern day, see Wickberg 1998: 57–68.
20. Freud 2002: 117.
21. Ibid. 144. Trans. Crick.
22. Kant 2007: 332.
23. Glick 2007.
24. Veatch 1998: 162.
25. Hall and Harrop 2010: 4.
26. Hall 2007a: 1.
27. Sommerstein 1973: 148–50; Steggle 2007; Hall 2007a: 1.
28. Goldhill 1991: 178.

Notes to pp. 6–15

29. Ibid. 179.
30. 2008: 4.
31. Ibid. 4.
32. Silk 2000: 82.
33. Ibid. 83.
34. Lowe 2008: 12.
35. 2009: 107. All quoted italics his.
36. Ibid. 111.
37. Ibid. 112.
38. Ibid. 110.
39. Solomos 1974: 3.
40. Ibid. 2.

Chapter 2

1. Attardo 2016 takes Beard to task, testily but not unfairly, for her arm's-length treatment of humour theory.
2. The open-access *European Journal of Humour Research* followed in 2013; less aligned with the GTVH agenda and debate, it has developed a distinctive specialism in comparative and non-Anglophone humour.
3. This is still the impression given by e.g. Eagleton 2019, whose first footnote waves away what he dismissively quote-marks as the '"scientific" studies' of Raskin and Attardo (with the latter's name garbled) as 'humourless' – not just palpably untrue, but a hoary category error whose corollary would be that the only studies of tragedy worth reading are those that make one weep. Attardo 1994 remains the fullest survey of humour theories to that date; see further Rockelein 2002, Ermida 2008: 1–40, Larkin-Galiñanes 2017. Other significant work from the past decade or so includes Morreall 2009, Weems 2014, and a growing reflective literature from within stand-up comedy practice, of which Lee 2010's commentaries on transcripts of his performed routines are the most closely detailed and illuminating.
4. See especially Ritchie 2004: 69–80, Oring 2011, 2019.
5. Oring's 'appropriate incongruity' model (1994, 2003, etc.) is argued by Raskin (2011: 224) to be compatible, rather than at odds, with the GTVH.
6. The English noun 'joke' is used in a variety of ways, including acts of joking or jokey utterances embedded in conversation, but is used here in the more limited sense of isolable humorous structures of narrative or propositional form, usually short, self-contained, context-independent, solo-performable, highly portable, and built from a situational setup with a humorous twist. It should be noted that this usage, like that of associated terms such as 'comedy' and 'humour', is culturally as well as linguistically localized; it is a familiar point in comparative humour studies that the classical western idea of a joke, as instantiated in texts as historically separate as the late antique *Philogelos* and its modern counterparts, does not map well onto the cultural productions of major Asian literatures. (See further n. 9 below.)
7. Wiseman 2002: 13 (slightly re-punctuated); see also Wiseman 2007: 179–225, and for a practitioner breakdown of a differently worded version Dean 2000: 9–12. The joke becomes incrementally edgier if 'grandfather' is substituted by 'father'.

8. 2001: 15.
9. I am grateful to Hannah Baldwin for sharing evidence that Confucian jokes predating Chinese contact with the Greek world use the same underlying structures, notwithstanding significant issues of cultural translation in classifying the stories as jokes in the western sense. On Chinese humour, see Yue 2018.
10. The terminology of Attardo 2001, who attempts to address the challenge of multiple sources of humour simultaneously active in an extended text through a model of comic 'strands'; these are nevertheless seen as textually rather than cognitively constituted.
11. Berlyne 1960, 1972; see Rockelein 2002: 162f., 169, 174, Martin 2006: 57–62, and for a concise summary of the problems with Berlyne's influential arousal-jag model see Strohminger 2014: 63. It has nevertheless proved hard to talk about audience sensitization to comic triggers – a key part of both diegetic (e.g. stand-up) and mimetic (e.g. dramatic) comic performance – without recourse to behavioural models.
12. On the pejorative implications of *Yauna*, see Olson 2002: 106.
13. For this aspect of ancient humour, see Baldwin 2019: 192.

Chapter 3

1. The three-plus-one formula did not last forever; at some point in the fourth century, before 341 BCE, the programme was altered so that only a single satyr play preceded the entire drama festival (*IG* II² 2319-2323).
2. Zanker 1998.
3. See the excellent study by Rosen 2000, and Hall 2006: 175f.
4. Hall 2007b.
5. Reproduced in Hall 2007b: 225 as Fig. 10.1 and Hall 2010a as the frontispiece.
6. It is now in New York (MMA 1924.97.250). It is reproduced in Hall 2007b: 230 as Fig. 10.3.
7. Reproduced in Hall 2007b: 232 as Fig. 10.4.
8. Brommer 1937: 4; Hedreen 1992: 10 n. 1.
9. Kossatz-Deissmann 1994.
10. Borg 2005.
11. Ibid. 192.
12. *ARV*² 1512.18.
13. Borg 2005: 196.
14. All translations in this chapter are my own.
15. I have elsewhere argued that she is *Tragōidia*; see Hall 2007b: 233–8 and 2010b: 176–9. I do not think that she is a personification of satyr play (see Csapo and Slater 1995: 69 and pl. 8).
16. Kossatz-Deissmann 1994: n. 9.
17. Further bibliography in Kossatz-Deissmann 1994. Kidd 2019 was not published in time for me to give it full consideration in this chapter, although its contents do not appear to be much concerned with fifth-century theatrical and comic *Paidiá*, but rather with Plato and Aristotle.
18. Hall 2006: 170–83.
19. Taplin 1983; Wright 2012: 17–19.

20. Hall 2006: 328–38.
21. Wright 2012: 201; Bakola 2010: 34–6.
22. See further Hall 2018a.
23. Frisk 1954–72: s.v. 'παῖς'.
24. Schiller 2004: 80.
25. Huizinga 1949 [1944]: 6; Aristotle, *De Part. Anim.* 673a8.
26. See Rosen 2004; Hall 2006: 347–9; Biles 2011.
27. Burckhardt 1941 [1893–1902]: vol. III, 68; Huizinga 1949 [1944]: 71.
28. Huizinga 1949 [1944]: 106, 109. See Strabo 14.692; Hesiod fr. 160 Merkelbach-West.
29. Huizinga 1949 [1944]: 18.
30. Ibid. 119–35.
31. Ibid. 122; see also 142.
32. Ibid. 144f.
33. Caillois 1962: 13, 27, 33–6.
34. Winnicott 1953.
35. See the section 'Play as the clue to ontological explanation' in Gadamer 1994: 101–34.
36. Suits 1990; Hurka and Tasioulas 2006.
37. Dieudonné 2008.
38. Quillin 2002; Teegarden 2007; Ober 2008.

Chapter 4

1. For a brief overview of Aristophanic humour, see Robson 2009: 48–76. Robson 2006 and Ruffell 2011: 54–213 engage with humour theory in their treatments of Aristophanic humour. Wright 2012: 103–40 and Kidd 2014: 118–60 analyse Aristophanic humour through explanatory frameworks that are often linguistic in nature, such as metaphor, nonsense and play. See also Kanellakis and Papachrysostomou in this volume.
2. Grice 1975: 45.
3. I do not intend that this list of social standards should be taken as exhaustive.
4. Grice 1975: 45.
5. Ibid. 45–6.
6. Raskin 1985: 102–4, Attardo 1993, Robson 2006: 18–22, Morreall 2009: 2–4.
7. For an overview of the release, superiority and incongruity theories of humour, see Morreall 2009: 2–23 and Hurley, Dennett and Adams 2011: 37–55, as well as the introduction of this volume.
8. Raskin 1985.
9. Attardo and Raskin 1991.
10. Hurley, Dennett and Adams 2011.
11. North 1966, Rademaker 2005.
12. Finkelberg 1998, Geuss 2013: 66–8.

13. Pollitt 1999: 3–8.
14. Sipiora 2002.
15. All translations my own, unless stated.
16. Morreall 1987.
17. Raskin 1985, Attardo and Raskin 1991.
18. Minsky 1975, Coulson 2001.
19. Euripides' use of lame characters was a running gag in Aristophanic comedy: *Acharnians* 410–11, 426–9, *Peace* 146–8, *Frogs* 846.
20. VΔgue 2013.
21. On the differences between funny-strange and funny-ha-ha, see Morreall 1987, Hurley, Dennett and Adams 2011: 27–30. Even 'arbitrary' jokes like this might still involve a frame violation, where an expected 'telling a joke with congruousness' frame is suddenly resolved to a 'telling a joke without congruousness' frame.
22. Olson 2002: 127, 129–33.
23. Keenan 1976.
24. Magnes' *Birds, Fig-Wasps, Frogs*; Pherecrates' *Ant-Men*; Callias' *Frogs*; Crates' *Beasts*; Eupolis' *Nanny-Goats*; Plato's *Ants*; Cantharus' *Nightingales, Ants*; Aristophanes' *Knights, Wasps, Birds, Frogs, Storks*; Diocles' *Bees*; Archippus' *Fishes*; Antiphanes' *Knights*, and Crates II's *Birds*. On animal choruses in comedy, see Sifakis 1971: 73–102, Rothwell 2007, Compton-Engle 2015: 110–43.
25. On women and gender in Aristophanes, see Taaffe 1993, Zeitlin 1996, Foley 2014.
26. On comedy's appropriation of other genres, see Bakola, Prauscello and Telò 2013.
27. On the concept of collision in Aristophanes, see Silk 1993, Robson 2006: 96–9, 184–6.
28. Wilkins 2000: 406–8.
29. Wilkins 2000: 407 n. 136 suggests an additional pun on the town of Meropis, which would create a layered humorous effect.
30. On paraepic in comedy, see Revermann 2013. On paratragedy in comedy, see Rau 1967, Silk 1993, Farmer 2017.
31. Wyles 2011: 61–85.
32. On costume reflecting one's identity in Greek drama, see Wyles 2011: 61–9, Wright 2012: 123–5, Compton-Engle 2015: 88–109.
33. On New Music, see Csapo 2004.
34. On the debate about whether women and non-citizens were able to watch theatrical performances, see Roselli 2011: 118–94, Powers 2014: 29–45.
35. On gender and androgyny in ancient Greece and Rome, see Brisson 2002.
36. See Swallow in this volume.
37. Farmer 2017: 22 provides one example from Callias' *Pedētai* (fr. 14), which mocks the sons of the tragic poet Melanthius as being the 'most white-assed' (μάλιστα λευκοπρώκτοι), a joke relying on the incongruity between the roots μελαν- 'black' and λευκο- 'white' as well as the sexual passivity implied in being 'white-assed'.
38. See n. 24.
39. On paratragedy in the comic fragments, see Farmer 2017: 11–113. On paratragedy in Cratinus, see Bakola 2010: 118–79. On paratragedy in Eupolis, see Telò 2007: 106–21. On paragedy in Strattis, see Miles 2009.

40. Bakola 2010: 252–61 suggests that Cratinus' *Dionysalexandros* staged Dionysus dressing up like Paris and a ram and that Eupolis' *Taxiarchoi* (fr. 280) may have featured Dionysus enacting some sort of costume change, or at least contemplating one.
41. Rosen 1997.
42. Storey 2011a: 188f.
43. Lissarrague 1990: 236.
44. On Cratinus' *Dionysalexandros*, see Bakola 2010: 81–102, 252–72, Shaw 2014: 90–4.
45. Revermann 2006a: 154.
46. Bakola 2010: 252–61.
47. Morreall 2009: 12–3, Hurley, Dennett and Adams 2011: 48–9.
48. Seidensticker 1978, 1982: 116–23.
49. McGraw and Warren 2010.
50. Hall 2010a.
51. Munteanu 2012: 141–50 also posits a tight link between emotions in the characters onstage and the audience.
52. One exception to this occurs in insult comedy, where the purpose is to transgress beyond the point where the audience feels safe and can consider the insults benign. But often this achieves a sense of discomfort, not laughter, or at best prompts a mixed response from the audience.

Chapter 5

1. Bataille 1971: 13.
2. The death drive was first theorized by Freud in *Beyond the Pleasure Principle* (1920). For an exploration of death-driven aesthetics in Greek tragedy, see Telò 2020.
3. Land 1992: xvii.
4. Sondheim 2011.
5. Here and elsewhere I reproduce Henderson's Loeb texts and translations of Aristophanes with adaptations (1998–2002). Italics mine.
6. The concept of the 'grotesque body' is famously theorized in Bakhtin 1984.
7. On this concept, see Bataille 1985, 1988. Parvulescu provides an important discussion of Bataille's 'joy in the face of death' and laughter (2010: 81–99).
8. See e.g. Bakhtin 1984: 62.
9. Bakhtin 1986: 135. Cf. Miller 1998.
10. Miller 1998: 267.
11. See esp. Bataille 1991b: 118. Cf. Land 1992: xvii, Privitello 2007: passim, Parvulescu 2010: 82f.
12. Bataille 1990: 25.
13. Ibid.
14. Critchley posits an important distinction between tragedy as the realization of one's finitude in death and comedy as the aesthetic domain where such finitude 'cannot be affirmed' (1999: 119). As a result of this radical impossibility, comedy 'is truly tragic', or 'is tragic by not being

tragic' (ibid.). Rather than seeing Bataille's 'joy in the face of death' univocally as a moment of 'tragic affirmation' (ibid. 113), I read it as permeated by a complex oscillation between ecstatic self-loss and lack thereof, that is to say, by an unresolvable coexistence of 'tragic' and 'comic' (in Critchley's terms); see Brennan 2015.

15. Bataille 1985: 237f.
16. Thus, Derrida (2005: 89), commenting on Bataille's notion of eroticism, which is germane to his conception of laughter.
17. On the anti-cathartic force of the orgasmic *petite mort*, see Telò 2020: Ch. 5.
18. Lacan 2014: 263. On dying of laughter in antiquity, see esp. Beard 2014: 14.
19. Privitello 2007: 180. On the convergence between Jacques Laplanche's and Leo Bersani's idea of self-shattering *jouissance* and Bataille's self-expenditure, see esp. Brintnall 2015.
20. Bataille 1970: 71. The translation is from Menninghaus 2003: 355.
21. In this scene, as I argue in Telò 2020: Ch. 5, Dionysus is in the typical position of the masochist dominated by the 'oral' mother, as theorized by Deleuze 1991; for Deleuze, humour is an expression of this masochism, while irony is a product of sadism, which, against Freud, he conceives of as fundamentally distinct from masochism.
22. Arist. *Poet.* 1449a34–6. Wiles points out that this notion of 'laughter ... without pain or harm', whereby 'the laughing audience feel superior to the ugly face of one who is in aesthetic, social, and moral terms *phaulos*', corresponds to the Aristotelian theory of catharsis (2008: 385). Like catharsis, such a notion presupposes a normative point of view, which preemptively polices the pleasures available to the spectator; see Telò 2020. Classicists recognize 'the normative slant of Aristotle's reading of the history ... of comic drama' (Halliwell 2008: 327), but they are reluctant to contest it. Bataille's theory of laughter is, in a sense, a response to Aristotle, or to be more precise, to the reformulation of Aristotle's ideas by Henri Bergson; see Parvulescu 2010: 86–7.
23. See Berlant and Ngai 2017: 238: 'The opposition between comedy and tragedy has itself come to seem theoretically mechanical and thus good fodder for joking.'
24. Halliwell 2008: 544 (my italics).
25. On the aesthetic continuity between the prologue of *Frogs* and the *parabasis* of *Clouds*, see esp. Rosen 2015a: 459–61.
26. On the ancient iconography of the tragic Andromeda, see Taplin 2007: 174–85; on the mythological character's ecphrastic use as an eroticized object of the male gaze, see esp. Morales 2004: 173–82.
27. See Taillardat 1965: 334. On gaping mouths in Aristophanes as Bakhtinian openings, symbols of voracious verbal aggression, see in general Worman 2008: Ch. 2.
28. Bataille 1988: 325.
29. Bataille 2014: 40. On this passage, see Parvulescu 2010: 84f.
30. When they talk about laughter, Christian writers dismiss it as a dangerous baring of the palate or loosening of the face; see e.g. Greg. Nyss. *Hom. in Ecc.* 44.645 M.: 'διάχυσις δὲ σώματος ἀπρεπής ... καὶ διαστολὴ παρειῶν καὶ γύμνωσις ... ὑπερῴας' ('an indecorous dissolution of the body ... and a dilatation of the cheeks and a baring ... of the palate'). On this passage, see Halliwell 2008: 9.
31. See Wyler 2008, Webb 2018.
32. Deleuze 1990.
33. Kaufman 2010: 79.

34. The phrase 'eternal present' is from Deleuze (1990: 311). Deleuze connects what he calls a 'return to the elements' with the Freudian death drive (1990: 317f.).
35. See Chitwood 1986.
36. Bataille refers to 'joy in the face of death' as a kind of becoming fire in *Inner Experience* (2014: 128); see Parvalescu 2010: 92.
37. It is significant that 'Φρέαρ' ('Well') appears among the titles of lost plays by Diphilus and Alexis. Can we imagine that the fall into a well was a frequent joke, a reliable comic crowd-pleaser?
38. Cavarero 1995: Ch. 2.
39. Ibid. 36.
40. On Democritus as the laughing philosopher, see esp. Halliwell 2008: 351–8, Stoholski 2017.
41. See esp. Thales 11 DK A 12 (= Arist. *Metaph*.A 3 983b18–22); Iren. *Adv haer*. 2.14.2 (R40 Most-Laks), another testimonium of Thales, observes that 'water' is the same as the 'abyss' (*idem autem est dicere aquam et Bythum*).
42. Laughter has specific associations with water. See e.g. [Aesch.] *PB* 89f.: 'ποντίων τε κυμάτων/ ἀνήριθμον γέλασμα' ('countless laughing waves of the sea').
43. 'Time empty and out of joint' is the phrase that Deleuze employs to define the death drive – that is, the same temporal/psychic register exemplified by the 'world without others' – in *Difference and Repetition* (1994: 136).
44. Mel Brooks, cited by Berlant and Ngai (2017: 239), once made this joke: 'Tragedy is when I cut my fingers. Comedy is when you fall into an open sewer and die.'
45. By 'Symbolic', I mean the regime of language and the Law that we enter at the moment of birth, as theorized by Lacan.
46. I follow the text of Arnott; 'βεβ[αμ]μένου' is Maas's widely accepted supplement.
47. Laughter seems to afford Knemon a momentary pre-Symbolic experience comparable to the condition of the 'aloof object' posited by object-oriented-ontology (OOO) – deceiving and subjugating the subject trying to know and capture it; see esp. Morton 2013.
48. Nancy 1987; 1993: 368–92. The phrase is from *Love's Labour Lost* (5.2): 'To move wild laughter in the throat of death,/It cannot be, it is impossible.' As Nancy puts it, 'to become the bursting joy of the deep throat' means 'devouring ... the realm of representation' (1987: 726). See also: 'Behind the ... very wideness of the mouth, as its indefinite and repetitive aperture, the throat of death bursts into laughter: coming forth from behind any presence, and going beyond any presence' (1987: 730).
49. Bataille 2001: 133.
50. Privitello 2007 (a wide-ranging discussion of Bataille's theory of laughter).
51. Privitello 2007: 170.
52. Bataille 1991a: 133.
53. Bataille 1989: 20.
54. Privitello 2007: 170.
55. On laughter as a cut in the throat, see Bataille 2011: 128.
56. Zeitlin notes that 'the policeman spectator ... unwittingly and fittingly plays the role of the sea monster' (1996: 395). I am focusing on how the second-person plural transforms the spectators – implicit metatheatrical addressees – from the original tragic helpers into monster-like laughers.

57. As suggested by the phrase 'λαιμότμητ' ἄχη' a few lines below (1054): see Austin and Olson 2004: 1054n. On the violence inflicted by the Scythian archer, see Hall 1989, 2006: Ch. 8.
58. On this passage's parody of 'Scythian' ways of speaking, see Hall 1989, 2006: Ch. 8.
59. Only aspiration separates a laughing interjection (ἃ ἅ) from a lamenting one (ἆ ἆ); see Kidd 2011.
60. On the 'obscure intimacy of the animal', see Bataille 1991a: 133.
61. My reading of Bataille's notion of animality is indebted to Marsden 2004.
62. Marsden 2004: 44. 'The rupture between the human and the animal' is, for Bataille, the '"open wound" of negativity constitutive for human society and history' (Timofeeva 2017: 168). In a sense, the Bataillean animal anticipates the Lacanian Real, the domain beyond language and subjectivization through language.
63. See Austin and Olson 2004: 1056f.n.
64. Σ^R *ad* 1059b (ἐπικοκκάστρια:) εἰωθυῖα γελᾶν, γελάστρια.
65. I discuss the association between Echo and the death drive in Telò 2020: Ch.3.
66. Deleuze and Guattari 1986: 13: 'To become animal is ... to find a world of pure intensities where all forms come undone ... to the benefit of an unformed matter of deterritorialized flux'. For Deleuze, 'becoming-animal is only one stage in a more profound becoming-imperceptible' (2003: 25). To an extent, echoey laughter is similar to the scream that, in Deleuze's view, is the bodily channel of this becoming.
67. Marsden 2004: 44.
68. Dover identifies the amphibian species of the chorus with the Eurasian marsh frog, technically known as *rana ridibunda* (1993: 119).
69. See, again, Bataille 1970: 71. The relation between laughter and defecation punningly emerges in *Clouds* through the resonance between 'καχασμῶν' (1073), cognate with 'καχάζω', 'to laugh', and 'κακκᾶν', a child's word for defecation (1384, 1390).
70. The citations are from Privitello (2007: 180), commenting on Bataille's idea of laughter as the 's/laughter' of subjectivity.
71. Ruffell observes that in this horridly misogynistic scene, 'the sexuality of older women is of course one object of humor ... but laughter and the aggressive gaze are aimed equally, if not more so, at Epigenes' (2013: 266). I want to read the treatment of Epigenes as a dramatization of laughter itself.
72. See above, first section. As Privitello (2007: 170) puts it, for Bataille 'laughter is the refusal of discourse'. See also Derrida 1978: 256: 'laughter bursts ... only on the basis of an absolute renunciation of meaning'. For Irigaray (1985: 163), this meaning is the law of patriarchy, which laughter as the feminine non-discourse subverts.
73. See esp. Bergren (2008: 341) on the fetishistic fantasies produced by the castration anxiety that pervades this speech.
74. The name of Empousa is cognate with the verb 'ἐμπίνειν', 'to gulp down' (literally 'to drink in').
75. See Bergren 2008: 341f.: 'Tarred alive and welded to his tomb by her feet, those perennial objects of the fetishist's sadistic adoration, female *metis* stands now wholly immobilised.'
76. On the death drive and the masochistic *jouissance* of sex, see esp. Bersani 1986: 201. On the connections between Bersani's position and Bataille's idea of 'joy in the face of death', see Brintnall 2015.

Notes to pp. 68–71

77. Nancy 1993: 374. The Baudelaire line reads: 'malheureux peut-être l'homme, mais heureux l'artiste que le désir déchire' ('unhappy is perhaps the man, but happy is the artist whom desire tears apart').
78. Ibid.
79. On humour and masochism, see Deleuze 1991: Ch. 7; cf. n. 21.

Chapter 6

1. On Demeter's laughter see Halliwell 2008: 161–6. The notion of laughter as therapy, cognate with what I describe, is already known in the Hippocratic corpus (Halliwell 2008: 16f.). On Democritus' philosophical laughter see Halliwell 2008: 343–71.
2. Freud 2002, Ramachandran 1998.
3. Plessner 1970; on the effect of social laughter on the threshold of pain see Dunbar et al. 2012; on the analogous pathologies of laughing and crying see Damasio 2004; cf. Halliwell 2008: 5 nn. 13–14.
4. Silk makes observations which overlap in part with what follows (2000: 26–33); Slater (2002) does not handle the baggage, while Dover only hints at the aspects that concern us here (1993: 44f., 191–4).
5. Translations mine except where stated.
6. The joke could be unfolded as follows: if the luggage can be said to be carried by both slave and donkey, since both feel the weight, doesn't that then redouble the weight? This logical paradox would reverse the notion that pain shared is pain divided, joy shared joy multiplied – the foundation of tragic pity. See e.g. Alford 1992: 147–60.
7. No use of 'χαλεπῶς φέρειν' is earlier than Thucydides. For 'συμφοράς/συμφορὰν φέρειν', Theognis (1085, 1322) offers only distant parallels.
8. The phrase 'συμφοράς/-ὰν φέρειν' appears also in Soph. OC 962 (produced after Frogs, although composed before it), Agathon fr. 34 (quoted in Ar. Thesm. 198), and later in Isocrates. It is also telling that Plato uses 'χαλεπῶς φέρειν' in Rep. 10.604b–c, a passage that echoes Pericles' sentiments in Thuc. 2.38. Summarizing Stesimbrotus, Plutarch similarly connects 'χαλεπῶς φέρειν' with Pericles' family life (Per. 36.2).
9. The Periclean intertext of Menexenus, on which see Monoson 1998, is reinforced by the anachronistic attribution of Socrates' speech to Aspasia (235e–236c, 249d). Socrates' speech is said to be indebted to Pericles' epitaphios (236b), whatever the phrase 'περιλείμματ᾽ ἄττα ἐξ ἐκείνου' means ('things left out' or 'leftovers'); yet it has little in common with Thuc. 2.35–46, so one might also think of the Samian oration as a possible source. The impact of the Samian epitaphios, possibly the first specimen of the genre, is attested in Plut. Per. 28.4–9; cf. 8.9.
10. While the notion of sailing is not explicit in 2.60.2, it can be shown to underlie Pericles' formulation through a comparison with the close parallel in S. Ant. 162f., 189f. See Griffith 1999: 156, 159. My general premise throughout is that Thucydides reproduces Pericles' idiolect in constructing his speeches.
11. On Arginusae in Frogs, see Dover 1993: 49f. On the Arginusae trial, the relative merit of our sources Xenophon and Diodorus, and the role of Theramenes, see Andrewes 1974.
12. On some implications of that for Frogs, see Sfyroeras 2008.
13. We may contrast the eight unconnected verbs in Acharnians to the four *connected* verbs in Peace 335 and the three *connected* verbs in Wealth 288.

14. On the idea conveyed by χαλεπ- as the basis of the ring composition from 14.2 to 16.2 see Hornblower 1991: 259, 269. He also points out (2008: 915) the echo of 2.16.1 in 8.54.1.
15. On the 'build-up of unrest' see Rusten 1989: 128.
16. On the contrast between Pericles' rationality and the 'emotional changeability of the δῆμος', see Rusten 1989: 198f.
17. Taylor stresses the psychological effects of the repeated invasions and ravaging of Attica (1998: 233–5); cf. Sfyroeras 2013. The scepticism of Hanson as to the extent of the devastation may be justified (1998: 131–73, 231–5; see Thuc. 7.27) but does not invalidate the *emotional* impact, as he acknowledges (e.g. 177–80).
18. For this type of psychological conditioning in Aristophanes see Reckford 1987: 10–13, 219–27.
19. Eupolis fr. 352 ('ῥιψάσπιδόν τε χεῖρα τὴν Κλεωνύμου', 'and the shield-throwing hand of Cleonymus') partly confirms the information in Schol. Ar. *Nub.* 353 that the other poets ridicule Cleonymus for his shield-throwing.
20. See e.g. Kakridis 1974: 257, Olson 1998: 167, Christ 2006: 29. Olson rightly rejects the suggestion that there was no actual 'ῥιψασπία', but 'merely an extension of Ar.'s earlier implication (*Eq.* 1369–72) that Cleonymus contrived to get himself removed from the city's hoplite-register'. Yet he may go too far in suggesting that *Knights* 1369–72 may be 'a malicious distortion of some serious proposal for military reform that Cleonymus put forward at the Assembly earlier that year'.
21. Aristophanes may graft the joke onto the mention of the shield handle in *Knights* 1369–72 (see previous note), a passage that seems to portray Cleonymus as a draft dodger about a year before Delium. This would render his shield-throwing all the more prominent.
22. On the battle and its time, see Gomme (1956: 558) and Hornblower (1996: 286–317).
23. On 'problem-solving' and its cognitive aspects as features of all jokes according to the incongruity theory, see Wild et al. 2003: 2131f.
24. 'Huge and trem ... ulous' comes from Sommerstein, who conveys the *para prosdokian* use of 'δειλὸν καὶ μέγα' instead of 'δεινὸν καὶ μέγα' (1987: 171, 296).
25. In addition to salient cowardice or hysterics, those reasons might include his obesity, his attempt to avoid conscription shortly before Delium (*Knights* 1369–72; cf. Christ 2006: 129), or his outspokenness in favour of the war; cf. Olson 1998: 167.
26. I find it psychologically telling that Plato has a rueful 'what if' moment in *Laches* 181b; if the rest had behaved in Socrates' manner at the Delium retreat, the *polis* would have remained 'upright' ('ὀρθή') and would not have suffered 'such a fall' ('τοιοῦτον πτῶμα').
27. Aristophanes is of course not concerned with the historical accuracy of the assemblies prior to the expedition (Thuc. 6.8.1–2), as noted by Henderson (1987: 119–20), who suggests that the account of Plutarch (*Nic.* 12.6) depends on this passage.
28. The Magistrate's remarks, including the bad-mouthing of Demostratus, make sense in the climate of recrimination following the disaster (Thuc. 8.1); cf. Henderson 1987: 119–20. Plutarch (*Nic.* 13) mentions a number of ill omens, including the Adonia.
29. See Henderson 1987: 194, Hornblower 2008: 367–81.
30. See Henderson 1987: 145f.
31. My reading is consonant with the insightful, though brief, comments of Reckford 1987: 295: 'Behind the scenes – hardly mentioned, because they are so very painful, but the very silence produces a deeply tragic effect in the midst of comedy – we feel the defeat of the Sicilian expedition, the loss of so many soldiers and ships, the scarcity of funds, the defection of

subject allies, the overall weariness and demoralization of Athens and of the rest of the Greek world.'

32. See Compton-Engle 2015: 52–5.

33. As verbal echoes and general context make clear, this passage is intentionally based on the exchange between Hector and Andromache in *Il.* 6.482–93; cf. Henderson 1987: 133–6. But while Aristophanes' 'ἀλγοῦσαι ... γελάσασαι' resembles Homer's 'δακρυόεν γελάσασα' ('having smiled/laughed through her tears', *Il.* 6.484), we should bear in mind that in Andromache's case, the smile is not feigned and the traumatic event has not yet occurred.

34. Regarding *Lys.* 512, Reckford rightly wonders, 'is this similar to Aristophanes' behavior as a concerned citizen/comic playwright?' (1987: 295 n. 16).

35. As summed up by Thucydides in 2.65.12 ('ἤδη ἐν στάσει ὄντες', 'being already in civil discord') and related more fully in 8.47f., 53f., 76, 89. On the 'dissolution of political coherence' or 'civic disintegration' as a significant theme and formal element in Book 8, see Connor 1985: 210–30; cf. Price 2001: 304–27.

36. See Halliwell 2008: 164 n. 22, 283. As in the case of comedy, Demetrius also uses the proverb to illustrate a misplaced attempt at rhetorical playfulness in a civic context. More generally, Aristophanes understands fully the co-dependence of the serious and the comic, e.g. *Ach.* 500; *Eccl.* 1154–6. On a related note, Aristophanes seems to anticipate Aristotle's definition of the laughable as 'ugly without pain' ('αἰσχρόν τι ... ἄνευ ὀδύνης', *Poet.* 5 1449a32–9) by implicitly wondering, if there is incompatibility between laughter and simultaneous pain, what happens if the pain is in the past?

37. A separate though related issue concerns the restrictions imposed on tragedy's ability to refer to recent trauma, as illustrated by Herodotus' account (6.21) of the Athenian reaction to Phrynichos' *Capture of Miletos*, on which see Rosenbloom 1993, Mülke 2000. The apparent solution – in general, tragic poets may only *allude* to specific events – stands in sharp contrast to comic poetics, but a full comparison would require a much longer treatment.

38. Halliwell 2008: 161–6.

39. Halliwell 2008: 16f.

40. Freud 2002; Ramachandran argues that laughter signals absence of threat (1998), but would it not make better evolutionary sense if one signalled threat instead of its absence?

41. Dunbar et al. 2012.

42. 00:22:45–00:23:45.

43. I wish to express my thanks to the conference organizers and editors of the volume Edith Hall and Peter Swallow and to the fellow participants, in particular Nick Lowe, Michael Silk, and Mario Telò. This paper would not have been written were it not for their hospitality, personal and intellectual.

Chapter 7

1. These lines mention Horace's debt specifically to Greek Old Comedy, but his *Epodes* were explicitly implicated in the Greek iambic tradition, affiliated with Old Comedy as a genre of comic satire and mockery. See e.g. Mankin 1995: 6–19, Barchiesi 2001, and Mankin 2010: 94–8.

2. Much has been written about these programmatic lines; see Rosen 2012a: 27–30; Gowers 2012: 147–52, with further bibliography, p. 152. Freudenburg 1993: 96–108 remains

fundamental in the more recent scholarship. On the thematizing of *libertas* in Roman satire, see Braund 2004.

3. All translations mine unless stated.

4. At the risk of redundancy, I use the phrase '*comic* satire' as a reminder that satire always implies comedy in one sense and to some degree (and conversely, that comedy does *not* always imply satire). While bona fide *satirists* (as opposed to authors working in non-satirical literary modes and genres who may *incorporate* satirical elements) often want audiences to believe they are saying serious (non-comic) things, they succeed as satirists only as a function of making an audience laugh, even if only quietly. Frye's comment on this (1957: 223) remains sound: 'Two things . . . are essential to satire; one is *wit or humor* founded on fantasy or a sense of the grotesque or absurd, the other is an object of attack. *Attack without humor, or pure denunciation, forms one of the boundaries of satire*' (my emphasis). For further discussion, see Rosen 2007: 19, 2013: 88–90.

5. 'And I hear that the son of *Cleisthenes*/was plucking his own arsehole among the graves/and scratching his cheeks . . ./. . . and they say that *Callias* the son of Hippofucker, dressed in a lionskin, does sea-battle with pussy' ('τὸν Κλεισθένους δ' ἀκούω/ἐν ταῖς ταφαῖσι πρωκτὸν/ τίλλειν ἑαυτοῦ καὶ σπαράττειν τὰς γνάθους· . . ./. . . καὶ *Καλλίαν* γέ φασι/τοῦτον τὸν Ἱπποκίνου/κύσθῳ λεοντῆς ναυμαχεῖν ἐνημμένον', *Frogs* 422–4; 428–30).

6. For a detailed discussion of how we define and conceptualize satire, see Rosen 2007: 17–20, with further bibliography at 18, n. 25. Griffin's comments (1994: 5) add nuance to any attempt to pin down satire as a stable category: 'satire is problematic, open-ended, essayistic, ambiguous in its relation to history, uncertain in its political effect, resistant to formal closure, more inclined to ask questions than to provide answers, and ambivalent about the pleasures it offers.'

7. Horace lays out these principles in *Sat.* 1.4.78–103 (among other places, such as in 2.1, on which see above, p. 79), where he objects to the fact that people often misunderstand a satirist's aggression as gratuitously malevolent. In fact, he would say, proper satire attacks only people who deserve it. The examples of such satire that he offers at *Sat.* 1.4.91–3, however, are humourously banal, leaving one to wonder how committed he actually is to something resembling a 'serious' or morally instructive agenda: 'if I laugh at the fact that Rufillus smells of breath-lozenges, or Gargonius smells like a goat, do I seem to you to be malevolent or biting?' ('ego si risi quod ineptus/pastillos Rufillus olet, Gargonius hircum,/lividus et mordax videor tibi?'). In other words, bad breath and bodily stench belong to the category of social transgressions that *deserve* to mocked.

8. Examples abound across Graeco-Roman satire, but Aristophanes offers plenty himself. Any of his *agōnes* can be seen to destabilize a singular ideological position, since the whole premise of a comic contest is to expose *both* sides of an argument to ridicule. The 'stronger argument''s position in the *agōn* of Aristophanes' *Clouds* – formally speaking at least – ends up prevailing by the end of the play, but what do we make of the fact that he actually 'loses' the contest itself? Similar forces are at play in the contest of 'πονηρία' between the Sausage Seller and Paphlagonian (the character standing in for the demagogue Cleon) in *Knights*, where each one tries to outdo the other in roguishness, leaving it uncertain which of the two is actually morally preferable. See Rosen 2007: 78–91 for further discussion of the difficulty in distinguishing satirist from target in episodes like this one where at least part of the point seems to be the exaltation of 'badness' ('πονηρία') rather than complaining about it – as one would expect from a satirist.

9. From Aristophanes' claim (ventriloquized through the character of Dicaeopolis) in *Acharnians* (498–501) that his comedy is designed to help the Athenians in the present moment ('I am going to speak among the Athenians about the city, while doing comedy

[*trugōidia*]. For even comedy knows what is just; and I will say things [that appear] terrifying, but they are just, 'ἐν Ἀθηναίοις λέγειν/μέλλω περὶ τῆς πόλεως, τρυγῳδίαν ποιῶν./τὸ γὰρ δίκαιον οἶδε καὶ τρυγῳδία. /ἐγὼ δὲ λέξω δεινὰ μέν, δίκαια δέ'), through Juvenal's claim in *Sat.* 1 that his entire satiric programme derives from his frustration at the state of his contemporary Rome, Graeco-Roman satirical writers typically insist (however disingenuously) that their work reflects their own lived experience within contemporary society. Bogel's summary of this classic dilemma in the context of eighteenth-century English satire (2004: 1f.), applies equally well to Graeco-Roman satire: 'The originating moment of satire is the satirist's perception of an object that exists anterior to the satiric attack. *This object is often assumed to belong to the real world . . . but it may also be an imaginary object constructed by the satirist*' (my emphasis).

10. For a full introduction to and discussion of the complex phenomenon of internet trolling, see Phillips 2015: 15–27, and further, below, pp. 82–4.

11. Further discussion in Rosen 2012b.

12. The distinction between an online existence and a counterpart, but different, existence 'in real life' has become a longstanding topic of debate in the quickly evolving history of internet culture, with the abbreviation IRL ('in real life') now in common use to refer to a life away from the largely unrestrained world of the internet, where personalities and behaviours can be constructed anew. Slater (2002) has argued that online and 'real' worlds might become functionally indistinguishable ten years hence, though many internet trolls in particular still seem invested in viewing their online presence as different from their 'real lives'.

13. Quite apart from the obvious differences in historical contexts and performative modes, there is also the fact that internet trolling is largely conducted anonymously or pseudanonymously, while Aristophanic comedy was a public event where neither author nor audience could hide.

14. Among the many psychological studies on this topic, see Johnson 1990, which considers the disconnect between a joke-teller's account of their personal attitudes and motivations in crafting a joke, and the *perception* of these attitudes by an audience. In a more detailed and nuanced study, Ford and Ferguson (2004) have found that audiences who are 'high in prejudice . . . are more likely to perceive a social norm of tolerance of discrimination against members of the disparaged group . . . That is, they are more likely to define the context as one in which people need not consider instances of discrimination against the targeted group in a serious, critical manner' (2004: 91). More recently, Ford (2016) has summarized the findings of such research: 'Regardless of its intent, when prejudiced people interpret disparagement humour as "just a joke" intended to make fun of its target and not prejudice itself, it can have serious social consequences as a releaser of prejudice.'

15. See Plato *Apol.* 19a7–d7. On the general problem of Socrates' portrait in *Clouds*, see e.g. Dover 1968: xxxi–lvii, Vander Waerdt 1994, Konstan 2011. On the question of how to understand Socrates' invocation of the *Clouds* in *Apol.*, see Rosen 1988: 61f., with 62 n. 8.

16. In my discussion of the passage in Plato *Apol.* 19a7–d7 (see previous note), for example; while I would still maintain that Socrates finds fault more with the audience who failed to 'get the joke' of Aristophanes' portrayal of him than with Aristophanes himself, one cannot ignore the *fact* (in Socrates' mind) that there was at least some causal link between the *Clouds* and Socrates' subsequent indictment.

17. There is a considerable body of sociological and psychological research on the effects of anonymity on online discourse. See Cho and Kwon 2015, which also collects much of the recent bibliography.

18. In an early cultural study of internet flame wars, Dery (1994: 4f.) notes analogies with other, pre-internet forms of invective and abuse: 'In some ways, flame wars are a less ritualised,

cybercultural counterpart to the African-American phenomenon known as "the Dozens", in which duelists one-up each other with elaborate, sometimes rhyming gibes involving the sexual exploits of each other's mothers. At their best, flame wars give way to tour-de-force jeremiads called "rants" – demented soliloquies that elevate soapbox demagoguery to a guerrilla art form ... Rants are spiritual kin to Antonin Artaud's blasphemous screeds and the Vorticist harangues in Wyndham Lewis's *Blast*.' Unstated by Dery is the fact that all his examples of invective – indeed, I would argue, all examples of invective – ultimately imply audiences who will find humour in them.

19. See Phillips 2015: 9–11, with further bibliography.
20. Ibid. 10.
21. Wikipedia 2018.
22. 'In no way are trolls affected by the havoc they wreak, except to the extent that said havoc is highly amusing – at least to them ... "I did it for the lulz" is often the only explanation trolls offer, and is indicative of what I have come to describe as the mask of trolling ... The mask worn by trolls precludes reciprocity; ... The recipient of the trolls' playful behavior, on the other hand, is expected to take things seriously, the more seriously the better. If the target does not, then the troll has failed' (Phillips 2015: 28).
23. Ibid. 28.
24. For this attitude in Greek culture, see Dover 1974: 182f. On battleground 'flyting' (a term borrowed from Germanic heroic literature) see Martin 1989: 67–88, who analyses Homeric *neikē* (formalized boast-and-insult quarrels between heroes) as examples of flyting, and Maciver 2012: 611–16. For broader cross-cultural background of flyting, see Parks 1990 and Jucker and Taavitsainen 2000, who also see through-lines from flyting to internet flaming when considered through the lens of linguistic pragmatics. For Parks (1990: 44), the central feature of flyting seems applicable to trolling behaviour as well, despite the obvious difference that in internet 'warfare' the contestants do not confront each other in the flesh; 'the eristic (querulous, disputatious, adversarial) impulse manifests in each contestant's attempt to force himself into a position of superiority to his foe and thereby to win *kleos* [glory/fame] at his adversary's expense. The presence of this motive constitutes a defining characteristic of the flyting activity.' It is surprising how rarely scholarly discussion of flyting ever thinks to mention *laughter* as, at the very least, an implicit goal of a flyter's boasting and abuse of a target. The fact that internet trolls privilege this aspect of their derision with their 'lulz' highlights, I would argue, an aspect always present to some degree as a goal in such discourse.
25. See e.g. Mead 2014 for an account of Mary Beard's (a classicist who has achieved an uncommon level of public celebrity) interactions with internet trolls.
26. 2015: 25.
27. Ibid. 29.
28. Ibid. 34.
29. Ibid. 35.
30. Ibid. 39.
31. Ibid. 34.
32. See ibid. 256, 264–6. Satirists are typically ambivalent about pushback from their targets – they become indignant when anyone blames them for their attacks, but at the same time enjoy the fact that antagonism from a high-profile target highlights the efficacy of their satire. Aristophanes thematizes this tension in his presentation of his quarrel with the demagogue Cleon across his plays. *Ach.* 502–6 mentions, with a hint of indignation, that Cleon had objected to the way in which Aristophanes had portrayed him the year before in his

Notes to pp. 84–87

Babylonians, but in *Wasps* 1029–36, he boasts of his his bravery in taking on a target as important and conspicuous as Cleon. See further Rosen 1988: 64, 2012b: 9–13.

33. *Encyclopedia Dramatica* 2018.
34. Ibid. (my emphasis).
35. Ibid.
36. See e.g. Jedrkiewicz 1989: 111–27, Compton 1990, Schauer and Merkle 1992, Rosen 2013: 24–7.
37. See Guilhamet 1985, who traces the satirical aspects of Socratic irony across the subsequent history of literary satire. See also McLean 2006 on the satirical Socrates of early modern France. More generally on Socratic irony, see Ferrari 2008, Vasiliou 2013.
38. See Long 1996, 1997, Prince 2006.
39. As, for example, in the *parodos* of *Frogs* (see above, pp. 79f.), where the laughter is programmatically thematized as an essential element of Aristophanic comedy. An exchange between Poverty and Chremylus at Ar. *Wealth* 557–600, while less explicitly programmatic, reveals the ongoing tension between Aristophanic comedy's *claims* to seriousness and its more immediate and urgent desire for an audience's laughter. Poverty here chastises Chremylus for constantly trying to 'mock and joke, without any concern for being serious' ('σκώπτειν πειρᾷ καὶ κωμῳδεῖν τοῦ σπουδάζειν μελήσας', 557), to which Chremylus responds, essentially, that he simply doesn't care: 'you won't persuade me, even if you do persuade me …' ('οὐ γὰρ πείσεις, οὐδ᾽ ἢν πείσῃς', 600). Further discussion at Rosen 2015b: 228f. Chremylus' anarchic, amoral insouciance in the face of Poverty's righteous indignation certainly seems analogous to typical lulzy troll responses from outraged targets.
40. See above n. 13.
41. A vast scholarly tradition has engulfed this topic. Modern discussion effectively began with Dover 1968, xxxii–lxvii. For more recent attempts to sift through the various conflicting ancient perspectives, see Vander Waerdt 1994, Waterfield 2013.
42. As Halliwell (2008: 244) has very usefully put it (I have italicized the many words and phrases which align his analysis with the dynamics of internet trolling), 'one of the main uses of laughter in Greek culture is as an agency for the *projection of dishonour onto people or things perceived as shameful*. "Shameful" (*aischros*) and "laughable" (*geloios*) are evaluations that can easily be coupled.' Later (266): 'If we attempt, therefore, to situate Old Comedy against the broader background of cultural attitudes … the question "when, or at what, is it wrong (for the audience) to laugh?" seems to be *entirely beside the point*. That is because within the purview of this spectacularly *uninhibited* genre, the dynamics of laughter and shame are exploited for *extraordinarily unruly* ends. What should (by prevailing social norms) count as shameful or ugly can be laughed at freely but also *"irresponsibly"*, without, it seems, any fear of shamefulness on the part of the audience itself, since the objects of laughter are turned into the material of a performance framed for the *collective pleasure of the spectators*.'
43. 2006: 226–35.
44. Ibid. 230.
45. See e.g. Phillips 2015: 97.
46. pp. 79f.
47. See above n. 32 on Cleon and the consequences of Aristophanes' portrait of him in *Bablylonians*, with Sommerstein 2004, and (contra) Halliwell 2008: 249–63.
48. Halliwell 2008: 262; '*Knights* allows us to see … how (Aristophanic) Old Comedy could celebrate its aischrologic freedom to the point of grotesque shamelessness, yet always, one

way or another, translate that shamelessness into theatrical artifice' – a formulation that applies remarkably well to internet trolls.

49. Line order followed from OCT.
50. As Halliwell (2008: 259) puts it, 'under the banner of Dionysiac festivity, it can become for spectators a linguistically and gelastically unshackled celebration of the frisson of hubristic outrage generated by aischrologic language, through a "safe" celebration that projects all its indecency onto the masked, padded figures of the performance'.
51. A recent psychological study (Buckels, Trapnell and Paulhus 2014) of internet troll personalities reached the unsettling conclusion that sadism as a personality trait most consistently correlates with the enjoyment trolls take in their online behaviour, allowing for the difficulty in determining whether the personality leads to the behaviour or vice versa (101). The authors attribute the extremity of this behaviour to the anonymity of the internet – an almost self-evident conclusion derived from what strikes me as an unnuanced methodology; online questionnaires that rely on self-reporting make it difficult to determine which 'self' (a 'real' personality or the constructed 'virtual self') was answering the questions. Still, wherever the 'real' sadism of such behaviour resides, the *perception* of antisociality sensed by an audience will remain the same coming from an internet troll or a literary satirist.
52. See further, Rosen 2012b: 25f.

Chapter 8

1. Hall 2011a: 208.
2. As Bowie points out, this pun has been preceded by the play on *aspis*, which can mean 'snake' (Hdt. 4.191) as well as 'shield', and on *dēmos*, which, if accented on the final syllable, means 'fat' rather than 'people' (1996: 78f.).
3. These dream-like and allegorical aspects of Old Comedy also overlap with the imaginary world conjured by the Aesopic fable, which is a prominent undertext in *Wasps*; see Hall 2013.
4. All translations are my own unless stated.
5. *Suda* s.v. 'Chionides'; see Csapo and Slater 1995: 120, 225.
6. Halliwell 2008: Ch. 5.
7. See Mirbach 2007: lxv and paragraph 44 of his German translation of Baumgarten's Latin text, with Stapleford 2012: 7–8.
8. Mendlesohn 2008, Stapleford 2012: 14–16.
9. Meister 2012.
10. Meister 2012: 25.
11. Ruffell 2011: 429.
12. Harmes and Bladen 2015: 1–14.
13. Bailey 2007: 3.
14. Griffith 1974.
15. See further Griffith 1974.
16. This suggestion was made by Müller-Strübing 1873.
17. Müller-Strübing 1873.
18. See Hall 2019: 271.

19. Hall 2006: 328–35.
20. If, in this context, winning Basileia from Zeus can function, as it does in Bacchylides fr. 41 (in Campbell *Greek Lyric* vol. IV), as a metaphor for winning immortality, then Peisetaerus is shattering the biggest human ontological constraint of them all.
21. Trans. Smith 2016. See Braund and Hall 2014: 371f. For similar tales about tyrants who believed or tried to persuade others to believe they were gods, see Aelian, *VH* 14.30; Athenaeus 3.98, 7.289.
22. [Apollodorus], *Bibliotheca* 1.9.7; Hyginus, *Fabulae* 60, 61; Strabo 8.356.
23. Hall 2006: 200 with n. 58.
24. Hall 2010c.
25. Sidney 1595: 10 (spelling updated).

Chapter 9

1. Unless stated otherwise, all translations are mine.
2. On Plutarch and Aristophanes, see Bréchet 2005. Bréchet not only picks up all the numerous other passages where Plutarch quite radically condemns Aristophanes, but also shows how Plutarch could at the same time admire and even emulate Aristophanes' style, which of course reminds one of Plato's same ambiguity towards the comedic poet.
3. E.g. Halliwell 1986: 273–5, 1987: 85–7, or Hunter 2009: 102. Notable exceptions are Janko 1984: 66–8, 205f. and Heath 1989; less recently Cooper 1924: 18–41.
4. See esp. 1454b1 against the *deus ex machina*; and 1454a29–33 against unjustified uses of the irrational.
5. On the importance of criticism in the *Poetics*, see esp. Ford 2015.
6. Halliwell 1986: 273, n. 30.
7. This is the implicit critique made in Chapter 14; the scene in *Antigone* where Haemon refrains from killing his father is ranked lowest (1453b37–1454a2).
8. This is one key argument in Chapter 26. It is also what (paradoxically) distinguishes Homer from other epic poets: 'Homer deserves to be praised for various reasons but mainly because he alone of all epic poets is not ignorant of what he must do in his own name. For the poet in his own name must say as little as possible as that is not what makes him an author of representations' (24.1460a5–8).
9. Interestingly enough, other sources credit Aeschylus with introducing a third actor (see *Vita Aeschyli* 13), which may indicate that it was Aristotle's firm decision to emphasize Sophocles' importance even against other opinions.
10. Storey 2011b: 200f.
11. On this, see Destrée 2016.
12. In fact, like Anaxandrides, Epicharmus is also quoted or referred to four times in the *Rhetoric*. In his *Ethics*, it comes as no surprise that Euripides is quoted more often than Sophocles to illustrate such-and-such an ethical feature, and that the most quoted poet remains Homer, for the evident reason that everyone knew their Homer by heart. (For references, see the useful lists in Moraitou 1994.)
13. See esp. Philo, *De aeternitate mundi* 11, from which one can recreate what Aristotle's joke against philosophers who argued for the ephemerality of the world may have sounded like:

'Whereas in the past I feared my own house being blown down by violent winds or terrific storms, now I have to live under the menace of our whole world collapsing one of these days.'

14. For a tentative reconstruction of this theory, see Destrée 2019.
15. On ancient appraisals of Aristophanes, see Slater 2016. For a more recent, no less enthusiastic, appraisal, see esp. Silk's book (2000: Ch. 3), which brilliantly demonstrates that indeed, 'Aristophanes is a master of words and a great poet' (98).
16. On this type of joke, see Kanellakis' chapter in this volume.
17. Comp: 'ὑπὸ ποσσὶν ἐδήσατο καλὰ πέδιλα ἀμβρόσια χρύσεια' (*Od*.1.96 and *Il*.24.340); 'αὐτὸς δ' ἀμφὶ πόδεσσιν ἑοῖς ἀράρισκε πέδιλα, τάμνων δέρμα βόειον ἐϋχροές' (*Od*.14.23).
18. Taillardat 1965: 156. Taillardat's explanation bears on the *ad loc*. Scholium: 'ἀντὶ ⌈δὲ V Γ [γὰρ Lh] τοῦ εἰπεῖν "πέττειν καὶ διαρτίζειν" <"κλάειν"> εἶπεν.' Curiously this very natural explanation, making this verse a very witty one, even if cruel for slaves, seems to have been neglected by more recent commentators. Sommerstein translates 'to cry at four tears to the quart', and understands that 'the beatings made them cry so hard that each tear would have filled a half-pint cup' (1983: 184); even less funny, Biles and Olson take 'τέτταρ' ἐς τὴν χοίνικα' as a colloquialism for 'to full measure' (2015: 227).
19. Heath 1989.
20. Interestingly enough, this is how Taylor (2006) translates it here, although he had rendered it by 'decent' in previous instances! In his translation of Aspasius' commentary on that passage, Konstan (2006) also renders 'ἐπιδέξιος' and 'ἐπιδεξιότης' by 'clever' and 'cleverness' (125, 29). For another instance where *epidexios* must mean 'clever', not 'decent', see Theophrastus, *Char*. 29.4.
21. Some interpreters have suggested that this Theodorus might refer to the fourth-century actor, but since this is a tragedy actor (as Aristotle himself says at *Pol*. 7.15, 1336b27) while the rhetorician is named a few lines before (1412a26), this seems to me much less likely.
22. The text of this joke is uncertain, and various readings have been proposed. I follow Cooper's reading (1920).
23. At least, if one considers this verse from Euripides' Hypsipyle (fr.752g): 'Ἀσιάδ' ἔλεγον ἰήιον/ Θρῇσσ' ἐβόα κίθαρις Ὀρφέως' ('Orpheus' Thracian lyre cried out a mournful Asian plaint') – I owe this reference to Stefan Hagel. Aristophanes (*Frogs* 678–82; cf. also Plato Com. fr.61) refers to Cleophon as 'Thracian', perhaps on the sole ground that he was a lyre-maker (a plausible suggestion Kidd makes in his 2014: 125, n. 22).
24. In addition to *Wasps* 440 I have quoted above, see e.g. *Birds* 92 where Tereus says to his slave: 'Open the ... woods' ('ἄνοιγε τὴν ὕλην') where the audience would have expected 'the door' (τὴν πύλην).
25. On all this, see the note by Kassel and Austin 1984: *ad loc*. Whether or not from another version of the *Clouds*, the tetrameter 'αὐτὸς δείξας ἕν <θ'> ἁρμονίαις χιάζων ἢ σιφνιάζων' as reconstructed by Toup (and followed by Kock) remains a very attractive suggestion.
26. See Taillardat 1965: 459, Henderson 1991: 213, Kassel and Austin 1984: *ad loc*.
27. My heartfelt thanks are due to the editors for their precious help in editing my paper, and to Ralph M. Rosen for his thoughtful comments (and critiques!) on a penultimate draft.

Chapter 10

1. Carey 1994: 69.
2. Silk 1993: 478, 2000: 351.

Notes to pp. 119–121

3. This specific meaning of the term 'parody' is the one adopted by the psychological studies by D'Errico and Poggi 2013, 2016. Since I borrow their interpretative model, I chose to keep the same terminology, so that a sense of both consistency and correspondence is sustained.
4. D'Errico and Poggi 2013.
5. Poggi and D'Errico 2016: 4–5.
6. Ibid. 5f., 11–3.
7. The present study does not seek to exhaustively (and pointlessly) register every single case of Aristophanic surface and deep parody; instead, the aim is to exemplify the pattern and subsequently reflect on a number of pertinent parameters.
8. Halliwell 2014: 191f.; cf. Halliwell 2008: 206–63.
9. Compared to the semi-defensive, semi-bantering tone that the chorus leader assumes at the beginning of the anapaests, 628ff.
10. Here and throughout this chapter (unless otherwise stated) I use Henderson's Loeb translations.
11. The term 'λακαταπύγων' is a *hapax*, coined especially for Cleon; the initial λα- is an emphatic prefix. There is no evidence whatsoever to support this accusation against Cleon. On 'καταπύγων', see Davidson 2007: 63f.
12. Thucydides' antipathy towards Cleon is made evident by the comments he makes at 4.28.5 and 5.16.1.
13. For a recent and analytical presentation of Cleon, see Lafargue 2013; cf. Lafargue 2017. On Cleon's relationship with Aristophanes (with reference to possible personal and local feuds between the two men), see Welsh 1978.
14. Trans. Rackham: 1935. For trenchant discussion of this passage and its far-reaching implications, see Rhodes 1981: 351–7.
15. On the bias of oligarchic sources, see Hall 2018b.
16. Despite Cleon's political prominence and despite his later military deeds (in various battlefields, such as in Sphacteria, and also in Amphipolis, where he died), he had not yet served as general by 425 BCE.
17. After all, this is what lines 300f. of *Acharnians* had aptly foreshadowed: 'I hate you even more than Cleon, whom I intend to cut up as shoe-leather for the Knights' ('ὡς μεμίσηκά σε Κλέωνος ἔτι μᾶλλον, ὃν/κατατεμῶ τοῖσιν ἱππεῦσι καττύματα'). For the portrait of Cleon drawn by Aristophanes in the *Knights*, see Lind 1990: 33–85, 165–257, Harder 1996, Hall 2018b.
18. See Lafargue 2013: 51–9.
19. Both Cleophon and Hyperbolus were portrayed by Plato as foreigners and low-born figures; for all relevant information and interpretation of surviving fragments from Plato's plays and other evidence (suggestive of deep parody), see Pirrotta 2009: 143–53, 319–37.
20. Eupolis' *Maricas* featured both similarities with and differences from Aristophanes' *Knights*; see the analysis by Olson 2016: 121–226. Cf. also Mnesimachus' treatment of the king of Macedon in his *Philip*, which may have been an analogous case; see Papachrysostomou 2008: 210–20.
21. Whether the tanner imagery is Aristophanes' own invention or not is a debatable issue; cf. Lind 1990: 87–164, Lafargue 2013: 89–110. In any case, it is instructive that Pollux includes the tanner's profession ('βυρσοδέψην') among his list of derisory occupations ('βίοι ἐφ' οἷς ἄν τις ὀνειδισθείη', 'means of living that one could live reproached by them', 6.128).

22. The '*eupatridai*' were the noble aristocrats of pre-Solonian Athens, as opposed to the occupational classes of '*agroikoi*' and '*dēmiourgoi*' ([Arist.] *Ath.* 13.2), although these terms, according to Rhodes (1981: 183), were the 'product of later theory'; cf. Rhodes 1981: 71f., 74-6. See also Duplouy 2003, Pierrot 2015.

23. Cleaenetus had assumed a *chorēgia* for men's dithyramb at the City Dionysia of 459 BCE (*IG* II² 2318.34).

24. After the monetization of the Greek economy. On ancient economy's monetization, see the monographs by Schaps 2004, Seaford 2004, Von Reden 2010. By the late sixth century BCE, more than one hundred mints were already operating throughout the Greek world (for their locations see Holle 1978).

25. Cf. [Arist.] *Ath.* 28.3 with Rhodes 1981: 354-5; Aeschin. 2.76.

26. Terminology borrowed from Edmunds' insightful article (1987) on Cleon and the ideological/political ramifications of the latter's satirical portrayal by Aristophanes in the *Knights*.

27. Cf. Ar. *Wasps* 894-972, *Peace* 313-15; D. 25.40; Thphr. *Char.* 29.4[a]; Plu. *Dem.* 23.5, X. *Mem.* 2.7.13-14. It is possible that this imagery of Cleon was used by Cleon himself (cf. Ar. *Knights* 1015-24). Plato Com. also called Cleon 'Cerberus' (fr. 236).

28. See Guthrie 1962: 181ff., Burkert 1972: 166-208, Zhmud 2012: 135-68. Attacking the Pythagoreans for (hypocritical) asceticism is a favourite subject of both Middle and New Comedy; cf. the plays *Pythagoristēs* by Aristophon, and *Pythagorizusa* by Alexis and Cratinus Junior (plus several individual fragments, e.g. Antiphanes frr. 133, 158, Mnesimachus fr. 1, etc.). See Imperio 1998.

29. Scientific interests, religious beliefs and content of teaching are the three areas where Aristophanes assigns to Socrates characteristics foreign to his true nature. See Dover 1968: xxxii-lvii, Bowie 1998.

30. For Pericles in Comedy see the monographs of Schwarze 1971 and Vickers 1997.

31. As put by Thucydides 2.65.10: 'in name it was a democracy, but in essence it was a government of the principal man' ('λόγῳ μὲν δημοκρατία, ἔργῳ δὲ ὑπὸ τοῦ πρώτου ἀνδρὸς ἀρχή'). The modern evaluations of Pericles are numerous (and often controversial); cf. Kagan 1991, Will 2003, Lehmann 2008, Azoulay 2010, Samons 2016.

32. See Cratinus fr. 258: 'Faction and ancient Time ... produced the greatest tyrant' ('Στάσις δὲ καὶ πρεσβυγενὴς/Χρόνος .../μέγιστον τίκτετον τύραννον'); fr. 73.1-2: 'here comes the squill-headed Zeus, Pericles' ('ὁ σχινοκέφαλος Ζεὺς ὅδε προσέρχεται/<ὁ> Περικλέης); fr. 118: 'come, Zeus, god of guests and lord of heads' ('μόλ' ὦ Ζεῦ ξένιε καὶ καραιέ'); and Teleclides fr. 18 (cf. Bagordo 2013: 128-30). Harsh criticism (albeit no deep parody) against Pericles also occurs in *Peace* 605-11, where Hermes describes how Pericles distanced himself from Pheidias (impeached at the time) and endorsed the enforcement of the Megarian decree that eventually caused the war to break out. Note that there is no surface parody by Aristophanes versus Pericles; i.e. Aristophanes (unlike Cratinus) nowhere makes fun of Pericles' shape of head ('σχινοκέφαλος', 'squill-headed').

33. Cf. Aristophanes fr. 178.

34. Agathon was in his thirties at the time of *Thesmophoriazusae*; cf. Austin and Olson 2004: 61. See also Given 2007.

35. E.g. the introduction of 'ἐμβόλιμα', choral interludes; Arist. *Po.* 1456a29-30, etc.

36. Cf. Austin and Olson 2004: 119.

37. See Dover 1978: 144. On Agathon's presence in *Thesmophoriazusae* see Davidson 2007: 444f., 607f., Davidson 2007 *passim*, but esp. 76–115, offers a radical reassessment on multiple aspects of Greek homosexuality, tangential to the present discussion about Agathon.
38. Throughout the surviving Aristophanic corpus there are mild political references to him; e.g. *Wasps* 1187 (participation in an embassy), *Lys.* 620–24 (perhaps the most important political piece – Spartan emissaries meeting with the dissident Athenian women at his house), *Frogs* 48 (he appears as a trierarch).
39. Dicaeopolis, meanwhile, is 'στρατωνίδης' (596, literally: 'son of the army'); as a comic patronymic). This was also a personal name, attested in Athens in the classical and Hellenistic periods (Olson 2002: 227).
40. The Generals were scrutinized and had their overall performance reviewed once during every prytany. If there were suspicions of incapacity, they were even liable to prosecution in court; cf. [Arist.] *Ath.* 61.2.
41. Cf. Csapo 2004.
42. Cleonymus – a pro-Cleon politician – was prominent in Athenian politics from 426/5 to 414 BCE (perhaps he died in Sicily). See Storey 1989.
43. Punishable by 'ἀτιμία' (loss of civic rights); cf. *Knights* 1369–72, *Clouds* 353f., *Wasps* 19–23, *Peace* 446, 673–8, *Birds* 1473–81.
44. Narrated by Thucydides 4.96.6–9 and alluded to by Plato *Smp.* 220e–221b (Socrates was a hoplite). (Cleonymus took part in this chaotic retreat.)
45. As Storey (1989: 256f.) inferred from *Knights* 1369–72.
46. At 1431f. Aeschylus warns against raising a lion cub in the city; cf. Dover 1993: 370f. Alcibiades is also mentioned in Aristophanes fr. 205, albeit without any political overtones. The only case where Alcibiades seems to have served as a substantial target is Eupolis' *Baptae* (cf. Olson 2017: 233–85). Vickers studies Aristophanes' use of political allegory regarding his attacks against prominent political figures (2015; for Alcibiades see esp. 1–18, 19–24, 33–41, 109–25, 129–48, 149–53; cf. Vickers 1989).
47. In comedy, Heracles is universally portrayed as the figure of excess *par excellence*; cf. Stafford 2012: 104–16.
48. Although both types of parody against gods are applicable, I consider it wise to exempt the gods from the following discussion, since religion and the depiction (and ridicule) of gods in Comedy asks for an entirely different chapter; cf. Revermann 2014 (with further bibliography).
49. Nabi et al. 2007.
50. For the Superiority Theory of humour, see the introduction of this volume, pp. 3f.
51. Aristophanes constantly complains about how the Athenians fail to listen to his advice; cf. *Wasps* 1043–59.
52. Sommerstein 1997, 1998a, Bowie 1998.
53. Dawson 1997, Wilson 2000, Revermann 2006b. What emerges is a model of stratified decoding by spectators – elite and non-elite – who share a considerable level of theatrical competence.
54. See Revermann 2006a: 159–61. There is also the crucial parameter of the audience's 'participation' in the performance. As Hall has demonstrated, ancient Greek audiences (of both theatres and lawcourts) were more interventionist than modern ones (1995: *passim*, esp. 44).

Chapter 11

1. Willi 2002: 17. A short chapter in that volume, Slings 2002, deals with anaphora, chiasmus and antithesis. Since then, only a few papers on Aristophanes' figures of speech have been published, e.g. Sommerstein 2009: 70–103 on euphemism.
2. TLG gives twenty occurrences of the term in the scholia on Aristophanes and nineteen occurrences in the scholia on all other authors for whom *para prosdokian* is attested (scholia on Epicharmus, Pindar, Sophocles, Euripides, Thucydides, Aristotle, Demosthenes, Aeschines, Apollonius of Rhodes and Lucian).
3. See Starkie 1909: lxvii f., Filippo 2001–2002, Bilbao Ruiz 2005, Napolitano 2007. A first taxonomy was made by Michael 1981: 171–81 but not deductively, and at the expense of interpretation.
4. Slater 2002: 4.
5. Storey 2007.
6. Ruffell 2011: 56.
7. In the same way, *Tractatus Coislinianus* (5–6, ed. Janko) puts *para prosdokian* under the category '*ek tōn pragmatōn gelōs*' rather than '*apo tēs lexeōs*'.
8. See McGing 2003: 199 n. 26, Lianeri 2016: 4f. Only once in Plutarch (*De tranq. anim.* 475a) does the term appear with reference to poetry, but again, with reference to situational surprise – Odysseus cries for his dog (*Od.* 17.302, 204) but not for his wife (*Od.* 19.211).
9. Demetr. *Eloc.* 152, Hermog. *Meth.* 34, Tib. *Fig. Demosth.* 16.
10. In Latin, the term appears as 'praeter exspectationem'; Cic. *De Or.* 2.63.255, 2.70.284. Quintilianus characterizes it as 'vel venustissima' ('the most elegant device', 6.3.84). As for the scholia, Rutherford correctly points out the terminological inconsistency of the annotators, who often used *para prosdokian* and *par' hyponoian* indistinguishably (1905: 449–51).
11. Silk 2000: 137.
12. Macquarie Dictionary 2013; this is the first, and thus far only, entry of the term in an English dictionary. Generally, the first identified occurrence of the term in print, in English, is Anstey 1891: 69.
13. See Burgers and Van Mulken 2017.
14. For the famous alliteration in Soph. *OT* 371, for instance, R. D. Dawe alone (*ad loc.*) insists that there is no emphatic effect – even though this does not have to be a foreshadowing of Oedipus's blinding.
15. Berk 1964: 138.
16. I use Henderson's Loeb translations, with a few exceptions or deviations.
17. For slaves stealing from their masters, cf. *Knights* 101f., 109–11, *Wasps* 449f., *Wealth* 1139.
18. Ching 1980: 181, on oxymoron. *Para prosdokian* works in the same way; in fact, oxymoron is a subcategory of logical *para prosdokian*, where the two parts are not merely incongruous ('to survey the sky'), but mutually exclusive ('to un-sky the sky').
19. This method originates from the Prague School. See Katz 1972: 37–42, Nida 1975.
20. Berk 1964: 138.
21. Cf. *Peace* 403, *Thesmo.* 581, Hom. *Il.* 11.10, *Od.* 3.322, Hes. *Theog.* 299, Soph. *Aj.* 205, Isoc. *Paneg.* 52.2.

22. Pomegranates were considered as the fruit of the dead; a certain number of grave statues of *korai* hold a pomegranate, and a series of fourth-century BCE *Totenmahl* reliefs depict the fruit in the funerary context. Most pertinently for our passage, Hades gave this fruit to seduce Persephone and take her to the Underworld (*Hymn Dem.* 372-4); as Hades' ferryman, Charon could reasonably (synecdochically) be expected here to use the same lure for the chorus.
23. Van Leeuwen 1904: 143.
24. Sommerstein 2001: 199.
25. See Parker 1996: 227-37, Stafford 2000: 173-7.
26. I have excluded those proposals that either mistake metonymy for *para prosdokian*, ignore textual or scenic information that renders the joke expected, or entail logical or grammatical errors. These cases are: *Acharnians* 18, 500, 889, 1002, 1021 (Olson 2002); 88, 118, 756, 967, 985 (Starkie 1909); 121 (Rennie 1909), 615, 684, 974 (scholia); 950 (Rogers 1910). *Peace* 34, 249, 1186 (Paley 1873); 95, 505 (scholia); 153, 199, 279, 557, 669, 728, 868 (Sharpley 1905); 235, 711, 795, 874, 1067 (Platnauer 1964); 627 (Olson 1998). *Thesmophoriazusae* 24, 158 (Rogers 1904); 53, 288, 334-7, 346, 515f., 1024f. (Austin and Olson 2004); 242, 804, 1050f., 1226 (Prato 2001); *Wealth* 290 (Rogers 1907). For a detailed analysis, see Kanellakis 2020: ch. 1.
27. Jokes with punchlines elicit brain response in such timings: detection of the incongruity comes 350-500 milliseconds after the acoustic stimulus; resolution of the incongruity comes 500-700ms after it; humour appreciation comes 800-1500ms after it. Laughter (the observable response) may come after the humour appreciation (Chen et al. 2017: 286).
28. In his brief discussion, Dover speaks of 'blending two tones' (1987: 288).
29. In Raskin's terms (1985: 100-4), there is a 'pretended *bona-fide* communication mode'; cf. *Ecclesiazusae* 773-6.
30. For triple rhyme of participles, cf. *Peace* 451-3, *Lysistrata* 26-8.
31. Cf. *Knights* 1014, *Clouds* 575, Cratinus fr. 484, Pherecr. 154.3, Isoc. 8.17.5-6.
32. For women being alcoholics, cf. *Lysistrata* 194-239, 466; *Thesmophoriazusae* 374-8, 393, 628-32, 733-57; *Ecclesiazusae* 132-57, 227, 1118-24.
33. Cf. Xen. *Hier.* 1.30.5.
34. Prato 2001: 206.
35. Cf. Euripides *Bacchae* 925ff. (Pentheus displaying feminine behaviour after wearing feminine clothes).
36. Even though the neo-Aristotelian trisection *eirōn – alazōn – bōmolochos,* applied in detail by Cornford (1914: 132-71), is nowadays rejected with the argument that those identities are only functions which may be transferred from one character to another, it is nevertheless clear that each character primarily performs one function. See Whitman 1964: 281-7, McLeish 1980: 53ff., Silk 1990: 163ff., Rosen 2014.
37. Arist. *Eth. Nic.* 2.7, 4.7.
38. Cf. Eur. *Electra* 1257, *Ion* 210.
39. Cf. *Peace* 473f., Xen. *Hell.* 4.4.17, Erinn. *SH* 401.25, Luc. *Philops.* 2.
40. Mitchell assumes that *Knights* has the most instances of *para prosdokian*, but he only names six of them, *ad.* 19, 98, 174, 508, 517 and 1238 (1835: l).
41. Translations from Henderson (1998-2002).

Chapter 12

1. Cf. Wiles 2008: 386.
2. 1900.
3. Bergson's main thesis was that we laugh at the inelasticity of the mind, the character and, also, of the body; specifically, a laughable moment could be when the living is encrusted with something mechanical (1911: 35). More precisely, he argued that 'mimesis is based on likeness and repetition, while the physical, the non-artificial should never repeat itself. To imitate anyone is to bring out the element of automatism he has allowed to creep into his person ... And as this is the very essence of the ludicrous, it is no wonder that imitation gives rise to laughter' (ibid. 15). For Incongruity Theory, see Jendza and Lowe in this volume.
4. For instance, Plato in *Meno* 97e–98a mentions Daedalic statues in a joke on why true opinions ('αἱ δόξαι αἱ ἀληθεῖς') should be tied up to prevent them from running away; see Morris 1992: 223, 236f., 257.
5. *Universität Paderborn* 2017. Specifically, on 'automatisms' see Bublitz, Marek, Steinmann and Winkler 2010, esp. Bublitz 2010. On automatic society see further Stiegler 2016; in antiquity see Gerolemou 2017, 2018.
6. See von Staden 1996: 93 and further Gundert 1992, Holmes 2010: 142–7, 2013, esp. 305f.
7. See Webster 2014: 1–30; further on that Kranz 1938, Solmsen 1963: 477–9, Tsitsirides 2001: 62.
8. Cf. *Regimen* 1.21; statue-makers imitate the outer form of the body but not the soul, as they are not interested in producing *gnōmē*, will and intelligence.
9. Newman and Bensaude-Vincent 2007: 5f., Schiefsky 2007.
10. See Schneider 1989: 220.
11. Gerolemou 2018, 2019.
12. On animated statues, see, among others, Steiner 2001, Pugliara 2003, Chaniotis 2017. On animated statues on stage, see e.g. the statue of the goddess Artemis in *IA* 1165–7 which allegedly gives a sign that should be perceived as a miracle; it moves from its place and closes its eyes automatically.
13. The issue of artificial physicality was partly raised and developed by Métraux 1995, who examined the results of the Hippocratic research on the human body, for example, the representation of respiration.
14. On prosthesis in antiquity see Bliquez 1983, Wiesing 2008, Draycott 2018.
15. Though Euripides is also described as 'καινὰ προσφέρων σοφά' ('offering novel ruses', *Thesmophoriazusae* 1130); on the ambiguous notion of Aristophanic novelty see Wright 2012: Ch. 3, Silk 2000: 45–51.
16. On gesture and voice, see further Dionysius Hal. 53 on Demosthenes; Athanasius' *Prolegomena* 14.177.4 on Theophrastus, the pupil of Aristotle, who argues on voice and bodily movement. See further Lada-Richards 1999: 169, n. 24.
17. See Wiles 1991: 22, 216; Graf 1991: 39, 51; Dutsch 2013: 422; Hanink 2017. See further esp. Torrance 2010: 224, Mueller 2016: 156. On the question of tragic plays as written scripts see Taplin 1977: 12–6, 1986: 168; Steiner 1994: Ch. 5; Revermann 2006: 87.
18. Cratinus in *Gods of Wealth*, Crates in *Wild Beasts*, Teleclides in his *Amphictyons*, Pherecrates in his *Miners* and *Persians*, Metagenes in *Thouriopersai*, Aristophanes in *Frying Pan Men*, Nicophron in *The Sirens*. On the *automatos bios* in Old Comedy, see Ceccarelli 1996, 453–55, Ruffell 2010, Farioli 2001, 214f., Konstan 2012.

19. Unfortunately, even illustrations of plays including theatrical devices do not reveal any information on the structure, materials, etc. of the machineries.
20. See Müller 1886: 152–5 for further ancient sources on theatrical machines. See also in Bekker 1814: 'γέρανος καὶ ἐν τῇ σκηνῇ ἅρπαξ κατεσκευασμένος ὑπὸ τοῦ μηχανοποιοῦ, ἐξ οὗ ὁ ἐσκευασμένος ὑποκριτικῶς τραγῳδεῖ' ('a crane and a grabber built in the *skēnē* by the crane-maker, from which a trained actor performs tragedy') – here the crane is pictured as a performer. On the *mēchanē* in particular see Rabkin 1979, Mastronarde 1990, Fiorentini 2013. On stage machinery more generally see Taplin 1978, Csapo-Slater 1994, Rehm 2002.
21. On the *ekkuklēma* see Hourmouziades 1965, 93–108, esp. 102 on Sophocles' avoidance of employing any technical expedient. Cf. the *scholion* ad A. *Eu.* 47 where the *ekkuklēma* is described as Euripides' invention, as cited in Hourmouziades 1965: 98. Neckel 1890 rejects the use of the *ekkuklēma* by Aeschylus and Sophocles but accepts it for Euripides and Aristophanes – for the purposes of comic parody. Against the 'improbable' use of the *mēchanē* (crane and *ekkuklēma*) in Sophocles, see Pickard-Cambridge 1946: 51, 111, Blume 1984: 72 (he argues for a *deus ex machina* in *Phil.* and *ekkuklēma* only in *Aj.* 346f., *Ant.* 1293f. and *El.* 1458ff.); Melchinger 1974: 191, 195–7, doubts the existence of a *deus ex machina* in *Phil.* but argues for the use of the *ekkuklēma* in some of Sophocles' plays. Newiger 1996: 99 argues for the use of the *ekkuklēma* in Soph. and rejects any possibility that a *mēchanē* could be used in *Phil.*; same Mastronarde 1990: 271, 286f. See further Taplin 1977: 443–7. Cf. Stiepel 1968: 252–63; he notes that it was not in fact a crane (what is called a *mēchanē*) but rather other forms of technical machines that supported divine *epiphaneia*.
22. See Ley 2005: 103.
23. Cf. Rau 1967: 96f., Melchinger 1974: 194, Blume 1984: 71, Lucarini 2016.
24. 2004: *ad loc.*
25. Antiphanes notes that when the tragic poets have nothing left to say they 'raise a *mēchanē* like a finger' (fr. 191 l.15).
26. For Aristophanes, I have used Henderson's Loeb translations throughout except where indicated.
27. See further for 'αὐτόματος' in Aristophanes, meaning 'without any interventions': *Ach.* 976, *Peace* 665, *Wealth* 1190.
28. Similarly, in a comedy by Plato (fr. 204), the wooden statue of the god Hermes declares that it enters the stage of its own accord ('Ερμῆς ἔγωγε Δαιδάλου φωνὴν ἔχων/ξύλινος βαδίζων αὐτόματος ἐλήλυθα', 'I am a wooden Hermes by Daedalus. I can talk and I have come here walking on my own', trans. Storey 2011c). The ambiguous outcomes of technology were also represented in Sophocles' satyr play *Pandora, or Sphyrokopoi*, where the creation of Pandora as well as the opening of the jar, along with its consequences, were enacted; on this see Seidensticker 2012: 218 and Uhlig: forthcoming. Cf. also the satyr drama perhaps called *Talos*, as cited at Hall 2006: 109 n. 41, in which Daedalus' gigantic bronze statue (cf. Apollonius *Argonautica* 4.1638–88) may have been operated by Medea.
29. Schwinge 2014: 69f. Cf. further Sörbom 1966: 76, Muecke 1982: 55f., Zeitlin 1996: 382–6, Stohn 1998 and Stehle 2002, esp. 381–5, argue that mimesis is accomplished through imitating physical traits and manners (*tropos*); see further Lada-Richards 1999: Ch. 4, esp. 169–72 and Lada-Richards 2002: 402f.: 'Mimesis cannot leave the imitator's own identity intact' (403). Duncan discusses the two kinds of mimesis that Agathon proposes and points out that the constructionist one is to be based on clothing and the essentialist one is to be based on the *phusis* of the body (2006: 27–46). See also Wyles 2011: Ch. 5.
30. See on that Taplin 1978: 76, Segal 1997: 225f., 257f., Falkner 1999: 189, Dobrov 2001: 11, 58, Rehm 2002: 201, Valakas 2002: 86, Gerolemou 2016.

31. Translations of *Bacchae* taken from Kovacs 2002.
32. On Dionysus' relation to mechanical automation see Csapo 2013, Bur 2016: 71.
33. On Pentheus' madness see e.g. Simon 1978, 118, Gerolemou 2011, 376–99.
34. On mirrors, reflections and mimesis see Vernant 1991: Ch. 7, Gerolemou and Diamantopoulou: 2020.
35. See on the philosophical influences implied in ll.16–18, Austin and Olson *ad loc*. Tsitsirides 2001, Clements 2014: 24–7. Empedocles, for instance, utilizes the image of a constructed (not born) human in a similar way; e.g. in B 96 DK, nature joins bones with glue.
36. My translation.
37. See further on the scene, Gerolemou 2018: 349.

Chapter 13

1. Telò views Philocleon's sickness as a reflection of the tragic disease of the audience of 423, who rejected the first production of Aristophanes' *Clouds*. He reads the prologue of *Wasps* against Euripides' *Hippolytus,* and later scenes involving Philocleon against the melancholic tragic characters of Niobe and Bellerophon, in order to show that 'the comic audience's impure judgment in rejecting *Clouds* is attributed to the tragic psychology of Cratinus's plays' (2016: 57). Harvey 1971: 363, Sidwell 1995: 70f., 2009: 73f., Ruffell 2002: 73f. and Biles 2011: 157 have viewed Philocleon's madness as reflecting Cratinus's manic addiction (to wine) in *Pytine*.
2. Beta 1999.
3. Dobrov 2001: 105–32.
4. Reckford 1991.
5. Euripides' *Bacchae*, which is not going to be discussed here in detail, offers many such examples. Pentheus' madness is most often cited for its explicit connection with mocking laughter (854, 1081; see Dobrov 2001: 83, Singer 2018: 305). Yet, Agave's triumphant entry with the head of Pentheus, and her pride and confidence which slowly give way to the realization of what she has done, is perhaps the most representative example of laughter placed in a grim context – and not the laughter of ridicule.
6. Singer 2018.
7. Ionesco 1964: 26. On comic absurdity in Beckett and Ionesco, see Brater 1974.
8. As Beckett's Arsene defines it in *Watt* (1953). See Janus 2009 and 2013.
9. For the incongruity theory of humour, see the discussions in Clark 1987 and Martin 1987. For a history of the theory, see Eagleton 2019: 67–93. See Kidd 2014: 120f., n. 12 for a helpful summary of incongruity theories of humour in Aristophanes. See also Swallow 'Introduction' and Jendza in this volume.
10. Eagleton 2019: 67.
11. For a psychological account of the theory, see McGhee 1972. See also Bruner 1976, Watson 1976.
12. Glasgow 1995: 8.
13. Ibid. 11.
14. Eagleton 2019: 90.

15. For the function of laughter in the face of disease and incongruity theory, see Kazantzidis and Tsoumpra 2018.
16. See Singer 2018.
17. With the exceptions of Euripides' *Orestes*, where Orestes' hallucinations and fit of madness are performed on stage (252–77), and the manic, bacchic-like dance of Cassandra in *Trojan Women*.
18. Cf. Galen's account of a patient with phrenitis who amuses passers-by with his absurd actions (*De locis affectis* 4.2 (8.225 K.)); he starts throwing glass vessels outside his window onto the street, which attracts the laughter of his 'audience'; the laughter stops ('γελῶντες μὲν ἐπαύσαντο') when the man proceeds to throw the woolworker out of the window too. For a discussion of the passage, see Kazantzidis and Tsoumpra 2018.
19. Peisetaerus is 'going mad', 'μαινόμενος', *Birds* 426; Chremylus is 'deranged' and 'overcome with black bile', 'παραφρονοῦντος' and 'μελαγχολῶντα', *Wealth* 2, 12. Carion accuses his master of insanity because he does the opposite of what one should do ('τοὐναντίον δρῶν ἢ προσῆκ' αὐτῷ ποιεῖν', 'doing the opposite of what he should do', 14). Cf. Xenophon, *Memorabilia* (3.9.6–7), where Socrates claims that acts of madness are measured by their distance from reality; madmen perform actions which, in the eyes of the majority, are completely divorced from reality or reflect a distorted idea of reality, and hence make no sense. Madness (*mania*) is a great delusion (*paranoia*). All translations of Aristophanes are Henderson 1998–2002.
20. See Ruffell 2018: 342: 'Protagonists (and other characters) may themselves be reacting against a social, cultural or political context that is insane, and where an effective counter is lacking.'
21. See Kidd 2014. Comedy echoes this form of political discourse; in *Thesmophoriazusae*, the Kinsman hurries to profess his hatred of Euripides to avoid an accusation of insanity (466–70), while in *Ecclesiazusae*, Praxagora, imitating a male speaker, plans to silence the proponents of opposing views in the assembly by hurling accusations of madness against them (249–52). See Ruffell 2018: 340–2 for the employment of a political discourse of madness as a female critique of patriarchy.
22. In classical antiquity there was no strict division between the mind and body, between mental and physical symptoms or afflictions, but mental illness was conceptualized as part of a larger psychosomatic continuum.
23. See Ruffell 2013.
24. Plato presents such a psychological script in his victim theory of comedy; in comic situations, be it in the theatre or in everyday life, laughter is principally aroused towards weak, self-ignorant characters (*Phlb.* 48a–50b), and our pleasure is linked to a feeling of 'spitefulness' ('φθόνος', 50a) against them. See Ruffell 2013: 248, Kazantzidis and Tsoumpra 2018.
25. Halliwell 1991: 280–7.
26. See Singer 2018.
27. Ruffell 2013: 249.
28. Ruffell 2013 discusses the political implications of comic violence and slapstick humour which, she argues, are marked out in sexual terms.
29. Eagleton claims that there is a touch of *Schadenfreude* in incongruity humour (and in all humour in general, 2019: 70f.). Even if we do not laugh at another's distress, we take a poke at our own rationality as the Freudian id triumphs over the superego.
30. For the medical connotations of *melancholia* in *Duskolos*, see Cusset 2014: 170.

31. For instance, at 173–7, he complains his house has turned into a meeting hub due to the presence of just one person.
32. Silk claims that there is no real breach of illusion because 'actually or potentially the complicity was always there; and comedy is not wholly containable within the aesthetic sphere in the first place' (2000: 91).
33. One can think here of the 'comedy of errors' which, similarly to madness, arouses laughter through situations of absurdity, confusion and embarrassment.
34. It is not without significance that feigned madness is very popular in the comic genre (Chaerestratus in Menander's *Aspis*, Menaechmus 2 in Plautus' *Menaechmi*, Casina in *Casina*). As a comic play-within-a-play, feigned madness shifts the ground between audience and action, and never allows the audience to settle in. See Smith 1987.
35. Beta 1999. See Harvey 1971 for Philocleon recalling Euripides' tragic heroines, Medea and Phaedra. See also the discussion below.
36. See Beta 1999: 148–55 for a discussion about the date of *Heracles*.
37. The comic affinities between *Thesmophoriazusae* and *Bacchae* have been long noted. See Seidensticker 1978, Segal 1997: 255f., 369–78, Dobrov 2001: 83f., Singer 2018.
38. See Wright 2013.
39. See Sidwell 1990: 10f.
40. For the political implications of Philocleon's madness, see Ruffell 2018.
41. Freud in his book on *The Joke* mentions the contribution repetition makes to comedy (2002: 225). On repetition and automatism as comic mechanisms see also Bergson 1911: 29–36.
42. *Helleborizomenoi* was the title of a play by the comic playwright Diphilus, which possibly dealt with the curing of Proetides by means of hellebore. Unfortunately only the title (and possibly a fragment) is preserved, but it is possible that acts of madness were depicted on stage.
43. Note the tossed-back head, which is the hallmark of the frenzied dance of the maenads in attic vase iconography; see Kefalidou 2009.
44. See Wright 2013: 221–5.
45. 'μετεωροκοπεῖς' is possibly a pun on 'παρακοπή', 'frenzy'.
46. Cf. also the aforementioned scene in *Wasps*, where Philocleon calls for the doors to be unbolted (1484) so that his insanity is displayed in its full comic splendour.
47. A good reason for this concealment is the concern of the afflicted individuals for their social standing and their sense of worth within their community, as well as the shame they may feel on account of their insanity and its manifestation. A clear reference to shame felt by patients who hide their heads when they sense an epileptic attack coming is found in Hp. *Morb. Sacr.* 15. Plato in the *Laws* (934c–d) ruled that a madman should be kept indoors by his relatives, with fines being levied against them if they failed to do so.
48. Singer 2018: 306f.
49. See Petrides 2013. Lada-Richards believes that the passage goes against the declared aim of Lycinus to defend pantomime from its attackers, as it clumsily displays the dangers of dramatic imitation (2006).
50. Trans. Harmon 1955.
51. Cf. the maddened Orestes in Euripides' *Orestes* who threatens (his visions of) the Furies with an imaginary bow (268–74). According to the ancient scholiast, Orestes was to use a real bow in the original staging, handed to him by Electra. It would be great (but unfortunately impossible) to know whether the original audience would have found this amusing.

52. Trans. Kaster 2011.
53. On the dangers of the affective power of theatrical representation, see Lada-Richards 2006.
54. Wilkins 2000: 321.
55. Trans. Olson 2008.
56. Funnily enough, Heracles is about to make the customary animal sacrifices when Lyssa strikes; if it were not for his other symptoms of madness (on which see below) excessive production of saliva could be attributed to his voracious appetite. My translations.
57. 375–355 BCE, London; British Museum n. 1867,0508.1287. See Trendall and Cambitoglou 1978: 298.
58. Green 1972.
59. Cf. also the Tarentine bell-krater with a frenzied pursuit of a naked young man by a pretend Heracles (Sydney 88.02). Rhinthon of Tarentum wrote a phlyax play with the name *Heracles*, which probably presented a burlesque madness modelled on the Euripidean tragedy (almost all nine titles preserved of his plays are burlesques of Euripidean subjects) but it is impossible to know with any certainty what it dealt with.
60. See also Singer 2018.
61. Trans. Kovacs 1998.
62. 2007: 144.
63. Tragicomedy: Bieber 1961: 130; hesitantly, Trendall 1989: 89f., Hughes 1996. Taplin maintains that the picture reflects a tragedy, perhaps a post-Euripidean one (2007: 145).
64. Pucci 1980: 185.
65. Kirpatrick and Dunn 2002: 35.
66. Ionesco 1964: 165.

Chapter 14

1. Fahrenthold 2016.
2. As the Introduction to this volume points out (p. 3), laughter and humour are not synonymous; it is of course possible that Bush is laughing awkwardly, and not because he finds Trump *funny*. This would be a generous interpretation.
3. 1987: 176.
4. 1998: 163f.
5. All translations my own.
6. 'Phrynichos and Ameipsias were contemporaries of Aristophanes and competed against him ... A Λυκ[won his first victory at the Dionysia some years after Aristophanes' first' (Dover 1997: 13fn.).
7. Hesk 2000: 235.
8. And indeed Hesk's invaluable analysis does just that (2000). See also Stanford 1963: 69–74, Dover 1993: 191–4, Telò in this volume pp. 54–6.
9. Veatch 1998: 175.
10. Fahrenthold 2016.
11. Veatch 1998: 172.

12. Keuls 1993: 47.
13. 2015: 316.
14. A notable exception to this, potentially, is the sexual groping of Lampito at *Lysistrata* 84; on which, see below, n. 27.
15. Or certainly, all the speaking roles were. Mute women may have been played by prostitutes, but this is a contentious issue. On the case of Festival and Harvest in *Peace*, see Olson 2003: 517–19 n.; they were 'more likely played by elaborately masked and costumed men'. For a more general discussion and summary of views, see Zweig 1992: 78–80, who likewise cautiously rejects the use of *hetairai*. I do not propose to set out a view here.
16. Robson 2015: 316.
17. Omitowoju 2002: 18.
18. Robson 2015: 317.
19. See Omitowoju (1997: 3–6) for a discussion of *hubris* in this context and why it 'does not work by reference to consent' when used to talk about sex acts.
20. Not that our concepts are necessarily so easily defined either. For an enlightening discussion on the competing narratives of rape in both the modern and ancient world, see Rabinowitz 2011.
21. 1998b: 105–9.
22. Namely the pig scene from the *Acharnians* and the captive scene from the *Thesmophoriazusae*.
23. Sommerstein 1998b: 105.
24. Cf. Halliwell's instructive discussion of the *Acharnians* passage (2002: 120–4). It is worth reflecting on the fact that Robson, Sommerstein and I are all men.
25. Compare with Lysias 1.12.
26. Ussher 1973: 1098ffn.
27. A similar joke-type can also be seen at *Lysistrata* 83f., where Calonice gropes Lampito. Here, the incongruity is that both victim and perpetrator are women. As noted above, n. 14, this scene is irregular in that there is no *threat* of sexual assault, but there is the *performance* of it (Calonice gropes Lampito's breasts). To an ancient Greek audience composed mostly or entirely of men, this comically incongruous display of female queerness between one Athenian and one Spartan character, both performed by male-bodied actors, would presumably have disarmed any moral tension around the assault. I do not propose to discuss this scene at any greater length because the sexual assault is not the focus of the scene, only a passing joke, and so it falls outside my scope.
28. Robson 2015: 324.
29. Dunbar 1995: 1196–261 n.
30. See Gerolemou, this volume.
31. Hall 2006: 248f.
32. The Scythian speaks broken Greek (more humour potential), but for the sake of clarity I have elided this in my translation.
33. Henderson 1991: 208.
34. A 'κηδεστής' indicates a connection by marriage – the Kinsman and Euripides are in-laws – so this is not incest of the first degree. The two men are nevertheless defined by their familial relationship to each other (*Thesmophoriazusae* 74, 210).

Notes to pp. 176–184

35. 2006: 227.
36. Henderson 1991: 60, 131.
37. Olson 2002: xxxvii–xxviii.
38. 1998: 181.
39. Olson 2002: xxxv, Aristophanes, *Peace* 609f.
40. As much as I have circumnavigated the examples selected by Robson (2015), I do not refute his or Sommerstein's (1998b) overall point.
41. For an analysis of Aristophanes' 'metrical playfulness' in this passage, see Robson 2015: 320–2.
42. Olson suggests that Festival has been nude since her entrance and that this line is referring to '"baggage" or "equipment"' and not clothing (1998: 517–19, 886 n.), but cf. *Frogs* 108.
43. Cf. *Peace* 658f.
44. Robson identifies this as a *para prosdokian* for the expected 'fist and legs' (2015: 321). For *para prosdokian* in Aristophanes, see Kanellakis in this volume.
45. Robson 2015: 322.
46. See Komornicka 2013: 219–21.
47. See Olson 1998: 905–6 n.; he 'leads Holiday down off the stage, through the orchestra, and over to the Council's seats . . . where he turns her over to one of the prytanic officers'.
48. Of course, whether Festival and Harvest were performed by male-bodied actors or by *hetairai* also has implications for the humour potential of this scene; see above, n. 15.
49. Omitowoju 2002: 116.
50. Ibid. 122.
51. 2006: 243.
52. Zeitlin 1986: 137.
53. Keuls 1993: 340f.
54. Harris 2015: 303.
55. Ogden 1997: 30.
56. Harris 2015: 310.
57. 1998b: 109.

Chapter 15

1. 1990; translated into English in 1993 as *Oedipus, Philosopher* (trans. Porter).
2. Goux 1993: 3.
3. On this topic, see Nussbaum 1981, Freydberg 2008, Clements 2014, Ruffell 2014.
4. See in particular Silk 2000: 42–97.
5. See Dobrov 2001: 89–104, Dixon 2014, Storey 2019: 126–8.
6. See further Riedweg 1990 and Whitmarsh 2016: 184f. for the atheistic traces in these fragments.
7. Goux 1993: 155.
8. In this respect Goux's focus on the myth of Bellerophon (along with Perseus and Jason) as an antecedent to the Oedipus myth is striking; see Goux 1993: 5–24.

9. See Clay 1994: 41, cited in Nightingale 1995: 172, for the idea that Plato formed his image of Socrates on the basis of Aristophanes' parody of the philosopher in *Clouds*. For the other references to tragedy and comedy in Plato's dialogues, see Clay 1975: 250–2.
10. See Clay 1975: 241.
11. All references to the *Symposium* are taken from Dover 1980, translations are my own.
12. For summaries of Aristophanes' speech, see Hunter 2004: 60–71, Cooksey 2010: 48–52; for more extensive studies see Ludwig 2002: 27–118, De Carvalho 2009.
13. Reeve 2007: 146.
14. Bataille 1986a: 80. See also Bataille 2001: 111–18 for another translation of this essay.
15. Ibid.
16. Ibid. 80, 81.
17. See Vrahimis 2012 and Marchessault 2017: 249–52.
18. Bataille 1986a: 83.
19. Bataille 1986b: 89. See also Bataille 2001: 133–50.
20. Cf. Kittler 2010: 19 and Pl. *R.* 508a–509c on the significance of the sun for philosophies ancient and modern.
21. On this see Loewenberg 1929: xxi, cited in Law 2000: 128 n. 3: 'The logic called dialectical is the logic of comedy par excellence.' See further Freydberg 2008: 3–4, 6, Desmond 1992: 301–42. Similarly, see Bataille 1986a: 84: 'there is, however, a perspective within which we can discern a true triumph for un-knowing: that of the end of history.'
22. See Dufresne 2000: 87 for discussion of these two 'beyonds'.
23. Nietzsche 2002: 3; see further Lampert 2004, Clay and Dudrick 2012 for this text. Cf. Gasché 1997: 175f. for the 'presuppositional' nature of Freud's *Beyond the Pleasure Principle*.
24. Nietzsche 2002: 27.
25. Ibid.
26. Trans. Lloyd-Jones 1994: 483.
27. Renger 2013: 54–6; for echoes of this in Theodor Adorno's decision to use Odysseus as motif in *Dialectic of Enlightenment*, see Hullot-Kentor 1989: 18–21, 24–7.
28. Nietzsche 2002: 5.
29. Ibid. 120f.
30. Ibid.
31. Nietzsche 1999: 83; Nietzsche's reference to 'instinct' here has striking resonances with the Freudian discussion of Aristophanes below.
32. Strong 1975: 183.
33. Nietzsche 2002: 30.
34. See Griffin 2015: 73f.
35. Nietzsche 2002: 4.
36. Ibid. 114.
37. All quotations are taken from Freud 2003: 43–102; see Freud 1955: 2–63 for Strachey's translation in the Standard Edition.

38. Jones 1957: 41, cited in Dufresne 2000: 14.
39. See Dufresne 2000.
40. Freud 2003: 76. Original emphasis.
41. Gasché 1997: 195. For the death drive in Aristophanes, see Telò in this volume.
42. Freud 2003: 52–4.
43. Ibid. 78. Original emphases. See further Freud 2003: 52.
44. Freud 2003: 77.
45. Ibid. 90. See also Freud 1953: 134 for a reference to 'the Eros of the divine Plato', in a preface to the fourth edition of *Three Essays on Sexuality* that was written in 1920 at around the same time as *Beyond the Pleasure Principle*.
46. Freud 2003: 96.
47. Ibid. 96f. Original emphasis.
48. Ibid. 97. For Freud's stress on the Platonic origin of this story to the detriment of Aristophanes, see Derrida 1980: 372, Weber 2000: 193f.; Armstrong 2005: 101 follows Freud in referring to it only as a 'Platonic myth'.
49. See Freud 1953: 136, Freud 1964: 149 n. 1; there also seems to be an echo at Freud 1959: 32, in his essay 'Delusions and Dreams in Jensen's *Gradiva*' (1907). Here, he draws attention to one of the characters in the story he is discussing describing the relationship between the two of them as a *Backfisch*, or a fish for frying (also an old-fashioned slang term for a young woman), just as Aristophanes describes the split creatures as similar to 'αἱ ψῆτται', 'flatfish' (191d4). These links with Plato were being drawn in Freud's lifetime; see Nachmansohn 1915, Pfister 1921.
50. Freud 2003: 97.
51. Dufresne 2000: 17.
52. See Abel-Hirsch 2010.

Chapter 16

1. *Lysistrata* produced by the National Theatre of Greece, translated by Dimitris Dimitriadis, directed by Michael Marmarinos, music by Dimitris Kamarotos, set design by Yiorgos Sapountzis, costume design by Mayiou Trikerioti, lighting design by Thomas Walgrave, movement by Christos Papadopoulos, artistic collaborator Efi Theodorou.
2. A few recent examples of productions of 'folk' Aristophanes: *Peace* by the National Theatre of Northern Greece, directed by Yiannis Iordanides (2005), *Acharnians* by the National Theatre, directed by Vangelis Theodoropoulos (2005), *Acharnians* by the State Theatre of Northern Greece, directed by Sotiris Hatzakis (2010), *Lysistrata* by the National Theatre of Greece, directed by Kostas Tsianos (2004).
3. Van Steen 2007: 164.
4. For the national and international impact of Koun's treatment of Aristophanes, see Van Steen 2000 and 2007.
5. A *fustanella* is a pleated kilt, the traditional men's costume in many areas of the Balkans and mainland Greece.
6. Georgousopoulos 1999.

7. Tsatsoulis 1999. In an interview about *Lysistrata*, Marmarinos also expresses his disagreement with the replacement of original historical references with current events in order to make Aristophanes funny for the contemporary audience, because he shares the opinion that this transforms a poetic text into a revue. He feels that the humour in Aristophanes is 'of another type' (Kaltaki 2016).
8. Sidiropoulou 2014: 127.
9. Ibid. 121.
10. Patsalidis and Stavrakopoulou 2014.
11. Ibid. 12.
12. This tonality was, of course, a frequently occurring feature of the original texts and performances of Aristophanic comedy. For example, Taplin (1983) suggests that the term *trugedy* (*trygōidia*), first documented in Aristophanes' *Acharnians* (499f.) and probably coined by the poet himself, referred to the instances when comedy can contain a serious message with didactic, edifying potential, such as the one attributed to tragedy in *The Frogs* (1009f.). Hall (2006: 330–3) applies this definition of *trygōidia* in her analysis of the character of Trygaeus in *Peace*, a protagonist with heroic traits who uses abundant references to tragic poetry, tragic plots and tragic characters to achieve his very serious goals. This character also has a strong relationship with Nicias, the politician responsible for the 421 BCE peace treaty with Sparta (Ibid.: 326f.). A theatrical realization of this serious tone is a relatively new area in contemporary revivals, that has been gaining momentum in recent years. The ancient and the contemporary contexts in this case have one crucial element in common – a political crisis so acute that it becomes an existential one.
13. Styan 1962: 260.
14. Foley 2010: 140. See also Zira 2019: 227.
15. Zira 2019: 227.
16. See also Zira 2019: 228, 230.
17. Sidiropoulou 2014: 126.
18. Tsatsoulis 2016. In an interview before the opening of the play, Marmarinos insisted on the importance of poetry, both as a quality in the translation and also as a means of enhancing the performance's emotional resonance with the audience (Zousi 2016.)
19. For more details see Charami 2016.
20. Kaltaki 2016. Translations mine.
21. Department of Theater, Aristotelian University of Thessaloniki 2019.
22. Zousi 2016.
23. Other performances by Marmarinos in which a chorus is the central device of the *mise-en-scéne* are, for example, *Dying as a Country* by Dimitris Dimitriadis (2007), in which he used a chorus of two hundred people, both professional actors and ordinary citizens, which he likened to a Greek tragic chorus; and his site-specific *Insenso* (2012), also by Dimitriadis, in which a chorus of twenty-one women actors perform the monologue of Livia Serpieri from Visconti's 1954 film *Senso*. On the several instances in which Marmarinos creates a chorus out of the audience by exploring the boundaries between performers and spectators, see Tsatsoulis 2017, Sidiropoulou 2014: 124.
24. Tsatsoulis 2017.
25. Marmarinos 2016.
26. See for example Mavridou 2018, Matthaiou 2017.

Notes to pp. 199–209

27. Marmarinos 2016.
28. See for example Kaltaki 2016.
29. There is no normal *parabasis* in the *Lysistrata*, since the chorus is divided, but this point in the play would be its natural place; see Sommerstein 1990: 186. Productions often make the decision to emphasize these lines by having the chorus address the audience, as in a typical *parabasis*.
30. See for example Lada-Richards 1999.
31. See Sella 2014.
32. On the cultural and ideological impact of the Epidaurus festival on contemporary Greeks, see Ioannidou 2010.
33. On the new dynamics of theatre production in Greece and Cyprus since the economic crisis, see Zira 2019.

Chapter 17

1. In 2013 and 2016, Eastman produced a tragedy/comedy double bill – first *Prometheus Bound* and *Frogs*, then *Antigone* and *Lysistrata*. The Cambridge Greek Play website has excellent documentation of these productions, including extensive photographs and links to reviews. A complete recording of *Frogs* and highlights from *Antigone* are available on YouTube.
2. See the Introduction to this volume (p. 3) for the distinction between laughter and humour.
3. As well as *Clouds*, I have adapted Sophocles' *Electra* and *Antigone*, Aeschylus' *Eumenides*, and Euripides' *Bacchae* and *Medea* for theatres in the UK and the US. Since 2015, I have produced the annual Greek Play at King's College London; most of the productions I have led have been tragedies, but the Greek Play in 2020 will be, in part, Aristophanes' *Frogs*. My ongoing work with By Jove Theatre Company engages with a range of classical material.
4. Details of the proposed cuts and the campaign against them can be found on the latter's blog; Support Classics at RHUL 2011.
5. See, for example, articles in the *Guardian* by Charlotte Higgins (2011) and the *Times Literary Supplement* by Mary Beard (2011).
6. Beard 2011.
7. Hall 2011.
8. Ibid.
9. Ibid.
10. Higgins 2011.
11. Hall 2011. The appearance of such universities was another part of the context that Hall saw as being symptomatic of the same kind of thinking that underpinned the Royal Holloway proposals to Classics. Hall notes in her brief that Grayling's university 'is ripping off syllabuses written by RHUL [Royal Holloway, University of London] Classicists but selling the degree for twice the money'.
12. Ibid.
13. Bullen 2011.
14. Ibid.
15. Ibid.

16. Ibid.
17. Ibid.
18. Ibid.
19. Ibid.
20. Ibid.
21. I am borrowing this extremely helpful phrase 'theatrical intelligence' from my colleague in the Department of Drama, Theatre and Dance at Royal Holloway, Professor Elizabeth Schafer.
22. For this, see Konstan 2010.
23. For a recent and highly accessible account of this association – couched in a broader argument in favour of Classics as a discipline – see the first chapter of Morley: 2018a. I discuss the book further in the next paragraph.
24. These were Classics, English and Drama. Hall has consistently turned to methodologies and perspectives outside of Classics to illuminate her scholarship on classical material and its reception. This is reflected in her frequent work with theatre makers.
25. 2018a.
26. Morley 2018a: 38f.
27. Jenkyns 2018.
28. Morley 2018b.
29. Jenkyns 2018.

BIBLIOGRAPHY

Abel-Hirsch, Nicola (2010) 'The Life Instinct', *International Journal of Psychoanalysis*, 91: 1055–71.
Alford, C. Fred (1992) *The Psychoanalytic Theory of Greek Tragedy*. New Haven, CT and London: Yale University Press.
Anchor, Robert (1978) 'History and Play: Johan Huizinga and His Critics', *History and Theory*, 17, 63–93.
Andrewes, A. (1974) 'The Arginousai Trial', *Phoenix*, 28 (1): 112–22.
Anstey, F. (1891) 'Voces Populi', *Punch*, 101: 69.
Armstrong, Richard H. (2005) *A Compulsion for Antiquity: Freud and the Ancient World*. Ithaca, NY and London: Cornell University Press.
Attardo, Salvatore (1993) 'Violation of Conversational Maxims and Cooperation: The Case of Jokes', *Journal of Pragmatics* 19 (6): 537–58.
Attardo, Salvatore (1994) *Linguistic Theories of Humor*. Berlin and New York, NY: De Gruyter.
Attardo, Salvatore (2001) *Humorous Texts: A Semantic and Pragmatic Analysis*. Berlin and New York, NY: De Gruyter.
Attardo, Salvatore (ed.) (2014) *Encyclopedia of Humor Studies*. 2 vols. Thousand Oaks, CA: Sage.
Attardo, Salvatore (2016) 'Review of Beard 2014', *Humor*, 29: 143–5.
Attardo, Salvatore (ed.) (2017) *The Routledge Handbook of Language and Humor*. New York, NY: Routledge.
Attardo, Salvatore and Victor Raskin (1991) 'Script Theory Revis(it)ed: Joke Similarity and Joke Representation Model', *Humor*, 4: 293–347.
Austin, Colin and S. Douglas Olson (eds) (2004) *Aristophanes: Thesmophoriazusae*. Oxford: Oxford University Press.
Azoulay, Vincent (2010) *Périclès: la démocratie athénienne à l'épreuve du grand homme*. Paris: Armand Colin.
Bagordo, Andreas (ed. and trans.) (2013) *Telekleides: Einleitung, Übersetzung, Kommentar*. Heidelberg: Verlag Antike.
Bailey, Michael D. (2007) *Magic and Superstition in Europe: A Concise History from Antiquity to the Present*. Lanham, MD: Rowman and Littlefield.
Bakhtin, Mikhail (1984) *Rabelais and His World*. Trans. Hélène Iswolsky. Bloomington, IN: Indiana University Press.
Bakhtin, Mikhail (1986) 'Notes Made in 1970–71' in *Speech Genres and Other Late Essays*. Trans. Vern W. McGee, ed. Caryl Emerson and Michael Holquist. Austin, TX: University of Texas Press. 132–58.
Bakola, Emmanuela (2010) *Cratinus and the Art of Comedy*. Oxford: Oxford University Press.
Bakola, Emmanuela, Lucia Prauscello and Mario Telò (eds) (2013) *Greek Comedy and the Discourse of Genres*. Cambridge: Cambridge University Press.
Baldwin, Hannah (2019) 'Was It You Who Died, or Your Brother?', *Humor*, 32: 179–94.
Barchiesi, Alessandro (2001) 'Horace and Iambos: The Poet as Literary Historian' in *Iambic Ideas: Essays on a Poetic Tradition from Archaic Greece to the Late Roman Empire*. Ed. Alberto Cavarzere, Antonio Aloni and Alessandro Barchiesi. Lanham, MD: Rowman and Littlefield. 141–64.
Bataille, Georges (1970) *Oeuvres complètes: premiers écrits (1922–40)*. Ed. D. Hollier. Paris: Gallimard.

Bibliography

Bataille, Georges (1971) *Oeuvres complètes: oeuvres littéraires posthumes*. Ed. T. Klossowski. Paris: Gallimard.

Bataille, Georges (1985) 'The Practice of Joy Before Death' in *Visions of Excess: Selected Writings, 1927-1939*. Ed., trans. and with an introduction by Allan Stoekl. Minneapolis, MN: University of Minnesota Press. 235-9.

Bataille, Georges (1986a) 'Un-Knowing and Its Consequences', *October*, 36. Trans. Annette Michelson: 80-5.

Bataille, Georges (1986b) 'Un-Knowing: Laughter and Tears', *October*, 36. Trans. Annette Michelson: 89-102.

Bataille, Georges (1988) 'Joy in the Face of Death' in *The College of Sociology, 1937-39*. Ed. Denis Hollier, trans. Betsy Wing. Minneapolis, MN: University of Minnesota Press. 322-8.

Bataille, Georges (1989) *Theory of Religion*. Trans. Robert Hurley. New York, NY: Zone Books.

Bataille, Georges (1990) 'Hegel, Death, and Sacrifice', *Yale French Studies*, 78: 9-28.

Bataille, Georges (1991a) *The Accursed Share*. Vol. I, trans. Robert Hurley. New York, NY: Zone Books.

Bataille, Georges (1991b) *The Accursed Share*. Vols. II-III, trans. Robert Hurley. New York, NY: Zone Books.

Bataille, Georges (2001) *The Unfinished System of Nonknowledge*. Ed. Stuart Kendall, trans. Michelle Kendall and Stuart Kendall. Minneapolis, MN and London: University of Minnesota Press.

Bataille, Georges (2011) *Guilty*. Trans. Stuart Kendall. Albany, NY: State University of New York Press.

Bataille, Georges (2014) *Inner Experience*. Trans. and with an introduction by Stuart Kendall. Albany, NY: State University of New York Press.

Beard, Mary (30 June 2011) 'Classics at Royal Holloway Under Threat', *Times Literary Supplement* [Online]. Available at: www.the-tls.co.uk/classics-at-royal-holloway-under-threat/ (Accessed 7 February 2019).

Beard, Mary (2014) *Laughter in Ancient Rome*. Berkeley, CA: University of California Press.

Bekker, Immanuel (1814) *Anecdota Graeca*. Berlin: G.C. Nauckium.

Bensaude-Vincent, Bernadette and William R. Newman (2007) 'Introduction: The Artificial and the Natural: State of the Problem' in *The Artificial and the Natural: An Evolving Polarity*. Ed. Bernadette Bensaude-Vincent and William R. Newman. Cambridge, MA and London: MIT Press. 1-19.

Bergren, Ann (2008) 'Female, Fetish, Urban Form' in *Weaving Truth: Essays on Language and the Female in Greek Thought*. Cambridge, MA: Harvard University Press. 304-54.

Bergson, Henri (1911) *Laughter. An Essay on the Meaning of the Comic*. Trans. Cloudesley Brereton and Fred Rothwell. New York, NY: Macmillan.

Berk, Lucas (1964) *Epicharmus*. Groningen: Wolters.

Berlant, Lauren and Sianne Ngai (2017) 'Comedy Has Issues', *Critical Inquiry*, 43: 233-49.

Berlyne, Daniel E. (1960) *Conflict, Arousal, and Curiosity*. New York, NY: McGraw-Hill.

Berlyne, Daniel E. (1972) 'Humor and its Kin' in *The Psychology of Humor*. Ed. Jeffrey H. Goldstein and Paul E. McGhee. London and New York, NY: Academic Press. 40-60.

Bersani, Leo (1986) *The Freudian Body: Psychoanalysis and Art*. New York, NY: Columbia University Press.

Beta, Simone (1999) 'Madness on the Comic Stage: Aristophanes' *Wasps* and Euripides' *Heracles*', *Greek, Roman, and Byzantine Studies*, 40: 135-58.

Bieber, Margarete (1961) *The History of the Greek and Roman Theater*. Princeton, NJ: Princeton University Press.

Bilbao Ruiz, Javier (2005) 'Procedimiento de humor ἐκ τῶν παρὰ προσδοκίαν en los scholia de *Acarnienses*' in *Actas del XI Congreso Español de Estudios Clásicos*. Ed. José Fco. González Castro, Antonio Alvar Ezquerra and Alberto Bernabé. Vol. 2. Madrid: Sociedad Española de Estudios Clásicos y Ediciones Clásicas. 245-52.

Biles, Zachary P. (2011) *Aristophanes and the Poetics of Competition.* Cambridge and New York, NY: Cambridge University Press.
Bliquez, Lawrence J. (1983) 'Classical Prosthetics', *Archaeology,* 36:5: 25–9.
Blume, Horst-Dieter (1984) *Einführung in das antike Theaterwesen.* Second revised edition. Darmstadt: WBG.
Bogel, Fredric V. (2001) *The Difference Satire Makes: Rhetoric and Reading from Jonson to Byron.* Ithaca, NY: Cornell University Press.
Borg, Barbara E. (2005) 'Eunomia or "Make Love not War": Eunomian Personifications Reconsidered' in *Personification in the Greek World.* Ed. Emma Stafford and Judith Herrin. Aldershot: Ashgate. 193–210.
Bowie, Angus (1996) *Aristophanes: Myth, Ritual and Comedy.* Cambridge: Cambridge University Press.
Bowie, Ewen (1998) 'Le portrait de Socrate dans les *Nuées* d'Aristophane' in *Le rire des anciens.* Ed. Monique Trédé-Boulmer and Philippe Hoffmann. Paris: Numilog. 53–66.
Boyd, Brian (2004) 'Laughter and Literature: A Play Theory of Humor', *Philosophy and Literature,* 28: 1–22.
Brater, Enoch (1974) 'Beckett, Ionesco, and the Tradition of Tragicomedy', *College Literature,* 1: 113–27.
Braund, David and Edith Hall (2014) 'Theatre in the Fourth-Century Black Sea Region' in *Greek Theatre in the Fourth Century BC.* Ed. Eric Csapo, J. R. Green, Hans Rupprecht Goette and Peter Wilson. Berlin: De Gruyter. 371–90.
Braund, Susanna Morton (2004) 'Libertas or Licentia? Freedom and Criticism in Roman Satire' in *Free Speech In Classical Antiquity.* Ed. Ineke Sluiter and Ralph M. Rosen. Leiden: Brill. 409–28.
Bréchet, Christophe (2005) 'Aristophane chez Plutarque', *PALLAS,* 67: 11–23.
Brennan, Eugene (2015) 'Mourning and Mania: Visions of Intoxication and Death in the Poetry of Georges Bataille' in *Literature and Intoxication: Writing, Politics, and the Experience of Excess.* Ed. Eugene Brennan and Richard Williams. London: Palgrave Macmillan. 67–80.
Brintnall, Kent L. (2015) 'Erotic Ruination: Embracing the "Savage Spirituality" of Barebacking' in *Negative Ecstacies: Georges Bataille and the Study of Religion.* Ed. Jeremy Biles and Kent L. Brintnall. New York, NY: Fordham University Press. 51–67.
Brisson, Luc (2002) *Sexual Ambivalence: Androgyny and Hermaphroditism in Graeco-Roman Antiquity.* Trans. Janet Lloyd. Berkeley, CA: University of California Press.
Brommer, F. (1937) *Satyroi.* Würzburg: K. Triltsch.
Bruner, Jerome S. (1976) 'Nature and Uses of Immaturity' in *Play: Its Role in Development and Evolution.* Ed. Jerome S. Bruner, Alison Jolly and Kathy Sylva. Harmondsworth: Penguin. 28–64.
Bublitz, Hannelore (2010) 'Täuschend natürlich. Zur Dynamik gesellschaftlicher Automatismen, ihrer Ereignishaftigkeit und strukturbildenden Kraft' in *Automatismen.* Ed. Hannelore Bublitz, Roman Marek, Christina Louise Steinmann and Hartmut Winkler. Munich: Wilhelm Fink. 153–72.
Bublitz, Hannelore, Roman Marek, Christina Louise Steinmann and Hartmut Winkler (eds) (2010) *Automatismen.* Munich: Wilhelm Fink.
Buckels, Erin E., Paul D. Trapnell and Delroy L. Paulhus (2014) 'Trolls Just Want to Have Fun', *Personality and Individual Differences,* 67: 97–102.
Bullen, David (adapt.) (2011) *Clouds* [Unpublished MS]. By Aristophanes.
Bur, Tatiana (2016) *Mechanical Miracles: Automata in Ancient Greek Religion* [Master's thesis]. University of Sydney.
Burckhardt, Jacob (1941) *Griechische Kulturgeschichte.* Stuttgart: Kröner.
Burgers, Christian and Margot van Mulken (2017) 'Humor Markers' in *The Routledge Handbook of Language and Humor.* Ed. Salvatore Attardo. New York: Routledge. 385–99.

Bibliography

Burkert, Walter (1972) *Lore and Science in Ancient Pythagoreanism*. Trans. Edwin L. Minar, Jr. Cambridge, MA: Harvard University Press.
Butler, Susan (ed.) (2013) *Macquarie Dictionary*. 6th ed. Sydney: Macquarie Dictionary Publishers.
Caillois, Roger (1962) [1958] *Man, Play, and Games*. Trans. Meyer Barash. London: Thames and Hudson.
Cambridge Greek Play (2013) 'Prometheus Bound/Frogs' [Online]. Available at: www.cambridgegreekplay.com/plays/2013/prometheusfrogs (Accessed 7 February 2019).
Cambridge Greek Play (2016) 'Antigone/Lysistrata' [Online]. Available at: www.cambridgegreekplay.com/plays/2016/antigonelysistrata (Accessed 7 February 2019).
Carey, Christopher (1994) 'Comic Ridicule and Democracy' in *Ritual, Finance, Politics. Athenian Democratic Accounts Presented to David Lewis*. Ed. Robin Osborne and Simon Hornblower. Oxford: Clarendon Press. 69–85.
Cavarero, Adriana (1995) *In Spite of Plato: A Feminist Rewriting of Ancient Philosophy*. Trans. Serina Anderlini-D'Onofrio and Áine O'Healey. Cambridge: Polity.
Ceccarelli, Paola (1996) 'L'Athènes de Périclès: Un « pays de cocagne »?: L'idéologie Démocratique et l'αὐτόματος βίος dans la Comédie Ancienne', *Quaderni Urbinati di Cultura Classica*, 54: 109–59.
Chaniotis, Angelos (2014) 'The Life of Statues of Gods in the Greek World', *Kernos*, 30: 91–112.
Charami, Stella (6 August 2016) 'Είδα: τη Λυσιστράτη σε σκηνοθεσία Μιχαήλ Μαρμαρινού [I Saw *Lysistrata* by Michael Marmarinos]', *To Spirto* [Online]. Available at: www.tospirto.net/theater/ive_seen (Accessed 6 August 2016).
Chen, Hsueh-Chih, Yu-Chen Chan, Ru-Huei Dai, Yi-Jun Liao and Cheng-Hao Tu (2017) 'Neurolinguistics of Humor' in *The Routledge Handbook of Language and Humor*. Ed. Salvatore Attardo. New York: Routledge. 282–94.
Ching, Marvin K. L. (1980) 'A Literary and Linguistic Analysis of Compact Verbal Paradox' in *Linguistic Perspectives on Literature*. Ed. Marvin K. L. Ching, Michael C. Haley and Ronald F. Lunsford. London: Routledge & Kegan Paul. 175–81.
Chitwood, Ava (1986) 'The Death of Empedocles', *AJP*, 107: 175–91.
Chłopicki, Władisław (1997) 'An Approach to the Analysis of Verbal Humor in Short Stories', *Humor*, 10: 333–47.
Cho, Daegon and K. Hazel Kwon (2015) 'The Impacts of Identity Verification and Disclosure of Social Cues on Flaming in Online User Comments', *Computers in Human Behavior*, 51A: 363–72.
Christ, Matthew R. (2006) *The Bad Citizen in Classical Athens*. Cambridge: Cambridge University Press.
Clark, Maudemarie and David Dudrick (2012) *The Soul of Nietzsche's* Beyond Good and Evil. Cambridge: Cambridge University Press.
Clark, Michael (1987) 'Humor and Incongruity' in *The Philosophy of Laughter and Humour*. Ed. John Morreall. Albany, NY: State University of New York Press. 139–55.
Clay, Diskin (1975) 'The Tragic and Comic Poet of the Symposium', *Arion*, New Series 2(2): 238–61.
Clay, Diskin (1994) 'The Origins of the Socratic Dialogue' in *The Socratic Movement*. Ed. Paul A. Vander Waerdt. Ithaca, NY and London: Cornell University Press. 23–47.
Clements, Ashley (2014) *Aristophanes'* Thesmophoriazusae: *Philosophizing Theatre and the Politics of Perception in Late Fifth-Century Athens*. Cambridge: Cambridge University Press.
Coleman, Gabriella (2014) *Hacker, Hoaxer, Whistleblower, Spy: The Many Faces of Anonymous*. London: Verso Books.
Compton, Todd (1990) 'The Trial of the Satirist: Poetic Vitae (Aesop, Archilochus, Homer) as Background for Plato's *Apology*', *AJP*, 111: 330–47.
Compton-Engle, Gwendolyn (2015) *Costume in the Comedies of Aristophanes*. Cambridge: Cambridge University Press.

Connor, W. Robert (1984) *Thucydides*. Princeton: Princeton University Press.
Cooksey, Thomas L. (2010) *Plato's Symposium*. London and New York, NY: Continuum.
Cooper, Lane (1920) 'A Pun in the *Rhetoric* of Aristotle', *AJP*, 41: 48–56.
Cooper, Lane (1924) *An Aristotelian Theory of Comedy*. New York, NY: Harcourt, Brace & Co.
Cornford, Francis Macdonald (1914) *The Origin of Attic Comedy*. London: Edward Arnold.
Coulson, Seana (2001) *Semantic Leaps: Frame-Shifting and Conceptual Blending in Meaning Construction*. Cambridge: Cambridge University Press.
Crisp, Roger (ed.) (2014) *Aristotle: Nicomachean Ethics*. Revised ed. Cambridge: Cambridge University Press.
Critchley, Simon (1999) 'Comedy and Finitude: Displacing the Tragic-Heroic Paradigm in Philosophy and Psychoanalysis', *Constellations*, 6: 108–22.
Csapo, Eric (2004) 'The Politics of New Music' in *Music and the Muses: The Culture of 'Mousikē' in the Classical Athenian City*, ed. Penelope Murray and Peter Wilson. Oxford: Oxford University Press. 207–48.
Csapo, Eric (20 February 2013) *The Dionysian Parade and the Poetics of Plenitude* [UCL Housman Lecture]. UCL Department of Greek and Latin, London.
Csapo, Eric and W. J. Slater (1995) *The Context of Ancient Drama*. Ann Arbor, MN: Michigan University Press.
Cusset, Christophe (2014) 'Melancholic Lovers in Menander' in *Menander in Contexts*. Ed. Alan H. Sommerstein. New York, NY and London: Routledge. 167–79.
D'Errico, Francesca and Isabella Poggi (2016) '*The Bitter Laughter*. When Parody Is a Moral and Affective Priming in Political Persuasion', *Frontiers in Psychology*, 7: 1–14.
Damasio, Antonio (2004) *Looking for Spinoza: Joy, Sorrow and the Feeling Brain*. London: Vintage.
Davidson, James N. (2007) *The Greeks and Greek Love: A Radical Reappraisal of Homosexuality in Ancient Greece*. London: Weidenfeld and Nicolson.
Dawson, S. (1997) 'The Theatrical Audience in 5th-Century Athens: Numbers and Status', *Prudentia*, 29: 1–14.
De Brasi, Diego 'Socrates and Alcibiades as Satiric "Heroes": The Socrates of Persius' in *Socrates and the Socratic Dialogue*. Ed. Alessandro Stavru and Christopher Moore. Leiden: Brill. 727–43.
De Carvalho, Mário Jorge (2009) *Die Aristophanesrede in Platons Symposium: Die Verfassung des Selbst*. Würzburg: Königshausen & Neumann.
Dean, Greg (2000) *Step by Step to Stand-Up Comedy*. Portsmouth, NH: Heinemann.
Deleuze, Gilles (1990) 'Michel Tournier and the World Without Others' in *The Logic of Sense*. Trans. Mark Lester, ed. Constantin V. Boundas. New York, NY: Continuum. 301–21.
Deleuze, Gilles (1991) *Coldness and Cruelty*. Trans. Jean McNeil. New York, NY: Zone Books.
Deleuze, Gilles (1994) *Difference and Repetition*. Trans. Paul Patton. New York, NY: Columbia University Press.
Deleuze, Gilles (2003) *Francis Bacon: The Logic of Sensation*. Trans. and with an introduction by Daniel W. Smith. Minneapolis, MN: University of Minnesota Press.
Deleuze, Gilles and Félix Guattari (1986) *Kafka: Toward a Minor Literature*. Trans. Dana Polan. Minneapolis, MN: University of Minnesota Press.
Department of Theater, Aristotelian University of Thessaloniki (2019) 'Μιχαήλ Μαρμαρινός' [Online]. Available at: www.thea.auth.gr/staff/michail_marmarinos (Accessed 25 March 2019).
Derrida, Jacques (1978) *Writing and Difference*. Trans. A. Bass. Chicago, IL: University of Chicago Press.
Derrida, Jacques (1987) *The Post Card: From Socrates to Freud and Beyond*. Trans. A. Bass. Chicago, IL and London: University of Chicago Press.
Derrida, Jacques (2005) 'Derrida's Response to Hent de Vries' in *Augustine and Postmodernism: Confessions and Circumfession*. Ed. John D. Caputo and Michael J. Scanlon. Bloomington and Indianapolis, IN: Indiana University Press. 88–90.

Bibliography

Dery, Mark (1994) 'Flame Wars' in *Flame Wars: The Discourse of Cyberculture*. Ed. Mark Dery. Durham, NC and London: Duke University Press. 1–11.

Desmond, William (1992) *Beyond Hegel and Dialectic: Speculation, Cult and Comedy*. Albany, NY: State University of New York Press.

Destrée, Pierre (2016) 'Aristotle on the Power of Music in Tragedy', *Greek and Roman Musical Studies*, 4/2: 231–52.

Destrée, Pierre (2019) 'Aristotle on Why We Laugh at Jokes' in *Laughter, Humor and Comedy in Ancient Philosophy*. Ed. Pierre Destrée and Franco V. Trivigno. Oxford: Oxford University Press. 35–51.

Dieudonné, J. (2008) 'Von Neumann, Johann (or John)' in *Complete Dictionary of Scientific Biography*. Ed. C.C. Gillispie. Seventh ed., vol. 14. Detroit, MI: Charles Scribner's Sons. 88–92.

Dixon, Dustin W. (2014) 'Reconsidering Euripides' *Bellerophon*', *Classical Quarterly*, 64: 493–506.

Dobrov, Gregory W. (2001) *Figures of Play: Greek Drama and Metafictional Poetics*. Oxford and New York, NY: Oxford University Press.

Dover, K. J. (ed.) (1968) *Aristophanes: Clouds*. Oxford: Clarendon Press.

Dover, K. J. (1978) *Greek Homosexuality*. London: Duckworth.

Dover, K. J. (ed.) (1980) *Plato: Symposium*. Cambridge: Cambridge University Press.

Dover, K. J. (1987) *Greek and the Greeks*. Oxford: Basil Blackwell.

Dover, K. J. (ed.) (1993) *Aristophanes: Frogs*. Oxford: Clarendon Press.

Draycott, Jane (ed.) (2018) *Prostheses in Antiquity*. London: Routledge.

Dufresne, Todd (2000) *Tales from the Freudian Crypt: The Death Drive in Text and Context*. Stanford, CA: Stanford University Press.

Dunbar, Nan (ed.) (1995) *Birds*. By Aristophanes. Oxford: Clarendon Press.

Dunbar, R. I. M. et al. (2012) 'Social Laughter is Correlated with an Elevated Pain Threshold', *Proceedings of the Royal Society B*, 279: 1161–7.

Duncan, Anne (2006) *Performance and Identity in the Classical World*. Cambridge: Cambridge University Press.

Duplouy, Alain (2003) 'Les Eupatrides d'Athénes, <<nobles defénseurs de leur patrie>>', *Cahiers du Centre Gustave Glotz*, 14: 7–22.

Dutsch, Dorota (2013) 'Towards A Roman Theory of Theatrical Gesture' in *Performance in Greek and Roman Theatre*. Ed. George W.M. Harrison and Vayos Liapis. Leiden and Boston, MA: Brill. 409–32.

Eagleton, Terry (2019) *Humour*. New Haven, CT and London: Yale University Press.

Edmunds, Lowell (1987) 'The Aristophanic Cleon's 'Disturbance' of Athens', *AJP*, 108.2: 233–63.

Encyclopedia Dramatica (2018) 'Socrates' [Online]. Available at: www.encyclopediadramatica.rs/Socrates (Accessed 30 May 2019).

Ermida, Isabel (2008) *The Language of Comic Narratives: Humor Construction in Short Stories*. Humor Research 9, Berlin and New York, NY: Mouton de Gruyter.

Fahrenthold, David A. (8 October 2016) 'Trump recorded having extremely lewd conversation about women in 2005', *Washington Post* [Online]. Available at: www.washingtonpost.com/politics/trump-recorded-having-extremely-lewd-conversation-about-women-in-2005/2016/10/07/3b9ce776-8cb4-11e6-bf8a-3d26847eeed4_story.html?utm_term=.c3537880246a (Accessed 21 January 2019).

Falkner, Thomas M. (1999) 'Madness Visible: Tragic Ideology and Poetic Authority in Sophocles' *Ajax*' in *Contextualizing Classics: Ideology, Performance, Dialogue*. Ed. Thomas M. Falkner, Nancy Felson and David Konstan. Lanham, MD: Rowman & Littlefield. 173–201.

Farioli, Marcella (2001) *Mundus alter: Utopie e distopie nella commedia Greca antica*. Milan: Vita e Pensiero.

Farmer, Matthew C. (2017) *Tragedy on the Comic Stage*. Oxford: Oxford University Press.

Ferrari, G. R. F. (2008) 'Socratic Irony as Pretence', *Oxford Studies in Ancient Philosophy*, 34: 1–33.
Filippo, Adele (2001–2), 'L'aprosdoketon in Aristofane', *Rudiae*, 13/14: 59–143.
Finkelberg, Aryeh (1998) 'On the History of the Greek ΚΟΣΜΟΣ', *HSCP* 98: 103–36.
Fiorentini, Leonardo (2013), 'Machines et deus ex machina dans les spectacles comiques' in *L'appareil scénique dans les spectacles de l'antiquité*. Ed. Brigitte Le Guen and Silvia Milanezi. Saint-Denis: Presses Universitaires de Vincennes. 122–36.
Foley, Helene (2010) 'Generic Ambiguity in Modern Productions and New Versions of Greek Tragedy' in *Theorising Performance*. Ed. Edith Hall and Stephe Harrop. London: Bloomsbury. 137–52.
Foley, Helene (2014) 'Performing Gender in Greek Old and New Comedy' in *The Cambridge Companion to Greek Comedy*. Ed. Martin Revermann. Cambridge: Cambridge University Press. 259–74.
Ford, Andrew (2015) 'The Purpose of Aristotle's *Poetics*', *Classical Philology*, 110: 1–21.
Ford, Thomas E. (2016) 'Psychology Behind the Unfunny Consequences of Jokes that Denigrate', *The Conversation* [Online Blog]. Available at: www.theconversation.com/psychology-behind-the-unfunny-consequences-of-jokes-that-denigrate-63855 (Accessed 20 May 2019).
Ford, Thomas E. and Mark A. Ferguson (2004) 'Social Consequences of Disparagement Humor: A Prejudiced Norm Theory', *Personality and Social Psychology Review*, 8.1: 79–94.
Freud, Sigmund (1953) *The Standard Edition of the Complete Psychological Works of Sigmund Freud, Volume VII (1901–1905): A Case of Hysteria, Three Essays on Sexuality and Other Works*. Trans. and ed. James Strachey. London: The Hogarth Press.
Freud, Sigmund (1955) *The Standard Edition of the Complete Psychological Works of Sigmund Freud, Volume XVIII (1920–1922): Beyond the Pleasure Principle, Group Psychology and Other Works*. Trans. and ed. James Strachey. London: The Hogarth Press.
Freud, Sigmund (1959) *The Standard Edition of the Complete Psychological Works of Sigmund Freud, Volume IX (1906–1908): Jensen's 'Gradiva' and Other Works*. Trans. and ed. James Strachey. London: The Hogarth Press.
Freud, Sigmund (1964) *The Standard Edition of the Complete Psychological Works of Sigmund Freud, Volume XXIII (1937–1939): Moses and Monotheism, An Outline of Psycho-Analysis and Other Works*. Trans. and ed. James Strachey. London: The Hogarth Press.
Freud, Sigmund (2002) [1905] *The Joke and its Relation to the Unconscious*. Trans. Joyce Crick. London: Penguin.
Freud, Sigmund (2003) *Beyond the Pleasure Principle and Other Writings*. Trans. John Reddick. London: Penguin.
Freudenburg, Kirk (1993) *The Walking Muse: Horace on the Theory of Satire*. Princeton, NJ: Princeton University Press.
Freydberg, Bernard (2008) *Philosophy & Comedy: Aristophanes, Logos, and Eros*. Bloomington and Indianapolis, IN: Indiana University Press.
Frisk, Hjalmar (1954–72) *Griechisches Etymologisches Wörterbuch*. Heidelberg: Carl Winter.
Frye, Northrop (1957) *The Anatomy of Criticism*. Princeton: Princeton University Press.
Gadamer, Hans-Georg (1994) *Truth and Method*. Trans. revised by Joel Weinsheimer and Donald G. Marshall. Second rev. ed. New York, NY: Continuum.
Gasché, Rodolphe (1997) 'The Witch Metapsychology' in *Returns of the "French Freud": Freud, Lacan and Beyond*. Trans. J. Patrick, ed. Todd Dufresne. London and New York, NY: Routledge. 169–208.
Georgousopoulos, G. (16 August 1999) 'Το άγχος της επίδρασης [The Stress of Influence]', *Ta Nea Newspaper*.
Gerolemou, Maria (2011) *Bad Women, Mad Women: Gender und Wahnsinn in der griechischen Tragödie*. Tübingen: Narr Verlag.

Bibliography

Gerolemou, Maria (2016) 'Homeric and Tragic Madness' in *The Concept of Madness from Homer to Byzantium*. Ed. Hélène Perdikogianni-Paleologou. Supplementi di Lexis N.S., Nr. V. Amsterdam: Verlag Adolf M. Hakkert. 1–34.

Gerolemou, Maria (2017) 'Thinking of Autonomy as Automatism: The Case of Autonomy in Thucydides' History', *Araucaria: Revista Iberoamericana de Filosofía, Política y Humanidades*, 19(37): 199–211.

Gerolemou, Maria (2018) 'Staging Artificial Intelligence: The Case of Greek Drama' in *The Routledge Handbook of Classics and Cognitive Theory*. Ed. Peter Meineck, William Michael Short and Jennifer Devereaux. London: Routledge. 345–55.

Gerolemou, Maria (2019) 'Why Can't I Have Wings? Aristophanes' *Birds*' in *Undoing the Human: Classical Literature and the Post-Human*. Ed. G. M. Chesi and F. Spiegel. London: Bloomsbury.

Gerolemou, Maria and Lilia Diamantopoulou (eds) (2020) *Mirrors and Mirroring*. London: Bloomsbury.

Geuss, Raymond (2013) 'The Wisdom of Oidipous and the Idea of a Moral Cosmos', *Arion* 20 (3): 59–89.

Given, John (2007) 'The Agathon scene in Aristophanes' *Thesmophoriazusae*', *Symbolae Osloenses*, 82: 35–51.

Glasgow, R. D. V. (1995) *Madness, Masks, and Laughter: An Essay on Comedy*. Madison, NJ, London and Toronto: Fairleigh Dickinson University Press.

Glick, Douglas J. (2007) 'Some Performative Techniques of Stand-Up Comedy: An Exercise in the Textuality of Temporalization', *Language & Communication*, 27: 291–306.

Goldhill, Simon (1991) *The Poet's Voice*. Cambridge: Cambridge University Press.

Gomme, A. W. (1956) *A Historical Commentary on Thucydides*. Vol. III. Oxford: Clarendon Press.

Goux, Jean-Joseph (1993) *Oedipus, Philosopher*. Trans. Catherine Porter. Stanford, CA: Stanford University Press.

Graf, Fritz (1991) 'Gesture and Conventions: The Gestures of Roman Actors and Orators' in *A Cultural History of Gesture*. Ed. Jan Bremmer and Herman Roodenburg. Ithaca, NY: Polity Press. 36–58.

Green, J. R. (1972) 'Oinochoe', BICS, 19: 1–16.

Grice, H. Paul (1975) 'Logic and Conversation' in *Syntax and Semantics, 3: Speech Acts*. Ed. Peter Cole & Jerry L. Morgan. New York, NY: Academic Press. 41–58.

Griffin, Dustin (1994) *Satire: A Critical Reintroduction*. Lexington, KY: University of Kentucky Press.

Griffin, Michael (trans.) (2015) *Life of Plato and On Plato First Alcibiades 1–9*. By Olympiodorus. London and New York, NY: Bloomsbury.

Griffith, John G. (1974) 'Amphitheus and Anthropos in Aristophanes', *Hermes*, 102, 367–9.

Griffith, Mark (ed.) (1999) *Sophocles: Antigone*. Cambridge: Cambridge University Press.

Guilhamet, Leon (1985) 'Socrates and Post-Socratic Satire', *Journal of the History of Ideas*, 46.1: 3–12.

Gundert, Beate (1992) 'Parts and Their Roles in Hippocratic Medicine', *Isis*, 83.3: 453–65.

Guthrie, W. K. C. (1962) *A History of Greek Philosophy*. Vol. 1. Cambridge: Cambridge University Press.

Hall, Edith (1989) 'The Archer Scene in Aristophanes' *Thesmophoriazusae*', *Philologus* 133: 38–54.

Hall, Edith (1995) 'Lawcourt Dramas: The Power of Performance in Greek Forensic Oratory', BICS, 40: 39–58.

Hall, Edith (2006) *The Theatrical Cast of Athens*. Oxford: Oxford University Press.

Hall, Edith (2007a) 'Introduction: Aristophanic Laughter across the Centuries' in *Aristophanes in Performance*. Ed. Edith Hall and Amanda Wrigley. London: Legenda. 1–30.

Hall, Edith (2007b) 'Tragedy Personified' in *Visualizing the Tragic: Drama, Myth & Ritual in Greek Art & Literature*. Ed. Chris Kraus, Simon Goldhill, Helene P. Foley and Jas Elsner. Oxford: Oxford University Press. 221–56.

Hall, Edith (2010a) *Greek Tragedy: Suffering Under the Sun*. Oxford: Oxford University Press.
Hall, Edith (2010b) 'The Pronomos Vase and Tragic Theatre: Demetrios' Rolls and Dionysus' Other Woman' in *The Pronomos Vase*. Ed. Oliver Taplin and Rosie Wyles. Oxford: Oxford University Press. 159–79.
Hall, Edith (2010c) 'The Many Faces of Lysistrata' in *Looking at Lysistrata*. Ed. David Stuttard. London: Duckworth. 29–36.
Hall, Edith (2011a) 'Playing Ball with Zeus: Strategies in Reading Ancient Slavery through Dreams' in *Reading Ancient Slavery*. Ed. Richard Alston, Edith Hall and Laura Proffitt. London: Bloomsbury. 204–26.
Hall, Edith (2011b) *Briefing for Clouds* [Unpublished MS].
Hall, Edith (2013) 'The Aesopic in Aristophanes' in *Greek Comedy and the Discourse of Genres*. Ed. Emmanuela Bakola, Lucia Prauscello and Mario Telò. Cambridge: Cambridge University Press. 277–97.
Hall, Edith (2018a) 'Hephaestus the Hobbling Humorist: The Club-Footed God in the History of Early Greek Comedy' in 'Morbid Laughter: Exploring the Comic Dimensions of Disease in Classical Antiquity', *Illinois Classical Studies*, 43(2). Ed. George Kazantzidis and Natalia Tsoumpra. 366–87.
Hall, Edith (2018b) 'The Boys from Cydathenaeum: Aristophanes versus Cleon Again' in *How to Do Things with History: New Approaches to Ancient Greece*. Ed. Danielle Allen, Paul Christesen and Paul Millett. Oxford: Oxford University Press. 339–63.
Hall, Edith (2019) 'The Black Sea Back Story to Euripides' *Medea*' in *Ancient Theatre and Performance Culture around the Black Sea*. Ed. David Braund, Edith Hall and Rosie Wyles. Cambridge: Cambridge University Press. 267–88.
Hall, Edith and Stephe Harrop (2010) 'Introduction' in *Theorising Performance: Greek Drama, Cultural History, and Critical Practice*. Ed. Edith Hall and Stephe Harrop. London: Bloomsbury. 1–9.
Halliwell, Stephen (1986) *Aristotle's Poetics*. London: Duckworth.
Halliwell, Stephen (ed. and trans.) (1987) *The Poetics of Aristotle*. London: Duckworth.
Halliwell, Stephen (1991) 'The Uses of Laughter in Greek Culture', *Classical Quarterly*, 41: 279–96.
Halliwell, Stephen (2002) 'Aristophanic Sex: The Erotics of Shamelessness' in *The Sleep of Reason*. Ed. Martha C. Nussbaum and Juha Sihvola. Chicago, IL: University of Chicago Press. 120–42.
Halliwell, Stephen (2008) *Greek Laughter*. Cambridge: Cambridge University Press.
Halliwell, Stephen (2012) *Between Ecstasy and Truth*. Oxford: Oxford University Press.
Halliwell, Stephen (2014) 'Laughter' in *The Cambridge Companion to Greek Comedy*. Ed. Martin Revermann. Cambridge: Cambridge University Press. 189–205.
Hanink, Johanna (2017) 'Archives, Repertoires, Bodies and Bones: Thoughts on Reperformance for Classicists' in *Imagining Reperformance in Ancient Culture*. Ed. Richard Hunter and Anna Uhlig. Cambridge: Cambridge University Press. 21–41.
Hanson, Victor Davis (1998) *Warfare and Agriculture in Classical Greece*. Revised ed. Berkeley, CA: University of California Press.
Harder, Ruth E. (1996) 'Zur Personenverteilung in Aristophanes' *Rittern*', *Hermes*, 124.1: 29–44.
Harmes, Marcus and Victoria Bladen (eds) (2015) *Supernatural and Secular Power in Early Modern England*. Farnham & Burlington, VT: Ashgate.
Harmon, A. M. (trans.) (1955) *Lucian*. Reprint, Vol. V. Cambridge, MA and London: Harvard University Press.
Harris, Edward M. (2015) '"Yes" and "No" in Women's Desire' in *Sex in Antiquity*. Ed. Mark Masterson, Nancy Sorkin Rabinowitz and James Robson. Abingdon: Routledge. 298–314.
Harvey, David and John Wilkins (eds) (2000) *The Rivals of Aristophanes: Studies in Athenian Old Comedy*. London and Swansea: University of Wales University Press.
Harvey, F. D. (1971) 'Sick Humour: Aristophanic Parody of a Euripidean Motif?', *Mnemosyne*, 24: 362–5.

Bibliography

Heath, Malcolm (1989) 'Aristotelian Comedy', *Classical Quarterly*, 39: 344–54.
Hedreen, G. M. (1992) *Silens in Attic Black-Figure Vase-Painting*. Ann Arbor, MN: Michigan University Press.
Henderson, Jeffrey (1991) *The Maculate Muse*. Oxford: Oxford University Press.
Henderson, Jeffrey (trans.) (1998a) *Aristophanes: Acharnians; Knights*. Cambridge, MA: Harvard University Press.
Henderson, Jeffrey (trans.) (1998b) *Aristophanes: Clouds; Wasps; Peace*. Cambridge, MA: Harvard University Press.
Henderson, Jeffrey (trans.) (2000) *Aristophanes: Birds; Lysistrata; Women at the Thesmophoria*. Cambridge, MA: Harvard University Press.
Henderson, Jeffrey (trans.) (2002) *Aristophanes: Frogs; Assemblywomen; Wealth*. Cambridge, MA: Harvard University Press.
Hesk, Jon (2000) 'Intratext and Irony in Aristophanes' in *Intratextuality*. Ed. Alison Sharrock and Helen Morales. Oxford: Oxford University Press. 227–62.
Higgins, Charlotte (15 September 2011) 'Classics at Risk at Royal Holloway, University of London', *Guardian* [Online]. Available at: www.theguardian.com/culture/charlottehigginsblog/2011/sep/15/educationdegreecourses-classics (Accessed 7 February 2019).
Hobbes, Thomas (1985) [1651] *Leviathan*. Ed. C. B. Macpherson. London: Penguin.
Holle, Bruce Fredric (1978) *Historical Considerations on the Origins and the Spread of Greek Coinage in the Archaic Age* [PhD thesis]. University of Michigan.
Holmes, Brooke (2010), *The Symptom and the Subject: The Emergence of the Physical Body in Ancient Greece*. Princeton, NJ: Princeton University Press.
Holmes, Brooke (2013) 'Causality, Agency, and the Limits of Medicine', *Apeiron*, 46.3: 302–26.
Holwerda, D. (1977) *Scholia Vetera in Nubes (Scholia in Aristophanem, pars I fasc. III 1*. Groningen: Bouma's Boekhuis.
Hornblower, Simon (1991) *A Commentary on Thucydides*. Vol. I. Oxford: Clarendon Press.
Hornblower, Simon (1996) *A Commentary on Thucydides*. Vol. II. Oxford: Clarendon Press.
Hornblower, Simon (2008) *A Commentary on Thucydides*. Vol. III. Oxford: Clarendon Press.
Hourmouziades, Nicolaos C. (1965) *Production and Imagination in Euripides: Form and Function of the Scenic Space*. Athens: Greek Society for Humanistic Studies.
Hughes, Alan (1996) 'Comic Stages in Magna Graecia: The Evidence of the Vases', *Theatre Research International*, 21 (2): 95–107.
Huizinga, J. (1949) [1944] *Homo Ludens: A Study of the Play-Element in Culture*. English translation. London, Boston, MA and Henley: Routledge & Kegan Paul
Hullot-Kentor, Robert (1989) 'Back to Adorno', *Telos*, 81: 5–29.
Hunter, Richard (2004) *Plato's Symposium*. Oxford: Oxford University Press.
Hunter, Richard (2009) *Critical Moments in Classical Literature*. Cambridge: Cambridge University Press.
Hurka, Thomas and John Tasioulas (2006) 'Games and the Good', *Proceedings of the Aristotelian Society*, Supplementary Volume 80, 217–35 and 237–64.
Hurley, Matthew M., Daniel C. Dennett and Reginald B. Adams, Jr. (2011) *Inside Jokes: Using Humour to Reverse-Engineer the Mind*. Cambridge, MA: MIT Press.
Imperio, O. (1998) 'La figura dell'intellettuale nella commedia greca' in *Tessere. Frammenti della Commedia Greca: Studi e Commenti*. Ed. A. M. Belardinelli, O. Imperio, G. Mastromarco, M. Pellegrino and P. Totaro. Bari: Adriatica Editrice. 43–130.
Ioannidou, Eleftheria (2010) 'Toward a National *Heterotopia*: Ancient Theaters and the Cultural Politics of Performing Ancient Drama in Modern Greece', *Comparative Drama*, 44(4): 385–403.
Ionesco, Eugène (1964) *Notes and Counter Notes: Writings on the Theatre*. Trans. Donald Watson. New York, NY: Grove Press.
Irigaray, Luce (1985) *This Sex Which Is Not One*. Trans. Catherine Porter. Ithaca, NY: Cornell University Press.

Janko, Richard (1984) *Aristotle on Comedy: Towards a Reconstruction of Poetics II*. London: Duckworth.
Janus, Adrienne (2009) 'From "Ha he hi ho hu. Mummum" to "Haw! Hell! Haw!": Listening to Laughter in Joyce and Beckett', *Journal of Modern Literature*, 32: 144–65.
Janus, Adrienne (2013) 'Laughter and the Limits of Identity: Joyce, Beckett and the Philosophical Anthropology of Laughter', *Études Irlandaises*, 38: 1–11.
Jenkyns, Richard (14 May 2018) Review of *Classics: Why It Matters* by Neville Morley, *Classics for All* [Online]. Available at: www.classicsforall.org.uk/book-reviews/classics-why-it-matters/ (Accessed 7 February 2019).
Johnson, A. Michael (1990) 'The "Only Joking" Defense: Attribution Bias or Impression Management?', *Psychological Reports*, 67: 1051–6.
Jones, Ernest (1957) *The Life and Work of Sigmund Freud, Volume III: The Last Phase, 1919–1939*. London: Hogarth Press.
Jucker, Andreas H. and Irma Taavitsainen (2000) 'Diachronic Speech Act Analysis: Insults from Flyting to Flaming', *Journal of Historical Pragmatics*, 1: 67–95.
Kagan, Donald (1991) *Pericles of Athens and the Birth of Democracy*. New York, NY: Free Press.
Kakridis, Phanis I. (1974) *ΑΡΙΣΤΟΦΑΝΟΥΣ ΟΡΝΙΘΕΣ*. Athens.
Kaltaki, M. (16 June 2016) 'Μιχαήλ Μαρμαρινός: Η Λυσιστράτη δεν είναι αρχαία φεμινίστρια, το έργο δεν αφορά την έμφυλη διαμάχη [Michael Marmarinos: Lysistrata is Not an Ancient Feminist, the Play is Not About Gender Conflict]', *Lifo.gr* [Online]. Available at: www.lifo.gr/articles/theater_articles/104426 (Accessed 29 May 2019).
Kanellakis, Dimitrios (2020) *Aristophanes and the Poetics of Surprise*. Berlin: De Gruyter.
Kant, Immanuel (2007) [1790] *Critique of Judgement*. Trans. James Creed Walker, revised and ed. Nicholas Walker. Oxford: Oxford University Press.
Karaoglou, Tonia (14 September 2016) 'Είμαι γυναίκα, μη με φθονείτε και γι' αυτό [I am a Woman, Don't Despise Me for It]', *Elculture.gr* [Online]. Available at: www.elculture.gr/blog/article/είμαι-γυναίκα-μη-με-φθονείτε (Accessed 29 May 2019).
Kaster, Robert A. (trans.) (2011) *Macrobius*. Vol. I. Cambridge, MA and London: Harvard University Press.
Katz, Jerrold J. (1972) *Semantic Theory*. New York: Harper and Row.
Kaufman, Eleanor (2010) 'Extreme Formality: Sadism, the Death Instinct, and the World Without Others', *Angelaki*, 15: 77–85.
Kazantzidis, George and Natalia Tsoumpra (2018) 'Morbid Laughter: Exploring the Comic Dimensions of Disease in Classical Antiquity', *Illinois Classical Studies*, 43(2): 273–97.
Keenan, Elinor Ochs (1976) 'The Universality of Conversational Postulates', *Language in Society* 5: 67–80.
Kefalidou, Eurydice (2009) 'The Iconography of Madness in Attic Vase-Painting' in *Athenian Potters and Painting*. Ed. John H. Oakley and Olga Palagia. Vol. 2. Oxford: Oxbow. 90–9.
Kennedy, George A. (trans.) (2007) *Aristotle on Rhetoric*. Second ed. Oxford: Oxford University Press.
Keuls, Eva C. (1993) *The Reign of the Phallus*. Berkeley and Los Angeles, CA: University of California Press.
Kidd, Stephen (2011) 'Laughter Interjections in Greek Comedy', *Classical Quarterly*, 61: 445–59.
Kidd, Stephen (2014) *Nonsense and Meaning in Ancient Greek Comedy*. Cambridge: Cambridge University Press.
Kidd, Stephen (2019) *Play and Aesthetics in Ancient Greece*. Cambridge: Cambridge University Press.
Kirkpatrick, John and Francis Dunn (2002) 'Heracles, Cercopes, and Paracomedy', *TAPA*, 132: 29–61.
Kittler, Friedrich (2010) *Optical Media: Berlin Lectures 1999*. Trans. Anthony Enns. Cambridge: Polity Press.

Bibliography

Komornicka, Anna Maria (2013) 'Personification in Aristophanes' Comedies', *Eos*, 100 Fasc. Electronicus: 211–32.
Konstan, David (ed.) (2006) *Aspasius: On Aristotle Nicomachean Ethics*. London: Duckworth.
Konstan, David (2010) 'Socrates in Aristophanes' *Clouds*' in *The Cambridge Companion to Socrates*. Ed. Donald R. Morrison. Cambridge: Cambridge University Press. 75–90.
Konstan, David (2012) 'A World without Slaves: Crates' *Thêria*' in *No Laughing Matter: New Studies in Athenian Comedy*. Ed. C.W. Marshall and George Kovacs. London: Bloomsbury. 13–18.
Kossatz-Deissmann, A. (1994) 'Paidia', *LIMC* 7.1, 141–3.
Kovacs, David (trans.) (1998) *Euripides*. Vol. III. Harvard, MA and London: Harvard University Press.
Kovacs, David (2002) *Euripides: Bacchae, Iphigenia at Aulis, Rhesus*. Cambridge, MA: Harvard University Press.
Kranz, Walther (1924) 'Das Verhältnis des Schöpfers zu seinem Werk in der althellenischen Literatur', *Neue Jahrbücher für das klassische Altertum, Geschichte und deutsche Literatur*, 27: 65–86.
Lacan, J. (2014) *Anxiety: The Seminar of Jacques Lacan, Book X*. Ed. Jacques-Alain Miller, trans. A. R. Price. Cambridge: Polity.
Lada-Richards, Ismene (1999) *Initiating Dionysus: Ritual and Theatre in Aristophanes'* Frogs. Oxford: Clarendon Press.
Lada-Richards, Ismene (2006) 'Becoming Mad on Stage: Lucian on the Perils of Acting and Spectating', *BICS*, 49: 145–64.
Lafargue, Philippe (2013) *Cléon: Le guerrier d'Athéna*. Bordeaux: Ausonius Éditions.
Lafargue, Philippe (2017) 'La bataille de Pylos. 425 av. J.-C. Athènes contre Sparte', *REA*, 119.2, 721–6.
LaFleur, Richard A. (1981) 'Horace and *onomasti komodein*: the Law of Satire', *ANRW*, 31.3: 1790–1826.
Lampert, Laurence (2004) *Nietzsche's Task: An Interpretation of* Beyond Good and Evil. New Haven, CT and London: Yale University Press.
Land, Nick (1992) *The Thirst for Annihilation: Georges Bataille and Virulent Nihilism (An Essay in Atheistic Religion)*. London: Routledge.
Larkin-Galiñanes, Cristina (2017) 'An Overview of Humor Theory' in *The Routledge Handbook of Language and Humor*. Ed. Salvatore Attardo. New York, NY: Routledge. 4–16.
Law, Stephen C. (2000) 'Hegel and the Spirit of Comedy: *Der Geist der stets verneint*' in *Hegel and Aesthetics*. Ed. William Maker. Albany, NY: State University of New York Press. 113–30.
Lee, Stewart (2010) *How I Escaped My Certain Fate: The Life and Deaths of a Stand-Up Comedian*. London: Faber.
Lehmann, Gustav Adolf (2008) *Perikles: Staatsmann und Stratege im klassischen Athen: eine Biographie*. Munich: C.H. Beck.
Ley, Graham (2005) 'The Nameless and the Named: Techne and Technology in Ancient Athenian Performance', *Performance Research*, 10(4): 97–104.
Lianeri, Alexandra (2016) 'Introduction: The Futures of Greek Historiography' in *Knowing Future Time in and through Greek Historiography*. Ed. Alexandra Lianeri. Berlin: De Gruyter. 1–56.
Lind, Hermann (1990) *Der Gerber Kleon in den 'Rittern' des Aristophanes. Studien zur Demagogenkomödie*. Frankfurt am Main: Peter Lang.
Lissarrague, François (1990) 'Why Satyrs are Good to Represent' in *Nothing to Do With Dionysos?: Athenian Drama in its Social Context*. Ed. John J. Winkler and Froma I. Zeitlin. Princeton, NJ: Princeton University Press. 228–36.
Lloyd-Jones, Hugh (ed., trans.) (1994) *Sophocles: Ajax, Electra, Oedipus Tyrannus*. Cambridge, MA: Harvard University Press.
Loewenberg, J. (ed.) (1929) *Hegel Selections*. Scribner's: New York.

Bibliography

Long, Anthony A. (1996) 'The Socratic Tradition: Diogenes, Crates, and Hellenistic Ethics' in *The Cynics: The Cynic Movement in Antiquity and its Legacy*. Ed. R. Bracht Branham and Marie-Odile Goulet-Cazé. Berkeley, CA and London: University of California Press, 28–46.

Lowe, N. J. (2008) *Comedy*. Cambridge: Cambridge University Press.

Lucarini, Carlo M. (2016), 'L'εκκυκυκλημα nel teatro greco dell'età classica', *Hermes*, 144.2: 138–56.

Ludwig, Paul W. (2002) *Eros and Polis: Desire and Community in Greek Political Theory*. Cambridge: Cambridge University Press.

Maciver, Calum Alasdair (2012) 'Flyte of Odysseus: Allusion and the *hoplōn krisis* in Quintus Smyrnaeus *Posthomerica* 5', *AJP*, 133.4: 601–28.

Mankin, David (ed.) (1995) *Horace: Epodes*. Cambridge: Cambridge University Press.

Mankin, David (2010) 'The Epodes: Genre, Themes, and Arrangement' in *A Companion to Horace*. Ed. Gregson Davis. Malden, MA and Oxford: Blackwell. 91–104.

March, Jennifer R. (1989) 'Euripides' *Bakchai*: A Reconsideration in the Light of Vase-Paintings', *Bulletin of the Institute of Classical Studies*, 36: 33–65.

Marchessault, Janine (2017) *Ecstatic Worlds: Media, Utopias, Ecologies*. Cambridge, MA and London: MIT Press.

Marmarinos, Michael (2016) 'Programme Note for *Lysistrata*' [Programme], *National Theatre of Greece*.

Marsden, Jill (2004) 'Bataille and the Poetics Fallacy of Animality' in *Animal Philosophy: Essential Readings in Continental Thought*. Ed. Matthew Calarco and Peter Atterton. London: Continuum. 37–44.

Martin, Mike W. (1987) 'Humor and the Aesthetic Enjoyment of Incongruities' in *The Philosophy of Laughter and Humour*. Ed. John Morreall. Albany, NY: State University of New York Press. 172–86.

Martin, Mike W. (2009) 'Humor and Aesthetic Enjoyment of Incongruities' in *The Philosophy of Laughter and Humor*. Ed. John Morreall. Albany, NY: State University of New York Press. 172–86.

Martin, Richard P. (1989) *The Language of Heroes: Speech and Performance in the Iliad*. Ithaca, NY: Cornell University Press.

Martin, Rod A. (2006) *The Psychology of Humor: An Integrative Approach*. New York, NY: Academic Press.

Mastronarde, Donald J. (1990) 'Actors on High: The Skene Roof, the Crane, and the Gods in Attic Drama', *Classical Antiquity*, 9.2: 247–94.

Matthaiou, Alexandra (2017) 'ΣΥΝΑΝΤΗΣΗ ΜΙΧΑΗΛ ΜΑΡΜΑΡΙΝΟΣ [Meeting Michael Marmarinos]', *Cyprus Theatre Organisation* [Online]. Available at: www.thoc.org.cy/event/synantisi-michail-marmarinos,3335,0,en,general (Accessed 22 April 2019).

Mavridou, Maria (24 July 2018) 'Μ. Κανείς δεν απαρνιέται το βλέμμα. Μια συνάντηση στο Θερινό Μαντείο [Nobody Refuses the Gaze: A Meeting at *Therino Manteion*]', *Art and Press.gr* [Online]. Available at: www.artandpress.gr/μιχαήλ-μαρμαρινός-κανείς-δεν-απαρνιέ (Accessed 29 May 2019).

McGhee, Paul E. (1972) 'On the Cognitive Origins of Incongruity Humour: Fantasy Assimilation versus Reality Assimilation' in *The Psychology of Humor*. Ed. Jeffrey H. Goldstein and Paul E. McGhee. New York and London: Academic Press. 61–80.

McGhee, Paul E. and Jeffrey H. Goldstein (eds) (1983) *Handbook of Humor Research*. 2 vols. New York, NY: Springer.

McGing, Brian (2013) 'Youthfulness in Polybius: The Case of Philip V of Macedon' in *Polybius and His World: Essays in Memory of F. W. Walbank*. Ed. Bruce Gibson and Thomas Harrison. Oxford: Oxford University Press. 181–200.

McGraw, A. Peter and Caleb Warren (2010) 'Benign Violations: Making Immoral Behavior Funny', *Psychological Science*, 21.8: 1141–9.

Bibliography

McLean, Donald R. (2006) 'The Private Life of Socrates in Early Modern France' in *A Companion to Socrates*. Ed. Sara Ahbel-Rappe and Rachana Kamtekar. Malden, MA and Oxford: Blackwell. 353–67.
McLeish, Kenneth (1980) *The Theatre of Aristophanes*. London: Thames and Hudson.
Mead, George Herbert (1934) *Mind, Self, and Society from the Standpoint of a Social Behaviorist*. Ed. Charles W. Morris. Chicago, IL and London: University of Chicago Press.
Mead, Rebecca (1 September 2014) 'The Troll Slayer: A Cambridge Classicist Takes On her Sexist Detractors', *The New Yorker*. Available online at: www.newyorker.com/magazine/2014/09/01/troll-slayer (Accessed 20 May 2019).
Meister, Jan Christopher (2012) '"It's Not What You See – It's How You See What You See": The Fantastic as an Epistemological Concept' in *Collision of Realities*. Ed. Lars Schmeink and Astrid Böger. Berlin: De Gruyter. 21–8.
Melchinger, Siegfried (1974) *Das Theater der Tragödie: Aischylos, Sophokles, Euripides auf der Bühne ihrer Zeit*. München: Beck Verlag.
Melfi, Milena (2010) 'Ritual spaces and performances in the Asklepieia of Roman Greece', *The Annual of the British School at Athens*, 105: 317–38.
Mendlesohn, Farah (2008) *The Rhetorics of Fantasy*. Hanover: Wesleyan University Press.
Menninghaus, Winfried (2003) *Disgust: Theory and History of a Strong Sensation*. Trans. Howard Eiland and Joel Golb. Albany, NY: State University of New York Press.
Michael, C. (1981) *Ο κωμικός λόγος του Αριστοφάνους* [PhD thesis]. University of Athens.
Miles, Sarah N. (2009) *Strattis, Tragedy and Comedy* [PhD thesis]. University of Nottingham.
Miller, Paul Allen (1998) 'The Bodily Grotesque in Roman Satire: Images of Sterility', *Arethusa*, 31: 257–83.
Minsky, Marvin (1975) 'A Framework for Representing Knowledge' in *The Psychology of Computer Vision*. Ed. P.H. Winston. New York, NY: McGraw Hill. 211–77.
Mirbach, Dagmar (ed.) (2007) 'Einleitung' in *Ästhetik*. By Alexander Gottlieb Baumgarten. Vol. I. Hamburg: Felix Meiner. xv–lxxx.
Mitchell, T. (1835) *The Knights of Aristophanes*. London: John Murray.
Monoson, S. Sara (1998) 'Remembering Pericles: The Political and Theoretical Import of Plato's *Menexenus*', *Political Theory*, 26 (4): 489–513.
Moraitou, Despina (1994) *Aristoteles über Dichter und Dichtung*. Stuttgart: Teubner.
Morales, Helen (2004) *Vision and Narrative in Achilles Tatius'* Leucippe and Clitophon. Cambridge: Cambridge University Press.
Morley, Neville (2018a) *Classics: Why It Matters*. Cambridge: Polity.
Morley, Neville (25 May 2018b) 'Neville Morley Replies to Richard Jenkyns', *Classics for All* [Online]. Available at: www.classicsforall.org.uk/book-reviews/neville-morley-replies-to-richard-jenkyns/ (Accessed 7 February 2019).
Morreall, John (1983) *Taking Laughter Seriously*. Albany, NY: State University of New York.
Morreall, John (1987) 'Funny Strange, Funny Ha-Ha, and Other Reactions to Incongruity' in *The Philosophy of Laughter and Humour*. Ed. John Morreall. Albany, NY: State University of New York Press. 188–207.
Morreall, John (2009) *Comic Relief: A Comprehensive Philosophy of Humour*. Malden, MA and Chicester: Blackwell.
Morris, Sarah P. (1992) *Daidalos and the Origins of Greek Art*. Princeton, NJ: Princeton University Press.
Morton, Timothy (2013) *Hyperobjects: Philosophy and Ecology after the End of the World*. Minneapolis, MN: University of Minnesota Press.
Muecke, Frances (1982) 'A Portrait of the Artist as a Young Woman', *CQ*, 32: 41–55.
Mueller, Melissa (2016) *Objects as Actors: Props and the Poetics of Performance in Greek Tragedy*. Chicago, IL: University of Chicago Press.

Mülke, M. (2000) 'Phrynichos und Athen: Der Beschluß über die *Miletou Halosis* (Herodot 6, 21, 2)' in *Skenika: Beiträge zum antiken Theater und seiner Rezeption*. Ed. Susanne Gödde and Theodor Heinze. Darmstadt: Wissenschaftliche Buchgesellschaft. 233–46.

Müller, Albert (1886) *Lehrbuch der griechischen Bühnenaltertümer*. Freiburg: J.C.B. Mohr.

Müller-Strübing, Hermann (1873) *Aristophanes und die historische Kritik. Polemische Studien zur Geschichte von Athen im fünften Jahrhundert*. Leipzig: B. G. Teubner.

Munteanu, Dana LaCourse (2012) *Tragic Pathos: Pity and Fear in Greek Philosophy and Tragedy*. Cambridge: Cambridge University Press.

Nabi, Robin L., Emily Moyer-Gusé and Sahara Byrne (2007) 'All Joking Aside: A Serious Investigation into the Persuasive Effect of Funny Social Issue Messages', *Communication Monographs*, 74: 29–54.

Nachmansohn, Max (1915) 'Freuds Libidotheorie verglichen mit der Eroslehre Platons', *Internationale Zeitschrift für Psychoanalyse*, 3(2): 65–83.

Nancy, Jean-Luc (1987) 'Wild Laughter in the Throat of Death', *MLN*, 102: 719–36.

Nancy, Jean-Luc (1993) *The Birth to Presence*. Trans. Brian Holmes et al. Stanford, CA: Stanford University Press.

Napolitano, Michele (2007) 'L'aprosdoketon in Aristofane: alcune riflessioni' in *Diafonie. Esercizi sul comico*. Ed. Alberto Camerotto. Padova: Sargon Editrice Libreria. 45–72.

Nida, Eugene A. (1975) *Componential Analysis of Meaning: An Introduction to Semantic Structures*. Hague: Mouton.

Neckel, Otto (1890) *Das Ekkyklema*. Friedland: Friedland i. Meckl.

Newiger, Hans-Joachim (1996) *Drama und Theater: Ausgewählte Schriften zum griechischen Drama*. Stuttgart: M&P.

Nietzsche, Friedrich (1999) *The Birth of Tragedy and Other Writings*. Ed. Raymond Geuss and Ronald Speirs, trans. Ronald Speirs. Cambridge: Cambridge University Press.

Nietzsche, Friedrich (2002) *Beyond Good and Evil: Prelude to a Philosophy of the Future*. Ed. Rolf-Peter Horstmann and Judith Norman, trans. Judith Norman. Cambridge: Cambridge University Press.

Nightingale, Andrea Wilson (1995) *Genres in Dialogue: Plato and the Construct of Philosophy*. Cambridge: Cambridge University Press.

North, Helen (1966) *Sophrosyne: Self-Knowledge and Self-Restraint in Greek Literature*. Ithaca, NY: University of Cornell Press.

Nussbaum, Martha (1981) 'Aristophanes and Socrates on Learning Practical Wisdom' in *Aristophanes: Essays in Interpretation*. Ed. Jeffrey Henderson. Cambridge: Cambridge University Press. 43–97.

Ober, J. (2008) *Democracy and Knowledge: Learning and Innovation in Classical Athens*. Princeton, NJ: Princeton University Press.

Ogden, Daniel (1997) 'Rape, Adultery and the Protection of Bloodlines in Classical Athens' in *Rape in Antiquity*. Ed. Susan Deacy and Karen F. Pierce. London: Duckworth. 25–42.

Olson, S. Douglas (ed. and trans.) (1998) *Aristophanes: Peace*. Oxford: Oxford University Press.

Olson, S. Douglas (ed. and trans.) (2002) *Aristophanes: Acharnians*. Oxford: Oxford University Press.

Olson, S. Douglas (trans.) (2008) *The Learned Banqueters*. Vol. 4. Cambridge, MA: Harvard University Press.

Olson, S. Douglas (ed. and trans.) (2014) *Eupolis frr. 326–497*. Heidelberg: Verlag Antike.

Olson, S. Douglas (ed. and trans.) (2016) *Eupolis: Heilotes-Chrysoun Genos (frr. 147–325)*. Heidelberg: Verlag Antike.

Olson, S. Douglas (ed. and trans.) (2017) *Eupolis: Einleitung, Testimonia und Aiges-Demoi (frr. 1–146)*. Heidelberg: Verlag Antike.

Bibliography

Omitowoju, Rosanna (1997) 'Regulating Rape: Soap Operas and Self-Interest in the Athenian Courts' in *Rape in Antiquity*. Ed. Susan Deacy and Karen F. Pierce. London: Duckworth. 1–24.

Omitowoju, Rosanna (2002) *Rape and the Politics of Consent in Classical Athens*. Cambridge: Cambridge University Press.

Oring, Elliott (1992) *Jokes and their Relations*. Lexington, KY: University of Kentucky Press.

Oring, Elliott (2003) *Engaging Humor*. Urbana and Chicago, IL: University of Illinois Press.

Oring, Elliott (2011) 'Parsing the Joke: The General Theory of Verbal Humor and Appropriate Incongruity', *Humor*, 24: 203–22.

Oring, Elliott (2019) 'Oppositions, Overlaps, and Ontologies: The General Theory of Verbal Humor Revisited', *Humor*, 32: 151–70.

Paley, F. A. (ed.) (1873) *The Peace of Aristophanes*. London: Bell and Daldy.

Palmer, Jerry (1987) *The Logic of the Absurd: On Film and Television Comedy*. London: BFI.

Palmer, Jerry (1994) *Taking Humour Seriously*. London: Routledge.

Papachrysostomou, Athina (2008) *Six Comic Poets: A Commentary on Selected Fragments of Middle Comedy*. Tübingen: G. Narr.

Parker, Robert (1996) *Athenian Religion: A History*. Oxford: Clarendon Press.

Parks, Wards (1990) *Verbal Dueling in Heroic Narrative: The Homeric and Old English Traditions*. Princeton: Princeton University Press.

Parvulescu, Anca (2010) *Laughter: Notes on a Passion*. Cambridge, MA: MIT Press.

Patsalidis, Savas and Anna Stavrakopoulou (2014) 'From the Years of Utopia to the Years of Dystopia' in 'The Geographies of Contemporary Greek Theatre: About Utopias, Dystopias and Heterotopias', *Gramma*, Vol. 22 No. 2. 7–16.

Petrides, A. K. (2013) 'Lucian's "On dance" and the Poetics of the Pantomime Mask' in *Performance in Greek and Roman Theatre*. Ed. George W. M. Harrison and Vayos Liapis. Leiden and Boston, MA: Brill. 433–50.

Pfister, Oskar (1921) 'Plato als Vorläufer der Psychoanalyse', *Internationale Zeitschrift für Psychoanalyse*, 7(3): 264–9.

Pickard-Cambridge, Arthur Wallace (1946) *The Theatre of Dionysos in Athens*. Oxford: Clarendon Press.

Pierrot, Antoine (2015) 'Who were the Eupatrids in Archaic Athens?' in *'Aristocracy' in Antiquity: Redefining Greek and Roman Elites*. Ed. Nick Fisher and Hans van Wees. Swansea: The Classical Press of Wales. 147–68.

Pirrotta, Serena (2009) *Plato Comicus: Die fragmentarischen Komödien; ein Kommentar*. Berlin: Verlag Antike.

Platnauer, Maurice (ed.) (1964) *Aristophanes: Peace*. Oxford: Clarendon Press.

Plessner, Helmuth (1970) *Laughing and Crying: A Study of the Limits of Human Behavior*. Trans. James Spencer Churchill and Marjorie Grene. Evanston, IL: Northwestern University Press.

Poggi, Isabella and Francesca D'Errico (2013) 'Towards the Parody Machine: Qualitative Analysis and Cognitive Processes in the Parody of a Politician' in *New Trends in Image Analysis and Processing – ICIAP 2013*. Ed. Alfredo Petrosino, Lucia Maddalena, Pietro Pala *et al.* Heidelberg: Springer. 491–500.

Polimeni, J. and P. J. Reiss (2006) 'The First Joke: Exploring the Evolutionary Origins of Humor', *Evolutionary Psychology*, 4: 347–66.

Pollitt, J. J. (1999) *Art and Experience in Classical Greece*. Cambridge: Cambridge University Press.

Powers, Melinda (2014) *Athenian Tragedy in Performance: A Guide to Contemporary Studies and Historical Debates*. Iowa City, IA: University of Iowa Press.

Pugliara, Monica (2003) *La mirabile e l'artificio: Creature animate e semoventi nel mito e nella tecnica degli antichi*. Rome: <<L'Erma>> di Bretschneider.

Prato, Carlo (ed.) (2001) *Aristofane: Le Donne alle Tesmoforie*. Milan: A. Mondadori.

Price, Jonathan J. (2001) *Thucydides and Internal War*. Cambridge: Cambridge University Press.

Bibliography

Prince, Susan (2006) 'Socrates, Antisthenes, and the Cynics' in *A Companion to Socrates*. Ed. Sara Ahbel-Rappe and Rachana Kamtekar. Malden, MA and Oxford: Blackwell. 75–92.

Privitello, Lucio Angelo (2007) 'S/laughter and *Anima-Lêthê*' in *Reading Bataille Now*. Ed. Shannon Winnubust. Bloomington, IN: Indiana University Press. 167–96.

Provine, Robert R. and Kenneth R. Fischer (1989) 'Laughing, Smiling, and Talking: Relation to Sleeping and Social Context in Humans', *Ethology*, 83: 295–305.

Pucci, Pietro (1980) *The Violence of Pity in Euripides' Medea*. Ithaca, NY: Cornell University Press.

Quillin J. (2002) 'Achieving Amnesty: The Role of Events, Institutions, and Ideas', *TAPA* 132, 71–107.

Rabinowitz, Nancy Sorkin (2011) 'Greek Tragedy: A Rape Culture', *Eugesta*, Issue 1. 1–21.

Rabkin, A. L. H. (1979) 'That Magnificent Flying Machine: On the Nature of the 'Mechane' of the Theatre of Dionysos at Athens', *ArchNews*, 8.1: 1–6.

Rackham, H. (trans.) (1935) *Athenian Constitution; Eudemian Ethics; Virtues and Vices*. By Aristotle. Cambridge, MA: Harvard University Press.

Rademaker, Adriaan (2005) *Sophrosyne and the Rhetoric of Self-Restraint: Polysemy & Persuasive Use of an Ancient Greek Value Term*. Leiden and Boston, MA: Brill.

Ramachandran, V. S. (1998) 'The Neurology and Evolution of Humor, Laughter, and Smiling: The False Alarm Theory', *Medical Hypotheses*, 51: 351–4.

Raskin, Victor (1985) *Semantic Mechanisms of Humor*. Dordrecht and Boston, MA: Reidel.

Raskin, Victor (2011) 'On Oring on GTVH', *Humor*, 24: 223–31.

Raskin, Victor (2017) 'Script-Based Semantic and Ontological Semantic Theories of Humor' in *The Routledge Handbook of Language and Humor*. Ed. Salvatore Attardo. New York, NY: Routledge. 109–25.

Rau, Peter (1967) *Paratragoidia: Untersuchung einer komischen Form des Aristophanes*. München: C. H. Beck.

Reckford, Kenneth J. (1987), *Aristophanes' Old-and-New Comedy*. Chapel Hill, NC and London: The University of North Carolina Press.

Reckford, Kenneth J. (1991) 'Strepsiades as a Comic Ixion', *Illinois Classical Studies*, 16: 125–36.

Reeve, C. D. C. (2007), 'A Study in Violets: Alcibiades in the *Symposium*' in *Plato's Symposium: Issues in Interpretation and Reception*. Ed. James H. Lesher, Debra Nails and Frisbee Sheffield. Washington, DC: Center for Hellenic Studies. 124–46.

Rehm, Rush (2002) *The Play of Space: Spatial Transformation in Greek Tragedy*. Princeton, NJ: Princeton University Press.

Renger, Almut-Barbara (2013) *Oedipus and the Sphinx: The Threshold Myth from Sophocles through Freud to Cocteau*. Trans. Duncan Alexander Smart and David Rice, with John T. Hamilton. Chicago, IL and London: The University of Chicago Press.

Rennie, W. (ed.) (1909) *The Acharnians of Aristophanes*. London: Edward Arnold.

Revermann, Martin (2006a) *Comic Business: Theatricality, Dramatic Technique, and Performance Contexts of Aristophanic Comedy*. Oxford: Oxford University Press.

Revermann, Martin (2006b) 'The Competence of Theatre Audiences in Fifth- and Fourth-Century Athens', *JHS*, 126: 99–124.

Revermann, Martin (2013) 'Paraepic Comedy: Point(s) and Practices' in *Greek Comedy and the Discourse of Genres*. Ed. Emmanuela Bakola, Lucia Prauscello and Mario Telò. Cambridge: Cambridge University Press. 101–28.

Revermann, Martin (2014) 'Divinity and Religious Practice' in *The Cambridge Companion to Greek Comedy*. Ed. Martin Revermann. Cambridge: Cambridge University Press. 275–88.

Rhodes, P. J. (1981) *A Commentary on the Aristotelian Athenaion Politeia*. Oxford: Oxford University Press.

Riedweg, Christoph (1990) 'The "Atheistic" Fragment from Euripides' *Bellerophontes* (286 N^2)', *Illinois Classical Studies*, 15(1): 39–53.

Bibliography

Ritchie, Graeme (2004) *The Linguistic Analysis of Jokes*. London: Routledge.
Robson, James (2006) *Humour, Obscenity and Aristophanes*. Tübingen: Gunter Narr Verlag.
Robson, James (2009) *Aristophanes: An Introduction*. London: Duckworth.
Robson, James (2015) 'Sexual Assault in Aristophanes' in *Sex in Antiquity*. Ed. Mark Masterson, Nancy Sorkin Rabinowitz and James Robson. Abingdon: Routledge. 315–31.
Rockelein, Jon E. (2002) *The Psychology of Humor: A Reference Guide and Annotated Bibliography*. Westport, CT: Greenwood Press.
Rogers, B. B. (ed.) (1904) *The Thesmophoriazusae of Aristophanes*. London: Bell and Sons.
Rogers, B. B. (ed.) (1907) *The Plutus of Aristophanes*. London: Bell and Sons.
Rogers, B. B. (ed.) (1910) *The Acharnians of Aristophanes*. London: Bell and Sons.
Rogers, B. B. (ed.) (1913) *The Peace of Aristophanes*. London: Bell and Sons.
Roselli, David Kawalko (2011) *Theater of the People: Spectators and Society in Ancient Athens*. Austin, TX: University of Texas Press.
Rosen, Ralph M. (1997) 'The Gendered Polis in Eupolis' *Cities*' in *The City as Comedy: Society and Representation in Athenian Drama*. Ed. Gregory W. Dobrov. Chapel Hill, NC and London: University of North Carolina Press. 149–76.
Rosen, Ralph M. (1988) *Old Comedy and the Iambographic Tradition*. Atlanta, GA: Scholars Press.
Rosen, Ralph M. (2000) 'Cratinus' *Pytine* and the Construction of the Comic Self' in *The Rivals of Aristophanes: Studies in Athenian Old Comedy*. Ed. David Harvey and John Wilkins. London and Swansea: University of Wales University Press. 3–39.
Rosen, Ralph M. (2004) 'Aristophanes' *Frogs* and the *Contest of Homer and Hesiod*', *TAPA*, 134, 295–322.
Rosen, Ralph M. (2007) *Making Mockery: the Poetics of Ancient Satire*. Oxford: Oxford University Press.
Rosen, Ralph M. (2012a) 'Satire in the Republic: From Lucilius to Horace' in *A Companion to Persius and Juvenal*. Ed. Susanna Braund and Josiah Osgood. Malden, MA: Blackwell. 19–40.
Rosen, Ralph M. (2012b) 'Efficacy and Meaning in Ancient and Modern Political Satire: Aristophanes, Lenny Bruce, and Jon Stewart', *Social Research*, 79.1: 1–32.
Rosen, Ralph M. (2013) 'Iambos, Comedy and the Question of Generic Affiliation' in *Greek Comedy and the Discourse of Genres*. Ed. Emmanuela Bakola, Lucia Prauscello and Mario Telò. Cambridge: Cambridge University Press. 81–97.
Rosen, Ralph M. (2014) 'The Greek "Comic Hero"' in *The Cambridge Companion to Greek Comedy*. Ed. Martin Revermann. Cambridge: Cambridge University Press. 222–40.
Rosen, Ralph M. (2015a) 'Laughter' in *A Companion to Ancient Aesthetics*. Ed. Pierre Destrée and Penelope Murray. Malden, MA: Blackwell. 455–71.
Rosen, Ralph M. (2015b) 'Aristophanic Satire and the Pretense of Synchrony' in *Diachrony: Diachronic Studies of Ancient Greek Literature and Culture*. Ed. José M. González. Berlin: De Gruyter. 213–32.
Rosenbloom, David (1993) 'Shouting "Fire" in a Crowded Theater: Phrynichos's *Capture of Miletos* and the Politics of Fear in Early Greek Tragedy', *Philologus*, 137 (2): 159–96.
Rothwell, Jr., Kenneth S. (2007) *Nature, Culture, and the Origins of Greek Comedy: A Study of Animal Choruses*. Cambridge: Cambridge University Press.
Ruch, Willibald, Salvatore Attardo and Victor Raskin (1993) 'Towards an Empirical Verification of the General Theory of Verbal Humor', *Humor*, 6: 123–36.
Ruffell, I. A. (2001) 'The World Turned Upside Down: Utopia and Utopianism in the Fragments of Old Comedy' in *The Rivals of Aristophanes: Studies in Athenian Old Comedy*. Ed. David Harvey and John Wilkins. London and Swansea: University of Wales University Press. 473–506.
Ruffell, I. A. (2002) 'A Total Write-off: Aristophanes, Cratinus, and the Rhetoric of Comic Competition', *Classical Quarterly*, 52: 138–63.

Ruffell, I. A. (2011) *Politics and Anti-Realism in Athenian Old Comedy*. Oxford: Oxford University Press.

Ruffell, I. A. (2013) 'Humiliation? Voyeurism, Violence, and Humor in Old Comedy', *Helios*, 40: 247–77.

Ruffell, I. A. (2014) 'Utopianism' in *The Cambridge Companion to Greek Comedy*. Ed. Martin Revermann. Cambridge: Cambridge University Press. 206–21.

Ruffell, I. A. (2018) 'Stop Making Sense: The Politics of Aristophanic Madness' in 'Morbid Laughter: Exploring the Comic Dimensions of Disease in Classical Antiquity', *Illinois Classical Studies*, 43(2). Ed. George Kazantzidis and Natalia Tsoumpra. 326–50.

Rusten, J. S. (ed.) (1989) *Thucydides: The Peloponnesian War Book II*. Cambridge: Cambridge University Press.

Rutherford, William G. (1905) *A Chapter in the History of Annotation: Scholia Aristophanica*. Vol. 3. London: Macmillan.

Samons II, Loren J. (2016) *Pericles and the Conquest of History*. Cambridge: Cambridge University Press.

Schaps, David M. (2004) *The Invention of Coinage and the Monetization of Ancient Greece*. Ann Arbor, MI: University of Michigan Press.

Schauer, Markus and Stefan Merkle (1992) 'Aesop and Socrates' in *Der Äsop-Roman: Motivgeschichte und Erzählstruktur*. Ed. Niklas Holzberg. Tübingen: Classica Monacensia. 85–96.

Schiller, Friedrich (2004) *On the Aesthetic Education of Man*. New York, NY: Dover Books.

Schmeink, Lars and Astrid Böger (eds) (2012) *Collision of Realities: Establishing Research on the Fantastic in Europe*. Berlin and Boston, MA: De Gruyter.

Schwarze, Joachim (1971) *Die Beurteilung des Perikles durch die attische Komödie*. Munich: Beck.

Seaford, Richard (2004) *Money and the Early Greek Mind: Homer, Philosophy, Tragedy*. Cambridge: Cambridge University Press.

Segal, Charles (1997) *Dionysiac Poetics and Euripides' Bacchae*. Princeton, NJ: Princeton University Press.

Seidensticker, Bernd (1978) 'Comic Elements in Euripides' Bacchae', *AJP* 99: 303–20.

Seidensticker, Bernd (1982) *Palintonos Harmonia: Studien zu komischen Elementen in der griechischen Tragödie*. Göttingen: Vandenhoeck and Ruprecht.

Seidensticker, Bernd (2012) 'The Satyr Plays of Sophocles' in *Brill's Companion to Sophocles*. Ed. Andreas Markantonatos. Leiden and Boston, MA: Brill. 211–44.

Sella, Olga (5 August 2014) 'Το πρώτο sold out της σεζόν, ένας θρίαμβος για τον Γιάννη Κακλέα [The First Sold-Out Performance of the Year, a Triumph for Yiannis Kakleas]', *Kathimerini Newspaper*. Also available at: www.kathimerini.gr/778702/article/politismos/8eatro/to-prwto-sold-out-ths-sezon-enas-8riamvos-toy-g-kaklea (Accessed 29 May 2019).

Sfyroeras, Pavlos (2008) '*Pothos Euripidou*: Reading the *Andromeda* in Aristophanes' *Frogs*', *AJP*, 129 (3): 299–317.

Sfyroeras, Pavlos (2013) 'The Battle of Marathon: Poetry, Ideology, Politics' in *Marathon: The Day After*. Ed. Kostas Buraselis and Elias Koulakiotis. Athens: European Cultural Center of Delphi. 75–94.

Sharpley, H. (ed.) (1905) *The Peace of Aristophanes*. Edinburgh and London: Blackwood and Sons.

Shaw, Carl A. (2014) *Satyric Play: The Evolution of Greek Comedy and Satyr Drama*. New York, NY: Oxford University Press.

Sidiropoulou, Avra (2014) 'Directors' Theatre in Greece: Stages of Authorship in the Work of Michael Marmarinos, Yiannis Houvardas, and Theodoros Terzopoulos' in 'The Geographies of Contemporary Greek Theatre: About Utopias, Dystopias and Heterotopias', *Gramma*, Vol. 22 No. 2. 121–33.

Sidney, Philip (1595) *An Apologie for Poetrie. Written by the Right Noble, Vertuous, and Learned, Sir Phillip Sidney, Knight*. London: Henry Olney.

Bibliography

Sidwell, Keith (1990) 'Was Philokleon Cured? The *Nosos* Theme in Aristophanes' *Wasps*', *Classica et Mediaevalia*, 41: 9–31.
Sidwell, Keith (1995) 'Poetic Rivalry and the Caricature of Comic Poets: Cratinus' *Pytine* and Aristophanes' *Wasps*' in *Stage Directions: Essays in Ancient Drama in Honour of E. W. Handley*. Ed. Alan Griffiths. London: Institute of Classical Studies. 56–80.
Sidwell, Keith (2009) *Aristophanes the Democrat: The Politics of Satirical Comedy during the Peloponnesian War*. Cambridge and New York, NY: Cambridge University Press.
Sifakis, G. M. (1971) *Parabasis and Animal Choruses: A Contribution to the History of Attic Comedy*. London: The Athlone Press.
Silk, M. S. (1990) 'The People of Aristophanes' in *Characterization and Individuality in Greek Literature*. Ed. Christopher Pelling. Oxford: Clarendon Press. 150–73.
Silk, M. S. (1993) 'Aristophanic Paratragedy' in *Tragedy, Comedy and the Polis*. Ed. Alan H. Sommerstein, Stephen Halliwell, Jeffrey Henderson and Bernhard Zimmermann. Bari: Levante. 477–504.
Silk, M. S. (2000) *Aristophanes and the Definition of Comedy*. Oxford: Oxford University Press.
Simon, Bennett (1978) *Mind and Madness in Ancient Greece: The Classical Roots of Modern Psychiatry*. Ithaca, NY: Cornell University Press.
Singer, Peter N. (2018) 'The Mockery of Madness: Laughter at and with Insanity in Attic Tragedy and Old Comedy' in 'Morbid Laughter: Exploring the Comic Dimensions of Disease in Classical Antiquity', *Illinois Classical Studies*, 43(2). Ed. George Kazantzidis and Natalia Tsoumpra. 289–325.
Sipiora, Phillip (2002) 'Introduction: The Ancient Concept of *Kairos*' in *Rhetoric and Kairos: Essays in History, Theory, and Praxis*. Ed. Phillip Sipiora and James S. Baumlin. Albany, NY: State University of New York Press. 1–22.
Slater, Don (2002) 'Social Relationships and Identity On-line and Off-line' in *Handbook of New Media: Social Shaping and Consequences of ICTs*. Ed. Leah A. Lievrouw and Sonia Livingstone. Thousand Oaks, CA: Sage Publications. 533–43.
Slater, Niall W. (2002) *Spectator Politics: Metatheatre and Performance in Aristophanes*. Philadelphia, PA: University of Pennsylvania Press.
Slater, Niall W. (2016) 'Aristophanes in Antiquity: Reputation and Reception' in *Brill's Companion to the Reception of Aristophanes*. Ed. Philip Walsh. Leiden and Boston, MA: Brill. 3–21.
Slings, Simon R. (2002) 'Figures of Speech in Aristophanes' in *The Language of Greek Comedy*. Ed. Andreas Willi. Oxford: Oxford University Press. 99–109.
Smith, Andrew (trans.) (2016) 'Memnon: History of Heracleia' [Online]. Available at: www.attalus.org/translate/memnon1.html [Accessed 20 May 2019].
Smith, Susan Harris (1987) 'Ironic Distance and the Theatre of Feigned Madness', *Theatre Journal*, 39 (1): 51–65.
Solmsen, Friedrich (1963) 'Nature as Craftsman in Greek Thought', *Journal of the History of Ideas*, 24: 473–96.
Solomos, Alexis (1974) *The Living Aristophanes*. Trans. and adapted by Alexis Solomos and Marvin Felheim. Ann Arbor, MI: University of Michigan Press.
Sommerstein, Alan H. (1973) 'On Translating Aristophanes', *Greece & Rome*, 20.2: 140–54.
Sommerstein, Alan H. (ed.) (1985) *The Comedies of Aristophanes: Peace*. Warminster: Aris & Phillips.
Sommerstein, Alan H. (ed.) (1987) *The Comedies of Aristophanes: Birds*. Warminster: Aris & Phillips.
Sommerstein, Alan H. (ed.) (1990) *The Comedies of Aristophanes: Lysistrata*. Warminster: Aris & Phillips.
Sommerstein, Alan H. (ed.) (1994) *The Comedies of Aristophanes: Thesmophoriazusae*. Warminster: Aris & Phillips.

Sommerstein, Alan H. (1997) 'The Theatre Audience, the *Demos* and the *Suppliants* of Aeschylus' in *Greek Tragedy and the Historian*. Ed. Christopher Pelling. Oxford and New York, NY: Clarendon Press. 63–79.
Sommerstein, Alan H. (1998a) 'The Theatre Audience and the Demos' in *La comedia griega y su influencia en la literatura Española*. Ed. J. López Férez. Madrid: Ediciones Clásicas. 43–62.
Sommerstein, Alan H. (1998b) 'Rape and Young Manhood in Athenian Comedy' in *Thinking Men*. Ed. Lin Foxhall and John Salmon. London: Routledge. 100–14.
Sommerstein, Alan H. (ed.) (2001) *The Comedies of Aristophanes: Wealth*. Warminster: Aris & Phillips.
Sommerstein, Alan H. (2004) 'Harassing the Satirist: The Alleged Attempts to Prosecute Aristophanes' in *Free Speech In Classical Antiquity*. Ed. Ineke Sluiter and Ralph M. Rosen. Leiden: Brill. 145–74.
Sommerstein, Alan H. (2006) 'Rape and Consent in Athenian Tragedy' in *Dionysalexandros*. Ed. Douglas Cairns and Vayos Liapis. Swansea: Classical Press of Wales. 233–53.
Sommerstein, Alan H. (2009) *Talking about Laughter and Other Studies in Greek Comedy*. Oxford: Oxford University Press.
Sondheim, Stephen (score and lyrics) (2011) *The Frogs*. By Aristophanes, freely adapted by Burt Shevelove, even more freely adapted by Nathan Lane, ed. Peter E. Jones. Milwaukee, WI: Hal Leonard.
Sörbom, Göran (1966) *Mimesis and Art: Studies in the Origin and Early Development of an Aesthetic Vocabulary*. Stockholm: Svenska Bokförlaget.
Spira, Andreas (1960) *Deus ex Machina: Untersuchungen zum Deus ex machina bei Sophokles und Euripides*. Kallmünz: Lassleben.
Stafford, Emma (2000) *Worshipping Virtues: Personification and the Divine in Ancient Greece*. London: Duckworth and The Classical Press of Wales.
Stafford, Emma (2012) *Herakles*. Abingdon and New York, NY: Routledge.
Stanford, W. B. (ed.) (1963) *The Frogs*. By Aristophanes. Second Edition. London: Macmillan.
Stapleford, Brian (2012) 'The Art and Science of Heterocosmic Creativity' in in *Collision of Realities*. Ed. Lars Schmeink and Astrid Böger. Berlin: De Gruyter. 7–19.
Starkie, W. J. M. (ed.) (1909) *The Acharnians of Aristophanes*. London: Macmillan.
Steggle, Matthew (2007) 'Aristophanes in Early Modern England' in *Aristophanes in Performance*. Ed. Edith Hall and Amanda Wrigley. Legenda: London. 52–65.
Steiner, Deborah Tarn (1994) *The Tyrant's Writ: Myths and Images of Writing in Ancient Greece*. Princeton, NJ : Princeton University Press.
Steiner, Deborah Tarn (2001) *Images in Mind: Statues in Archaic and Classical Greek Literature and Thought*. Princeton, NJ : Princeton University Press.
Stiegler, Bernard (2016) *Automatic Society: The Future of Work*. Vol. 1. Trans. Daniel Ross. Cambridge: Polity Press.
Stiepel, Gert Roland (1968) *Die Bühne des Euripides: Theaterwissenschaftliche Studien zu den Problemen des altgriechischen Bühnenwesens*. Köln-Lindenthal: Wienand.
Stohn, Günther (1993) 'Zur Agathonszene in den ‚Thesmophoriazusen' des Aristophanes', *Hermes*, 121.2: 196–205.
Stoholski, Mark (2017) 'Laughing Matters: On Democritus', *Oxford Literary Review*, 39: 101–15.
Storey, Ian C. (1989) 'The "Blameless Shield" of Kleonymus', *Rheinisches Museum für Philologie*, 132: 247–61.
Storey, Ian C. (2007) 'Review of J. Robson, *Humour, Obscenity and Aristophanes*, Tübingen 2006', *BMCR*, 2007.12.38.
Storey, Ian C. (ed. and trans.) (2011a) *Fragments of Old Comedy*. Vol. 2. Cambridge, MA and London: Harvard University Press.
Storey, Ian C. (ed. and trans.) (2011b) *Fragments of Old Comedy*. Vol. 1. Cambridge, MA and London: Harvard University Press.

Bibliography

Storey, Ian C. (ed. and trans.) (2011c) *Fragments of Old Comedy*. Vol. 3. Cambridge, MA and London: Harvard University Press.

Storey, Ian C. (2019) *Aristophanes: Peace*. London and New York, NY: Bloomsbury.

Strohminger, Nina (2014) 'Arousal Theory (Berlyne)' in *Encyclopedia of Humor Studies*. Ed. Salvatore Attardo. 2 vols. Thousand Oaks, CA: Sage. i.62–3.

Strong, Tracy B. (1975) *Friedrich Nietzsche and the Politics of Transfiguration*. Berkeley, CA: University of California Press.

Styan, J. L. (1962) *The Dark Comedy: The Development of Modern Tragic Comedy*. Cambridge: Cambridge University Press.

Suits, Bernard (1990) *The Grasshopper: Games, Life and Utopia*. Boston, MA: Godine.

Support Classics at RHUL (2011) [Online]. Available at: www.supportclassicsatrhul.wordpress.com/ (Accessed 7 February 2019).

Taaffe, Lauren K. (1993) *Aristophanes and Women*. London and New York, NY: Routledge.

Taillardat, J. (1965) *Les images d'Aristophanes: études de langue et de style*. Paris: Les Belles Lettres.

Taplin, Oliver (1977) *The Stagecraft of Aeschylus: The Dramatic Use of Exits and Entrances in Greek Tragedy*. Oxford: Clarendon Press.

Taplin, Oliver (1978) *Greek Tragedy in Action*. Berkeley, CA: Methuen.

Taplin, Oliver (1983) 'Tragedy and Trugedy', *Classical Quarterly*, 33(ii): 331–3.

Taplin, Oliver (1986) 'Fifth-Century Tragedy and Comedy: A Synkrisis', *JHS*, 106: 163–74.

Taplin, Oliver (2007) *Pots & Plays*. Los Angeles, CA: Getty Publications.

Taylor, C. C. W. (ed. and trans.) (2006) *Aristotle: Nicomachean Ethics, Books II–IV*. Oxford: Oxford University Press.

Taylor, Jeremy G. (1998) 'Oinoe and the Painted Stoa: Ancient and Modern Misunderstandings?', *AJP*, 119 (2): 223–43.

Teegarden, D. (2007) *Defending Democracy: A Study of Ancient Greek Anti-Tyranny Legislation*. Princeton, NJ: Princeton University Press.

Telò, Mario (2007) *Eupolidis Demi*. Florence: Felice Le Monnier.

Telò, Mario (2016) *Aristophanes and the Cloak of Comedy*. Chicago and London: University of Chicago Press.

Telò, Mario (2020) *Archive Feelings: A Theory of Greek Tragedy*. Columbus, OH: Ohio State University Press.

Timofeeva, Oxana (2017) ' "The Only Real Outlaws": Animal Freedom in Bataille' in *Georges Bataille and Contemporary Thought*. Ed. Will Stronge. London: Bloomsbury. 155–72.

Torrance, Isabelle (2010) 'Writing and Self-Conscious Mythopoesis in Euripides', *Cambridge Classical Journal*, 56: 213–58.

Trendall, A. D. (1989) *Red Figure Vases of South Italy and Sicily: A Handbook*. London: Thames and Hudson.

Trendall, A. D. and Alexander Cambitoglou (1978) *The Red-Figured Vases of Apulia*. Vol. 1. Oxford: Clarendon Press.

Tsatsoulis, Dimitris (17 September 1999) 'Ο Αριστοφάνης, ως επιθεώρηση [Aristophanes as a Review]', *Imerisia Newspaper*.

Tsatsoulis, Dimitris (20 September 2016) 'Ανα-προσεγγίζοντας τα μνημεία των προγόνων [Reapproaching the Monuments of Our Ancestors]', *Ημεροδρόμος* [Online]. Available at: www.imerodromos.gr/marmarinos-lusistrath (Accessed 29 May 2019).

Tsatsoulis, Dimitris (15 April 2017) 'Ζητήματα χώρου και μνήμες κειμένων στη σκηνική δραματουργία του Μιχαήλ Μαρμαρινού [Issues of Space and Memories of Texts in the Staged Dramaturgy of Michael Marmarinos]', *The Greek Play Project* [Online]. Available at: www.greek-theatre.gr/public/gr/greekplay/index/reviewview/80 (Accessed 29 May 2019).

Tsitsirides, Stavros (2001) 'Euripideische Kosmogonie bei Aristophanes (Thesm. 14–18)', *Ἑλληνικά*, 51: 43–67.

Bibliography

Uhlig, Anna (forthcoming) 'Birth by Hammer: Pandora and Somatic Construction' in *Exploring Gender Diversity in the Ancient World*. Ed. Jennifer Dyer and A. Surtees. Edinburgh: Edinburgh University Press.

Universität Paderborn (2017) 'Graduiertenkolleg Automatismen' [Online]. Available at: www.uni-paderborn.de/graduiertenkolleg-automatismen (Accessed 18 March 2019)

Ussher, R.G. (ed.) (1973) *Ecclesiazusae*. By Aristophanes. Oxford: Oxford University Press.

VΔgue (2013) 'Taylor Swift – Trouble (Goat Remix)' [Online Video]. Available at: www.youtube.com/watch?v=-aLYvZ5sX28 (Accessed 17 April 2019).

Valakas, Kostas (2002) 'The Use of the Body by Actors in Tragedy and Satyr-Play' in *Greek and Roman Actors: Aspects of an Ancient Profession*. Ed. Pat Easterling and Edith Hall. Cambridge: Cambridge University Press. 69–92.

Van Leeuwen, J. (ed.) (1904) *Aristophanis Plutus*. Leiden: A. W. Sijthoff.

Van Steen, Gonda A.H. (2000) *Venom in Verse: Aristophanes in Modern Greece*. Princeton: Princeton University Press.

Van Steen, Gonda A.H. (2007) 'From Scandal to Success Story: Aristophanes' *Birds* as Staged by Karolos Koun' in *Aristophanes in Performance*. Ed. Edith Hall and Amanda Wrigley. London: Legenda. 155–78.

Vander Waerdt, Paul A. (1994) 'Socrates in the Clouds' in *The Socratic Movement*. Ed. Paul A. Vander Waerdt. Ithaca: Cornell University Press. 48–86.

Vasiliou, Iakovos (2013) 'Socratic Irony' in *Bloomsbury Companion to Socrates*. Ed. John Bussanich and Nicholas D. Smith. London: Bloomsbury Academic. 20–34.

Veatch, T. C. (1998) 'A Theory of Humor', *Humor*, 11(2): 161–215.

Vernant, Jean-Pierre (1991) *Mortals and Immortals: Collected Essays*. Ed. Froma I. Zeitlin. Princeton, NJ: Princeton University Press.

Vettin, Julia and Dietmar Todt (2005) 'Human Laughter, Social Play, and Play Vocalizations of Non-Human Primates: An Evolutionary Approach', *Behaviour*, 142.2: 217–40.

Vickers, Michael (1989) 'Alcibiades on Stage: *Thesmophoriazusae* and *Helen*', *Historia*, 38.1: 41–65.

Vickers, Michael (1997) *Pericles on Stage: Political Comedy in Aristophanes' Early Plays*. Austin, TX: University of Texas Press.

Vickers, Michael (2015) *Aristophanes and Alcibiades: Echoes of Contemporary History in Athenian Comedy*. Berlin: De Gruyter.

Von Reden, Sitta (2010) *Money in Classical Antiquity*. Cambridge: Cambridge University Press.

Von Staden, Heinrich (1996) 'Body and Machine: Interactions between Medicine, Mechanics and Philosophy in Early Alexandria' in *Alexandria and Alexandrianism*. Ed. Kenneth Hamma. Malibu, CA: J. Paul Getty Museum. 85–106.

Vrahimis, Andreas (2012) ' "Was There A Sun Before Men Existed?" A. J. Ayer and French Philosophy in the Fifties', *Journal for the History of Analytical Philosophy*, 1(9): 1–25.

Waterfield, Robin (trans.) (2018) *Aristotle: The Art of Rhetoric*. Oxford: Oxford University Press.

Watson, J. (1976) 'Smiling, Cooing and "The Game" ' in *Play: Its Role in Development and Evolution*. Ed. Jerome S. Bruner, Alison Jolly and Kathy Sylva. Harmondsworth: Penguin. 268–76.

Webb, Ruth (2018) 'Attitutes Towards Tragedy from the Second Sophistic to Late Antiquity' in *Greek Tragedy After the Fifth Century*. Ed. Vayos Liapis and Antonis K. Petrides. Cambridge: Cambridge University Press. 297–323.

Weber, Samuel (2000) *The Legend of Freud*. Expanded ed. Stanford, CA: Stanford University Press.

Webster, Colin A. (2014) *Technology and/as Theory: Material Thinking in Ancient Science and Medicine* [PhD thesis]. University of Columbia.

Weems, Scott (2014) *Ha! The Science of When We Laugh and Why*. New York, NY: Basic Books.

Wehgartner, I. (1987) 'Das Ideal massvoller Liebe auf einem attischen Vasenbild', *JdL*, 102, 185–97.

Bibliography

Welsh, David (1978) *The Development of the Relation Between Aristophanes and Cleon to 424 B.C.* [PhD thesis]. King's College London.

White, E.B. (1941) 'Preface' in *A Subtreasury of American Humor*. Ed. E.B. White and Katharine S. White. New York, NY: Coward-McCann. xi–xxii.

Whitman, Cedric H. (1964) *Aristophanes and the Comic Hero*. Cambridge, MA: Harvard University Press.

Whitmarsh, Tim (2016) 'Diagoras, Bellerophon and the Siege of Olympus', *Journal of Hellenic Studies*, 136: 182–6.

Wickberg, Daniel (1998) *The Senses of Humor*. Ithaca, NY and London: Cornell University Press.

Wiesing, Urban (2008) 'The History of Medical Enhancement: From Restitutio ad Integrum to Transformatio ad Optimum?' in *Medical Enhancement and Posthumanity*. Ed. Bert Gordijn and Ruth Chadwick. New York, NY: Springer. 9–24.

Wikipedia (2018) 'Internet Troll' [Online]. Available at: www.en.wikipedia.org/wiki/Internet_troll (Accessed 21 June 2018).

Wild, Barbara *et al.* (2003) 'Neural Correlates of Laughter and Humour', *Brain*, 126: 2121–38.

Wiles, David (1991) *The Masks of Menander: Sign and Meaning in Greek and Roman Performance*. Cambridge: Cambridge University Press.

Wiles, David (2008) 'The Poetics of the Mask in Old Comedy' in *Performance, Iconography, Reception: Studies in Honour of Oliver Taplin*. Ed. Martin Revermann and Peter Wilson. Oxford: Oxford University Press. 374–94.

Wilkins, John (2000) *The Boastful Chef: The Discourse of Food in Ancient Greek Comedy*. Oxford: Oxford University Press.

Will, Wolfgang (2003) *Thukydides und Perikles: der Historiker und sein Held*. Bonn: Habelt.

Willi, Andreas (ed.) (2002) *The Language of Greek Comedy*. Oxford: Oxford University Press.

Wilson, Peter (2000) 'Powers of Horror and Laughter: The Great Age of Drama' in *Literature in the Greek and Roman Worlds: A New Perspective*. Ed. Oliver Taplin. Oxford: Oxford University Press. 88–132.

Winnicott, D. (1953) 'Transitional Objects and Transitional Phenomena – A Study of the First Not-Me Possession', *International Journal of Psycho-Analysis*, 34, 89–97.

Wiseman, Richard (2002) *LaughLab: The Scientific Search for the World's Funniest Joke – Final Report* [Online]. Available at: www.laughlab.co.uk (Accessed 1 August 2019).

Wiseman, Richard (2007) *Quirkology: The Curious Science of Everyday Lives*. London: Macmillan.

Worman, Nancy (2008) *Abusive Mouths in Classical Athens*. Cambridge: Cambridge University Press.

Wright, Matthew (2012) *The Comedian as Critic: Greek Old Comedy and Poetics*. London: Bristol Classical Press.

Wright, Matthew (2013) 'Comedy versus Tragedy in *Wasps*' in *Greek Comedy and the Discourse of Genres*. Ed. Emmanuela Bakola, Lucia Prauscello and Mario Telò. Cambridge: Cambridge University Press. 205–25.

Wyler, Stéphanie (2008) 'Faire peur pour rire? Le masque des *Erotes*', *La Part de l'Oeil*, 23: 105–21.

Wyles, Rosie (2011) *Costume in Greek Tragedy*. London: Bristol Classical Press.

Yue, Xiaodong (2018) *Humor and Chinese Culture: A Psychological Perspective*. London and New York, NY: Routledge.

Zanker, Paul (1998) *Eine Kunst für die Sinne: Zur Bilderwelt des Dionysos und der Aphrodite*. Berlin: Wagenbach.

Zeitlin, Froma (1986) 'Configurations of Rape in Greek Myth' in *Rape*. Ed. Sylvana Tomaselli and Roy Porter. Oxford: Basil Blackwell. 122–51.

Zeitlin, Froma (1996) *Playing the Other: Gender and Society in Classical Greek Literature*. Chicago, IL: University of Chicago Press.

Zhmud, Leonid (2012) *Pythagoras and the Early Pythagoreans*. Trans. Kevin Windle and Rosh Ireland. Oxford: Oxford University Press.

Zira, Magdalena (2019) *The Problem of the Chorus in Contemporary Productions of Greek Drama and Directorial Solutions in the Last Forty Years* [PhD thesis]. King's College London.

Zousi, Mania (2016) 'Μιχαήλ Μαρμαρινός: Η Λυσιστράτη είναι σαν ρεμπέτικο, ένας καημός [Michael Marmarinos: Lysistrata Is Like a *Rembetiko*, It Is a Sadness]', *Avgi.gr* [Online]. Available at: www.avgi.gr/article/10971/7327402/e-lysistrate-einai-san-rempetiko-enas-kaemos (Accessed 29 May 2019).

Zweig, Bella (1992) 'The Mute Nude Female Characters in Aristophanes' Plays' in *Pornography and Representation in Greece & Rome*. Ed. Amy Richlin. Oxford: Oxford University Press. 73–89.

INDEX

Aeschylus xiv, 35, 43–4, 47, 88, 91, 103, 105, 109, 148, 180, 201, 214, 232, 236, 240, 250
Agathon 47–9, 51, 101, 124, 135–7, 142, 148–9, 184–5, 189, 224, 235, 236, 240
Alcibiades 89, 104, 125, 184, 236
Athens (Athenian) xiii, xv, 6, 8, 19–20, 23, 28–9, 32–4, 36–7, 45, 49–50, 52, 70–2, 74–5, 79, 83, 89–91, 93–4, 96–9, 102, 104–5, 114, 119–22, 125–7, 129, 147, 149, 171, 174–5, 177–81, 193, 195, 197, 199, 200, 203, 212, 226, 227, 235, 236, 245
Arginusae 69, 71–2, 97, 99, 224
Aristophanes, plays
 Acharnians 17–19, 32, 42–3, 69, 71–3, 92–4, 109, 121–5, 132–9, 151, 167, 172, 176–7, 183, 219, 224, 227, 234, 238, 245, 248, 249
 Birds frontispiece, 33, 45, 73–4, 91, 95–7, 124–5, 131, 133, 155, 167, 172–3, 219, 233, 236, 242
 Clouds 9, 33, 35, 54, 58, 60, 61, 63, 73, 81, 86, 92, 95, 115, 123–5, 147–9, 151, 153, 155, 183, 205–14, 221, 223, 227, 228, 233, 236, 238, 241, 247, 250
 Ecclesiazusae 45, 66–7, 70, 108, 109, 125, 167, 172, 174, 179, 238, 242
 Frogs 28, 30, 32, 34, 35, 43, 46, 54, 56, 65–7, 69–72, 79, 87, 91, 97, 108, 124, 125, 132, 147, 149, 162, 163, 168–70, 183, 200–3, 219, 221, 224, 227, 233, 236, 249, 250
 Knights 35, 73, 87, 94, 121–7, 219, 225, 227, 230, 234, 235, 236, 238
 Lysistrata 28, 29, 46, 74–5, 79, 98, 99, 124, 132–3, 148–9, 172, 180–1, 183, 193, 196–203, 238, 245, 248, 249, 250
 Peace 29, 32, 35, 46, 73, 95, 125, 129, 131, 133–6, 139–42, 148, 155, 158–9, 167, 172, 178, 183, 184, 219, 224, 235, 236, 237, 238, 240, 245, 246, 248, 249
 Thesmophoriazusae 30, 41, 45, 47–9, 63–4, 66, 70, 98, 124, 133–9, 142–3, 148–51, 157, 167, 174–5, 183, 235, 236, 238, 239, 242, 243, 245, 246
 Wasps 2, 32, 44, 70, 73–4, 89, 109, 123, 125, 147, 155, 156–7, 162, 183, 219, 230, 231, 233, 236, 237, 241, 243
 Wealth 27, 29, 98, 130, 132, 134–5, 137–9, 142–4, 149, 155, 201, 203, 224, 230, 237, 238, 239, 240, 242

Aristotle (Aristotelean) ix, xiii, 3–4, 8, 35, 54, 56, 101–16, 120, 129, 137, 146, 149, 194, 205, 217, 218, 221, 226, 232, 233, 237, 238, 239, 244

Bakhtin, Mikhail (Bahktinian) 5–6, 9, 54, 55, 58, 66, 220, 221
Bataille, Georges (theory of laughter) 8, 53, 55–6, 58, 63, 65–8, 185–7, 220, 221, 222, 223, 247
Bergson, Henri 14, 72, 145, 221, 223, 239

chorus 23, 26–33, 36, 44, 46, 50–2, 63–4, 65, 67, 73, 75, 79, 87, 89, 93–5, 98, 103, 120, 131–3, 135, 147, 159, 180, 187, 196–9, 201, 203, 208, 210, 219, 223, 234, 238, 249, 250
Cicero 116, 130, 147
Cleisthenes 124, 137, 227
Cleon 87–88, 89, 115, 120–4, 126–7, 227, 229, 230, 234, 235, 236
Cleonymus 73–4, 125, 131, 225, 236
Crates 29, 104–6, 124, 219, 239
Cratinus 23, 29, 50, 87, 124, 219, 220, 235, 238, 239, 241

Dionysia 23–4, 29, 30, 107, 184, 235
Dionysus (Dionysiac) xiv, xv, 8, 23–4, 26–30, 32–3, 43, 46–7, 51, 54, 56, 65–7, 69–73, 79, 91, 95, 97, 98, 125–6, 149, 150, 157, 162–3, 168–9, 201, 220, 221, 235, 239, 240

Eupolis 32, 50, 56, 58, 64, 121, 125, 219, 220, 225, 234, 236
Euripides xii, xiv, 1, 29, 35, 41, 43–4, 46, 51, 63, 65, 70–1, 88, 94, 102–3, 109, 124–5, 146–51, 153, 156–7, 159, 162–4, 174–6, 183–4, 189, 201, 219, 232, 233, 237, 238, 239, 240, 241, 242, 243, 246, 250

femininity (feminizing) 24, 28, 29, 47–9, 124, 142, 164, 170, 172, 180–1, 200, 223, 238
Freud, Sigmund (Freudian) 4, 9, 14, 53, 56, 69, 77, 183, 187–8, 109–92, 215, 220, 221, 222, 224, 226, 242, 243, 247, 248

Grice, H. P. (Gricean) 13, 39–40, 44, 218

Hegel 183, 187
Heracles 46–8, 51, 66, 91, 96–8, 125, 146, 153–4, 156–7, 162–5, 180, 236, 243, 244

Index

Hippocrates (Hippocratic) 4, 69, 76, 145–6, 224, 239
Homeric Hymn 28, 69, 76
Horace 79–80, 226, 227
Huizinga, Johan 2, 24, 35–7, 218
humour (comic) theory 1, 5–8, 13–17, 22, 39, 52, 108, 167, 216, 218
    Incongruity Theory 4–6, 9, 40–1, 51, 154, 167, 225, 239, 241, 242
    Play Theory 2, 5–6, 8, 37
    Release Theory 40
    Relief Theory 4–8, 77, 155, 236
    Superiority Theory 3–5

Lacan, Jacques 55, 58, 221, 222, 223
Lucian 59, 160, 222

Marmarinos 193, 196–203, 248, 249, 250
Menander 62, 101, 135, 156, 143

neuroscience, -scientists 13, 69, 77
Nietzsche ix, xiv, 9, 183, 187–90, 192, 247

Oedipus 104, 168, 183–4, 187–8, 190, 237, 246, 247
Old Comedy xii, xv, 1, 4, 6, 8, 9, 23, 29, 30, 32, 46, 50, 54, 56, 68, 87, 89–91, 95, 99, 101, 105–6, 110, 114, 116, 122, 138, 147, 167, 171–2, 181, 226, 230, 231, 239

Paidiá (play, game play, goddess of) 3, 8, 24–34, 36–7, 217
parody xv, 5, 8, 41, 46, 48, 63–4, 108–10, 119–27, 148, 176, 183–4, 207–8, 223, 234, 235, 236, 240, 247
Pericles 70, 72, 121, 123–5, 224, 225, 235
Phrynichus 56, 58, 63–4, 68, 169, 226, 244
Plato (Platonic) xiii, 3–4, 24, 33–7, 40, 49, 61, 70, 73, 81, 84–6, 93, 110, 113, 121, 123, 125, 180, 183–6, 189–92, 201, 213, 217, 219, 224, 225, 228, 232, 233, 234, 235, 236, 239, 240, 242, 243, 247, 248
Plessner 69, 224
Plutarch 101, 116, 225, 232, 237
pottery (images on, krater, vase) 3, 8, 23–8, 34, 37, 56, 163–5, 243, 244
Presocratic(s) 40, 115, 145

Rabelais 5, 55
Ramachandran 69, 77, 224, 226

satyr drama 8, 23–4, 27, 29, 36, 41, 49–51, 174, 190, 217, 240
Schadenfreude 56, 79–80, 83, 86, 242
Schiller, Friedrich 35–7, 218
scholia, -iast 33, 65, 129–30, 132, 135, 139–44, 148, 237, 238, 243
Shakespeare (Shakespearean) 6, 63
Socrates (Socratic, Socratism) 60–2, 73, 81–2, 84–6, 88, 93, 115, 123–4, 126, 148, 151, 184–5, 189, 190, 208–9, 211, 213, 224, 225, 228, 230, 235, 236, 247
Sondheim, Stephen 54–5, 220
Sophocles xii, xiv, 83, 102–3, 105, 154, 158–9, 180, 183, 184, 187, 232, 237, 240, 255
Sparta xv, 18, 28, 71–2, 75, 93–4, 177, 236, 245

Thucydides 70, 72, 121, 123–5, 224, 226, 234, 235, 236, 237
tragedy (tragic, *also* paratragedy, tragicomedy) xv, 2, 4–9, 20, 23–4, 26–9, 32, 41, 46, 48, 50–2, 53, 55–6, 59, 63–5, 72, 77–8, 86, 89, 98, 101–6, 109, 111, 124–5, 129, 130, 135, 148, 150, 153–9, 163–166, 172, 174, 176, 180, 183–90, 192, 193–5, 201, 205, 212, 216, 217, 219, 220, 221, 222, 224, 226, 233, 239, 240, 241, 243, 244, 247, 249, 250

www.ingramcontent.com/pod-product-compliance
Lightning Source LLC
Chambersburg PA
CBHW072126290426
44111CB00012B/1792